THE SOUL OF A UNIVERSITY

Why excellence is not enough

Chris Brink

BRISTOL
UNIVERSITY
PRESS

First published in Great Britain in 2018 by

Bristol University Press
1-9 Old Park Hill
Bristol BS2 8BB
UK
t: +44 (0)117 954 5940
www.bristoluniversitypress.co.uk

North American office:
c/o The University of Chicago Press
1427 East 60th Street
Chicago, IL 60637, USA
t: +1 773 702 7700
f: +1 773-702-9756
e:sales@press.uchicago.edu
www.press.uchicago.edu

© Bristol University Press 2018

British Library Cataloguing in Publication Data
A catalogue record for this book is available from the British Library.

Library of Congress Cataloging-in-Publication Data
A catalog record for this book has been requested.

ISBN 978-1-5292-0034-8 paperback
ISBN 978-1-5292-0036-2 ePub
ISBN 978-1-5292-0037-9 Mobi
ISBN 978-1-5292-0035-5 ePdf

Cover design by blu inc, Bristol
Author photo: Jean Pretorius
Printed and bound in Great Britain by CMP, Poole
Bristol University Press uses environmentally responsible print partners

For Tobea in particular,
and all long-suffering academic
spouses and partners in general

The supreme good open to man is to know the true, to do the good, and to delight in both.
Boethius of Dacia, *De Summo Bono*, ca.1270s

Contents

List of Illustrations

List of Abbreviations

CHE	Centre for Higher Education
CHEPS	Centre for Higher Education Policy Studies
CHERI	Centre for Higher Education Research and Information
CMA	Competition and Markets Authority
ECU	Equality Challenge Unit
EU	European Union
EUA	European University Association
FTE	full-time equivalent
GPA	grade point average
HEFCE	Higher Education Funding Council for England
HEIDI	Higher Education Information Database for Institutions
HESA	Higher Education Statistics Agency
HMC	Headmasters' and Headmistresses' Conference
IMHE	Institutional Management in Higher Education
INQAAHE	International Network for Quality Assurance Agencies in Higher Education
LERU	League of European Research Universities
LSE	London School of Economics
NCEE	National Council for Educational Excellence
NSS	National Student Survey
OECD	Organisation for Economic Co-operation and Development
OFFA	Office of Fair Access
OfS	Office for Students
PISA	Programme for International Student Assessment
QAA	Quality Assurance Agency
QR	quality related
QS	Quacquarelli Symonds (ranking)
RAE	Research Assessment Exercise

REF	Research Excellence Framework
TEF	Teaching Excellence Framework
UCL	University College London
UUK	Universities UK

Acknowledgements

Most of this book was written while I was Vice-Chancellor of Newcastle University in the north-east of England, up to the end of 2016. I am grateful to the university for a pleasant and stimulating work environment, and to many colleagues at Newcastle for many conversations on the idea of a world-class civic university.

Various people kindly read the manuscript, in whole or in part. I am indebted to them for their comments and suggestions, all of which I thought about and most of which I adopted or adapted. Grateful thanks to Dame Janet Beer, Tobea Brink, Suzanne Cholerton, Nicola Dandridge, Danny Dorling, Simon Fanshawe, Jon File, John Goddard, Ellen Hazelkorn, John Hogan, Lord Judd, Dianne Nelmes, Sir Howard Newby, Jaana Puukka, Brian Randell, Ingrid Rewitzky, Matt Ridley, Julie Sanders, Mark Shucksmith, Adam Swallow, Liz Todd, Anton van Niekerk and Sir Mark Walport. Rebecca Walker devoted a lot of time to the project, and did a great deal of work on the technical material, desk research and critical reading. Alison Pickard was always available to help when I needed someone with a sharp eye for English grammar and idiom. Alison Shaw of Bristol University Press championed the book from the outset, and the friendly and professional BUP staff made publication look easy.

Grateful thanks to all.

Prologue

Aristotle characterised the soul as 'the essential what-ness' of a living body. On this definition, and if we accept the university as a living body, the question of the soul of the university is a question about its essence.

Universities are among the most durable institutions society ever invented. You can trace the idea of a university back to Greek philosophers, or Chinese sages, or Islamic madrassas. Even just its European manifestation goes back almost a thousand years. Somehow, despite their wide variety, there is something recognisable about a university. We feel that if a time machine dropped us into a university of say 500 years ago, we would recognise it, and not feel out of place there. Likewise, we hope that if the time machine brought us forward in time to the year 2500, we would still find universities recognisable, and flourishing.

Such durability must be a consequence of the unchanging essence, the soul, of a university. And while we might dispute details and offer different formulations, there can be little doubt that the essence of a university has to do with the exercise of reason. Reason exercised, in particular, in the pursuit of knowledge and the search for truth. When we engage in learning and scholarship we do so in a certain way, and we try to inculcate that way in our students. We follow the way of rationality. This is not to say that universities do not adapt. They do. They may be maddeningly slow, and they may wander off into detours and dead ends, but they are not ignorant of what happens in society, because professors are people, and students even more so. So when we say there is something unchanging about the university – that there is an identifiable essence that characterises it – this is not an indictment of resistance to change. It is an affirmation of enduring value.

Having said that, it must be recognised that at present universities are confronted with a societal change so fundamental it is hard to know how it will turn out. The very essence of a university, it seems, is under threat. Throughout the history of universities, the exercise of reason, the pursuit of knowledge and the search for truth have enjoyed the respect and support of society. But no longer. Or at least no longer to the extent to which universities have always taken such respect for granted. It is hard to think of any earlier time when the very concept of truth itself has been undermined and constrained as at present.

Towards the end of 2016, the *Oxford English Dictionary* selected 'post-truth' as its word of the year. In a post-truth world, appearance matters more than reality, and what people can be led to believe takes precedence above what they ought to know.

With hindsight we can see the signs. In the penultimate chapter of his 1997 book *Truth: A History and a Guide for the Perplexed*, the historian Felipe Fernández-Armesto traces what he calls 'the death of conviction', and the role of intellectuals in its demise. Deconstruction, postmodernism, relativism: the intellectual white-anting of truth is well documented. Since the millennium, the decline of truth has accelerated. Iraq was invaded on the grounds of weapons of mass destruction, which were not found. The financial crisis of 2007–8 destroyed trust in the probity of banks and the veracity of governments. The widening inequality gap led to the rage of the Occupy movement. And, increasingly, a disenchanted electorate refused to vote as they were supposed to, turning to unexpected charismatics stronger on promise than on experience.

In the UK, the leader of a political party signed a pledge, on camera, against any increase in student fees, and then, as part of a coalition government, voted to triple them. Another party elected as leader a man with no clear expertise but a messianic message, and although 80% of his parliamentary colleagues initially declared that they had no confidence in him, the electorate gave him an extra 30 seats in parliament. A former secretary of state for education declared that the people have had enough of experts. A new prime minister called a general election in the confident expectation of significantly increasing the government's majority, and lost it. The United States of America elected as president a billionaire with no experience whatsoever of government, but an instinctive mastery of social media and an oceanic reservoir of self-belief as an exponent of the art of the deal. France swept aside both the established left and the established right, and elected a president who had never fought an election, and a party which had not existed a year before.

At the same time, we see a new isolationism taking shape. Three decades after the wall came down in Berlin, new walls, physical or metaphysical, are being constructed. Scotland threatens to leave the United Kingdom, Catalonia may leave Spain, and England voted to leave the European Union. A post-referendum secretary of state re-affirmed the government's intention of bringing immigration into the UK down from the hundreds of thousands to the tens of thousands, starting with a clampdown on international students. A prime minister declared that 'If you see yourself as a citizen of the world you are a citizen of nowhere. You do not understand the concept of citizenship.'

Both the post-truth and isolationist developments are contrary to the idea of a university. Universities are where experts come from. The search for truth is what makes an expert. Truth knows no boundaries and no national identity. Universities, for hundreds of years, have welcomed anybody, regardless of national or cultural identity, who has the ability to contribute to, or the potential to benefit from, an environment concerned with knowledge and understanding. That is why universities have always been international entities, ever since medieval wandering scholars commuted between Bologna and Paris and Oxford. The post-truth conception of the world undermines the idea of a university, and the new isolationism constrains it.

It may be argued that the current developments are just a new manifestation of the old tension between logic and rhetoric. But that would be to flatter the post-truth Twitterati. Socrates, Plato and Aristotle were all fairly scathing about the sophists, but they took rhetoric seriously, and no sophist would have openly flouted logic, though they were adept at twisting it. It used to be the case that public figures who contradicted themselves were held up to ridicule. *Reductio ad absurdum* has long been a powerful weapon for destroying the credibility of an opponent. But no longer. The Trumpeters have discovered that contradicting yourself is a way of validating any opinion. In the post-truth world of social media you can always refer back to the currently convenient half of your previous contradiction, and trust to the short attention span of your audience to forget the other half.

Any thought of a response must begin with an admission. As academics, we have been complacent in watching the new post-truth spirit develop, complicit in facilitating it, and compliant in accommodating its consequences. Which is odd. How can we say that we strive for knowledge when we disdain truth?

There are two key questions we should always ask about our academic work. The first is: what are we good at? The second is: what are we good for? The first question is about excellence: who is expert at what? The second question is about purpose: how do we respond to the needs and demands of society? Both questions are important and legitimate. We have been complicit in a relentless focus on the first question, and complacent in the face of a growing revolt about our lack of focus on the second.

Inequality is about the distance between the haves and the have-nots. In the UK and the US the economic distance between the top and the bottom is greater now than it has ever been. This is worth taking note of, because there is a strong argument that social ills proliferate in direct correlation with economic inequality. The greater the distance between the rich and the poor, the more social problems the state will face. The same, I hold, is true for educational inequality. The UK and US like to boast about the world-class excellence of their top academics, counting their Nobel prizes like their Olympic gold medals. At the same time, just as the rich are stratospherically above the poor, and the super-athletes are on another plane than the obese masses, the star academics float above an underclass of barely literate and largely innumerate people who, we now know, are very angry. They have been fed a sugary diet of appearances rather than a healthy dose of truth, to the extent that they cannot recognise the difference any more. They do not understand the experts, nor do they interact with them. Whatever lingering vestiges of respect there might have been for clever people has been eroded by a lack of evidence that their work benefits everybody. There has not been a clear educational trickle-down effect, just as there has not been an economic trickle-down effect. The knowledge gap, like the wealth gap, has become too large to endure.

The central thesis of this book is that universities should pay attention to the question of what they are good *for* with the same rigour and determination as they pursue the question of what they are good *at*. This is not entirely a new idea. I quote a somewhat obscure medieval scholar called Boethius of Dacia as saying that the supreme good open to man is to know the true and pursue the good – and to take delight in both. You can read his own words on this topic in the Epilogue, and you can trace his idea back to Aristotle.

We have not been paying sufficient attention to parity between the two guiding questions about the true and the good. We have self-indulgently been focusing on the former. Some have done so by undermining the very idea of truth. Among the remainder, who have no problem with truth, there is a school of thought that the search for truth is an end in itself – that advancing the frontiers of knowledge will suffice as a response to the question about societal benefit. We may call this the 'invisible hand' argument: that knowledge will always, in the fullness of time, through the workings of an invisible hand, bring benefit to society. Many of us accept this maxim as true, but some of us feel that it cannot be the whole truth. The pursuit of knowledge for its own sake is necessary, but not sufficient, for addressing the needs and demands of civil society. Its benefits are unpredictable in nature and slow in coming.

In global society space has shrunk and time has accelerated to the extent that responsiveness to the challenges facing us cannot wait for the workings of the invisible hand in the knowledge economy. Universities need to engage with the challenges faced by civil society, global and local. We should do so with a proper understanding of when the pursuit of knowledge should be challenge-led rather than curiosity-driven, and how these two methodologies differ from and interact with each other. The societal benefit of having experts should be made manifest. We have not been clear about the feedback loop between excellence and relevance.

In expounding my thesis, I have found it necessary to introduce some new ideas and debunk some common assumptions. 'Applied research', for example, is almost exactly what I am not talking about when I speak of 'challenge-led research'. Applied research is a solution looking for a problem, challenge-led research is the opposite. I also have severe concerns about the fashionable idea of 'merit', and the accompanying socio-political construct of a meritocracy. A meritocracy, I argue, is much the same as an aristocracy, except that those at the top have higher self-esteem. Third, I am somewhat impatient with bogus quantification, and the deferential respect commonly paid to any conclusion arising from the application of a formula. We are prone to confusing accuracy of calculation with legitimacy of conclusion. This tendency is well illustrated by the current craze for university rankings. It takes only a little scrutiny to realise that these rankings are normative at least as much as they are substantive. They create a reality more than reflect a reality. Any competent arithmetician could easily find a perfectly plausible formula and a decent data set that will deliver pretty much any ranking you want.

Rankings are a perfect manifestation of the post-truth society. They give the appearance of certainty and avoid the complexities of truth. In response to a question about quality they offer a single number, which is your university's position on their ranking. And they get away with it, on the apparently unimpeachable grounds that the result was obtained by a mathematical calculation.

Behind almost any discussion about universities is the question of quality. What makes a 'good university'? This question, which occupies not only academics but millions of parents and prospective students, is of course only a proxy for a more fundamental question: what do we mean by 'good'? Following Boethius of Dacia, I hold that 'good' has at least two dimensions: good as in excellent, and good as in virtuous. On the latter, less explored axis, quality is inseparable from equality. Likewise, equality is inseparable from diversity, which leads me to conclude that quality needs diversity.

I have now said what my book is for. If you ask, on the other hand, what my book is against, it is the poverty of linearism. 'Linear' just means 'as if on a straight line', which is how ordinary numbers are arranged. A straight line is the simplest representation of one-dimensionality. When we assign everything a number we have enforced a situation where, of any two things, one of them has a higher number than the other, and so is presumed to be better. Linearism, then, is a lazy preference for the apparent certainty of one dimension rather than the multidimensional complexities of truth. A ranking, of universities or anything else, is a numbered list, which is a one-dimensional representation of whatever reality we started with. The problem is not that it is done, but that it is so easily and uncritically accepted as a true representation of reality, rather than a preferential ordering. I can easily rank apples above oranges; that will tell you something about my preferences but nothing about fruit.

The antidote to one-dimensionality is more dimensions. I advocate an academic landscape, the two axes of which are excellence and purpose. The excellence axis is our response to the question of what we are good at; the axis of societal purpose is our response to the question of what we are good for. As in any landscape, the two axes are conveniently thought of as being orthogonal: at right angles to each other. Such a conceptualisation is half metaphorical and half practical. Metaphorically, I argue, we should envisage the good as orthogonal to the true. In practical terms, what this means is that challenge-led research cuts across disciplinary research (for which we use words like 'cross-disciplinary'), and the idea of knowledge in service of society cuts across the idea of knowledge for its own sake.

One advantage of the landscape metaphor is that we are not trapped by another common assumption, which is that academic debate presents itself as a series of binary oppositions. It is not the case that we are talking of excellence versus purpose; the good versus the true. Instead, we can talk of excellence *and* purpose, knowing the true *and* pursuing the good. We can delight in both, because each can reinforce the other.

On the metaphor of an academic landscape each university could determine for itself its desired coordinates. What subjects do you wish to be good at? And what contribution do you wish to make to the challenges facing civil society? Given your circumstances, location, history, opportunities and responsibilities, where would you like to be located on the axis of excellence, and where on the axis of societal relevance? And how do these two ambitions interact, and mutually reinforce each other?

In the same way as we all strive to be a 'world-class' university on the axis of excellence, we can all strive to be a 'civic' university on the axis of societal purpose. 'Civic' is nicely ambiguous: it can refer to your interaction with your city or region, but it can also refer to your responsibility to civil society – local, national or global. Just as a world-class university knows what it is good at, and has the evidence to back it up, a civic university is one that knows what it is good for, and has the evidence to back it up.

For better or for worse, the good-at axis has developed as a competitive one – a fact the rankers have clearly perceived and ruthlessly exploited. The good-for axis, however, is intrinsically a collaborative one. Tackling climate change, or clean energy, or antimicrobial resistance, or obesity, or inequality, or extremism, or any other grand challenge facing global society, is unlikely to be the work of some lone genius. It will be the work of committed teams with various forms of expertise, interacting on different fronts. Locating ourselves on an academic landscape means we can compete when competition will suffice and collaborate where joint action is necessary.

And so, in summary, this book is one of advocacy. It is a set of academic considerations regarding the soul of a university. In a post-truth society we need to keep up the search for truth and understanding, but we need to do so with a better understanding of why we are doing it, and a clear commitment that academic excellence must respond to the challenges facing civil society. In an increasingly fractured world, we need to combat isolationism with the simple truth that your problem will no longer stop at my border, nor mine at yours. It is up to us to demonstrate that the world can still benefit from wandering scholars.

Chris Brink
Franschhoek
31 January 2018

Introduction

As an aid to the reader I give a chapter-by-chapter outline of how the central thesis of the book develops.

Chapter One begins with a mathematician called G.H. Hardy, who extolled and exemplified the idea of 'pure' research. From Hardy's views I extrapolate some general features of research, not least the manner in which it may rely on Platonic preconceptions. One such Platonic preconception is 'the idea of a university', which has much to do with a voluminous 19th-century tome by John Henry Newman, on the pursuit of knowledge for its own sake. In the cold war era such thoughts solidified into what I call the *standard model university*, aloof from society, where the academic discipline is central, research matters more than teaching, and 'pure' research enjoys the highest esteem. By the 1990s, a number of authors were starting to question such an inward focus of higher education, calling for a return to the idea of the university as a public good. Just as this move was gaining traction, however, a new phenomenon arose to reinforce the standard model: university rankings and league tables.

Chapter Two is on rankings and league tables. I give some background and examples, to show how rankings focus mostly on research, and specifically on the kind of research paradigmatic to the standard model university. I also play around with the technicalities a bit, just enough to make the point that constructing a ranking involves so many choices that what you end up with is an ordering of preference more than a reflection of reality. As a reality check we may note that even the periodic national Research Assessment Exercise (or Research Excellence Framework), which deliberately produces research *profiles* as an evaluation of research quality, almost immediately gets turned into different kinds of rankings. Rankings have become astoundingly influential – so much so that the leading expert on the topic compares their growth to the spread of a virus.

Which raises a challenge for those who argue, as I do, that ranking is a poor way of reflecting quality. Namely: what do we mean by quality?

Chapter Three, therefore, is on the notion of quality in higher education. When we speak of a 'good university', do we mean good as in excellent, or good as in virtuous? We treat excellence and virtue as separate notions, and the standard model university is focused on the former, but when Plato and Aristotle spoke of quality as *arête* they meant both. There is a whole regulatory regime in higher education called 'quality assurance', which features some helpful articulations of what quality might mean, but in practice is confined to an evaluation of the efficacy of processes of education. Thus, while rankings are focused on research, quality assurance is focused on teaching, but there is neither connection nor complementarity between these exercises. As a marker for later discussion, I raise the thought that quality may be more like a shape than a number, in the sense that it can lend itself to comparison, but not to ranking. I also offer a short reality check on the Teaching Excellence Framework, introduced in addition to the quality assurance regime as a kind of counterpart to the Research Excellence Framework. And I conclude with the observation that, while the Teaching Excellence Framework (and many other features of higher education) may be well-intentioned, we have multiplied good intentions to the point where they have become a burden, the effect of which is an erosion of trust.

Chapter Four relates quality to equality and diversity. It is written in the first person, relating personal experiences in South Africa and England, leading up to some general principles. I tell the story of how, at the Mathematics Department of the University of Cape Town in the 1990s, we tried to deal with the legacy issues of the infamous rhetorical question posed by Dr Hendrik Verwoerd, the architect of grand apartheid: 'What is the use of teaching a black child mathematics?' I also relate how, when I took up the vice-chancellorship of Stellenbosch University in the 2000s, we tried to bring diversity to the institution which had been, for most of the 20th century, the intellectual home of the apartheid regime. Later, in England, I drew on these experiences in conducting a thought experiment: what are the arguments *against* the equality agenda?

In the final section I draw some conclusions and elaborate some principles, notably that quality needs diversity.

Chapter Five questions the easy assumption that problems of equality and social mobility have a silver-bullet solution called meritocracy. The word 'meritocracy' was originally coined as satire. Decades later its originator (a social activist called Michael Young) lamented that exactly what he feared had in fact transpired: those at the top believe that they have made it on their own merit, and that their success is for the common good, whereas in fact their ability and hard work have very often been liberally supplemented by privilege or patronage. I therefore start this chapter with an essay on merit, followed by a short detour about schools, where the wheels of what Michael Young called 'the engine of education' are oiled by parent power and influence. I then posit that a meritocracy is only virtuous if it is based on equal opportunity and enhances social mobility. Unfortunately the evidence points the other way. Instead of acquiring a good education on the basis of merit, we have reached the stage where we gain merit on the basis of a good education. This becomes a problem when the 'good education' is not equally available to all – which it isn't, when it must be bought. As regards social mobility, the simple fact is that the gap between the advantaged and the disadvantaged is growing – and that 'the engine of education' seems to be exacerbating rather than ameliorating this circumstance.

Chapter Six is a discourse on linearism – our predilection for listing things in a presumed rank order of worth. We are fond of metaphors of linearity, like the 'ladder of success', which narrows our thinking on issues such as quality, merit and social mobility into one-dimensionality. At the same time we are over-trusting of quantification, in the sense that we often mistake accuracy of calculation for legitimacy of conclusion. Numbers cannot do our thinking for us. A choice of calculation for constructing a ranking is just as much an expression of preference as simply ranking the items themselves in terms of preference. That is why compressing multiple single-metric rankings into a single multiple-metric ranking will always be normative, even when the original rankings are substantive. We do wish to compare things, but comparison does not need to involve ranking, and ordering does not need to be linear. Linearism, I argue, is an impoverished kind of thinking.

Chapter Seven explores the possibility of thinking about quality in more than one dimension, starting with a consideration of the life and work of Alan Turing, a mathematician who was just as intellectually creative as G.H. Hardy. They differ in that Turing's work also served a societal purpose beyond knowledge creation. That takes us back to an apparent dichotomy between 'useful' and 'useless' research, first encountered in Chapter One, and the identification of many such juxtapositions of apparent opposites in debates about higher education. Many of these arise from the uncritical application of two Aristotelian precepts: the law of excluded middle, which has the effect of creating dichotomies, and the principle of the mean, which has the effect of linearising the alternatives. I argue that a better way of representing many of the so-called binary oppositions in higher education is to consider them as orthogonal: at right angles to each other. As an implementation of this thought, I outline a paradigm and a terminology for a kind of research which is orthogonal to the conception of 'curiosity-driven', 'pure', or 'blue-sky' disciplinary research. *Lateral* research is 'challenge-led', 'participative', 'responsive' and cross-disciplinary. Classic 'vertical' research is about depth, lateral research is about breadth.

Chapter Eight pulls it all together by considering ideas of a civic university. There are two key questions every university should ask itself: 'What are we good *at?*' and 'What are we good *for?*' The first question is about excellence, the second about responsiveness to societal needs. The original civic universities – the 'redbricks' – of Victorian England provide an example of universities with a clear sense of societal purpose. Going back even further into history, I look at an attack on academic freedom at the University of Paris in 1277. That leads to a medieval scholar called Boethius of Dacia, who said that the supreme good – what we have been calling 'quality' – consists of two dimensions: to know the true and to do the good. The dimension of 'the true', for universities, is what we call excellence, while the dimension of 'the good' consists of civic engagement and responding to societal challenges. As a reality check we need to note that the latter is not risk-free – particularly for research-intensive universities. Which brings us to the key idea of this book: that we may think of the good as orthogonal to the true. For universities, that means thinking of societal purpose as orthogonal to academic excellence. This two-dimensionality gives us a conceptual framework within which to resolve our earlier conundrums. It also has practical significance for the governance and management of universities. The question 'Which societal challenges does your university respond to?' should be as common, and as insistent, as the question 'Which academic disciplines do you excel at?' And so, finally, the soul of the university can be characterised by the dimensions of excellence and societal purpose. Not only will this re-emphasise the societal value of truth and rational argument, it will also reinforce the kind of universalism that transcends national boundaries.

1

The Standard Model University

A mathematician's apology

> What is the proper justification of a mathematician's life?
> *G.H. Hardy*

In 1940 a Cambridge don called G.H. Hardy published an essay titled *A Mathematician's Apology*.[1] This was not an apology in the sense of saying sorry. It was an apology in the original sense of the word: a robust and combative justification of Hardy's subject and the way he had lived his life. The little book became a minor classic, and is still in print today. It is complemented very well by a long Foreword written by Hardy's friend and admirer C.P. Snow, added after Hardy's death. The Foreword is a kind of mini-biography of Hardy, which also evokes something of the atmosphere of Cambridge and Oxford universities around and between the two world wars. That Oxbridge world lingers in higher education as part of a collective academic unconscious, and so Hardy's apology is well worth paying attention to.

Hardy put forward his view of academic life with great clarity and precision. He writes as someone exemplifying academic excellence in a specialised subject. At his peak he was, by his own rather precise estimate, the fifth best mathematician in the world. His area of specialisation was number theory, one of the first, most enduring and more highbrow parts of mathematics. For most of his life he lived and worked in Trinity College Cambridge, and that was his home until he died. He did mathematics in the mornings, spent his afternoons at Fenners cricket ground, then had dinner in college. He was an introvert who did not teach, solved no real-life problems, had no administrative duties, never married and is not known to have had any romantic liaisons.

Hardy was the Sadleirian Professor of Pure Mathematics,[2] and he lived and breathed the idea captured in the name of his chair. The adjective 'pure' should be understood as having its conventional meaning: pure as in untouched, unsullied, uncontaminated, and, in particular, pure as in not having any connection with the messy world around us. The essence of pure mathematics is that it is not there for any particular purpose. It is there for itself.

This is a topic on which another Cambridge man, Bertrand Russell, had already waxed eloquent a few decades before.

> Mathematics, rightly viewed, possesses not only truth, but supreme beauty — a beauty cold and austere, like that of sculpture, without appeal to any part of our weaker nature, without the gorgeous trappings of painting or music, yet sublimely pure, and capable of a stern perfection such as only the greatest art can show. The true spirit of delight, the exaltation, the sense of being more than Man, which is the touchstone of the highest excellence, is to be found in mathematics as surely as in poetry.[3]

Russell knew what he was talking about. With Alfred North Whitehead he was the author of *Principia Mathematica*, a massive three-volume work intended to derive mathematics entirely from logic. An idle hour would not be wasted by going to your local university library and paging through this work. It is beautiful, in somewhat the same way as the Sphinx or Stonehenge is beautiful: imposing, inscrutable, and best admired from afar. To all appearances it might be written in hieroglyphics. If you wonder whether there is any relief in the unremitting reams of mathematical results, have a look at Proposition 110.643 in the second volume, where, having started out a few hundred pages earlier with nothing but logical principles, the authors are eventually able to prove that $1+1 = 2$. 'The above proposition', they drily comment, 'is occasionally useful.'

As counterpoint to this demonstration of logical certainty, it is worth adding that Russell, around the same time, also wrote that mathematics may be defined as the subject in which we never know what we are talking about, nor whether what we are saying is true.[4] Perhaps certainty is not so far removed from doubt.

G.H. Hardy, however, was untroubled by doubt. He knew exactly what mathematics consisted of, and he was not shy about sharing his opinion. Indeed, he is very quotable, if not always agreeable, on any topic he felt qualified to comment on, including cricket. He is also, as may be expected, entirely consistent. His very first observation is that it is a melancholy experience for a professional mathematician to find himself writing about mathematics, rather than doing mathematics. 'There is no scorn more profound', Hardy said, 'than that of the men who make for the men who explain. Exposition, criticism, appreciation, is work for second-rate minds.' This is as pithy a formulation as you could wish for of the view that, in academic life, research counts for more than teaching. Hardy hated teaching, and was not afraid to say so. Perhaps fortunately for everybody concerned, he had to do very little of what an academic would today regard as the day job, since his 'teaching' (and he used the quotation marks himself) consisted almost entirely of research supervision. He did profess to love lecturing, which presumably differed from teaching in his being able to maintain some distance from his audience. He was also pleased to say that 'I have had very little trouble with the duller routine of universities.'

Hardy was a prolific researcher. It is known that mathematicians generally publish less than, say, physicists or chemists, and an average output of two or three papers a year is not uncommon for a professional mathematician. Hardy published more than 300 mathematical papers – testimony both to his creative powers and to the fact that doing mathematics was the only thing he had to do. He had complete freedom to work on whatever he liked. He did not work to any external schedule, demands, targets or constraints. He did not have to apply for any funding grants, or need any equipment, or work with research assistants. His work followed nothing but his own interests and his own schedule. He was a specialist in pure mathematics, and his professional interests did not stray very far beyond the boundaries of his field. His mathematical papers (of which a complete list appears with his obituary in the *Journal of the London Mathematical Society* of 1950)[5] are nuts-and-bolts results from the workshop of mathematics, making no concessions to a wider audience.

'Pure' research, disciplinary specialisation, excellence, research above teaching, scorn for administration − one can already see some of the more prominent clichés of academic life formulated with great authority. On no topic, however, was Hardy clearer or more authoritative than on the creative process. He was interested in mathematics only as a creative art − the 'austere beauty' that Russell spoke of. A mathematician, like a painter or a poet, makes patterns, and the mathematician's patterns are the more durable because they are made with ideas. But to be durable they must be beautiful. 'Beauty is the first test: there is no place in this world for ugly mathematics.'

This beauty must also be ethereal − it should have nothing to do with the real world. Hardy proudly claimed never to have done anything of the slightest practical use. He also believed, or perhaps just hoped, that his work would never turn out to be useful in future. 'No discovery of mine', he said, 'has made, or is likely to make, directly or indirectly, for good or ill, the least difference to the amenity of the world.' Earlier on, indeed, during the First World War, his view had been that 'A science is said to be useful if its development tends to accentuate the existing inequalities in the distribution of wealth, or more directly promotes the destruction of human life.' (Although he did, 25 years later in the *Apology*, dismiss this particular remark as 'a conscious rhetorical flourish'.)

Hardy was also very clear that in mathematics creativity goes with youth. Young mathematicians should prove theorems; old ones could write books. The *Apology*, therefore, is not only an explanation and a justification of a way of life, it is also a lament that it is over. 'It is plain now,' Hardy says, 'that my life is finished, and that nothing I can do can perceptibly increase or diminish its value.'

Such views do not add up to a contented old age. Hardy felt that he had lost his mathematical creativity, and therefore he lost the will to live. He had remained physically vigorous until 1939, when at the age of 62 he had a coronary thrombosis, and his health deteriorated.

In 1947 he tried to commit suicide, but, embarrassingly, failed. God, whom he had always seen as a personal adversary, none the less allowed him to die shortly afterwards.

Extrapolation

> Applied mathematics is bad mathematics.
> *Paul Halmos*

From G.H. Hardy's life and work we may extrapolate some general comments on research. First, a fundamental part of academic work, and a core function of a university, is knowledge creation. Hardy is an extreme example: knowledge creation is all he did. His entire professional life consisted of pumping out new knowledge into the world. His work was, as we now say, curiosity-driven, blue-sky, basic, fundamental, or, deploying his own terminology, 'pure' research. Whether there was any need or demand for these results out there in the world was of no concern to him. He might be drawn into creative thinking by a result or a problem stated by another mathematician, but nothing of what he produced came from outside the realm of 'pure' mathematics. Beauty, he would have repeated, was the only test. There was as much or as little need or demand for his theorems as there was for poems or paintings or sculpture. His results stand on their own, and should be appreciated for their own sake. If, in the long term, anything he did in pure mathematics turned out to be useful in any way, that was immaterial to him. We may take this as a definition of 'pure' research: the creation of knowledge without any ultimate aim in mind, and with no motive other than the desire to know. It is about knowledge for its own sake.

Second, the curious and fascinating thing is that, having disclaimed utility as a motive, 'pure' research often does turn out to be useful. It may be a long time coming, and it frequently crops up in totally unexpected ways and places, but results that originated from nothing but curiosity do, as a body, pay off in the end. Despite his protestations, Hardy's own work can serve as an example. In fact, it can serve as an example in two ways, specific and general.

A specific example is the Hardy–Weinberg principle of population genetics, formulated independently by Hardy and a German physician, Wilhelm Weinberg. For Hardy this must have been an entirely trivial matter – little more than a throwaway remark. It does not, for example, appear in the publications list of his obituary. It was none the less a published result, appearing as a letter to *Science* of 10 July 1908 under the heading 'Mendelian proportions in a mixed population'. The letter is in characteristic Hardy style.

> TO THE EDITOR OF SCIENCE: I am reluctant to intrude in a discussion concerning matters of which I have no expert knowledge, and I should have expected the very simple point which I wish to make to have been familiar to biologists. However, some remarks of Mr. Udny Yule, to which Mr. R.C. Punnett has called my attention, suggest that it may still be worth making.
>
> In the *Proceedings of the Royal Society of Medicine* (Vol. I, p. 165) Mr Yule is reported to have suggested, as a criticism of the Mendelian position, that if brachydactyly is dominant 'in the course of time one would expect, in the absence of counteracting forces, to get three brachydactylous persons to one normal.'
>
> It is not difficult to prove, however, that such an expectation would be quite groundless....
>
> In a word, there is not the slightest foundation for the idea that a dominant character should show a tendency to spread over a whole population, or that a recessive should tend to die out.[6]

The Mr Punnett who is credited with having called the matter to Hardy's attention was a geneticist with whom he played cricket. It may be that Hardy thought that any mathematical observation arising from a social interaction on the cricket field could not be 'pure', and hence not meet the test of beauty and creativity. It is, however, not inconceivable that Hardy may be remembered for this apparent triviality long after his creative works on mathematically profound questions have passed into obscurity.

Hardy was also wrong in his more general observation, that 'pure' mathematics, or at least his own brand of it, will remain unsullied by utility. What had long counted as esoteric parts of abstract number theory have in fact become of practical importance in a number of ways, not least in computer security. So-called *public key cryptography*, for example, essentially relies on the fact that while it is very easy to multiply numbers, even very large numbers, it is really hard to factorise a large number – that is, break it down into the numbers of which it is a product.

In particular, if you have a very large number, it is hard to tell whether or not that number is prime – that is, whether or not it is the product of some other numbers (other than 1 and itself). In public key cryptography a security code would have two kinds of key required to unlock it: one public and two private. If you and I want to exchange coded messages, you would have a private key and so would I. The public key would be a really large number, so large that even very powerful computers could not easily factorise it, but which is in fact the product of two primes. One of the secret prime numbers would serve as your private key, and the other as mine. When one of us sends a message to the other, it is accompanied by the public key, which anybody can see. However, the message is coded in such a way that it cannot be read unless you can break down that public key into its two constituent private keys. You can do so, because you have one of the keys, and so you can easily divide the large number by your number to get my number. That is, by using your private key you can decode the publicly coded message I sent you, and likewise I can read any similarly coded message you send me. Anybody else who tried to obtain the private keys required to read the message would have to spend many years trying to factorise the public key.

Of course, there is more to the matter than this somewhat oversimplified example. The point is, however, that really sophisticated number theory is used in constructing (and trying to break) the security of information. In the internet age, with cyber-security and hacking and identity theft becoming ever greater risks, the 'pure' mathematics of numbers really matters in everyday life. It is a good example of the unexpected long-term practical outcomes of 'pure' research.

Which leads us to a third conclusion: when we ask about the usefulness (or declaim about the uselessness) of blue-sky research, it is unrealistic to expect that utility must lie, item for item, with any particular results. Such micro-utility can happen – as for example in the case of the Hardy–Weinberg principle – but mostly it won't. It is the whole package of number theory, for example, that is useful for computer security. All those apparently esoteric single results, such as in Hardy's publication list, add up to a body of knowledge and expertise which provides the tools for public key cryptography or other applications.

The misapprehension that utility lies with specific results is an easy mistake to make. Anybody who has ever taught mathematics will be familiar with the pupil's question 'Where will I ever use this theorem in real life?' This may be about a result in geometry, or algebra, or calculus, or any other part of mathematics – it is the level of abstraction that raises the question, rather than the topic. The right answer, then, is rarely to show some actual application of that particular result (although, to repeat, that might happen). More often, the right answer is about macro-utility: that a particular area of mathematics, or of research generally, is useful as a whole.

Calculus, for example, indisputably makes a contribution to many aspects of daily life, whether in the design of the bridge you drive over, the modelling behind the weather report, or the computer program that determines the way your pension fund invests your money. Its very pervasiveness, however, renders it invisible. While we daily experience the consequences of designs or models or decisions determined by mathematical means, and more generally by pure research, mostly we do not see the actual workings out of the process by which that design or decision was reached.

If you hold a calculator or a mobile phone in your hand, you do not actually see the electronic circuits that make it work. Much less do you see the mathematics behind the design of those circuits. It might not occur to you, for example, that electronic circuit design makes extensive use of so-called 'imaginary numbers'. The layman's explanation of what these imaginary numbers are is that they are constructed on the basis of something that seems impossible, namely the square root of minus one. It turns out that such numbers, imaginary or not, are really useful. Every undergraduate electrical engineering student, for example, will learn about something called Euler's equation. (Leonhard Euler, 1707–83, is sometimes claimed to be the greatest mathematician ever. Hardy followed in the footsteps of Euler on some topics.) Euler's equation relates four numbers. The first is the archetypal 'imaginary' number, called i, which is the square root of minus one. The next two are what are called 'irrational numbers' – which is not to say that they are mad, but to say that neither can be expressed as a ratio of two ordinary whole numbers. One of these irrational numbers is called e, which is the base of something called the natural logarithm – rounded off to five decimals it is 2.71828, although the full decimal expansion carries on without repetition to infinity. The other irrational number is called π (the Greek letter pi), which is the ratio of the circumference of any circle to its diameter – rounded off to five decimals it is 3.14159, although again the full decimal expansion carries on without repetition to infinity.[7] Euler's equation says that if you raise e to the power of π-multiplied-by-i, then the answer is minus one.

Euler's equation is often called the most beautiful equation in mathematics – a sentiment Hardy would have agreed with, although he is likely to have had other candidates for the title. There is no conflict here between beauty and utility.

The issue of utility brings up a fourth observation, which is about applied research. Since the utility of 'pure' research is so slow and unpredictable in becoming apparent, we may well want to speed up and direct the process of translating curiosity into utility by going out to look for applications. That is the basic idea of 'applied' research. To illustrate the point, let us consider the topic of applied mathematics. This is a subject on which Hardy was particularly scathing.

> But is not the position of an ordinary applied mathematician in some ways a little pathetic? If he wants to be useful, he must work in a humdrum way, and he cannot give full play to his fancy even when he wishes to rise to the heights. 'Imaginary' universes are so much more beautiful than this stupidly constructed 'real' one; and most of the finest products of an applied mathematician's fancy must be rejected, as soon as they

have been created, for the brutal but sufficient reason that they do not fit the facts.[8]

We should not dismiss these ideas lightly, because many have been swayed by them. Even in the 1980s Paul Halmos, an esteemed mathematician, could in all seriousness publish an article with the title 'Applied mathematics is bad mathematics'.[9] Halmos was of a decidedly Hardyesque frame of mind, echoing the idea that mathematics is a creative art.[10] On the website of the Mathematical Association of America it is related that once, when Halmos was interviewed, he was asked: 'What is mathematics to you?' He responded: 'It is security. Certainty. Truth. Beauty. Insight. Structure. Architecture. I see mathematics, the part of human knowledge that I call mathematics, as one thing – one great, glorious thing.' A few years later, he was asked about the best part of being a mathematician. He said: 'I'm not a religious man, but it's almost like being in touch with God when you're thinking about mathematics.'[11] It is worth noting that Halmos was not only a gifted creative mathematician in the Hardy mould, he was also a respected teacher and expositor, with awards to show for both.

There is a terminological ambiguity about 'applied mathematics'. Used in one sense it is a subject area, and used in another sense it is an activity. For Hardy, and for many mathematicians for decades after Hardy, 'applied mathematics' was a subject, also called 'theoretical physics'. This goes right back to Isaac Newton, who invented the differential and integral calculus in order to describe the world around us. Newton held the Lucasian Chair of Mathematics at Cambridge, a recent incumbent of which was Stephen Hawking. That Chair is situated at Cambridge in the Department of Applied Mathematics and Theoretical Physics, whereas Hardy's Sadleirian Chair of Pure Mathematics is held in the Department of Pure Mathematics and Mathematical Statistics. Old demarcations die hard in universities. From Newton to Hawking, and in applied mathematics departments across the world, there is a strong sense of a particular discipline which tries to model the cosmos, on all scales from the sub-atomic to the supra-universal, and which employs mathematical means to do so. For many academics this is what applied mathematics consists of.

Over time there have been many and varied debates about distinguishing 'applied mathematics', as a discipline, from 'pure mathematics', as a discipline. Many battles have been fought over academic turf, to decide whether a university should have a department of applied mathematics as well as a department of pure mathematics (not to mention a department of statistics), or just an overall department of mathematical sciences. There is also, however, another discussion, more to the point for present purposes, which sees applied mathematics as the activity of using mathematical methods and results to model situations and solve problems from the world of experience. In this sense, applied mathematics is not a discipline but a methodology. This line of thinking is consistent with topics such as biomathematics, financial mathematics, computational mathematics, game theory, cryptography, computer security, population dynamics, and modelling of many kinds. The practitioners of such areas of work are unlikely to see what they do as some kind of mathematics different from 'pure' mathematics. Their interest is typically in modelling situations from the world around us in such a manner that useful conclusions may be drawn and practical decisions may be taken, for which purpose they will use whatever methods will come in useful no matter what part of mathematics they come from.

As a fifth observation we should take note of the philosophical basis of the Hardy/Halmos view of mathematics. As any student of philosophy would have surmised by now, it is Platonism.

One of the most enduring questions in philosophy is the ontological question. What is the world made up of? Two and a half millennia ago, Plato, speaking through the voice of Socrates, put forward an answer which has proved to be very durable. The world around us, Plato said, is but a poor imitation of a world which is made up of *ideas*. These ideas, or forms, or – as the philosophers would say – universals, have a reality of their own, divorced from and primary to any physical reality. The world of ideas is more real, more pure, more beautiful, more structured and altogether less messy than the world we experience.

So what are these ideas or universals? You can get to a universal by considering an adjective as denoting an object. 'Red', for example, is an adjective, and you may consider this adjective to denote an object called 'redness', which is a universal. The advantage of doing so is that you can now say that any physical object is red only in so far as it manifests the *real* object, which is redness. 'Good' is an adjective, and if you reify that then you get 'the good' as a universal. Then our actions and intentions are good only in so far as they reflect the universal good. The key idea is that universals are abstract objects, that it is the abstract object that is real, and that in our physical lives we sense or experience only imperfect copies of that ultimate reality. In an ironic terminological twist, this point of view is known among philosophers as 'realism'.

The ontological question also crops up in mathematics. What is it that mathematicians are actually studying? You may feel on solid ground by saying that, among other things, mathematicians study numbers. But what is a number? You have five fingers on your hand, there are five rings in the Olympic logo and five corners to a pentagon – but is there such thing as the number five? And if so, what kind of an entity is it? Platonism gives a convenient answer. Numbers, and number theory, align well with the view that reality is not about things but about ideas. On this view, your hand and the Olympic logo and the pentagon all have an attribute in common, namely having five parts or members, and that attribute reflects a Platonic form, the idea of 'fiveness'. This idea or form or universal of fiveness is what we commonly call the number five. So the number five is a real entity, just as much (and maybe more so) as the chair you are sitting on or the book you have in your hand. On the Platonic view numbers exist independently, aphysically and atemporally. And if you think this is not a good answer then you may legitimately be challenged to provide a better one.

Once you have grasped the idea of numbers as Platonic ideas, any discomfort with 'irrational' or 'imaginary' numbers disappears. It is no longer a concern that π or i seems quite abstract, because so is five. All numbers, of any kind, in fact, are of the same kind of abstractness, inhabiting a Platonic universe. In this universe there will be many mathematical galaxies, one of which will be a galaxy of numbers. Such a Platonic universe is one in which many mathematicians choose to live, and spend their time exploring galaxies where they can access and appreciate that supreme beauty of which Bertrand Russell spoke.

When Hardy dismissed 'this stupidly constructed' world that we live in, therefore, that was not so much a conscious rhetorical flourish as a statement of his Platonistic beliefs. He was adamant, for example, that a mathematician is in much more direct contact with reality than a physicist, because to the Platonist numbers are more real than physical objects.

Which brings us to a sixth point about 'pure' research. When we speak about 'knowledge creation', say for example in mathematics, we are skirting an old and difficult question. Are mathematical results invented, or discovered? When Euler produced his equation, did he invent that result, just as Edison invented the phonograph, or did he find it, like Columbus found America? On this question, Hardy himself was never in any doubt. Mathematical results, for him, are not invented. They are discovered.

> I believe that mathematical reality lies outside us, that our function is to discover or observe it, and that the theorems which we prove, and which we describe grandiloquently as our 'creations', are simply our notes of our observations. This view has been held, in one form or another, by many philosophers of high reputation from Plato onwards, and I shall use the language which is natural to a man who holds it.[12]

Finally, Hardy's observation that he will use the language natural to a Platonist is also not to be passed over lightly. It grasps the point that language is a powerful tool. The terminology of 'pure' mathematics, or 'pure' research, is a case in point. If the world of numbers is 'pure', then only politeness prevents us from saying that bringing mathematics to bear on the world of experience is 'impure'. And sometimes not even politeness, as in the case of Halmos. Presumably the phrase 'applied mathematics' was sufficiently polite terminology, which none the less served to make the point that such endeavours are not of the same aesthetic standard as the 'pure' ones. Likewise, with 'pure' and 'applied' research. There is a value judgement built into the terminology, and that is something to be aware of.

The Platonic idea of a university

> It is not at all clear whether people should be trained
> in what is useful for life, in what conduces to virtue,
> or in something out of the ordinary.
> *Aristotle, Politics, Book VIII, chapter two*

For many people 'the university' exists as a Platonic idea. In this view, the universities in which we live and work are each but an imperfect imitation of the real idea of a university. There are good approximations, like the Oxbridge of G.H. Hardy, but none actually fully capture the 'real' idea of a university.

The phrase 'the idea of a university' has a lot of academic currency. It comes from the title of a canonical text, *The Idea of a University*, by John Henry Newman, later Cardinal Newman, now well under way to being declared a saint by the Catholic Church. The origin of the book is a series of nine 'Discourses' delivered in Dublin in 1852, after Newman had taken up post there as the founding rector of a new Catholic university. The institution did not last, but may be considered a precursor to what is today University College Dublin. On the occasion of its 150th anniversary in 2005, University College Dublin brought out a new edition of the definitive version of Newman's *Idea*, as it appeared in 1889, under the full title *The Idea of a University Defined and Illustrated; I In Nine Discourses delivered to the Catholics of Dublin, II In Occasional Lectures and Essays addressed to the members of the Catholic University*.[13]

This book is well worth browsing through, even if you are not inclined to read all 500-odd pages. As the editor says in her Preface, Newman's *Idea* is a classic which shares with Plato's *Dialogues* the quality of being both a work of literature and a work of philosophy. The opening sentence of Newman's own Preface gives an idea of what is to follow:

> The view taken of a University in these Discourses is
> the following:- That it is a *place* of *teaching* universal
> knowledge. This implies that its object is, on the one
> hand, intellectual, not moral; and on the other, that
> it is the diffusion and extension of knowledge rather
> than the advancement. If its object were scientific and

philosophical discovery, I do not see why a University should have students; if religious training, I do not see how it can be the seat of literature and science.

If we momentarily delete the word 'religious', this makes two disputable but quite contemporary points. First, that the true function of a university is not the creation of knowledge, but its dissemination. So the university is not about research but about teaching. Second, Newman means education of a particular kind, which is the opposite of what we would call training. These debates are very much still with us: research vis-à-vis teaching as core functions of the university, and the nature of both.

Just as Newman may be regarded as the great advocate of university teaching, we can also find a founding father of the idea of research as a core function of the university. His name is Wilhelm von Humboldt, a Prussian intellectual and government functionary around the time of the Napoleonic wars. You can see a statue of von Humboldt outside the University of Berlin, of which he is regarded as the founder.

[In 1810] Wilhelm von Humboldt wrote a memorandum[14] that led to the creation of the University of Berlin. He envisaged a university based on three principles: unity of research and teaching, freedom of teaching and academic self-governance. The first was critical both of research divorced from teaching, undertaken by private scholars or in separate research institutes, without the stimulation of sharing those investigations with young minds, and of higher education divorced from original enquiry. The second, *Freiheit der Lehre und des Lernens*, was that professors should be free to teach in accordance with their studiously and rationally based convictions. The third principle, of academic self-government, only implicit in Humboldt's memo but increasingly apparent as an integral component of his vision, was meant to protect academic work from the distortions of government control.[15]

As is clear from this quote von Humboldt had a holistic idea of a university, situated within the German educational tradition of intellectual self-cultivation called *Bildung*. John Henry Newman, on the other hand, in defining a university as a place of teaching, simultaneously ruled out a second core function of 'scientific and philosophical discovery'. While it is useful, therefore, to contrast von Humboldt's advocacy of research with Newman's advocacy of teaching (and I will do so), we should not forget that von Humboldt had a broader vision of the university than Newman.

Before von Humboldt, a university was, more or less, a place where the classic seven liberal arts would be studied at what we would now call undergraduate level, whereas professional subjects such as law or medicine or – importantly – theology would be studied at postgraduate level. In the wake of von Humboldt's reforms came the idea of 'disciplines': subjects beyond the liberal arts, but not necessarily 'professional'. These were the kind of disciplines familiar to us today, on which I will say more in the next section. From these disciplines, in turn, came the practice of academic specialisation. What you do, as an academic, is to profess a discipline. That is what makes you a professor.

The idea of the liberal arts is an old an enduring one: it is the kind of education deemed suitable for a free citizen. It would prepare people to take an active part in civic life, including the capacity to participate in debate. In the 5th century AD one Martianus Capella, a contemporary of St Augustine and a fellow North African, defined the liberal arts as three plus four subjects, known as the *trivium* and the *quadrivium*.[16] The *trivium* formed the basis for reasoning, and consisted of grammar, logic and rhetoric. The *quadrivium* was more mathematical, comprising arithmetic, geometry, astronomy and music (a classification coming from the Pythagoreans). And so we got our idea of 'reading, writing and arithmetic', and so it remained for many centuries: a set curriculum with set textbooks. Aristotle's logic of syllogisms and Euclid's *Elements of Geometry*, for example, remained required study until the 19th century.

Today there are still many liberal arts colleges all over the world, particularly in America, and most academics anywhere in the world will know, more or less, what is meant by a liberal arts education. It is a strong and durable tradition. There is a lovely book, for example, titled *The Trivium: The Liberal Arts of Logic, Grammar and*

Rhetoric: Understanding the Nature and Function of Language, by Sister Miriam Joseph of Saint Mary's College in South Bend, Indiana, first published in 1937, then reverently edited and republished in 2002. For Sister Miriam, who taught the *trivium* at Saint Mary's for 25 years, 'the liberal arts denote the seven branches of knowledge that initiate the young into a life of learning'. Her views would not have been out of place in Newman's *Idea of a University*:

> The utilitarian or servile arts enable one to be a servant – of another person, of the state, of a corporation, or of a business – and to earn a living. The liberal arts, in contrast, teach one how to live; they train the faculties and bring them to perfection; they enable a person to rise above his material environment to live an intellectual, a rational, and therefore a free life in gaining truth.[17]

John Henry Newman would have no truck with the idea of research as a core function of the university, as he made clear in his opening sentence. Since he went to Dublin only a few decades after the Napoleonic wars he may well have been uncontaminated by radical ideas from Prussia. Until the 1830s there were still only two universities in England – the same two that had been there since the 13th century. Neither of these were active at that time in what we would now call research, let alone playing any part in the industrial revolution which was rapidly unfolding. Then, with the rise of the new manufacturing cities, came the first civic universities: Manchester, Liverpool, Birmingham and so on. Again, however, Newman, as is clear from his 'Discourses', kept his thoughts at a sanitary distance from such poor imitations of the idea of a university.

Knowledge, Newman emphasises repeatedly and at length, is an end in itself. This is a powerful idea, which Newman was neither the first nor the last to espouse, and which is still an article of faith for many academics. Mathematicians like Hardy are a good example.

Newman devotes one entire discourse (the fifth) to elaborating the point. 'I consider, then', he says, 'that I am chargeable with no paradox, when I speak of a Knowledge which is its own end, when I call it liberal knowledge, or a gentleman's knowledge, when I educate for it, and make it the scope of a University.' The basic premise of knowledge as its own end allows us to understand the university as a community of scholars, and the benefit which accrues to students in such a community, namely absorbing a liberal education.

> This I conceive to be the advantage of a seat of universal learning, considered as a place of education. An assemblage of learned men, zealous for their own sciences, and rivals of each other, are brought, by familiar intercourse and for the sake of intellectual peace, to adjust together the claims and relations of their respective subjects of investigation. They learn to respect, to consult, to aid each other. Thus is created a pure and clear atmosphere of thought, which the student also breathes, though in his own case he pursues only a few sciences out of the multitude. He profits by an intellectual tradition, which is independent of particular teachers, which guides him in his choice of subjects, and duly interprets for him those which he chooses. He apprehends the great outlines of knowledge, the principles on which it rests, the scale of its parts, its lights and its shades, its great points and its little, as he otherwise cannot apprehend them. Hence it is that his education is called 'Liberal'. A habit of mind is formed which lasts through life, of which the attributes are, freedom, equitableness, calmness, moderation, and wisdom; or what in a former Discourse I have ventured to call a philosophical habit. This then I would assign as the special fruit of the education furnished at a University, as contrasted with other places of teaching or modes of teaching. This is the main purpose of a University in the treatment of its students.[18]

Satisfied that this point has been sufficiently made, Newman then turns to the obvious follow-on question: 'And now the question is asked of me, What is the use of it? and my answer will constitute the main subject of the Discourses which are to follow.' Which indeed is what happens, through four more discourses. First he elaborates on the question:

> Now this is what some great men are very slow to allow; they insist that Education should be confined to some particular and narrow end, and should issue in some definite work, which can be weighed and measured. They argue as if every thing, as well as every person, had its price; and that where there has been a great outlay, they have a right to expect a return in kind. This they call making Education and Instruction 'useful', and 'Utility' becomes their watchword. With a fundamental principle of this nature, they very naturally go on to ask, what is there to show for the expense of a University; what is the real worth in the market of the article called 'a Liberal Education', on the supposition that it does not teach us definitely how to advance our manufactures, or to improve our lands, or to better our civil economy; or again, if it does not lead to discoveries in chemistry, astronomy, geology, magnetism and science of every kind.[19]

This is all very topical in the second decade of the 21st century. What is the use of a liberal education? For Newman, the matter is clear. First, the question itself is essentially based on a lack of understanding of the relationship between the good and the useful.

> I say, let us take 'useful' to mean, not what is simply good, but what *tends* to good, or is the *instrument* of good; and in this sense also, Gentlemen, I will show you how a liberal education is truly and fully a useful, though it be not a professional, education. 'Good' indeed means one thing, and 'useful' means another, but I lay it down as a principle, which will save us a great deal of anxiety, that, though the useful is not always good, the good is always useful....
>
> I say then, if a liberal education be good, it must necessarily be useful.[20]

This is a nice little piece of sophistry: lay down an axiom that the good is always useful, and then deduce that a liberal education is useful because it is good. But Newman is not done yet. In magisterial style, with mile-long sentences, he explicates the proposition that a liberal education is an instrument of preparation for life, and as such is good for anything and everything.

> Again, as health ought to precede labour of the body, and as a man in health can do what an unhealthy man cannot do, and as of this health the properties are strength, energy, agility, graceful carriage and action, manual dexterity, and endurance of fatigue, so in like manner general culture of the mind is the best aid to professional and scientific study, and educated men can do what illiterate cannot; and the man who has learned to think and to reason and to compare and to discriminate and to analyze, who has refined his taste, and formed his judgment, and sharpened his mental vision, will not indeed at once be a lawyer, or a pleader, or an orator, or a statesman, or a physician, or a good landlord, or a man of business, or a soldier, or an engineer, or a chemist, or a geologist, or an antiquarian, but he will be placed in that state of intellect in which he can take up any one of the sciences or callings I have referred to, or any other for which he has a taste or special talent, with an ease, a grace, a versatility, and a success, to which another is a stranger. In this sense, then, and as yet I have said but a very few words on a large subject, mental culture is emphatically *useful*.[21]

We may take issue with Newman's claim (in this, his seventh discourse) about having 'as yet said but a very few words' on the subject. But his point has been emphatically made. And it has been long-lasting. To turn to a contemporary version, consider a book published in 2012, titled *What Are Universities For?*, by Stefan Collini, Professor of Intellectual History and English Literature at Cambridge University.[22] In his third chapter, Professor Collini opens with a warning:

Anyone who attends to the history of debates about the values and purposes of universities needs to cultivate a high tolerance for repetition. The topic's capacity to generate eye-glazing truisms of various kinds seems matched by its tendency to recur to a small set of binary oppositions. In Britain, though also elsewhere, these debates fall into a particularly dispiriting pattern, which might be parodied as the conflict between the 'useful' and the 'useless'.

And, continues Collini, besides harping on about the useful and the useless, 'another, more minor but in its way no less striking, piece of repetition, [is] the constant invocation in the literature on higher education of John Henry Newman's *The Idea of a University*'.[23]

Professor Collini then poses an interesting and illuminating question: why has this debate about the useful and the useless not been settled a long time ago? Why doesn't the 'useful' side of the debate win once and for all? Why does Newman keep coming back?

Indeed so. And the answer Professor Collini arrives at, after factoring out Newman's religious predispositions and the persuasive effect of his wonderful prose, is surely the only one possible: the 'useless' side of the debate keeps getting up from the floor because Newman has a point. A valid point. The so-called 'useless' focus on knowledge for its own sake has something about it that we want, and that we always return to, no matter how much we also value utility. In the remainder of (the first half) of his book, Collini proceeds to give, in contemporary terms, his own outline of the character and value of the humanities and the idea of universities as a public good. It is phrased in a different context, and a different (though no less elegant) style of prose, but Collini's main contention is essentially Newmanesque, and none the worse for that.

There is ample evidence of an appetite in society for knowledge that has no immediately apparent 'useful' outcome, and a capacity to value such knowledge for its own sake. The only two preconditions seem to be that the subject matter must either be understandable, or generally understood to be so profound that understanding cannot generally be expected. In 2012–13, for example, Britain was transfixed by the story of the 'the king in the car park' – the exhumation of what proved to be the bones of King Richard III in the grounds of the former Greyfriars church in Leicester. Print and broadcast media ran with the story for months. A TV documentary was made about it (and won an award). A book was written. York fought Leicester for the honour of interring the remains (but lost). Leicester University, whose archaeologists led the search, enjoyed a jump in public esteem. Finding some old bones in a car park is not a particularly 'useful' thing to do, in the sense that it is unlikely to make us any healthier or wealthier. But perhaps it made us a little bit wiser. Anybody could understand the story, many people could relate to it in some way, and nobody said a word about it being a 'useless' thing to do.

At the other end of the scale, there are many things we support without understanding them, as long as we are persuaded that some really clever people do understand them, and that it helps those people – and therefore ultimately us – understand the world better. So, for example, we do not mind – indeed, we positively support – a large taxpayer-funded organisation called CERN spending £2.6 billion to build a 27 km circular tunnel 100 m under the ground to smash protons together at almost the speed of light, in order to search for an elementary particle called the Higgs Boson, the existence of which was hypothesised in a piece of 'pure' research decades ago. Dimly, perhaps, we are aware that finding the Higgs Boson will somehow help us understand why things have mass, which would be interesting to know.

Such examples of the appreciation of 'useless' but interesting knowledge are easily multiplied. We love the story of dinosaurs, and would like to know more about them, although they are millions of years removed from us and pose no current threat or advantage. We are thrilled to hear that, about 1,400 light years away, there is a planet called Kepler 452b which looks pretty much like the earth, because we keep wondering whether we are alone in the universe. We avidly read Booker Prize-winner Hilary Mantel's historical fiction about the Tudors, and 4 million people watch the TV programme, because the Tudors seem so much like us.[24] Such fiction also gets a reaction from the scholars, researching and debating the respective roles of Thomas Cromwell and Thomas More.

Little of this would have been possible without an underlying structure and network of 'pure' research, and little of those structures and networks would have been possible unless there was a space, conceptual and physical, for 'pure' research to thrive. Such a space can easily be conceived of as part of the Platonic idea of a university. And for such an idea, of an ideal university beyond the blue sky, society seems to have an appetite. Even if the idea is not fully understood, or its nature hotly disputed, it is somehow understood to be profound.

And many people would like to go there. Parents would like their children to go to a 'good' university. Academics like to trade up from their current place of employment to one which they believe more closely approximates the Platonic idea of a university. Business and industry may grumble about graduates not being work-ready, but it is clear from which universities they prefer to recruit. Governments, while busily trying to make universities more useful, will boast that their country is one of the best in the world at pure research.

The era of the ologies

> Expanded federal research support in the 1960s and early 1970s to meet the needs of the Cold War and to pursue a competitive space exploration program prompted the rapid growth of graduate enrollments, Ph.D. production, and an expanded resource base for the research university.
>
> *The United States Country Report: Trends in Higher Education from Massification to Post-Massification, 1997*[25]

It is not a long way from the Platonic idea of a university to its caricature as an ivory tower. How convenient if those who contemplate a universe of pure ideas, who strive for 'certainty, truth, beauty, insight', were to be safely ensconced in a protected environment, at some distance from the 'stupidly constructed' world around us, and shielded from 'the duller routines' of a university. Newman clearly thought that early 19th-century Oxford was as close an approximation to the idea of a university as a gentleman could desire. (He spent a large part of his seventh discourse defending Oxford against some criticisms from Edinburgh, where the spirit of von Humboldt had materialised.) G.H. Hardy, sitting at Fenners cricket ground in the afternoon or at high table in the evening, may well have thought the same about Trinity College Cambridge in the 1930s. And many academics of today, particularly those nearing what used to be called retirement age, think back rather nostalgically to the university they grew up in between the early 1960s and the late 1980s.

In considering the nature and function of universities, the period between the ascent of Sputnik and the fall of the Berlin wall is worth special consideration. During this time a certain standard model of the university took shape: something like the Platonic idea, but here on earth. There are three reasons why. First, it was the time of the cold war, which, from the moment President Kennedy promised to put a man on the moon, put a lot of money and incentive into scientific research. Second, it was the beginning of the computer age, with the first mainframe computers in the 1960s and the first personal computers from the 1980s, before the internet changed everything again in the 1990s, and then social media in the 2000s. And, third, it was, in the UK, the time of the welfare state, when you could go to university for free, study what you like, and be pretty much assured of a job when you left.

Any one of these three factors – cold war, computers and welfare state – could have caused an expansion of higher education. Together, they caused an explosion. In 2012, the London-based magazine *Times Higher Education*, in one of its increasingly common university league tables, published a list of what it considered to be the world's best 100 universities under 50 years old.[26] The list is interesting not so much for its ranking as for reminding us of what happened in the 1960s and 1970s: the sudden and simultaneous creation of many new universities around the world. That was when, in the UK, well-known universities such as Brunel, Essex, Lancaster, Loughborough and York came into being – sometimes out of nothing, as in the case of Warwick (which is actually not in the town of Warwick, but just outside the somewhat bigger city of Coventry). In Australia, a big country with a small population, a large number of universities were created in the 1960s, such as Curtin, Deakin, Flinders, Griffith, La Trobe, Macquarie and Wollongong – sometimes referred to as the 'gumtree' universities, after the ubiquitous eucalypts, to distinguish them on the one hand from the older 'sandstone' universities, and on the other hand from the later universities created in the so-called 'Dawkins revolution' of 1989–92. Many new universities contemporaneously came into being in Europe (Aalborg, Bielefeld, Maastricht, Pierre et Marie Curie, Trento, Tromsø, Twente, Umeå), the United States (California at Irvine and at Santa Cruz, George Mason, Illinois at Chicago, Maryland at Baltimore, Texas at Dallas and at San Antonio) and Canada (Calgary, Concordia, Guelph, Simon Fraser). In the east, Taiwan alone had five entries on the *Times Higher*'s inaugural list of young universities, and Hong Kong had four, with others from Korea, Malaysia and Singapore.

More universities meant more students, and vice versa. With the drivers of expansion, particularly the welfare state, came the expansion of student numbers. Later this came to be called massification – the idea that many more students, not just by numbers but by proportion, can and should go to university.

In the UK, massification can be traced back to a 1963 report with the bland title *The Report of the Committee appointed by the Prime Minister under the Chairmanship of Lord Robbins.* Known then and now as the Robbins Report, it set higher education in the UK on a new track. At the time of the Robbins Report, fewer than 5% of young Britons went to university, and of these fewer than a quarter were women. Fifty years later, just under half of young people in the UK went to university, and of these just over half were women. Key to this change was what has become known as the Robbins Principle: that university places 'should be available to all who are qualified by ability and attainment to pursue them, and who wish to do so'.[27]

At the same time, within the university, disciplinarity became the norm. Investment in knowledge spurred investment in specialisation. Therefore, as every shrewd academic and university manager divined, expansionism would work not only within the sector but also within a university. The way to get ahead was to create more departments, units or structures, for ever more specialised disciplines and subdisciplines. Thus, in the standard model era, a university would typically have three mathematical departments: 'pure', 'applied' and 'statistics'. In addition, it might have a department of cosmology and/or astronomy and/ or theoretical physics, and possibly a department of mathematics education as well. Any university of reasonable size would have at least ten academic divisions, or 'faculties', as they are known in the British Commonwealth (to the confusion of Americans, where 'faculty' refers to academics). A faculty would delineate some category of academic work: agriculture, arts, commerce, dentistry, engineering, fine art, forestry, humanities, law, medicine, music, pharmacy, science, social sciences, theology, veterinary science – not by any law or regulation, nor even by convention, but by whatever sort of categorisation that particular university preferred. A faculty would then break down into departments, and these departments would typically represent whatever the prevailing view at that university was about academic disciplines.

Disciplines ruled, and disciplines demanded structures. A faculty of medicine could have upward of 30 departments, to accommodate what medical professors call 'ologies': cardiology, dermatology, gynaecology, hepatology, immunology, nephrology, oncology, pathology, rheumatology, toxicology, urology, virology – and this is before you get to anaesthetics, dietetics, genetics, obstetrics, paediatrics and so on. Likewise, a faculty of science would not only have several departments for mathematical sciences, but also more than one department for physics, quite possibly separate departments of organic chemistry, inorganic chemistry, physical chemistry and biochemistry, departments of biology and microbiology, botany and zoology, computer science and information systems, geography, geology and so on, to whatever extent the university, the faculty or individual professors could argue the case and afford its implementation.

Similarly for other faculties. A commerce faculty could have departments for accounting, actuarial science, business management, economics, finance, industrial psychology, information systems, logistics, marketing and public administration. Even a small faculty like law could easily have departments for administrative law, commercial law, constitutional law, environmental law, international law, labour law, private law, and public law. In a faculty of theology, no matter how tiny, the possibilities for subdisciplinary structures are practically infinite, being defined only by what faith demands. The idea of disciplines as 'ologies', manifested as structures, is not confined to medicine.

A distinguishing feature of the standard model of a university, therefore, is the way academic structures reflect a taxonomy of disciplines. Big structures – faculties – go with broad disciplinary areas, like humanities or natural sciences or commerce. Basic structures – departments – go with ologies which are considered to be basic disciplines, like anthropology or biology or cosmology – or history or logic or statistics. Substructures go with specialisations like economic history or political philosophy or organic chemistry. For special purposes there may be further intersections and aggregations, like medieval French literature, or PPE (politics plus philosophy plus economics).

After structure, a second important feature of the standard model is function. What does a university do?

In the standard model, the answer is simple: a university does research and it does teaching. It puts von Humboldt and Newman alongside each other. And here function follows form: in the standard model, research is carried out within disciplines, and so is teaching. As an academic, you are a representative of your discipline, and you identify yourself as such: you are an anthropologist or a biologist or a cosmologist, a historian or a logician or a statistician. This is the von Humboldt paradigm, which still defines social interaction between academics. To the standard question 'What do you do?', the socially correct response is to say what your subject is. What you actually do do is then understood: you profess your subject. On the one hand you profess by expanding the subject, through creating new knowledge, and on the other hand you profess your subject by disseminating it – which means you publish results and you produce graduates. In other words, you do research and you do teaching. And as long as you do these two things well, then that is your job done.

What this means is that the standard model of a university operates mostly on the supply side of the knowledge economy. This point is worth exploring.

The idea of a knowledge economy was popularised by Peter Drucker in his 1969 book *The Age of Discontinuity*.[28] The basic premise is that the wealth of nations will depend, not on what we can grow on the land, or mine from the earth, or manufacture, or trade, or transact. In a knowledge economy, prosperity will depend primarily on knowledge and ideas that exist in our minds, and the way we use that knowledge and those ideas to make changes in the world and in society. If we accept this premise, there is an obvious general question to ask: in a knowledge economy, what are the drivers of supply and demand?

The question is relevant to universities because a university is about knowledge. In the standard model university, in particular, it is all about creating and disseminating knowledge. Presumably, therefore, universities can and should play a key part in the knowledge economy. The follow-on question is, how?

The standard model offers an answer, which is this: the university is a producer and supplier of knowledge. Its role is to pump out knowledge into the world, and it does so through its two core functions of research and teaching. On the standard model, the university is a knowledge production factory, the products of which are publications and graduates. This factory is organised into units of increasing specialisation, at the base of which is the individual worker – the academic. And this is where we find the driver of supply in the knowledge economy: it is the curiosity of the individual.

In the standard model university, the academic credo is that it is not only accepted, but expected, that academics will investigate topics they are curious about, and are therefore quite likely to produce knowledge for which there has not initially been any particular need. We have seen G.H. Hardy as an exemplar. He was an autonomous knowledge generator, who worked exclusively on the supply side of mathematical knowledge. He and his peers believed, implicitly or explicitly, that creating and disseminating new knowledge was sufficient justification for the life of a mathematician and the existence of a university.

To researchers and institutions in this frame of mind, the value of the research endeavour lies with the quality of what is produced. Their quality judgement is about intrinsic quality – whether the product is good, rather than what it is good for. And the mechanism by which quality is judged is through peer evaluation. When a mathematician produces a new piece of mathematical knowledge, it is evaluated by those other mathematicians who actually understand the result, and the methods used to obtain that result. These peers are able to judge whether the result is correct and significant, and whether the methods of obtaining it are valid and elegant. In practice, peer evaluation unfolds during the process of refereeing the result, once it has been submitted for publication in a professional journal. Should the piece of work pass muster it will get published, and thereby 'extend the frontiers of knowledge'. In that phrase lies the response to the value question about the supply side. In the standard model, the primary task of the university and the academic is to contribute to the sum total of knowledge.

There is then a follow-up question. If the value of academia lies in building an edifice of knowledge and understanding, how do we judge the value of the edifice? How does all that knowledge that has been created contribute to society, or to individuals? We have already seen two answers on offer, each a variation on the theme of knowledge for its own sake. The first is the aesthetic response, along the lines of G.H. Hardy: that true knowledge is beautiful, and that the beautiful needs no further justification. On this way of thinking the edifice of knowledge stands like a sculpture – as Bertrand Russell thought of mathematics. It is there to be appreciated, overall or in parts, as far as we are able, and for us to be uplifted by that experience. The second response is moral: gaining knowledge is part of the search for truth, this is what distinguishes us from other organisms on the planet, it expands the mind and exalts our higher faculties, and makes us better human beings. This is the Newmanesque response (after factoring out, again, the religion and the rhetoric).

Each of these responses justifies 'knowledge for its own sake' as an attempt to comprehend a Platonic idea: the beautiful, or the good. The standard model of a university absorbed these two responses and added a third and more pragmatic one. Namely, that the knowledge edifice is valuable because, very often, it turns out to be useful – despite the fact that utility was not its original purpose, and that we have no idea about where or when utility might come to light. We can be confident of striking gold without looking for it. And so we get, for free, an additional utilitarian response to the value question: knowledge brings benefits, both for individuals and for society. The standard model goes further than Newman's abstract argument that the good is always useful. It actually demonstrates the point, building up a stock of examples where curiosity-driven research in the end proved to be of practical benefit. 'Practical benefit' we may take to mean yielding, for the individual, community or society, an increase of wellbeing, security, health or wealth. In short, knowledge is a good thing because it can make life better. (It can also make life worse, as Hardy rather pessimistically pointed out, but that is different strand of argument.)

In terms of the knowledge economy, we may call the idea that knowledge becomes useful in a non-deterministic fashion the 'invisible hand argument'. Adam Smith argued in *The Wealth of Nations*[29] that if the producer is free to choose what to produce and the consumer is free to choose what to buy then an invisible hand will regulate the market to the maximum benefit of society. So, accepting and adapting this metaphor, the best way for the knowledge economy to work is for academics to produce knowledge in any manner they like, for this knowledge to be freely available, and for society to pick whatever bits it finds useful. The fact that utility was not part of the knowledge producer's intention is immaterial. It might even be a good thing. As Adam Smith said, of the producer:

> [He] is in this, as in many other cases, led by an invisible hand to promote an end which was no part of his intention. Nor is it always the worse for the society that it was not part of it. By pursuing his own interest he frequently promotes that of the society more effectually than when he really intends to promote it.[30]

Standard model academics love the invisible hand argument. It can conveniently be deployed to justify 'knowledge for its own sake' even to philistines who do not appreciate the beautiful or the good, but insist on usefulness as a quid pro quo for support. For this purpose, convincing examples can be given.

The task is complicated only by an embarrassment of riches. We have already seen the example of number theory. Logic, likewise, gives an example of how a very old and established discipline, one of the original seven liberal arts, can unexpectedly turn out to be useful. From Aristotle onward, logic had been thought of as the formalisation of reasoning. For many centuries, and still today, the subject has been an integral part of philosophy, sometimes taking rather strange and esoteric turns. (Try reading Hegel on logic, for example.) Even George Boole, who initiated the algebraic phase of logic, titled his seminal publication of 1854 *The Laws of Thought*. As if logic-as-philosophy had not been abstract enough, logic-as-mathematics added its own layers of abstraction, as the recommended look at *Principia Mathematica* will confirm. None the less, by the mid-1970s, with the computer era well under way, something quite unexpected had become quite clear: that the supposedly abstract and esoteric discipline of logic is a crucial foundation of the very practical discipline of computer science. In fact, logic stands to computer science in much the same relationship as calculus stands to engineering. The abstractions of logic are as necessary to the understanding of computing as the abstractions of imaginary numbers and Euler's equation are to the practical results delivered every day by engineers.

Natural science delivers many more examples of curiosity-driven research which eventually yields practical and beneficial outcomes, often stumbled upon rather than consciously sought. X-rays had been observed by various researchers for about 20 years before Wilhelm Röntgen photographed the bones in his wife's hand in 1895. The theoretical foundation for lasers can be traced back to a 1917 paper by Einstein, but it took decades of various studies before the term 'laser', for 'light amplification by stimulated emission of radiation', was coined in 1959. The first functioning laser device was constructed in 1960, at which time the idea was called 'a solution looking for a problem'.[31] Similar stories can be told about applications ranging from penicillin to microwave ovens to what happened at CERN in Switzerland, where the Large Hadron Collider was the largest and most expensive piece of scientific equipment ever built. Constructed to further our understanding of particle physics, CERN was also, in a major but unexpected side-effect, the birthplace of the worldwide web, which started as a means of enabling physicists to share data, news and information, before branching out 'to allow links to be made to any information anywhere'.[32] Some discoveries are so accidental as to be amusing. Sucralose, an artificial sweetener marketed by Tate & Lyle, was reputedly discovered when a graduate student in a lab at King's College London misheard an instruction to *test* a compound as a request to *taste* it.[33]

While we are sometimes able, in retrospect, to pinpoint a particular moment or event as the point where some piece of abstruse knowledge turned out to be seminal for application, mostly such specific information is well hidden in a web of knowledge and a tangle of predecessors. Even the creativity of G.H. Hardy in number theory builds on previous results going back many centuries, to Euler and others. And beyond mathematics the whole web of scientific knowledge is now so large, so intricate, and so dynamic, that it is difficult to comprehend even in parts, let alone in full.

One sustained effort at comprehension is the scientific discovery journal *Nature*.[34] Published continuously since 1869, it takes all of science as its domain. It is one of the most cited journals in the world. Publishing a paper in *Nature* is a major career boost for any academic. *Nature* makes a considerable effort to keep an overview of science, and make it understandable. At its heart is the publication of new scientific discoveries, but it also publishes summaries, news, editorials and feature articles on matters of general interest relating to science.

In 2003 *Nature* published a compendium called *A Century of Nature: Twenty-one Discoveries that Changed Science and the World*.[35] The editors are careful not to claim that these are the most important scientific discoveries of the 20th century, nor even that these are the most important papers published in *Nature* during that time. However, 'What we do claim is that these are all papers that transformed their subject – even, in some cases, the world.'[36] In that distinction lies the heart of the matter: 'pure' research may transform the subject, but 'applied' research transforms the world. Importantly, however, 'no discovery, no matter how startlingly original, stands alone'.

Helpfully the editors situate their 21 seminal papers within a chronological listing, year by year, of the overall highlights of scientific discovery in the 20th century. The topics are fascinating. They deal with the very small, the very large, the very old, life, and the earth. There is Planck on quantum theory, Rutherford on atoms and Einstein on relativity. There are neutrons, positrons, neutrinos and quarks. There are cosmic rays, galaxies, quasars, pulsars, the expansion of the universe and the big bang theory. There is *Australopithecus africanus* and *afarensis*, the impact hypothesis for the extinction of the dinosaurs and the 'Out of Africa' hypothesis of human evolution. There is the fact that the earth has a core, the idea of continental drift, the Richter scale for earthquakes and the theory of plate tectonics. All of this could be considered as purely academic considerations – interesting, but not particularly useful. But then consider the rest.

There is the discovery of human blood groups, the existence of vitamins, the isolation of insulin, the discovery of penicillin and the polio vaccine – and that just takes you up to mid-century. There is then the discovery of the double helix structure of DNA, from which comes genetic engineering techniques, DNA sequencing and genetic fingerprinting (and after the turn of the millennium the dawn of personalised medicine). There is the synthesis of ammonia, the start of the Mexican wheat improvement programme, the explanation of photosynthesis, the greenhouse effect and the ozone hole. There is superconductivity, the electron microscope, nuclear fission, radiocarbon dating, the transistor, the laser, magnetic resonance imaging, buckminsterfullerene and the cloning of Dolly the sheep. There is plenty of what has changed the world.

Indisputably, then, knowledge generated without purpose of utility can turn out to be useful, and often does. We cannot tell in advance which piece or part will turn out to be useful, nor how long it will take, but if we keep investing in the overall web of knowledge we can be sure of a return.

All of this is very comforting for the professors. But not everyone is content. Business people, industrialists, politicians and journalists, for example, are irritated by the fact that the process through which knowledge becomes useful is random, unpredictable and slow. They are not always content to wait for the invisible hand to do its work. They would really prefer the process to be managed, and preferably speeded up. Explicitly or implicitly, they tend to invoke an argument of causality. If knowledge causes utility, then surely there must be ways of analysing and enhancing that causal process, so as to reach the desired beneficial outcomes somewhat more directly, more quickly and more efficiently.

On this point too, the standard model has a response, which is the idea of applied research. The thought is that once pure research has generated knowledge – out of nothing, so to speak, and with no motive other than curiosity – applied research will go out and connect that knowledge to the real world. It will do so by looking for beneficial uses, problems to solve and opportunities to exploit, in real life. Here, 'real life' does not mean the reality of Platonic ideas, but the realities of life around us – getting up, going to work, paying the mortgage, having friends and family, living life and participating in society.

Consider graphene. In 2004, at the University of Manchester, Andre Geim and Konstantin Novoselov famously produced this new material by using sticky tape to split graphite crystals into increasingly thinner layers. The result is essentially a two-dimensional sheet of single atoms arranged in a hexagonal lattice structure. Graphene is one of the strongest materials ever tested, with a breaking strength 100 times greater than a hypothetical steel film of the same thickness. It is very light, with a sheet of one square meter weighing less than a milligram. It has unique mechanical, electronic, optical and thermal properties. It won Professors Geim and Novoselov the 2010 Nobel Prize in Physics. It has also started a gold rush of searching for applications.

In a *Nature Materials* paper titled 'The rise of graphene',[37] Geim and Novoselov summarise the matter as follows.

> Graphene is the name given to a flat monolayer of carbon atoms tightly packed into a two-dimensional (2D) honeycomb lattice, and is a basic building block for graphitic materials of all other dimensionalities. It can be wrapped up into 0D fullerenes, rolled into 1D nanotubes or stacked into 3D graphite. Theoretically, graphene (or '2D graphite') has been studied for sixty years, and is widely used for describing properties of various carbon-based materials. Forty years later, it was realized that graphene also provides an excellent condensed-matter analogue of (2+1)-dimensional quantum electrodynamics, which propelled graphene into a thriving theoretical toy model. On the other hand, although known as an integral part of 3D materials, graphene was presumed not to exist in the free state, being described as an 'academic' material and was believed to be unstable with respect to the formation of curved structures such as soot, fullerenes and nanotubes. Suddenly, the vintage model turned into reality, when free-standing graphene was unexpectedly

found three years ago – and especially when the follow-up experiments confirmed that its charge carriers were indeed massless Dirac fermions. So, the graphene 'gold rush' has begun.

This passage illustrates a number of points made earlier. First, graphene existed before it was created. That is, it existed theoretically, as 'pure' research, long before the possibility of its physical existence was demonstrated. Second, progress was slow – 60 years. Geim and Novoselov meticulously assign credit where credit is due, referencing papers on 'the band theory of graphite' that go back to 1947. Third, graphene is a classic case of 'pure' research eventually feeding into 'applied' research. The Nobel citation for Geim and Novoselov did not award them the prize for discovering a new material. It awarded them the prize 'for groundbreaking experiments regarding the two-dimensional material graphene'.[38] Fourth, and most strikingly: once the possibility of actually making graphene has been proven, its accumulated reserve of known theoretical properties becomes a rich seam which can be mined for applications. Geim and Novoselov conclude their paper by enumerating a few possibilities. 'It is most certain', they say, 'that we will see many efforts to develop various approaches to graphene electronics.' In parallel, they see applications being developed, very likely on a shorter timescale, in composite materials, electric batteries, plasma displays, solid-state gas sensors, hydrogen storage and even in the holy grail of computer science – quantum computing.

The commercial rewards of any or all these applications could be enormous. That has made governments and investors very interested in graphene. Shortly after the announcement of the Nobel Prize for Geim and Novoselov, the British government announced a fund of £50 million for graphene research. That was soon dwarfed by a fund of €1 billion made available by the European Union (EU) for research into the applications of graphene.

In summary, applied research will mine the results of pure research for applications. This is a convenient response to the question of how the supply-side model of knowledge production becomes useful, and applied research has therefore been a convenient add-on to the standard model of a university. Since the

1990s most universities will have, either in-house or outsourced, a 'tech transfer' structure and process of some kind, which tries to systematise the intellectual property generated by its research, and periodically trawls through this intellectual property portfolio to look for potential commercial applications.

In terms of structure and function, then, we may say that the standard model of the university is Newmanesque in valuing knowledge for its own sake, and Humboldtian in the pre-eminence of research. Both approaches focus on the individual as the fountainhead of knowledge. Knowledge emanates from the individual, and it is structured in ways which make sense to the producer. Knowledge is structured in terms of the scientific paradigm, and flows through the conduits called disciplines.

The way for new knowledge to become respectable was for it to be regarded as 'scientific'. And so, to quite a remarkable extent, all of academia developed science envy. The ultimate role models in science trying to understand the world were Aristotle, Newton and Einstein, and so the model for being scientific was physics. All of science thus developed physics envy. And finally, to complete the chain, all of physics had maths envy. This is what allowed G.H. Hardy to speak contemptuously of applied mathematicians, meaning theoretical physicists.

Which brings us to culture. The standard model strongly professes the idea of a community of scholars. What are the shared values, norms and beliefs of such a community? We may distinguish two fundamental principles, and three common beliefs.

The two fundamental principles of the standard model are academic freedom and institutional autonomy. Academic freedom is a principle that fits well with the standard model's emphasis on individual creativity. For individual curiosity to work best as a driver of knowledge production, there should be no constraint on exercising that curiosity. In their field of academic expertise, professors should be able to pursue whatever topic they like, and profess whatever conclusion they come to. There should be no prescription and no proscription. Results and conclusions should be made freely available. There should be free and open debate, in which no topic is beyond scrutiny. Academics should harbour neither fear nor favour. Their task is to question, their right is to speak, their obligation is to be objective. They should pursue 'certainty, truth, beauty, insight'. When necessary, they should be ready, able and willing to speak truth to power.

Academic freedom is primarily an attribute of the individual academic. Freedom of the individual, however, is best exercised from a base of collective security, and in the standard model the secure base for academic freedom is institutional autonomy. The university must be able to take its own decisions on how to conduct itself. It should be self-governing and not beholden to anyone. It will not issue instructions to any other part of society, but neither will it take them. It should be free from the state, free from the church, free from the military, free from the press, free from strictures of culture or language. As an autonomous institution, it may choose to align itself with, and even promote, a community, a culture or a religion, but in its academic function it should not be subordinate to any of these.

Academic culture in the standard model university may be summarised in three common beliefs. These are: that research trumps teaching, that pure research trumps applied research, and that anything academic trumps anything non-academic. We have seen these three beliefs play out in the life and work of G.H. Hardy. They unfold further into a number of features of the standard model university which will be familiar to many.

For all the idea of a community of scholars, the culture of the standard model encourages and rewards the work of the lone researcher. The best strategy towards promotion is to focus on your research. Pursuing that strategy, all or some of a number of tactics may be deployed. It is advantageous, for example, to establish your reputation as a disciplinary specialist – an ologist of some kind. To do so, you should try to publish in the best journals in your field – the so-called discovery journals, which focus on curiosity-driven research. The topic is really immaterial, as long as your work gets to be cited by other disciplinary experts. Single-author papers are better than collaborative publications, because they unambiguously establish your originality. 'Narrow it down' was good advice to a young academic in the 1970s and 1980s: better know more and more about less and less than the other way round. It does not matter if there are only five other people in the world who know what you are talking about, as long as those five people think you are a top expert in the disciplinary area the six of you have defined.

For the same reason, doing pure research is better than doing applied research. Since the standard model operates on the supply side of the knowledge economy it is the creation of knowledge that is prized above all. Applied research is not ruled out, but if practised it is best positioned in such a manner that you may call your work 'applied' when it feeds into the theory of another discipline. Thus what Hardy calls 'applied mathematics' a physicist would call 'theoretical physics', what counts as applied to a physicist would count as theory to an engineer, and what seems like an application to the engineer is theory to the technician. In this manner applied research essentially remains part of a knowledge production continuum.

In the standard model, teaching easily comes to be seen as a second-rate activity – a necessary part of the day job, but something to be performed as a duty rather than developed as a career. Many and ingenious are the excuses professors will invent in order to minimise their teaching duties on the departmental workload model. For many, it is a happy day when they can say 'I've been bought out of my teaching for this semester'. When it comes to supervision of research students, however, the situation is reversed, and professors will compete in enticing promising students to come and work with them. Partly, this is because teaching, in the standard model, is seen as a kind of academic procreation. The rationale for teaching is not so much to give the students what they want or need by way of an education, but to identify and train the very few, at the very top, who can become the next generation of disciplinary specialists. The idea of knowledge for its own sake plays into this quite nicely, because the students are supposed to study the subject in its own right, rather than in the context of their own career aspirations.

Finally, in the standard model, both the institution and the individual academic should be spared the inconvenience of having to concern yourself with money. In the standard model era the university was state-funded, usually through some kind of formula funding which, though complicated, was reasonably predictable. The unexamined assumption behind state funding, which really means taxpayer funding, is that higher education is a public good, and therefore the public should pay for it. There is another paradox here. Conceptually, the idea of state funding for the university does not fit well with the ideas of institutional autonomy and academic freedom, since there is inevitably a tension when you vigorously assert your independence from your paymaster. By and large, however, both the state and the university managed to accommodate this tension, possibly because of the benign climate for higher education at the time (which started breaking down in the Thatcher era).

At the individual level, the standard academic could reasonably assume that although they would never be rich neither would they ever be poor. A modest but adequate salary was acceptable, partly because being an academic puts you in the happy position of being paid to pursue your hobby, and partly because a good pension in retirement was assured. You also did not have to concern yourself about income generation of any kind, neither for your department nor for your university. There was no causal relationship between what the individual academic did and the finances of the university, and any such idea would have been foreign to standard model thinking.

Cracks in the ivory tower

> Science, by itself, provides no panacea for individual, social, and economic ills.
> *Vannevar Bush, Science: The Endless Frontier, 1945*

The standard model is very powerful and very appealing, and surely much of what it says is true. But is it anywhere near the whole truth? It tells us what universities are good *at*, which is the creation and dissemination of knowledge, but it does not really tell us what they are good *for*. Are we satisfied that the standard model gives an adequate representation, not just of how knowledge is produced, but why? Does it suffice for societal needs and demands? Can our questions about the role of knowledge in our lives, individually and collectively, be adequately addressed by reference to the standard model?

Five years after the fall of the Berlin wall, a short book with a long title appeared which comprehensively said no. This was *The New Production of Knowledge: The Dynamics of Science and Research in Contemporary Societies*,[39] a collaborative effort by six authors. An indication of its influence appears on the inside front cover, which records that the book has been reprinted 15 times since 1994. The lead author, Michael Gibbons, who wrote the Preface, was a science policy expert with a PhD in theoretical physics, and served as the Secretary General of the Association of Commonwealth Universities from 1996 to 2004.

Gibbons et al introduced into academic discourse two bland terms signifying different kinds of knowledge production. These became part of the academic lexicon: 'Mode 1' and 'Mode 2'.

> By contrast with traditional knowledge, which we will call Mode 1, generated within a disciplinary, primarily cognitive context, Mode 2 knowledge is created in broader, transdisciplinary social and economic contexts.[40]

And:

> In Mode 1 problems are set and solved in a context governed by the, largely academic, interests of a specific community. By contrast, Mode 2 knowledge is carried out in a context of application. Mode 1 is disciplinary while Mode 2 is transdisciplinary. Mode 1 is characterised by homogeneity, Mode 2 by heterogeneity. Organisationally, Mode 1 is hierarchical and tends to preserve its form, while Mode 2 is more heterarchical and transient. Each employs a different type of quality control. In comparison with Mode 1, Mode 2 is more socially accountable and reflexive. It includes a wider, more temporary and heterogeneous set of practitioners, collaborating on a problem defined in a specific and localised context.

Mode 1, in our terminology, was the knowledge-generation paradigm behind the 20th-century standard model of universities. It is based on the academic characterisation of scientific disciplines – a fact also pointed out by Gibbons et al:

A history of knowledge production since the seventeenth century could be written in terms of the efforts of the proponents of previously non-scientific forms of knowledge production to gain recognition as scientific. In Western cultures to be involved in non-scientific knowledge production is to place oneself beyond the pale, so that there is, today, a distinct sense of social isolation associated with participation in a non-scientific activity. But, the term scientific in this context already implies a distinct form of knowledge production. Its ideal is Newtonian empirical and mathematical physics.

The point made here is about what I have called science envy, morphing into physics envy. The more general point of Gibbons et al is that Mode 1 knowledge production is valuable but it is not sufficient. The standard model does not fully account for what academics do, and even less for what they could be doing.

This general point had already been made earlier by another author. Equally well known, and just as enduring as the distinction between Mode 1 and Mode 2 is a categorisation of academic activity introduced by Ernest L. Boyer in a Carnegie Foundation Report of 1990, titled *Scholarship Reconsidered: Priorities of the Professoriate.*[41] Whereas Gibbons et al are British and concerned almost entirely with research, Boyer is American and starts with teaching.

Today, on campuses across the nation, there is a recognition that the faculty reward system does not match the full range of academic functions and that professors are often caught between competing obligations. In response, there is a lively and growing discussion about how faculty should, in fact, spend their time. Recently, Stanford University president Donald Kennedy called for more contact between faculty and students, especially in the junior and senior years, a time when career decisions are more likely to be made. 'It is time', Kennedy said, 'for us to reaffirm that education – that is, teaching in all its forms – is the primary task' of higher education.[42]

But this is only the starting point. The central theme of Boyer's book is the question of what it means to be a scholar. And here, too, the question is essentially about the validity of the standard model.

> According to the dominant view, to be a scholar is to be a researcher – and publication is the primary yardstick by which scholarly productivity is measured.

However:

> The time has come, we believe, to step back and reflect on the variety of functions academics are expected to perform. It's time to ask how priorities of the professoriate relate to the faculty reward system, as well as to the missions of America's higher learning institutions. Such an inquiry into the work of faculty is essential if students are to be well served, if the creativity of all faculty is to be fully tapped, and if the goals of every college and university are to be appropriately defined.
>
> While we speak with pride about the great diversity of the American higher education, the reality is that on many campuses standards of scholarship have become increasingly restrictive, and campus priorities are frequently more imitative than distinctive. In this climate, it seems appropriate to ask: How can each of the nation's colleges and universities define, with clarity, its own special purposes? Should expectations regarding faculty performance vary from one type of institution to another? Can we, in fact, have a higher education system in this country that includes multiple models of success?

The idea of different missions for different universities, and multiple models of success, leads Boyer beyond the question of the relationship between research and teaching, to the role of universities in society.

Beyond the campus, America's social and economic crises are growing – troubled schools, budget deficits, pollution, urban decay, and neglected children, to highlight problems that are most apparent. Other concerns such as acid rain, AIDS, dwindling energy supplies, and population shifts are truly global, transcending national boundaries. Given these realities, the conviction is growing that the vision of service that once so energized the nation's campuses must be given a new legitimacy. The challenge then is this: Can America's colleges and universities, with all the richness of their resources, be of greater service to the nation and the world? Can we define scholarship in ways that respond more adequately to the urgent new realities both within the academy and beyond?

Out of these questions grew Boyer's response, which became known as 'the four scholarships'. The basic premise is that scholarship has four aspects: the creation of knowledge, the integration of knowledge, the application of knowledge and the dissemination of knowledge. Boyer himself referred to the scholarships of *discovery*, of *integration*, of *application* and of *teaching*. He carefully defined each of these in turn, in an attempt to inculcate a wider understanding of scholarship than that allowed by the standard model.

In particular, Boyer speaks up against the paradigm of scholarship narrowly understood as research.

Today, when we speak of being 'scholarly', it usually means having academic rank in a college or university and being engaged in research and publication. But we should remind ourselves just how recently the word 'research' actually entered the vocabulary of higher education. The term was first used in England in the 1870s by reformers who wished to make Cambridge and Oxford 'not only a place of teaching, but a place of learning', and it was later introduced to American higher education in 1906 by Daniel Coit Gilman. But scholarship in earlier times referred to a variety of creative work carried on in a variety of places, and its integrity was measured by the ability to think, communicate and learn.

What we now have is a more restricted view of scholarship, one that limits it to a hierarchy of functions. Basic research has come to be viewed as the first and most essential form of scholarly activity, with other functions flowing from it. Scholars are academics who conduct research, publish, and then perhaps convey their knowledge to students or apply what they have learned. The latter functions grew *out of* scholarship, they are not to be considered a part of it. But knowledge is not necessarily developed in such a linear manner. The arrow of causality can, and frequently does, point in *both* directions. Theory surely leads to practice. But practice also leads to theory. And teaching, at its best, shapes both research and practice.[43]

Boyer thus recognises and challenges the standard model view that discovery always precedes application. Moreover, he recognises that the role of universities in the knowledge economy lies not only on the supply side, but also on the demand side. 'Can social problems themselves', he asks, 'define an agenda for scholarly investigation?' And he refers to institutions such as the land-grant colleges, Renssellaer Polytechnic Institute, and the University of Chicago, all founded on the principle that higher education must serve the interests of the larger community. So applications do not only arise from previous curiosity-driven research. The scholarship of application takes its raw material from life and the world around us.

Given the similarity of their central theses, it is interesting that Gibbons et al make no mention of Boyer's book. Perhaps this omission is due to the research/teaching divide, or perhaps to the Atlantic Ocean, or perhaps because Boyer's book is named after the priorities of the professors and concerned with *their* understanding of scholarship. In that sense Gibbons et al made a more decisive transition, considering knowledge, research and scholarship also from the perspective of society. Once that line has been crossed, it is only a small further step to ask how, through their research and their teaching, universities engage with civil society.

The standard model fits best with the idea of universities remaining at arm's length from the world, indiscriminately spinning out knowledge and applications. None the less, following the era of the standard model, through Boyer, Gibbons et al and others, from the 1990s onward the idea of situating the university within the context of civil society took root and became legitimate.

It also took on a variety of forms. Boyer's idea of 'service to the nation and the world', which he resurrects from earlier times, easily morphed into a word that became a standard part of the university lexicon, namely 'outreach'. Like many other words commonly used by academics, there is no clear definition, and only superficial consensus as to what is meant. The basic premise is that the university should reach out and engage with society, but this can take place in many different ways. I will pick up on this topic a number of times, and sum up in Chapter Eight, but it is worth a preview here.

The first and most enduring version of outreach is, as Boyer said, that the university should render service. Quite often this takes the shape of what in business and industry would be called corporate social responsibility – doing good deeds. In principle, the exercise of social responsibility is not place-bound, but since charity starts at home, it is often locally focused. Local focus is in fact a separate variation of outreach, construed as engaging and interacting with your local community, or city, or region. This may or may not be from a platform of corporate social responsibility. It could also be, for example, from a platform of playing a part in civic discourse, or economic development, or cultural activities. And culture itself is a separate strand of engagement – when a university associates itself with a certain community, be that a community of culture or practice or religion or language, irrespective of geography.

One aspect of outreach that has received a lot of attention is the manner and extent to which universities respond to the massification of student numbers, and in particular to diversifying the social profile of the student population. In England this is called 'widening participation'. It has a more specific aspect called 'fair access', which asks in particular about the social mix of students entering what are regarded as leading universities. And it has a more general aspect, which is about the role of higher education in social mobility.

Another aspect of outreach is the manner and extent to which universities engage with business and industry, sometimes called 'third strand' activities. Gibbons et al devote an entire chapter to 'The marketability and commercialisation of knowledge', starting from the observation that the mutual acceleration of both the supply of, and demand for, knowledge, is being driven by an intensification of the international competition in business and industry, and that, in economic terms, the only safe haven for any country is pre-eminence in technological innovation.[44] That observation introduces the term 'innovation', of which much has been made in more recent times. For example, Gibbons et al also make the point that knowledge production in Mode 2 involves a more fluid and collaborative give-and-take approach between universities and industry, and indeed between competing parts of industry, than the traditional in-house development of knowledge favoured in Mode 1. A later continuation of this line of argument came to be known as 'open innovation'.[45]

A specific manifestation of 'third strand' activities was the idea of the university itself creating businesses, usually called 'spin-out companies', by commercialising the intellectual property that arises as part of its research. This line of thinking gave rise to a new characterisation: the entrepreneurial university. In 1998 Burton R. Clark, an emeritus Professor from the Graduate School of Education at UCLA, published a book that quickly became the gospel of a new movement: *Creating Entrepreneurial Universities: Organisational Pathways of Transformation*.[46] Mainly, it is a book of five case studies of universities regarded as exemplars of entrepreneurship: Warwick, Twente, Strathclyde, Chalmers and Joensuu. The heart of the book, however, is Clark's summary chapter, titled 'Entrepreneurial pathways of university transformation'. It characterises the entrepreneurial university, and it gives a kind of roadmap of how to become one.

> 'Entrepreneurial' is taken in this study as a characteristic of social systems; that is, of entire universities and their internal departments, research centers, faculties and schools. The concept carries the overtones of 'enterprise' – a wilful effort in institution-building that requires much special activity and energy. Taking risks

when initiating new practices whose outcome is in doubt is a major factor. An entrepreneurial university, on its own, actively seeks to innovate in how it goes about its business. It seeks to work out a substantial shift in organisational character so as to arrive at a more promising posture for the future. Entrepreneurial universities seek to become 'stand-up' universities that are significant actors on their own terms. Institutional entrepreneurship can be seen as both process and outcome.[47]

Who, then, would not want to be an entrepreneurial university? So quickly did the idea catch on, and so quickly did Burton Clark become something of a cult figure, that the Organisation for Economic Co-operation and Development (OECD)[48] Programme for Institutional Management in Higher Education (IMHE) devoted its Year 2000 Conference in Paris to the topic of 'Beyond the Entrepreneurial University', at which Burton Clark gave the keynote address.

> The many demands and challenges of the day in themselves are not going to determine the fate of universities. Rather, how universities respond to and shape the many forces that play upon them becomes the heart of the matter. The conference properly drives home this point.
>
> And of course I could not be more pleased that the organisers of the conference have picked up on my slim 1998 book, *Creating Entrepreneurial Universities*, to set categories for panel discussions, group sessions, and case reports from diverse institutions around the world. Rare is the book in the social sciences, and especially in educational research, that receives, just two years after publication, such a concentrated international effort to critically review the ideas set forth to see whether they can be put to work. Such organised critical attention has never happened to me before in a half-century of scholarly writing, and it will surely never happen to me again. I am grateful, and I am deeply indebted.[49]

The concepts of innovation, enterprise and entrepreneurship, coupled with the new way of thinking about the role of universities, gave rise to a wave of books and studies about the relationship between universities and the marketplace, with titles such as *Engines of Innovation: The Entrepreneurial University in the Twenty-first Century*,[50] or *The Innovative University: Changing the DNA of Higher Education from the Inside Out*,[51] or *Reinventing Higher Education: The Promise of Innovation*.[52] (There does seem to be a trend for two-phrase titles with a colon in the middle.)

Quite properly, cautionary notes were also sounded. Derek Bok, the respected long-serving President of Harvard, wrote a book on *Universities in the Marketplace: The Commercialization of Higher Education*,[53] arguing that the opportunities for making money via the academic pathway has become so plentiful and so seductive that universities are at risk of compromising their fundamental mission and value system. Other titles express concern in less restrained terms (although still in two-phrase format), such as *University Inc.: The Corporate Corruption of American Higher Education*,[54] or *Academic Capitalism and the New Economy: Markets, State and Higher Education*,[55] or *The Fall of the Faculty: The Rise of the All-administrative University and Why It Matters*.[56]

With all this discussion and debate one might have expected a steady move towards complementing the supply-side orientation of the standard model with increasing accommodation of the demand side of the knowledge economy. In fact, however, a countervailing force has been pressurising universities back towards uniformity, and reinforcing many of the precepts of the standard model.

This new force is the phenomenon of rankings and league tables.

2

Rankings and League Tables

The rise of the rankers

> The modern curse of bogus quantification.
> *John Kay*[1]

In 2003, the Institute of Higher Education at the Shanghai Jiao Tong University in China published a list of what it considered to be the top 500 universities in the world. The next year a London magazine called the *Times Higher Education Supplement* published its own list of what it viewed as the top 200 universities in the world. Neither list was given alphabetically, or clustered into sectors or bands. Each was a numerical ranking of universities in presumed order of quality: best in the world, 2nd best in the world, 3rd best, and so on, right down to 200th best or 500th best in the world.

These endeavours met with astounding success. No scepticism greeted the idea that such a list represents some kind of objective reality. On the contrary, it soon became common practice to talk about *the* list of top universities in the world. Both lists have, since their inception, been updated annually. Journalists have found this a fruitful topic: who's up, who's down, why are they up or down, and what does that say about the state of higher education? Universities started taking note, because prospective students (and their parents) had started taking note. Football clubs are ranked in league tables, so why not universities? Then politicians started to take note. It was not long before national pride was awakened. In somewhat the same way as countries compete in the medals table at the Olympics, the idea took root that countries compete for pre-eminence in 'the world ranking of universities'.

This phenomenon impacts on our views of what universities are for. It also impacts on our understanding of quality. It not only affects the way society sees universities, but also how universities see themselves.

The first thing to understand is that there is no such thing as *the* world ranking of universities. Within a decade or so of university rankings first arising there were lots of them. Potentially there are infinitely many. Besides the Shanghai Jiao Tong index and the *Times Higher* ranking, another early ranking was the Quacquarelli Symonds ranking, generally known as QS. Quacquarelli Symonds is an educational company specialising in study-abroad programmes, founded in the 1990s by Mr Quacquarelli. QS was in fact initially partnered with the *Times Higher Education* in the ranking business, until 2009, when the *Times Higher* divorced them and partnered with Thomson Reuters instead (but only up to 2014, when there was another parting of the ways). Since 2010, therefore, the *Times Higher* ranking has been different from the QS ranking. The presence of an educational company in the rankings business shows that anybody can do a ranking. And frequently anybody does. In England most of the national newspapers now do an annual national ranking of universities. You could do so yourself, as I will show in the next section.

Another entry into the rankings game has been the University of Leiden, in the Netherlands, which produces a 'top 500' list of universities based on bibliometric indicators of their performance in science. There is also a ranking called Webometrics, produced by the Cybermetrics Lab of the Spanish National Research Council, which is 'a directory of world universities ranked according to their presence on the web'.[2] Beyond that there are a number of other special-purpose rankings, such as the People & Planet University League Table on sustainability, or the International Student Barometer, which claims feedback from over a million students and 'benchmarks drawn from hundreds of the world's leading universities'.[3]

An interesting development arising from the European Commission has been U-Multirank, which is 'a multi-dimensional, multi-level and user-driven'[4] global university ranking. After a three-year feasibility study with a sample of 150 institutions, the European Commission announced in late 2011 that the first U-Multirank results would be available in 2013. Following that announcement, in early 2012, the *Times Higher* ran an article titled 'U-Multirank may be a waste of taxpayers' money'.[5] The author of the article was the person in charge of the *Times Higher* rankings. It reported a discussion in the House of Lords European Union Committee, which slated U-Multirank and made approving noises about the *Times Higher* ranking. It also reported the then-Minister for Universities and Science David Willetts (later Lord Willetts, and chair of the *Times Higher Education* advisory board[6]), as saying that U-Multirank could be viewed as 'an attempt by the EU Commission to fix a set of rankings in which [European universities] do better than they appear to do in the conventional rankings'. (I will return to U-Multirank as a case study in Chapter Three.)

Presumably the 'conventional rankings' to which the minister referred would be the ones mentioned earlier, including the *Times Higher* ranking. The minister had perhaps not noticed that 'conventional' rankings often gave quite widely differing results. At the time he wrote, Cambridge University, for example, was ranked 2nd in the world by the QS ranking, 5th by the Shanghai Jiao Tong index, 7th by the *Times Higher*, 20th by Webometrics and 31st by the Leiden ranking. The University of Oslo was ranked 111th by QS, 75th by Shanghai, outside the top 200 by the *Times Higer*, 73rd by Webometrics and 276th by Leiden. The London School of Economics and Political Science (LSE) was ranked 39th in the world by the *Times Higher*, and outside the top 200 by Shanghai Jiao Tong.

Once you start looking into the matter, there are many reasons why different rankings give different results.[7] The period around a decade or so after rankings started provides a useful illustration. To begin with, different rankings measure different things – even when laying claim to such a generic title as 'the world ranking of universities'. The Shanghai Jiao Tong index, for example, believes that Nobel prizes are an integral part of the quality of a university, and so their ranking assigns a weight of 30% to whether or not that institution has any Nobel Laureates[8] among its staff or alumni. If not, it would be hard to do well in their league table, no matter how meritorious that university may be in other respects. Another 20% of the Shanghai Jiao Tong index is based on how many highly cited researchers a university has. This is different from asking how many research citations the university has, and would favour an institution with some big research stars above an institution with a larger number of well-performing but less stellar researchers, even when the two institutions generate the same number of research citations. Another 10% of the Shanghai Jiao Tong index goes to a parameter called 'size', presumably on the belief that bigger is better.

On the other hand, the Shanghai Jiao Tong index does not do something which both QS and the *Times Higher* do, which is to incorporate a 'reputational survey' into its ranking. No less than 50% of the QS ranking, and 33% of the *Times Higher* ranking, arises from such a survey. It appears that QS holds a database of academics who it consults annually about the reputation of universities. Academics are free to add themselves to this database, or be nominated by their own, or another, university. In the *Times Higher* ranking, 33% of the eventual outcome is determined by a reputational survey, which was for some years conducted by Thomson Reuters. Of this, 18% arises from a survey of research reputation, and 15% from a similar survey on teaching. Participants in this survey cannot self-select. At the time when the *Times Higher* was in partnership with Thomson Reuters, participants were selected from a list of authors publishing in journals covered by the Web of Science (which is provided and maintained by Thomson Reuters).

The *Times Higher* survey is not a complicated one. Its key feature is that every respondent begins by identifying their own academic discipline – or 'subject area', as it is called. This is not altogether a free choice. During the collaboration with Thomson Reuters, the subject areas with which respondents could identify were from the Thomson Reuters classification used for their academic publications. There were six main categories (Clinical, Pre-clinical and Health; Life Sciences; Physical Sciences; Arts and Humanities; Engineering & Technology; and Social Sciences) and $40+20+9+17+26+27 = 139$ subject areas, which are almost exclusively classic academic disciplines. In Clinical, Pre-Clinical and Health, for example, the subject areas are pretty much the ologies of medicine: cardiology, dermatology, hepatology, oncology, pathology, rheumatology, toxicology, urology, and so on.

Respondents are invited to nominate up to 15 universities which they regard as 'the best' in that subject area. For example: 'Please choose up to 15 institutions around the world that you regard as producing the best research in the subject area of Archaeology'. The same question is asked again later, with the word 'research' replaced by 'teaching'. There are also geographically more specific versions of these two questions, about the 15 best universities in the respondent's region (that is, their continent, more or less).

There are two drawbacks to this methodology. The first is that 'research' is entirely identified with classic supply-side disciplinary research (and likewise for 'teaching'). There is very little scope for identifying, or giving any credit to, cross-disciplinary research. Second, any university not reckoned to be in the top 15 is nowhere. Even if every respondent to the survey thought that your university is around 20th best in the world at every one of its academic disciplines, that response will get you no credit whatsoever. Instead, your university will be outranked by any institution, no matter how small or specialised, that does well enough on only one of the 139 subject areas for just one respondent somewhere to consider it among the top 15 in the world.

If you unleash a professional statistician on the *Times Higher* reputation survey you will learn a few interesting things. First, quite a lot of mathematical massaging is applied to the raw scores. That means that the outcome is dependent not only on the data, but also on which mathematical techniques you choose to apply. Second, if you disaggregate the overall 'world ranking' into the data-based part and the reputational part you will find no strong correlation. In other words, for most universities there is not much of a relationship between how well that university is doing and how well people think it is doing. Third, there is a very close correlation between the survey results on 'research reputation' and the results on 'teaching reputation'. Clearly respondents make up their mind about how to rate a university on the basis of its research, and then just repeat that rating as regards its teaching. And what else could you expect? Research has an aspect of externality to the university that teaching does not have.

Finally, the number of respondents involved in the reputational ranking of any particular university could be tiny. The *Times Higher* and Thomson Reuters boasted that they have of the order of 16,000 responses to their survey. However, there are also of the order of 16,000 universities in the world, any one of which could potentially be mentioned by somebody as being among the top in the world in one of the 139 subject areas under discussion. By reverse engineering the outcome of the reputational rankings of the 'top 200' universities it is possible to get a good idea of how many respondents would have mentioned each one of them, and the number could be as low as a few dozen. Tiny variations can therefore make an appreciable difference. Just a few more votes for a particular university, as few as five or ten, could cause a noticeable change in ranking.

To summarise the point that different rankings measure different things, Table 2.1 shows what the five above-mentioned rankings might actually measure, and how they compare.[9]

As a rider, it should be mentioned that both the selection of what to measure, and the weights assigned to what is measured, can be varied at will by those who do the rankings. Such adjustments are often done. For example, without any fuss or bother, the *Times Higher* quietly readjusted its rankings two years in a row after its big change in 2010 of moving from QS to Thomson Reuters (the deal later discontinued). In 2011 they introduced a new measure and got rid of one. In 2012 they adjusted their weightings. It is in the nature of the rankings game that universities may differ from each other only by very small fractions of a percentage, and so any small tweak in weightings can result in quite a big difference for any university in its place on the eventual ranked list.

That brings up a further point. Not only do rankings differ from each other, but there can be considerable fluctuation within each ranking from one year to the next. A university can move up or down any ranking quite considerably, without, it seems, anything very much having happened in such a short space of time, either at that institution or in the sector overall. Between 2004 and 2007, for example, the School of Oriental and African Studies in London was successively ranked 44th, 103rd, 70th and 243rd in the world by the *Times Higher*. By 2012 it did not feature in the top 400 at all. Webometrics ranked Ghent University as 275th, 291st and 214th from 2009 to 2011 – and then as 93rd in 2012. In the space of one year, from 2011 to 2012 the University of New South Wales moved from 173rd to 85th on the *Times Higher* ranking, the

University of Wisconsin Milwaukee moved from 230th to 430th in the Webometrics ranking, while Sungkyunkwan University moved from 259th to 179th on the QS ranking.

It is also quite possible that a university may rise in one ranking while falling in another. In one year, from 2011 to 2012, the University of East Anglia rose 25 places in the QS ranking, but dropped 31 places in the *Times Higher*. At the same time the Free University of Berlin dropped 21 places in QS, but rose 23 places in the *Times Higher*.

A particular discontinuity in the *Times Higher* rankings occurred in 2010 when they had broken away from QS. Consider, for example, the case of Warwick University. It was ranked 58th in the world by the *Times Higher* (with QS) in 2009, and had featured in the top 100 of that list in each earlier year. Following the new collaboration between *Times Higher* and Thomson Reuters in 2010, however, Warwick was ranked 220th. That, and similar moves, the *Times Higher* argued, was due to its 'improved methodology'. None the less, the fluctuation created some adverse comment, along the lines of 'any ranking that does not have Warwick in the top 200 cannot be right'. As noted above, the *Times Higher* weightings were quietly tweaked over the next two years, presumably as further improvement of its methodology. At the same time Warwick rose to 157th in 2011 and 124th in 2012.

'Improving the methodology' is a neat euphemism for 'making the ranking conform to what you think should be the case'. Another example occurred in 2015, when it was QS which 'improved its methodology', reducing the weight assigned to medicine and life sciences in order to address what it felt was an anomaly in the rankings. The head of research at QS explained the matter thus:

> That the LSE is a world–class institution is not news. Indeed, they have been a firm fixture in the QS top 100 for over a decade, but in any ranking system that places emphasis on medicine and sciences, their strength in their areas of specialty are never likely to shine as brightly as they ought to. The QS methodology now evens the playing field and LSE climbs 36 places to be counted, rightfully, amongst the world's top 40.[10]

Table 2.1: Measures used by five university ranking systems

Exact definitions for each measure vary between rankings	QS World University Rankings	Times Higher Education World Rankings	Academic Ranking of World Universities (Shanghai Jiao Tong)	Leiden ranking	Webometrics ranking
STUDENT MEASURES					
Teaching reputation		15%			
Student:staff ratio	20%	4.5%			
International students	5%	2.5%			
Graduate employer reputation	10%				
Doctorates per academic		6%			
Doctorates per bachelor student		2.25%			
RESEARCH MEASURES					
Research reputation	40%	18%			
Nobel prizes and Fields medals – staff			20%		
Nobel prizes and Fields medals – alumni			10%		
Research papers published		6%	20%	✓	
Articles published in *Science* and *Nature*/high-prestige journals			20%		35%
Citations	20%	30%		✓	
Highly cited researchers			20%	✓	10%
International co-authors/collaboration		2.5%			
Research Income		6%			
Research Income from Industry		2.5%			
STAFF MEASURES					
International staff	5%	2.5%			
OTHER MEASURES					
Institutional income		2.25%			
Per capita performance on other measures			10%		
Size of the main web domain of the institution					5%
Count of external inlinks received from third parties					50%
Total	100%	100%	100%		100%

In other words, the previous ranking must have been wrong because the result for LSE did not look right. At the same time, inevitably, those institutions which do focus on medicine and life sciences experienced a corresponding drop in rankings – also, presumably, 'rightfully'. Something similar happened when the *Times Higher*, realising that they are on to a good thing, started recycling their university rankings to produce subject rankings. To get the right results, some adjustment needed to be made.

> The THE [*Times Higher Education*] subject rankings use the same 13 performance indicators as the flagship World University Rankings but are recalibrated with different weightings to suit each field.[11]

How to build a ranking

> Oh, my name is John Wellington Wells
> I'm a dealer in magic and spells.
> *Gilbert and Sullivan, The Sorcerer*

Should you wish to make up your own ranking of universities, you will find it easy. Your main difficulty will be that you are spoilt for choice, at a number of levels.

The first level of choice is to decide what categories of university activity you wish to evaluate. We have already seen a few: research, teaching, income, and international presence, for example. There are many other possibilities to choose from. You could focus on specific disciplines, for example, or clusters of disciplines, and this is what is most commonly done. Or you could try to evaluate institutional efforts in internationalisation, innovation, entrepreneurship, industrial collaboration or public relations activities. Your choice of categories will reflect your view of the nature and function of the university. Since there are different views about such matters, there are few grounds for insisting that any particular choice of categories is uniquely the right one. You may think that including Nobel prizes is a sensible category, but I may differ. In exercising your choice, therefore, you are already shaping the eventual outcome. If my university does very well in some categories which you choose not to include, or does not focus on some categories which you do include, then we will have little chance of doing well in your ranking. The universities which do have a chance of doing well in your ranking will be the ones whose choices of what to focus on happen to match the categories you chose to include.

Having chosen some categories, your second level of choice is how to measure each of them. This is by no means straightforward, because again you are spoilt for choice. Consider, for example, the category most likely to be included in any university ranking, which is research. By what criteria would you like to measure success in research? 'Research publications' seems an obvious choice, but as any academic will tell you the number of your publications is not an indication of their quality, so the parameter that is easy to measure does not necessarily tell you what you want to know. One way round this is to count, not the publications of an academic or a university, but the number of times their publications are cited by other academics in their own publications. These can not only be counted, nowadays they can also be looked up on the internet, so that is handy. On the other hand, this rather discriminates by subject, because citations are less used in the humanities and social sciences than in medicine or natural sciences.

A simple way out of this conundrum, it seems, is just to look at research income, on the argument that the value or quality of your research is reflected by the fact that somebody – a research council, or a grant-giving charity, or the government, or business or industry – is willing to pay you money to do it. Research income has the advantage that it is a simple numerical measure, and the numbers are publicly available in the institution's annual financial statements. Likewise, there are other criteria relating to research which are quite legitimately expressed by numbers. You could count the number of researchers, for example, and/or the number of research students. Or you could count the number of doctorates awarded annually, on the argument that this is where knowledge creation begins to happen.

It seems like a sound principle, then, to try to find, in each of your selected categories of evaluation, some criteria that are legitimately expressed by a verifiable set of numbers. When you do so, you will soon, like any other ranker, realise that when you rank universities according to things you can count your ranking tends to reflect the size of the institution. Clearly, if you just take into account the overall number of publications or citations, or the total research income, or the total number of doctorates awarded, then bigger institutions will have higher numbers and so will do better on your ranking. So bigger will be better. At this stage you therefore have to exercise a third level of choice: whether to stick with the raw numbers or to normalise them. 'Normalised' just means 'taken relative to size', which means that you will deal with fractions or percentages rather than whole numbers.

One difficulty with taking your numbers relative to size is that there is no unique definition of the size of a university. Even for me and you, size could mean height or weight or girth, or any two of these, or all three. Likewise, for a university, you could measure size as the number of students, or the number of staff, or the size of the budget, or any combination of these. What this means is that normalising also involves making choices. This happens even when you wish to normalise something as seemingly straightforward as research income: you could calculate research income relative to overall income (which would give you an idea of research intensity), or per academic staff member (which would be a measure of research productivity). It depends on what you want.

You will also have to take account of the fact that, while gross numbers favour bigger institutions, normalised measures tend to favour smaller institutions. This is not difficult to understand. If your university has only a few academics, each of them a top specialist in a single niche subject, then, on the normalised measure of 'research output per academic staff member', your university could easily beat a large research-intensive university, because their average is taken over a bigger number and a broader range. For example, following the 2008 Research Assessment Exercise the *Times Higher* published a 'research excellence' ranking.[12] Top of the list was the Institute of Cancer Research, which had entered 97 researchers, beating into second place Cambridge University, which had entered 2,040 researchers.

Consider an example. Let us suppose – not a far-fetched supposition – that you wish to do a ranking of the 24 UK universities which are members of the Russell Group.[13] These are generally thought of as research-intensive universities, so you decide to focus mainly on the category of research. There are many possible criteria for evaluating research but you decide on three basic ones: research income, research citations and doctorates awarded. You also decide to compensate for size by having each of these both in terms of gross numbers and normalised for size. As a measure of size, you choose the number of full-time equivalent (FTE) academic staff.

You do not wish to be one-sided, so you also want to bring in the category of teaching. Because teaching is less easy to measure than research you decide to go with only one criterion, which is student satisfaction, as measured by the annual National Student Survey (NSS).[14] The main outcome of the NSS is the percentage of students who 'definitely agree' or 'mainly agree' with the assertion 'Overall, I am satisfied with the quality of the course'. From this, each university would get a percentage for its level of student satisfaction, these percentages are then ranked and the ranking is made publicly available.

You may at this stage note that your research criteria are matters of fact, while your teaching criterion is a matter of opinion, but for the sake of your ranking you decide to gloss over this difference. You may also note that the NSS ranking does not sensibly allow of normalisation, so in that respect too it differs from the other criteria.

For your ranking experiment, you have now come up with the following seven criteria:

A. Total research income (in, say, millions of pounds)
B. Average research income per academic FTE (in thousands of pounds)
C. Total research citations
D. Average citations per academic FTE
E. Number of doctorates awarded
F. Average number of doctorates awarded per academic FTE
G. NSS student satisfaction score (as a percentage)

What you have to do next is get the data. That too introduces some variability, because of the data changes from one year to the next, and so when you 'get the data' you are actually taking a snapshot of some given year. Also, inconveniently, the data will not all be from the same year. Research income data, for example, will typically be at least two years old, because it first has to be compiled at the institutional level, then published in the annual report, then reported to the regulators, and only then can it be aggregated at the national level and made publicly available.

None the less, data is available, and plenty of it. So you may select a moment in time – say, for example, the end of 2012 – and then find the relevant data. Which, for the 24 Russell Group universities, listed in alphabetical order, is shown in Table 2.2.[15]

At this stage you have reached a fourth level of choice. You have already chosen, at the first level, what categories of activity to measure, at the second level what criteria to measure them by, and at the third level whether to use raw scores or scores relative to size (or both). At the fourth level, you have to decide on a method for turning the resulting table of numbers (such as the one above) into a single list of numbers, which will then be your ranking. In other words, for each university you have to compress its seven scores for the seven criteria into a single score.

This is a very important stage in designing your ranking. You are going to combine seven numbers into one number, and there are infinitely many ways of doing so. A very common way, for example, is to apply weightings to your seven criteria, and then make up the combined number as a weighted aggregate of the others.[16] In the table of comparison given in the first section of this chapter (Table 2.1) we saw that most rankings – QS, *Times Higher*, Shanghai Jiao Tong and so on – assign different weights to their various criteria. We also saw that they do so in widely different ways, which again illustrates the point that you can make up a ranking any way you want. And you may reflect on the fact that there is no 'right way' of assigning weights. Choosing weights, like choosing categories, is just a reflection of your own views on what is important in a university. None the less, having noted these points, you decide to go ahead and do so.

You have now reached your fifth level of choice: what are the weights? You could, for example, decide to give a weighting of 60% to research and 40% to teaching. You have picked six criteria for measurement of research, and you may decide (again, for example) to give them equal weight, so 10% each. This seems like good progress, because all you have to do now to get your ranking is, for each university, to calculate 10% of the number under each of the first six criteria and 40% of the number under the seventh criterion and then add them up.

However, trying to be rigorous about the exercise, you realise that you first have to address a small technical problem, which is that the numbers sitting in each column of your table are of

Table 2.2: Illustrative Russell Group data

University	A Research income	B Research income/FTE	C Research citations	D Citations/ FTE	E PhDs given	F PhDs/FTE	G NSS score
Birmingham	101,540	80	9,348	7.35	555	0.44	88
Bristol	110,120	114	11,462	11.82	445	0.46	86
Cambridge	283,718	188	32,563	21.61	1095	0.73	92
Cardiff	84,633	64	9,222	7.02	380	0.29	89
Durham	48,740	66	7,060	9.61	310	0.42	89
Edinburgh	180,990	128	17,638	12.43	640	0.45	83
Exeter	46,327	71	5,700	8.69	265	0.40	91
Glasgow	128,047	117	10,983	10.04	350	0.32	89
Imperial	299,238	245	27,808	22.79	760	0.62	86
King's	147,099	94	14,988	9.53	520	0.33	82
Leeds	123,975	93	9,880	7.38	480	0.36	87
Liverpool	110,310	106	8,564	8.23	380	0.37	86
LSE	25,596	48	876	1.65	190	0.36	85
Manchester	196,242	105	15,424	8.26	965	0.52	83
Newcastle	88,483	81	7,458	6.86	405	0.37	89
Nottingham	100,295	64	8,730	5.58	640	0.41	88
Oxford	372,256	236	36,866	23.41	955	0.61	92
Queen Mary	73,657	95	8,272	10.63	265	0.34	87
Queen's	63,069	72	4,532	5.20	335	0.38	87
Sheffield	101,336	89	9,856	8.69	555	0.49	90
Southampton	93,624	91	10,336	10.09	435	0.42	88
UCL	283,383	161	29,852	16.95	780	0.44	85
Warwick	86,334	93	5,289	5.72	370	0.40	87
York	51,566	79	4,944	7.61	245	0.38	88

different orders of magnitude. Your criterion A (Research income) is typically measured in the hundreds of millions, criterion B by hundreds of thousands, criterion C by tens of thousands, and so on, with criterion F, for example, given by a very small number, usually less than 1. So you cannot really use these numbers as they are and just assign your preferred weights to them, because then the large numbers will dominate and the small numbers will be insignificant.

Once again, you have many techniques at your disposal for addressing this inconvenience. You could, for example, in every column find the middle number by size (called the median), and then divide every entry by that number. That will bring all numbers in every column within the same range, somewhere around 1, so you can then go ahead with your chosen weightings and compute your overall ranking. Or, if you feel a need for more sophistication, you can use the spreadsheet facility on your computer to calculate something called 'z-scores'. This is a technique for measuring, in each column, how far each entry is above or below the mean value of that column. So, same story really, just a different calculation, and starting from the mean rather than the median. However, 'z-scores' sounds very impressive, and so you decide to use them – perhaps also because you have noticed that some other rankers do so (including the *Times Higher*).

You are now ready to compute your first-ever own ranking of Russell Group universities, and it comes out as shown in Table 2.3.

At this stage you may well say to yourself 'job done', and go and have a cup of tea. Or perhaps you decide to do a bit more experimenting. You may, for example, want to see what happens if you tweak your weightings just a little bit – that is, make an adjustment at your fifth level of choice. So you could adjust the relative weights between research and teaching from 60:40 to, say, two thirds against one third, which is not a big change at all. You also decide to keep equal weightings for the six criteria of research, so they now have a weight of 11.1% each, rather than 10% – again not a big change. You then run exactly the same calculations as before. And this time your ranking comes out as in Table 2.4.

Now you notice that things have changed. The first four places remain the same, and so does the last place, but in the middle things have changed quite a bit. On the first ranking Manchester was 5th, on the second ranking it is 14th. Cardiff, on the other hand, was only 22nd in the first ranking, but on the second ranking it is 15th. Depending on which ranking you use, therefore, Manchester is either 17 places higher in the Russell Group than Cardiff, or they lie right next to each other. Other universities also bounce around. Exeter could be 6th or 18th, depending on which ranking you use, King's could be 13th or 23rd, and Newcastle could be 10th or 17th.

Table 2.3: Illustrative Russell Group ranking 1

Ranking 1	University
1	Oxford
2	Cambridge
3	Imperial
4	UCL
5	Manchester
6	Edinburgh
7	Sheffield
8	Bristol
9	Birmingham
10	Southampton
11	Glasgow
12	Nottingham
13	King's
14	Leeds
15	Liverpool
16	Durham
17	Newcastle
18	Exeter
19	Queen Mary
20	Warwick
21	York
22	Cardiff
23	Queen's
24	LSE

Table 2.4: Illustrative Russell Group ranking 2

Ranking 2	University
1	Oxford
2	Cambridge
3	Imperial
4	UCL
5	Sheffield
6	Exeter
7	Glasgow
8	Southampton
9	Birmingham
10	Newcastle
11	Nottingham
12	Durham
13	Bristol
14	Manchester
15	Cardiff
16	Edinburgh
17	Leeds
18	Queen Mary
19	York
20	Warwick
21	Liverpool
22	Queen's
23	King's
24	LSE

A tiny tweak in the weightings therefore, can produce a marked effect in the league table. Having noticed that, you may wonder whether the problem lies with your method being too complicated. Going right back to Table 2.2 which gives the scores on all seven criteria, you decide that it may be simpler just to treat each column on its own as a ranking rather than using z-scores and weightings. If you do that, the results come out as shown in Table 2.5.

Table 2.5: Russell Group data recast

University	A Research income	B Research income FTE	C Research citations	D Citations/FTE	E PhDs given	F PhDs/FTE	G NSSscore
Birmingham	12	17	13	18	8	9	=9
Bristol	11	7	8	6	12	6	=17
Cambridge	3	3	2	3	1	1	=1
Cardiff	18	22	14	19	15	24	=5
Durham	22	21	19	10	20	11	=5
Edinburgh	6	5	5	5	6	7	=22
Exeter	23	20	20	13	21	13	3
Glasgow	8	6	9	9	18	23	=5
Imperial	2	1	4	2	5	2	=17
King's	7	11	7	11	10	22	24
Leeds	9	13	11	17	11	19	=13
Liverpool	10	8	16	15	15	18	=17
LSE	24	24	24	24	24	20	=20
Manchester	5	9	6	14	2	4	=22
Newcastle	16	16	18	20	14	17	=5
Nottingham	14	23	15	22	6	12	=9
Oxford	1	2	1	1	3	3	=1
Queen Mary	19	10	17	7	21	21	=13
Queen's	20	19	23	23	19	15	=13
Sheffield	13	15	12	12	8	5	4
Southampton	15	14	10	8	13	10	=9
UCL	4	4	3	4	4	8	=20
Warwick	17	12	21	21	17	14	=13
York	21	18	22	16	23	16	=9

Now you still have to combine these seven separate rankings into a single ranking, and, still trying to keep things really simple, you decide to do so by just adding them up. You then get a third ranking, shown in Table 2.6. On this attempt Manchester is 6th, Cardiff is 21st, Exeter is 19th, King's is 12th and Newcastle is 16th – all of them having changed position for the third time.

Table 2.6: Illustrative Russell Group ranking 3

Ranking 3	University
1	Oxford
2	Cambridge
3	Imperial
4	UCL
5	Edinburgh
6	Manchester
7	Bristol
8	Sheffield
9	Glasgow
10	Southampton
11	Birmingham
12	King's
13	Leeds
14	Liverpool
15	Nottingham
16	Newcastle
=17	Durham
=17	Queen Mary
19	Exeter
20	Warwick
21	Cardiff
22	York
23	Queen's
24	LSE

If you are a determined ranker, none of this will worry you. You will simply argue that your own ranking is sensible, or fair, or scientific, or perhaps even 'right'. On the other hand, it may occur to you that if a tiny change at your fifth level of choice can result in such big changes in the ranking, then perhaps, given the rich variety of choice across all five levels, almost any outcome is possible. It may also occur to you that there is no strong reason, at any level, to think that one set of choices is better than any other set of choices, or does anything more than express your preferences. Which means that there is no strong reason to think that any ranking really does anything more than express your preferences. Is it conceivable, then, that with some ingenuity you could pretty much get any result you want?

15 varieties of ranking

Heinz 57, Heinz 57
You've a family to feed
Heinz have everything you need
Ready when you are, yes indeed
That's Heinz 57!
Advertising jingle, 1959

Sometimes a picture is worth a thousand numbers. The conclusion emerging from our case study of the 24 Russell Group universities is that reality can be pretty messy. However, we may still harbour some lingering wishful thought that, if only we were clever enough, there might be a way of corralling that messy reality into an authoritative linear ranking.

That is not the case. The cleverer we become at choosing categories, criteria, parameters and weights, the more possibilities there are for different eventual rankings. To see why that is so, consider the following thought experiment.

Imagine that we are interested, not in universities and their research, but in cities and their restaurants. That is, we would like to rank cities by the quality of their restaurants. How would we do it?

Let us suppose, first, that we invent a *rating* system for restaurants, which is to award each restaurant between zero and four stars, based on how good it is. As follows:

4 stars = world-leading
3 stars = of continental renown
2 stars = of national renown
1 star = acceptable, popular in the city
0 stars = not rateable

We then invite each city to enter a number of restaurants for rating by a panel of gourmets. The panel's job is to judge the quality of each of these restaurants and decide how many stars it should be awarded.

So far, so easy. Next, we wish to evaluate each city according to the ratings of its restaurants. This is done as follows: we list, in each city, the percentage of entered restaurants which have been awarded four stars, the percentage that has been awarded three stars, and so on.

Imagine, for example, that we are in the city of Someburgh, and that 10% of the restaurants visited were awarded four stars, 25% were awarded three stars, 40% were awarded two stars, 20% were awarded one star, and 5% received no star. That gives what we may call the *quality profile* of restaurants in Someburgh, as in Figure 2.1.

The picture gives us, quite literally, a profile, in the sense that we can see that in Someburgh the quality of restaurants has a concentration towards the middle of the scale, with smaller representation at the two extremities. In other words, in Someburgh the quality profile of the restaurants is like a simple version of a normal curve.

Figure 2.1: Quality profile of restaurants in Someburgh

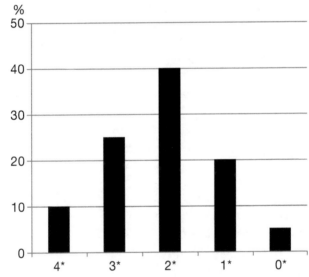

Now imagine the same exercise being conducted in a number of other cities, such as Otherville, Thistown and Elseport, and that we get a collection of quality profiles as shown in Figure 2.2.

It is easy to see that in Otherville the quality profile is quite level, in Thistown there is a high proportion both of world-class restaurants and poor ones, and in Elseport there is quite a low proportion of world-class restaurants but a very high proportion of nationally renowned ones. After a while one grows accustomed to this mode of representation, to the extent that the mere listing of the percentages will suffice to evoke the profile. Thus:

Someburgh: 10-25-40-20-5
Otherville: 20-20-20-20-20
Thistown: 30-20-10-10-30
Elseport: 5-50-30-15-0

Figure 2.2: Quality profiles of restaurants in Someburgh, Otherville, Thistown and Elseport

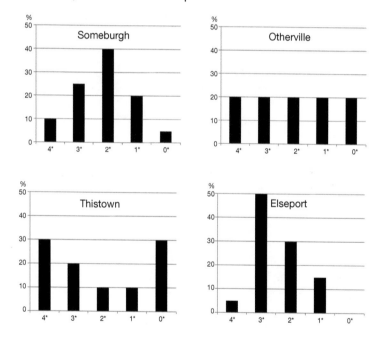

This is good progress, but of course we are not done yet. The original intention was to produce a *ranking* system. For that purpose, we now have to turn the collection of quality profiles into a league table, which will tell us which city is first, second, third and so on.

Doing so is a bit of a conundrum, but only (again) in the sense of being spoilt for choice. There are many methods we could use. Let us suppose, however, that the weekly magazine *Culinary Times* comes up with the following method, which they call a 'weighted grade point average', commonly referred to as GPA. First, they argue that being world-class is surely more important and prestigious than being nationally renowned, or just popular in the city. Accordingly, they give a weighting to each of the categories (4-star, 3-star and so on), as follows: the percentage of 4-star restaurants is multiplied by 4, the percentage of 3-star restaurants is multiplied by 3, and so on, giving a numerical score in each category. The sum of these scores is then divided by 100 to give the GPA, which is a number between 0 and 4. The cities are then neatly ranked in order of their GPA. As follows:

Someburgh: $[(10\times4)+(25\times3)+(40\times2)+(20\times1)+(5\times0)] \div 100 = 2.15$

Otherville: $[(20\times4)+(20\times3)+(20\times2)+(20\times1)+(20\times0)] \div 100 = 2.0$

Thistown: $[(30\times4)+(20\times3)+(10\times2)+(10\times1)+(30\times0)] \div 100 = 2.1$

Elseport: $[(5\times4)+(50\times3)+(30\times2)+(15\times1)+(0\times0)] \div 100 = 2.45$

In the culinary league table published by *Culinary Times*, therefore, Elseport is first, Someburgh is second, Thistown is third, and Otherville is fourth.

A rival publication, however, called *Restaurant Fortnight*, thinks that this is not quite right. First, they notice that the 'average' part of the GPA (in other words division by 100) is just arithmetical candy, since it makes no difference to the rankings. Second, and more substantively, they argue that the weightings used by *Culinary Times* do not give enough credence to the difference between the categories. Being 'world-leading', they argue, is not just being of a better quality than 'nationally renowned', it is being of a *much* better quality. Accordingly, they decide to do a ranking along the same lines, but with the 4-star category getting a weighting of 16, 3-star with a weighting of 9, 2-star with a weighting of 4, 1-star with a weighting of 1, and 0-star weighted zero. In other words, as weightings they use the *squares* of the previous weightings. These new weightings then give rise to the following scores:

Someburgh: $[(10x16)+(25x9)+(40x4)+(20x1)+(5x0)] = 565$
Otherville: $[(20x16)+(20x9)+(20x4)+(20x1)+(20x0)] = 600$
Thistown: $[(30x16)+(20x9)+(10x4)+(10x1)+(30x0)] = 710$
Elseport: $[(5x16)+(50x9)+(30x4)+(15x1)+(0x0)] = 665$

Accordingly, *Restaurant Fortnight* publishes a league table in which Thistown is first, Elseport is second, Otherville is third and Someburgh is last.

Clearly we could continue playing with the weightings, and arrive at different rankings. At this stage, however, having read the *Culinary Times* and *Restaurant Fortnight*, the Association for Haute Cuisine (AHC) decides to publish its own league table. In fact, it does better: it publishes three separate league tables. First, it re-names the categories, as follows: a 4-star award is called a Gold Medal, a 3-star award is called a Silver Medal, and a 2-star award is called a Bronze Medal. The other awards are simply disregarded. The AHC then publishes a Gold Medal Table, which is of the utmost simplicity: it ranks each city by its percentage of gold medals. On the Gold Medal Table, therefore, Thistown is first, Otherville is second, Someburgh is third, and Elseport is last.

Next, the AHC publishes a Gold and Silver Medal Table, in which it counts a gold medal as being worth two silver medals. Thus:

Someburgh: $(10x2)+25 = 45$
Otherville: $(20x2)+20 = 60$
Thistown: $(30x2)+20 = 80$
Elseport: $(5x2)+50 = 60$

On this table, therefore, Thistown is first, Elseport and Otherville are joint second, and Someburgh is third and last. For completeness, the AHC finally does an All Medals Table, in which a gold medal is worth three bronze medals, and a silver medal is worth two bronzes. Thus:

Someburgh: $(10x3)+(25x2)+40 = 120$
Otherville: $(20x3)+(20x2)+20 = 120$
Thistown: $(30x3)+(20x2)+10 = 140$
Elseport: $(5x3)+(50x2)+30 = 145$

Which means that in the All Medals Table Elseport is first, Thistown second, and Otherville and Someburgh joint third and last.

What the AHC may or may not have realised is that all this talk about medals is just another way of assigning weights to the various ratings. On the Gold Medal Table a 4-star award is given a weight of 1 and all other awards get a weight of zero. On the Gold and Silver Medal Table a 4-star award gets weight 2, a 3-star award gets weight 1, and all other awards get a weight of zero. Likewise, on the All Medals Table the weights are respectively 3, 2, 1 and zero.

We may now pause for breath, and note that the five methods have produced five different rankings. In keeping with our initial intention, we may refer to all of these rankings as *GPA rankings*, or (if you want to push the idea that your ranking captures quality) as *quality* rankings. To keep track, we summarise these five rankings as follows, representing each city by the first letter of its name, and putting shared positions in parentheses:

Culinary Times Table: ESTO
Restaurant Fortnight Table: TEOS
AHC Gold Medal Table: TOSE
AHC Gold and Silver Medal Table: T(EO)S
AHC All Medals Table: ET(OS)

We may, perhaps, be disappointed that there is no unambiguous winner (or loser), and in fact no clear pattern of ranking. At best, if we wish to draw any conclusions at all, we may note that either E or T is always first, that O, S and E have all been last, that T has never been last, and that S and O have never been first.

At this stage (to continue our thought experiment) a new player enters the arena. The Tourist Board points out that in each city it is relevant to ask, not just about the percentage breakdown of ranked restaurants, but also how many restaurants were actually submitted for ranking. When they look into the matter, they find that the numbers vary quite a bit: Someburgh submitted 40 restaurants, Otherville submitted 30, and Thistown and Elseport only submitted 20 each. The Tourist Board then argues that the right way to do a ranking is to factor in the size of the submissions, because that would give the public a good idea of what a city actually offers, which gives more information about the gastronomic quality of that particular city. Accordingly, it reworks the five 'quality' rankings as *power rankings*, by the simple expedient of multiplying the number produced by each quality ranking for each city by the number of restaurants submitted for ranking by that city. It is easy enough to do the calculations, which then yield the following results:

Culinary Times Power Ranking: SOET
Restaurant Fortnight Power Ranking: SOTE
AHC Gold Medal Power Ranking: (OT)SE
AHC Gold and Silver Medal Power Ranking: (OS)TE
AHC All Medals Power Ranking: SOET

With these rankings, the previous situation has almost been reversed. With the 'quality' rankings, either E or T was always first; with the 'power' rankings either E or T is always last. Either S or O is always first under the power rankings, whereas they were never first under the quality rankings.

At this stage, therefore, with two competing methodologies and ten different ranking methods, we already have nine different outcomes. We may, however, still hope that there is some pattern to these outcomes. We note, for example, that so far S and O are often grouped together, and likewise for E and T.

Suppose now (to take the thought experiment even further) that the matter has gained considerable prominence and a number of further opinions are voiced. The Chamber of Commerce, for example, points out that we have only taken account of the number of restaurants *submitted*, instead of the *total number* of restaurants in each city. The culinary quality of a city, they argue, is not just about those restaurants carefully selected for submission (probably by the Tourist Board). No, culinary quality is about what the city offers in the totality of its restaurants. Therefore the power ranking, while correctly putting a size factor into the calculation, errs in using only the number of restaurants submitted. The size factor that should be used instead is the ratio of the submitted restaurants to the total number of restaurants in the city. That will give you a better idea of what your chances are of getting a good culinary experience in each city.

Fortunately the Chamber of Commerce already has a database listing the total number of restaurants per city. From that database they know that Someburgh has 64 restaurants in total, Otherville has 33, Thistown has 40 and Elseport has 30. That gives the Chamber of Commerce an easy way of calculating what we might call *intensity rankings*. Namely, you follow the same procedure as for power rankings, but multiply by ratios rather than sizes: 40 over 64 for Someburgh, 30 over 33 for Otherville, 20 over 40 for Thistown and 20 over 30 for Elseport. This yields the following results:

> *Culinary Times* Intensity Ranking: OEST
> *Restaurant Fortnight* Intensity Ranking: OETS
> AHC Gold Medal Intensity Ranking: OTSE
> AHC Gold and Silver Medal Intensity Ranking: O(ET)S
> AHC All Medals Intensity Ranking: OEST

With this method of ranking, any supposition that we might have some natural pairings (S with O, or E with T) has disappeared. Moreover, the intensity rankings feature something absent from the other rankings: a single clear winner (Otherville).

With the extra data now accumulated we may conveniently enhance our quality profiles. We simply have to use actual numbers instead of percentages, and add another column giving the number of unranked restaurants (labelling them NS, for 'Not Submitted'). The updated quality profiles are shown in Figure 2.3.

There is much to be said for these enhanced profiles. They still give us a visual impression of quality – indeed, exactly the same profile as before, since the numbers of ranked restaurants are in the same ratio as the original percentages. However, since they are presented in terms of numbers rather than percentages, they also tell us, more or less at a glance, the size of what each city has to offer by way of gastronomic satisfaction – that is, the total number of restaurants. Moreover, by simply looking at the height of the last column (the non-submitted remainder), and comparing it with the combined size of the other columns, we have a very clear idea of the tactical approach adopted by each city in the rankings game. Thus we see that Otherville played a very straight game, submitting almost all their restaurants (30 out of 33). Thistown, on the other hand, only submitted half their restaurants (20 out of 40) – possibly because they knew the unsubmitted ones to be very poor. Elseport and Someburgh are somewhere between these two extremes, having submitted two thirds (20 out of 30) and five eighths (40 out of 64), respectively.

Figure 2.3: Enhanced quality profiles of restaurants in Someburgh, Otherville, Thistown and Elseport

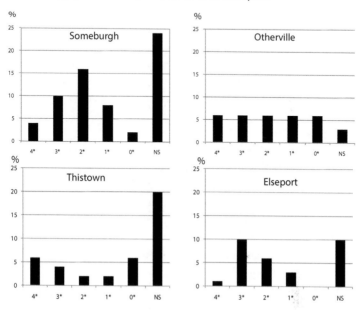

We could easily carry on inventing yet further ranking methodologies. We may, for example, start the whole game over, by calculating, for each city and for each category of rating, the number of restaurants in that category as a percentage of the total number of restaurants in the city, not just as the percentage of restaurants submitted. That would lead to another 15 varieties of ranking, on top of the 15 we have covered already. And, as pointed out earlier, we could obtain yet more variations simply by changing, in any calculation, the relative weightings. So you really can have pretty much any ranking you want, just by choosing an appropriate method. Instead, let us put aside our thought experiment and return to reality.

Reality check

> We allocate funding selectively by reference to robust
> judgements of research quality.
> *Higher Education Funding Council for England*[17]

Every six years or so the entire higher education sector in the
United Kingdom goes into a mighty convulsion, known until 2008
as the Research Assessment Exercise, and renamed from 2014 as
the Research Excellence Framework. Immediately acronymised,
the RAE and then the REF has played and continues to play an
important part in every academic's life, and in the institutional life
of each university.

For about 25 years the body responsible for carrying out
the RAE/REF was the Higher Education Funding Council for
England, known as the HEFCE. As the name implies, the key
idea behind the HEFCE was that there should be a buffer body
between the state and the higher education sector which disburses
taxpayers' money to universities. Part of that disbursement was
to fund research, and the rationale behind such funding was that
it should be quality related. But then of course you have to have
some kind of periodic evaluation of the quality of research of
each university, and that was the function of the RAE/REF. It is a
serious business, because the outcome of the RAE/REF not only
fixes the disbursement of billions of pounds for six or seven years,
it also brings considerable bragging rights and reputational benefit
for those who do well.

The rationale for a funding council was seriously eroded by the
decision of the 2010 Coalition government that students should pay
more and taxpayers less of the cost of higher education. After some
to-ing and fro-ing the HEFCE metamorphosed into a regulatory
body called the Office for Students (from 2018), but planning for
REF 2021 continued seamlessly under the auspices of another body,
called Research England.

What happens with the RAE and the REF is that it starts out
as a research *rating* system for informing funding decisions, but
then gets transmuted in the public domain into a research *ranking*
system. Our little thought experiment of a culinary league table
of cities already illustrates most of the technical aspects of how a

rating system can, in many different ways, be turned into a ranking system. In fact, the detail exactly parallels that of the RAE 2008.

For the RAE, each university was invited to submit information on its research outputs in up to 67 research areas, called units of assessment. These submissions were then assessed, mainly on the best four academic papers of each member of academic staff selected for entry. Each unit of assessment was given a profile based on the percentage of work judged to fall within each of the following ratings:

4★ = world-leading
3★ = internationally excellent
2★ = recognised internationally
1★ = recognised nationally
0★ = unclassified; below standard

The HEFCE stated the aim of the exercise as follows:[18]

> The primary purpose of RAE2008 is to produce quality profiles for each submission of research activity made by higher education institutions. The results will be used by the four UK funding bodies to determine the funding for research to the institutions which they fund from 2009–10.

The quality profiles in question are exactly as in our thought experiment, explained by the HEFCE as follows:[19]

> Sub-panels assessed the research submitted against the published criteria. They then made a recommendation to the main panel for endorsement. The judgement indicates the proportion of the research that met each of four quality levels or is unclassified. In each case, the panel took account of three overarching components of the submission – research outputs, research environment and indicators of esteem. The results are published as a graded profile for each UOA [unit of assessment] for each submission. An example of quality profiles for two hypothetical submissions is [in the table] overleaf.

Unit of assessment A	Full-time equivalent research staff submitted for assessment	Percentage of research activity in the submission judged to meet the standard for:				
		4*	3*	2*	1*	Unclassified
University X	50	15	25	40	15	5
University Y	20	0	5	40	45	10

The point to note is that the HEFCE felt no need to move from the notion of a quality profile to the calculation of some quality ranking. The profile itself sufficed for decision making. The HEFCE's job was to deliver research funding, not to rank universities. The RAE was one input, but not the only one, into the HEFCE's decision on how to allocate what academics know as QR, which is 'quality related' research funding. Besides the RAE results, the HEFCE would also apply whatever strategic funding principles it had adopted at that time (or been instructed by the government to adopt). A perennial strategic choice, for example, is whether to fund 'research concentration', which means lumping the money, or 'quality wherever it is found', which means smearing it.

Once QR funding had been allocated, universities could of course be ranked in terms of their funding, by gross amount or by normalised amount or some such. But that really illustrates the point: the profiles lead to a quality judgement, which in the context of strategy leads to a decision, and the decision determines the ranking, not the other way around.

Others were not so restrained. Many of the ranking formulae we saw for our culinary league tables were published for the RAE with great fanfare, as though capturing some true reality. The *Times Higher Education* turned the RAE profiles of the 159 participating higher education institutions into what it called a 'Research Excellence Ranking', also known as the 'quality ranking'. This was done by calculating a 'weighted grade point average', exactly as in our thought experiment, with the same weightings and also without regard to size. Not surprisingly, small specialist institutions tended to do well on this ranking. For example, as noted earlier, on the *Times Higher* ranking the Institute of Cancer Research, with a submission of 97 researchers in 2 units of assessment, beat into second place Cambridge University, which submitted 2,040 researchers in 50 units. Perhaps recognising this as an anomaly, another newspaper, *The Times* of London, adapted the *Times Higher* ranking by simply leaving out small institutions (which of course involved another level of decision: how big is small?). A different publication, *Research Fortnight*, adopted the methodology of power rankings, using essentially the algorithm in our thought experiment. This reversed some of the earlier rankings. The LSE, for example, which was ranked 4th by the *Times Higher* (and 2nd by *The Times*), came 27th in the *Research Fortnight* ranking. The Russell Group published its own version of power rankings, called the Gold Medal Table and Gold and Silver Medal Table, again as illustrated in our thought experiment (adopting a power ranking). On these tables Russell Group universities tended to do well.

Our imaginary culinary league table, therefore, is no mere figment of the imagination. It is a small illustration of what happens in reality. And that brings us to the core point. Using quality profiles, we are able to rate universities, and compare them. This comparison, however, is by shape, and shapes do not come in any particular order. Nor do they determine an order. There is no unique ranking determined by the ratings.

Any linear ranking obtained from such quality profiles or shapes is the result of a subsequent calculation, to which all the caveats noted earlier apply. Typically, it involves reducing a set of numbers to one number. The mere fact that we have correctly performed such a calculation does not by itself mean that the outcome has any particular meaning or credence – other, perhaps, than what we designed it to have, by some decision or belief. You could, if you wished to, take the square root of the sum of the numbers, or the logarithm of the product, or do any other clever calculation, and arrange the results in a linear order. Apart from looking tidy, or representing what you have already decided, it is unlikely to mean anything.

The HEFCE reserved to itself the decision making on how to turn RAE quality profiles into funding decisions. It never published an algorithm for doing so ahead of time, only finalising its strategy once the results were in. The reason for doing so is fairly obvious: once you know the algorithm on which a system is based you can game the system by optimising your input according to the algorithm.

That is exactly what happens with rankings generally, and exactly what happened with RAE rankings in particular. Some universities decided to optimise their 'grade point average', because once it became known as a 'research excellence' ranking it was such wonderful PR to be able to say that you scored highly for research excellence. And it was very simple to do: you just submit fewer and better people into the exercise. If you are in England (but not in Wales or Scotland) this would have the downside that your smaller submission may then earn you less QR research funding from the HEFCE, but you could easily decide that the reputational benefits will in the long term outweigh a medium reduction in research cash. Other universities may decide to do the opposite: optimise the power ranking by submitting more people, which will get you more cash, which you can then invest in the quality of your research.

After the 2008 RAE the new Coalition government decided to improve the system, and turned it into what became universally known as the REF. One change was to add a parameter called 'impact', which I will have occasion to mention again in Chapter Eight. Overall, however, if anything, the opportunities for gaming the system increased. And so that is exactly what happened.

For REF 2014, universities were ranked in all three ways seen in our thought experiment: GPA 'quality' or 'excellence' ranking, power ranking, and intensity ranking. Naturally, results varied, and none more so than for Cardiff University. Cardiff is in Wales, which does not fall under the funding regime of the HEFCE. The financial restraint on optimising your submission according to the 'quality' ranking therefore does not apply to Cardiff, and so they went full-tilt for this strategy, submitting a smaller percentage of researchers than any of their Russell Group rivals. The outcome was predictable, but none the less interesting in the disparities it showed up. Once the REF 2014 numbers had been crunched, Cardiff was ranked fifth in the Russell Group[20] on 'excellence'. That was a tremendous PR coup, and within weeks of the result coming out Cardiff ran an advertisement in the *Times Higher Education* for 'Exceptional Opportunities at the University ranked 5th in the UK for Research Excellence'.[21] What the advertisement did not mention was that on the power measure Cardiff ranked 18th in the UK, and on the intensity ranking it was 50th. All three these outcomes are equally valid or invalid. Each is just an artefact of

Cardiff's submission strategy for gaming the system. On the basis of the REF 2014 results you could say that Cardiff ranks 50th in the country with just as much and just as little justification as you can say that it ranks 5th.

Other universities played a different game. University College London, for example, submitted almost all its staff, and so only came seventh in the Russell Group on the 'excellence' ranking. It did have the consolation, however, of coming first in the Russell Group (and the sector) on the power ranking, which was also a highly advantageous position to be in in terms of HEFCE funding. But the conclusion remains the same. UCL would play up its power ranking for public consumption just as much as Cardiff would play up its 'excellence' ranking. Neither has more credence than the other, and none of the rankings had substance beyond what was created by the rankings methodology.

The rankings effect

> Rankings have spread like a virus.
> *Professor Ellen Hazelkorn, Dublin*

Universities reacted to rankings like a baby given a rattle. They waved them about and made a noise. Five years after the first appearance of the Shanghai Jiao Tong index, it had already become commonplace for universities appearing on 'the world ranking' to use this fact in staff recruitment. Thus, for example, in the jobs section of a single edition of the *Times Higher* in 2008 the University of Auckland describes itself as 'a top 50 University in a top 5 City', the University of Sydney is 'rated as one of the top 40 universities across the globe', and Imperial College London is 'ranked 5th best in the world by the THES', while the City University of Hong Kong's growing international reputation is 'evidenced by its surge up the THES rankings'.[22] Another five years later, making use of rankings – any rankings – had become accepted practice, and indeed expected behaviour, on university websites and in student recruitment. The University of Melbourne's website said 'Welcome to Australia's No. 1 University', and went on to say that Melbourne is 'consistently ranked among the leading universities in the world, with its international peers placing it in the top 20 worldwide, and employers placing it in the top 10'. Teesside University was 'the best new university for student experience, according to the *Times Higher Education* survey'. The 2012 Christmas card from the president of National Taiwan University (NTU), besides saying 'Season's greetings and best wishes for the new year', also had an insert mentioning that the NTU ranked 121st on the Shanghai Jiao Tong index, in the 61st–70th band of the *Times Higher* ranking, and 80th in the QS ranking.

Of course, you can only boast about your ranking if you *have* a ranking, and so envy followed in the wake of pride. Those who found themselves without a ranking decided that they should pursue one. Universities started characterising themselves by their ranking aspirations, usually encoded in the institutional strategic plan. The University of Iceland 'has set itself the long-term goal to become one of the 100 best universities in the world'. Haceteppe University in Turkey 'aims to reinforce its respectful status and improve its position in international rankings within the next five years'. RMIT University aims to 'improve RMIT's ranking amongst Australian universities in the UK *Times Higher Education Supplement World University Rankings*'. The University of Botswana wants a strong international reputation, 'indicated by presence in the THES top 200 or Shanghai Index of top 500 world universities'.[23] An international survey carried out in 2006 found that 70% of universities surveyed desired to be in the top 10% nationally and 71% in the top 25% internationally.[24]

Countries displayed the same reaction to rankings as universities did. The Australian federal minister for science and training said in 2007 that 'more of our universities should aim to be within the top 100 internationally and I would like some of our universities to aspire to the top 10'. The Taiwanese vice-minister of education said in 2003 that the ministry would like at least one of its universities to be among the top 100 leading international institutions, and six years later the minister said 'with National Taiwan University now on the list of the world's top 100 universities ... [our] next goal is to help other universities to make the top 100 rankings'. For the higher education minister of Malaysia, the matter was clear: 'The task given to them [the universities] was simple. They knew the measurement criteria of the *THES* rankings. All they had to do was to identify how their existing plans for improving the quality of their institutions matched those criteria.'[25] In other words, universities in Malaysia should re-engineer themselves to match a set of criteria for excellence devised by a newspaper in London.

Because of their desire to do well in the rankings, re-engineering themselves is exactly what many universities started to do. In fact, universities, which would often tell secondary schools not to 'teach to the test', seem to find it natural that they should 'plan to the ranking'. There are many small things universities can do to improve their place in league tables: clean up their data, improve their public relations, publish more in English-language journals, create incentives for publishing in high-impact journals and so on. Such tactical responses are, however, only the least of what universities are actually doing. Often, they change their entire strategy. The overall strategic goal becomes, explicitly or implicitly, to achieve a higher ranking. The levers available for doing so may include structural changes, such as greater investment in subjects that generate high citation levels, or even dropping subjects that don't.

None played the rankings game better than Nanyang Technological University in Singapore. Led by an astute and charismatic president with excellent international connections (a former chief executive of the European Science Foundation and chair of the Nobel Committee for Chemistry), and backed by substantial investment, both from the Singaporean government and from philanthropy, Nanyang Technological University rose in the QS rankings from 74th in 2010 to 13th in 2016. Even more impressively, they rose in the *Times Higher* ranking from 174th in 2010 to 55th in 2015. And they became number one on the ranking of universities under the age of 50.[26]

On a larger scale, at supra-national level, having top-ranked universities became the educational equivalent of having one of the tallest buildings in the world. Within months of the appearance of the first Shanghai Jiao Tong ranking, Ireland's minister for education and science, speaking in his capacity as president of the European Council of Education Ministers, told a conference that Europe was 'behind not just the US but other economies', on the basis that the Shanghai ranking showed only 10 European universities among the top 50 compared with 35 for the United States.[27] This sentiment was echoed by the European Commissioner Jan Figel, who asked at the first meeting of the Commission's University/Industry Forum in February 2008 why Europe could not be as globally successful in higher education as it was in football.[28] Soon voices were raised to champion the creation of an EU ranking[29] (which created the space for U-Multirank, on which more in Chapter Three).

Governments started shaping higher education systems with the aim of improving their national rankings profile. Mostly, this would take the shape of prioritising some universities, namely those who are considered to fit the mould rewarded by ranking parameters. The name of the game is 'research concentration'. France, Germany, Russia, Spain, China, South Korea, Taiwan, Malaysia, Finland, India, Japan, Singapore, Vietnam and Latvia all launched initiatives aimed at creating 'world-class' universities, where 'world-class' is a thinly disguised synonym of 'top-ranked'. Russia's Project 5–100, for example, aimed to propel 5 universities into the top 100 of the world rankings by 2020.[30] Germany launched its *Exzellenzinitiative*, worried that they were being disadvantaged in the ranking by having much of their research carried out in Max Planck Institutes or Fraunhofer Institutes (which, ironically, was at that time seen in the UK as a model worth emulating). The French Senate issued a report arguing that its researchers were disadvantaged relative to English-speaking institutions, and launched *Operation Campus*, spending about €8 billion to establish centres of excellence. The University of Paris-Saclay, for example, which opened in 2015, brought together 19 higher education institutions, in a bid to create a university rivalling Harvard, MIT and Oxbridge. China started Project 211 in 1995 to build up 100 top universities, and followed that in 1998 by Project 985 which is to produce a dozen or so universities able to compete on level terms with the best in the US and Europe. Malaysia's Action Plan for Higher Education of 2007 aimed to establish one or two 'Apex Universities', and for at least one university to achieve a top 100 ranking.[31] In Saudi Arabia, when opening the King Abdullah University of Science and Technology (and endowing it with a $10 billion grant), the king stated that 'It is my desire that this new University become one of the world's great institutions of research'.[32]

By 2014, with the release of their latest rankings, the *Times Higher* press release was able to say that 'the THE rankings have been built into government policy and institutions' strategic plans across the globe'. It is worth pondering the fact that this was no idle boast. Governments around the world were shaping national higher education policy in response to a cocktail of metrics and formulae shaken up in the offices of a small newspaper in London. It is also rapidly became true that students worldwide were making career choices based on rankings, rather than the extent to which a university's offering actually matches their own needs and aspirations. And it is sadly true that universities, who are so insistent on their institutional autonomy and academic freedom, not to mention their intellectual depth and academic rigour, slavishly follow the crude arithmetic of the rankers.

They really must be pinching themselves over at the offices of the *Times Higher Education*. Students and parents believe in their omniscience. Newspapers put them on the front page. Vice-chancellors fawn upon them. Ministers of state dance to their tune. All this power, and a goldmine too. The data sets on which the rankings are based can be recycled at will into different types of special-purpose rankings, dangling a carrot in front of those aspiring to make it onto the main list of the 'world rankings'. Geographically, there are rankings of Asian universities, African universities, Arab universities and Latin American universities. By age, there is a (very popular) ranking of universities under 50 years old. Economically, there are rankings of universities in BRICS (Brazil, Russia, India, China, South Africa) countries and emerging economies. There is a ranking of 'international presence', a ranking of universities on no other criterion than 'reputation', and, conversely, a ranking of universities whose subject rankings are better than their reputation rankings. These types of rankings are all in addition to very many subject rankings, which focus on one subject of faculty at a time.

In this manner, everybody can aspire to do well in some ranking. With appetites thus whetted, a market is created for helping universities improve their rankings, typically by selling back to them a repackaged version of the information that came from them in the first place. Seminars can be offered, international conferences can be arranged, data sets can be sold. It is a wonderful business model. Somewhat like the cosmetics industry, it is based on the vanity of the consumer, with the added advantage that the consumers themselves supply the basic ingredients from which the various nostrums are compounded.

The situation is not devoid of humour. There is the case of Princeton, which is reputed to have one of the best law schools in the US, despite the inconvenience that Princeton does not have a law school.[33] There is the University of Alexandria, whose good showing in the 2010 *Times Higher* rankings was due to a cluster of highly cited papers by one researcher in one journal.[34] There is the very idea of ranking in one list the wide diversity of 1,000 American universities and colleges, and being able to proclaim very precisely that Chatham University in Pennsylvania ('recognised as a leader in sustainability')[35] is joint 499th best in the country, together with Southern Nazarene University in Oklahoma ('a Christian community of scholars').[36] There is the proud claim of that same ranking that for the parameter of 'quality of staff–student interaction' it 'draws on a survey of 100,000 students' – not noticing, apparently, that this means it consulted on average only 100 students per institution.[37] There is the difference it can make to a university's ranking when the rankers decide to take a ratio of averages rather than the average of ratios.[38] There are the stories about university presidents who get a bonus if their university moves up in the rankings – and about what might happen if it drops in the rankings.[39] And there is the rather delicious irony that by their compliance universities provide a veneer of legitimacy to a methodology which any one of their own statisticians could tell them is highly questionable.

The 'reputation survey' part of the ranking would have its own idiosyncrasies. For example, if yours is an old and committed standard model university, there will be a higher than usual proportion of academics among your many alumni, probably distributed around the world, who can then be relied upon to vote for you. Or, if you are the best in a poorly performing region, the geographical slant of the survey will lift you out above an equal university in a better performing region. And, as mentioned before, if you are voted to be in the top echelon by one person in one discipline, you will rank above another university which 100 voters had top in the second echelon in a number of disciplines.

Decisions on rankings can cut close to the bone. There's the experience of a Scottish university which had the third-highest standard of student entry after Oxford and Cambridge, only to hear that the ranker refused to accept these figures because they were, to his mind, counter-intuitive.[40] And there is my personal experience when writing this chapter of receiving from Thomson Reuters an indication of just how casually 'editorial discretion' can be deployed.

> For example some universities would show up in the Clinical Health ranking but on investigation do not actually have a Medical School and would therefore [be] manually removed from the ranking. We have the opposite too, for example University X has a small Engineering faculty that would appear to be too small a proportion of the university to warrant inclusion in the rankings, but *actually their Engineering faculty is small but highly regarded and editorial discretion is used to manually include them in the ranking even though they ordinarily would not qualify.*[41] (My anonymisation and my italics – CB)

Given all the interest it has generated, the rankings phenomenon has attracted the attention of social scientists, educationists, think tanks and government agencies, and so there is by now quite a literature on the subject. Within five years of the first appearance of the Shanghai Jiao Tong index, the HEFCE started taking an interest. They commissioned a report on the topic which was published on the web in April 2008, titled *Counting What Is Measured, or Measuring What Counts? League Tables and Their Impact on Higher Education Institutions in England.*[42] The HEFCE report looked at three national league tables (the *Sunday Times*, the *Times* and the *Guardian*) and two international ones (Shanghai Jiao Tong and *Times Higher*). It presented an early version of some conclusions which have since then become quite familiar. About the league tables themselves: they do not provide a complete picture of the sector; some of the measures included are poor proxies for the qualities identified; the rankings are not transparent, and they reflect reputation more than quality or performance. About their impact: universities are strongly influenced by league tables, and:

> The influence of league tables is increasing both nationally and internationally, and cannot be ignored despite serious methodological limitations. They are being used for a broader range of purposes than

originally intended, and being bestowed with more meaning than the data alone may bear.

Starting from about the point where the HEFCE left off, the European University Association (EUA) felt the need to commission a report on rankings, because of increasing questions from its members, the interest shown by European governments, and the European Commission's decision to develop a European ranking. Its report was published in 2011,[43] as a 'first review' in an ongoing project. The report is a clearly written information brochure on the methodologies behind 13 of 'the most popular global rankings', and their potential impact. More interesting, perhaps, to those who want an overview of the rankings phenomenon rather than the details of indicators, weights, parameters and formulae, are the comments headed 'Implications of the rankings in brief'. Here is a selection.

> Those who compile and publish rankings usually claim that rankings are 'objective' and that the position of a university in a ranking table corresponds to its 'quality'. Critics argue that the result of rankings depends strongly on the choice of indicators and weights assigned to the indicators and that, because it is difficult (if not impossible) to measure quality itself, rankings use various more or less distant proxies and claim that these measurements represent quality or excellence itself. As stated by Marginson and van der Wende,[44] 'A better approach to rankings begins from the recognition that all rankings are partial in coverage and contain biases, and that all rankings are purpose driven.'
>
> At the same time society, including politicians, often like to see universities arranged in a neat league table according to the results attained through indicators, and truly believe that, in much the same way as for sports teams, each university in the table is 'better' than the one below, and 'not as good' as the one above.... Growth of interest in the results of rankings has changed the context in which universities function: for a university to be seen as 'successful' it has now become necessary

to improve performance specifically in those aspects that are measured by rankings....

It would be naïve to imagine that the media will ever give up a tool such as the global university rankings, which attract thousands of readers when the new results are published and which allows suspense to be maintained over an entire year by publishing tiny snippets of information about minimal changes in ranking methodologies. The general public as well as politicians will always like easily readable tables, which clearly state which universities are the very best in the world.

As regards universities, they are often either flattered or ashamed depending on their current position in the league table or the change of position since the previous year. There are forces both inside and outside the university encouraging it to make every effort to improve its position in the rankings or simply to be included in the league tables at all costs. As S. Marginson puts it,[45] 'Rankings are the meta-performance indicator, with a special power of their own. Rankings are hypnotic and become an end in themselves without regard to exactly what they measure, whether they are solidly grounded or whether their use has constructive effects. The desire for rank overrules all else.'

The report also lists some 'biases and flaws' of rankings. These include the bias towards research rather than teaching or other university functions, the bias within research towards the natural sciences and medicine, away from the social sciences, the built-in biases of normalisation techniques, health warnings about 'impact factors', peer review bias, language bias and regional bias.

Biases and flaws notwithstanding, however, the growth of the rankings phenomenon seems unstoppable, and the consequences increasingly apparent. Universities, as we have seen, increasingly comply with the paradigm rewarded in the rankings. The second report of the EUA on *Global University Rankings and Their Impact*[46] was sent to members in April 2013. The covering letter says:

The report underlines that there have been significant new developments in the field of international rankings since EUA's first ranking review report, in 2011. It reveals that the number of international ranking and other 'transparency tools' continues to grow, with the arrival of new rankings and new products developed by ranking providers. The report also shows that rankings are beginning to impact on public policy making. The developments indicate the need for all stakeholders to reflect on the extent to which global rankings are no longer a concern only for a small number of elite institutions but have become a reality for a much broader spectrum of universities as they seek to be included in, or improve their position in one or the other rankings.

The definitive biography, so to speak, of rankings, is a 2011 book titled *Rankings and the Reshaping of Higher Education: The Battle for World-class Excellence*,[47] by Ellen Hazelkorn, at that time vice-president at the Dublin Institute of Technology. Comprehensively researched, well contextualised and meticulously documented, this book documented in detail the various rankings, their impact and influence on universities, their relation to student choice and recruitment, their influence on national policy and planning, and, most interestingly, how they reshape our understanding of universities and of higher education. (Expanding on the topic and updating developments, Professor Hazelkorn also produced in 2016 an edited volume titled *Global Rankings and the Geopolitics of Higher Education: Understanding the Influence and Impact of Rankings on Higher Education, Policy and Society*,[48] consisting of specially commissioned chapters which examine the changes affecting higher education and the implications for society and the economy.)

Professor Hazelkorn's key observation is that rankings have spread like a virus. Her key conclusion can be paraphrased, without taking too much of a liberty, as saying that rankings have all the health benefits of a virus. She variously uses phrases like 'a growing obsession with rankings', 'a mantra for governments', 'the fetishization of world-class status', 'an annual feeding frenzy', 'policy hysteria', 'policy panic', 'the maelstrom' and 'a storm which has blown around the world'. The key consequence is a new kind of arms race: the reputation race.

There is a growing obsession with university rankings around the world. What started as an academic exercise in the early 20th century in the US became a commercial 'information' service for students in the 1980s and the progenitor of a 'reputation race' with geo-political implications today. Around the world, rankings consciousness has risen sharply and, arguably inevitably, in response to globalisation and the pursuit of new knowledge as the basis of economic growth, and the drive for increased public accountability and transparency. Rankings are a manifestation of what has become known as the worldwide 'battle for excellence' and are perceived and used to determine the status of individual institutions, assess the quality and performance of the higher education system and gauge global competitiveness. As internationalisation has become a priority for both government and higher education, the talent-catching and knowledge-producing capacity of higher education has become a vital sign of a country's capacity to participate in world science and the global economy. In the process, rankings are transforming universities and reshaping higher education.[49]

The trouble with rankings reshaping higher education is that it works against institutional diversity. Rankings are a straitjacket which universities have been keen to wear as a fashion item. The uniformity towards which we are heading is not one defined by the universities themselves, but by those who make a business out of rankings, and reinforced by perception, vanity and politics. We are drifting towards a new version of an old model of what a university should look like. We are, in short, heading back towards the standard model.

As discussed in Chapter One, the 20th-century standard model of a university emphasises individual curiosity-driven research, sees teaching as secondary to research, and does not feel any particular responsibility towards civic engagement. It is mostly interested in the self-referential opinions of academics about other academics. What the most influential rankings do is to take that model as a gold standard, and then attempt to measure the distance of universities from it. The new version of the old model is that to be a 'world-class university' amounts to nothing more than occupying a high position on league tables and rankings. Value has been replaced by position on a list. Quality has become a positional good.

For those universities which, by history or choice, exemplify the standard model anyway, the growth of rankings has come as a welcome turn of events. For those that choose to adopt the standard model as a goal it provides clarity of purpose. To any other university which had been trying to tread a different path it creates a dilemma: whether to stick to your principles and risk being seen as second-rate, or to conform to the new model. Many universities choose the latter path, and thus become complicit in 'the fetishization of world-class status' by chasing a (higher) ranking, and bending to conform to a particular model whether it suits their beliefs and circumstances or not.

How, then, should we react to rankings? At a tactical level, it would make sense to encourage their proliferation. The more rankings and league tables there are, the more they will add to the welter of information, satisfying those who believe that increase in information is always a good thing. Also, the more rankings there are the more they will contradict each other, illustrating the fact that since they cannot all be true very likely none of them is true. This may help to establish the point that rankings are just arithmetic games, not theorems. Third, the more rankings there are the more each university will have a chance to find some ranking somewhere to boast about. And if they cannot find one they like they can always construct their own.

At a strategic level, however, we should respond to rankings by considering their effect on the sector, even if only out of self-interest. Rankings are forcing a return to the pre-eminence of Mode 1 knowledge production. Mode 1, we recall from our discussion of Gibbons et al in Chapter One, is the traditional, discipline-based, curiosity-driven, individual pursuit of new knowledge, in the paradigm of Newtonian science. Mode 2 knowledge production, on the other hand, takes place in response to societal needs and demands, is typically conducted by interdisciplinary teams, problem-oriented and solutions-driven, in active engagement and collaboration with society. As the title of their book indicates, Gibbons et al thought that Mode 2 was the new production of knowledge, and the way of the future.

Not so, in a new era when rankings dictate policy. The ivory tower is being refurbished.

> Thus, rankings fetishize a narrow definition of research, undermine the value of the arts, humanities and social sciences, and fail to give adequate recognition to the breadth of knowledge's contribution to society and the economy. By hierarchically ordering or stratifying knowledge – for example, through the practice of ranking journals – rankings reinforce the status of elite institutions and particular countries as the primary knowledge producers and generators of intellectual property....
>
> By elevating rankings and their indicators to god-like status, rankings and their many cheerleaders threaten to undermine the breadth of higher education's contribution and benefit to society and the economy. They perversely ask which HEI [higher education institution] is better, without also asking for whom and for what? There is plenty of evidence that rankings, or more precisely doing well and being seen to do well, is now a significant factor driving institutional and government policy with priorities and resources aligned to indicators.... The public policy imperative has been lost in the (self-interested) belief that elite research universities have a bigger impact on society and the economy, or have higher quality.[50]

These are strong words. They are, however, representative of a growing unease with the effect of rankings on public policy, and the way universities have simply given away the power to determine their own destiny.[51] Ironically, we have given it away, not to government, as many discussions about academic freedom over the years have warned, nor to big business, which was a concern when the model of 'the entrepreneurial university' came to the fore, but to nothing more substantial than a one-size-fits-all caricature of what universities are supposed to be like. The greatest danger of loss of institutional autonomy now comes, not from the state, nor from big business, not from globalisation, but from our own vanity.

Again, then: what to do? Analysis of the problem comes first, of course, but as we have seen there is plenty of that already, and sufficiently many warning bells have been sounded so that we cannot plead ignorance. Trying to tame the beast comes next, and there are plenty of academics and institutions who try to invent 'better rankings' – some sit on boards, some speak at conferences, and some try to invent something different.

My own view is that we need to understand the social context within which rankings flourish, and I will in later chapters give it a name: linearism. Then, once we understand the context, we need a credible alternative approach. I will give a name to that too: orthogonality. But first we have to talk about quality.

3

Quality in Higher Education

Plato, Aristotle and *arête*

Everyone is born either a Platonist or an Aristotelian.
Samuel Taylor Coleridge

In trying to figure out what makes a good university we should engage with the idea of the good, otherwise the question lacks content. We then seem to be confronted with an ambiguity. When we speak of 'a good university', do we mean good as in excellent, or good as in virtuous?

The perception of ambiguity is interesting in itself, because it indicates that we draw a distinction between excellence and virtue. This is a point worth exploring. And the exploration takes us back about two and a half millennia, to Athens.

Plato would reify the concept of the good, add capital letters, and talk about 'The Good' as a universal. He had quite a lot to say about it, and so it is worth saying something about him. This may seem like a mere exercise in repetition, because an entire library could be filled with opinions about Plato, coming from professionals who devote their life to the task. None the less, there is a simple fact worth pointing out, which is this: he never spoke with his own voice. He never said 'I am Plato the philosopher, and my view is – '. Instead, Plato spoke through others, and mainly through the voice of Socrates.[1]

Socrates was a real person who made a real nuisance of himself in the streets of Athens. He went around and about trying to find out what wisdom consists of. His method was to ask people who professed to know to explain it to him. He would then engage them in conversation, and through dialogue would invariably succeed in showing that the matter was in no way as simple as the self-assured interviewee had thought. In these endeavours Socrates had quite a fan club of young men from the leisured class. One of them was Plato, and Plato took it upon himself to record these Socratic dialogues.

Or so it seems. Socrates spoke a lot, but he never bothered to write anything down. And so we have a man who never spoke for himself reporting the views of a man who never wrote for himself. The difficulty is obvious: it is not easy to figure out when you are hearing the voice of Socrates, and when you are hearing the voice of Plato.

One thing is accepted historical fact: Socrates willingly chose to die for his beliefs. When sufficiently many upright Athenians had been sufficiently annoyed by Socrates for sufficiently long, they charged him before the court of Athenian citizens with corrupting the young. His defence is recorded in one of the few pieces of Platonic writing that is not in dialogue form, but as a Socratic monologue. This is the celebrated *Apology*: the spirited and robust defence by Socrates of his life and ideals.

It is worth quoting a piece of the *Apology*, because it tells us what Socrates believed, and it also illustrates the style in which Plato wrote. The *Apology* comes in three parts: Socrates speaking in his own defence before the verdict (guilty), then before the sentence is pronounced (death), and finally in response to the sentence. The following quote comes from the third part, with Socrates reflecting on the nature of death, and finding nothing to fear.

> Let us reflect in another way, and we shall see that there is great reason to hope that death is a good, for one of two things: either death is a state of nothingness and utter unconsciousness, or, as men say, there is a change and migration of the soul from this world to another. Now if you suppose there is not consciousness, but a sleep like the sleep of him who is undisturbed even by

the sight of dreams, death will be an unspeakable gain. For if a person were to select the night in which his sleep was undisturbed even by dreams, and were to compare this with the other days and nights of his life, and then were to tell us how many days and nights he had passed in the course of his life better and more pleasantly than this one, I think that any man, I will not say a private man, but even the great king, will not find many such days or nights, when compared with the others. Now if death is like this, I say that to die is gain; for eternity is then only a single night. But if death is the journey to another place, and there, as men say, all the dead are, what good, O my friends and judges, can be greater than this? ...

Wherefore, O judges, be of good cheer about death, and know this of a truth – that no evil can happen to a good man, either in life or after death. He and his are not neglected by the gods; nor has my own approaching end happened by mere chance. But I see clearly that to die and be released was better for me; and therefore the oracle gave no sign. For which reason also, I am not angry with my accusers, or my condemners; they have done me no harm, although they did not mean to do me any good; and for this I may gently blame them. Still I have a favor to ask of them. When my sons are grown up, I would ask you, O my friends, to punish them; and I would have you trouble them, as I have troubled you, if they seem to care about riches, or anything, more than about virtue; or if they pretend to be something when they are really nothing, – then reprove them, as I have reproved you, for not caring about that for which they ought to care, and thinking that they are something when they are really nothing. And if you do this, I and my sons will have received justice at your hands. The hour of departure has arrived, and we go our ways – I to die, and you to live. Which is better God only knows.[2]

We should keep the *Apology* in mind when we encounter Socrates again in the later writings of Plato. Of these, Plato's most famous work is *The Republic*, where he pursues the proposal that The Good is actually about the best kind of government – because the best kind of state would have the best kind of citizens. Something quite astonishing then happens. That same Socrates who died for the right to freedom of enquiry now becomes the mouthpiece for a proposed dictatorship. This dictatorship is exercised by an elite, who are superior in intellectual capacity and attainment to the lower classes. Karl Popper, the philosopher of science who had to flee the Nazis, hated this line of thought so much that he elevated Plato – not Socrates, but Plato – to one of the three main enemies of an open society (along with Hegel and Marx).[3]

What has this got to do with the university? This much: that Plato's thoughts took shape in his Academy, which is commonly taken to be the original prototype of a university. The origin of the university, therefore, our perceived bastion of academic freedom, is tainted with an original sin in putting forward an idea of the good which smacks of intellectual arrogance: that knowledge and understanding makes you superior – not just intellectually, but morally.

Among the 'students' at the Academy was a younger man called Aristotle, who did not really buy in to Plato's ideas about Ideas. Besides metaphysics, he was also interested in other things. Many other things, as it turned out. Aristotle wrote on aesthetics, astronomy, biology, ethics, logic, metaphysics, meteorology, physics, poetics, politics, rhetoric and zoology. In doing so, he more or less invented many of the academic disciplines still with us today. He distinguished between the natural philosopher, the mathematician and the metaphysician. He had views on the soul, on youth and old age, and life and death. He pointed out that one swallow does not make a summer, and that a story must have a beginning, a middle and an end. He wrote solemnly on the meaning of the terms 'heavy' and 'light', on prophesying by dreams, and on the habits of the elephant.

Quite often he was just plain wrong. He thought a vacuum was impossible. He believed men have more teeth than women. He nailed down for two millennia the idea that the world is made up of just four elements: earth, air, fire and water. He casually asserted that a heavier object would fall faster than a lighter one, and this remained an accepted fact until disproved by Galileo. The great thing about Aristotle, though, is that so much of what he wrote allows of falsification. He may therefore properly be called a scientist, in a sense in which Plato was not. He investigates many phenomena in what we would call a scientific manner. Plato is interested mostly in the way the world ought to be, but Aristotle is interested mostly in the way the world is. He believes in observation, and he did a lot of it (although he missed out on some obvious ones, like counting Mrs Aristotle's teeth). Nothing is beyond his scope. His great overall strength is that he tries to make sense of his observations. He is the great systematiser, the ultimate conceptual tidier-upper.

As a writer, as well, Aristotle is entirely different from Plato. Try this, for example:

> There cannot be an intermediate between contradictories, but of one subject we must either affirm or deny any one predicate. This is clear, in the first place, if we define what the true and the false are. To say of that which is that it is not, or of what is not that it is, is false, while to say of what is that it is, and of what is not that it is not, is true, so that he who says of anything that it is, or that it is not, will say either what is true or what is false; but neither what is nor what is not is said to be or not to be.[4]

Philosophers and logicians can recognise here a correspondence theory of truth, which has to do with the relationship between words and facts, and a formulation of the law of excluded middle, which says that a declarative statement is either true or false. Most other people just find it deadly dull. They would not read Aristotle for pleasure, and if forced to read him anyway he makes their head hurt. If Plato writes prose which reads like poetry, then Aristotle writes prose which reads like algebra. But some of us *like* algebra.

Aristotle is always in rational mode, proceeding methodically from premises to conclusions by logical argument. And so he is when discussing the nature of the good. Opening the *Nicomachean Ethics* with the claim that the good is that at which all things aim, he moves, with various clarifying digressions along the way, to the good as happiness, which is 'the best, noblest and most pleasant thing in the world'.[5] Happiness, it turns out, is an activity of the soul in accordance with perfect virtue, which takes us on to a discussion of virtue. And here Aristotle makes an important distinction: virtue can be intellectual, or it can be moral.

> Virtue, then, being of two kinds, intellectual and moral, intellectual virtue in the main owes both its birth and its growth to teaching (for which reason it requires experience and time), while moral virtue comes about as a result of habit.

This is exactly the apparent ambiguity with which we started, and which still confronts us today: the good as intellectual excellence, or the good as moral virtue. And this is where you really need your professor of Greek. Plato and Aristotle come down to us over the course of two millennia by the vehicle of translation, and understanding what they actually said informs our understanding of how the ideas they expressed in classical Greek translate into ideas of 21st-century English. That is why many books on Greek philosophy will carry parenthetical remarks on Greek words, and try to explain that some of the connotations we attach to some words today may not have existed for the Greeks, or the other way round. What is translated as 'happiness' for example, was *eudaimonia* to the Greeks, which literally translates into 'good spirit', and could also be taken as a state of contented wellbeing or human flourishing. ('Quality of life' may be a better expression, in so far as it refers to the state of mind of the individual, rather than their material circumstances.)

When we talk about the good, therefore, and we take the concept back to Plato or Aristotle, we should know that in their language they were talking about *arête*. Our translation comes out either as excellence or as virtue, and we experience this as an ambiguity to be cleared up, but the original sense of *arête* would encompass both nuances, as separate dimensions rather than separate meanings. Here is Aristotle, mixing it up:

> We may remark, then, that every virtue or excellence both brings into good condition the thing of which it is the excellence and makes the work of that thing be

done well; e.g. the excellence of the eye makes both the eye and its work good; for it is by the excellence of the eye that we see well. Similarly the excellence of the horse makes a horse both good in itself and good at running and at carrying its rider and at awaiting the attack of the enemy. Therefore, if this is true in every case, the virtue of the man also will be the state of character which makes a man good and which makes him do his own work well.

Arête, then, is the virtue of being good at what you are supposed to be, and doing well at what you are supposed to be doing. Anything, and anybody, can have *arête,* if you live up to your full potential, or truly fulfil your core purpose. In Greek philosophy, 'living up to your full potential' would translate into realising your *essence.* This in turn relates to a distinction between substance and essence, where the substance of a thing is that to which its properties adhere, and essence is what its true nature is. So, really, any substance can have *arête,* which it will attain by realising its essence, and this is a good thing both in the sense of being excellent and in the sense of being a virtue.

Having come this far with Plato and Aristotle on the question of the good, we should take note of a cult book of the 1970s called *Zen and the Art of Motorcycle Maintenance,* by Robert M. Pirsig. In the 40th anniversary edition, the author reflects that it is really three books: an account of a father-and-son motorcycle trip from Minnesota to California, a philosophical meditation on the concept of quality, and an account of a man pursued by the ghost of his former self. It is the middle book that is of interest here, but the narrator tells that story in the first person by reference to his own previous persona, a self-absorbed hyper-intellectual whom he calls Phaedrus.

It is this modern Phaedrus who becomes obsessed with trying to understand what quality is, and descends into insanity in the process. On his mental descent, Phaedrus delves into Greek philosophy, encounters the concept of *arête,* and equates that with a true pre-Socratic understanding of quality. Unfortunately, however, this Phaedrus concludes, true understanding of *arête* was damaged by Plato, who subordinated the good to the true, and then virtually killed off by Aristotle, who is the arch-villain of the piece.

> Under Aristotle the 'Reader', whose knowledge of Trojan *arête* seems conspicuously absent, forms and substances dominate all. The Good is a relatively minor branch of knowledge called ethics; reason, logic, knowledge are his primary concerns. *Arête* is dead and science, logic and the university as we know it today have been given their founding charter: to find and invent an endless proliferation of forms about the substantive elements of the world and call these forms knowledge, and transmit these forms to future generations.[6]

This is hardly complimentary to the university as we know it today. It does, however, raise a fair question: how do universities treat quality?

Quality and standards

> They sought it with thimbles, they sought it with care;
>   They pursued it with forks and hope;
>   They threatened its life with a railway-share;
>   They charmed it with smiles and soap.
>   *Lewis Carroll, The Hunting of the Snark*

To use rankings and league tables as a response to the question of what makes a good university is to commit a category error, because a ranking represents quality as quantity. In a ranking, the question of whether or how your university is a good university is answered by a number, which is your position on the list. This is effective in the sense that it does produce an answer, but fallacious in the sense that it is the answer to a formula, not an answer to the question. It is suitable at best for those who prefer certainty to truth.

Academics, however, pride themselves on being truth-seekers. So it is a reasonable challenge to ask whether the higher education sector itself has come up with a better approach to quality. The answer is not entirely edifying, but that in itself is a good reason for unpacking it. It lies in an activity called quality assurance.

In 2008, Universities UK (UUK), the representative body for vice-chancellors of universities in the United Kingdom, published a pamphlet titled *Quality and Standards in UK Universities: A Guide to How the System Works*. The executive summary of that pamphlet opens as follows:

> UK universities are widely regarded as being amongst the best in the world. Maintaining the highest academic quality and standards is crucial to that reputation. This paper explains how universities ensure that students can have confidence that the time and money that they invest in their education are well spent.[7]

This is saying a number of things. First, the opening sentence carefully does not say that UK universities *are* among the best in the world, only that they are *regarded* as such. None the less, such a claim does give credence to the idea of 'best in the world'. Second, the high reputation of UK universities is grounded in something presumed to be objective, namely academic quality and standards. Third, the matter of quality and standards essentially relates to the educational experience of students. And fourth, that one reason why this matters is about return on investment.

UUK therefore starts off from the same basic premise as those who produce rankings and league tables: that it is a valid question to ask which universities are the best in the world, and that there is some way of giving a sensible answer to that question. However, UUK then takes another tack. While league tables are mostly about research, using comparative data and quantitative formulae, UUK ties the question about 'best in the world' to the idea of 'the highest academic quality and standards'.

The qualitative starting point sounds eminently sensible. For it to lead anywhere, however, there needs to be some common understanding about what quality in higher education means, and how quality judgements may objectively be made. It is the pursuit of such a common understanding which has, at times, resembled the hunting of the Snark. We are not quite sure what we are looking for, we are not quite sure where to look, or how, and sometimes we may even doubt whether what we are looking for exists at all.

So, what do we mean by quality in higher education? The question first seems to have made its way into academic consciousness during the late 1980s and early 1990s, when universities, particularly in British Commonwealth countries, suddenly found a 'Higher Education Quality Assurance Agency' of some kind being set up at national level. Perhaps the idea fell on fertile ground towards the end of the era of the standard model, when politicians and policy makers were no longer content to leave academia alone. Perhaps it blew over from the manufacturing sector, where quality assurance is standard practice to ensure that products meet customer expectations and comply with minimum standards. Perhaps the cult status of *Zen and the Art of Motorcycle Maintenance* had something to do with it.

Quality assurance quickly became an industry, and it is still going strong. Almost every university in the world is subject to some kind of periodic quality audit by some kind of government agency. There is an international association of such national quality assurance agencies, with over 200 members.[8] A lay person might be forgiven for thinking that these would be the bodies best able to respond to the question of which universities are 'amongst the best in the world'. Not so, however. Anybody who would like to verify or dispute a claim that some particular university or group of universities are 'amongst the best in the world' will soon find that the quality assurance industry is almost entirely irrelevant to their efforts.

The first reason for this anomaly is that quality assurance in higher education has become firmly coupled to only one of the core functions of universities, namely teaching and learning. It is on the Newman side of the fence, with no presence on the von Humboldt side. It plays a different game altogether from the attempt to rate and rank research, even though the quest of finding 'the best' universities is the same.

One might think that if the rankings game is mainly focused on research, and the quality assurance game is mainly focused on teaching, then perhaps there is a way of putting these together to get better coverage in the quest of finding 'the best'. That would be good if it could be made to work. However, the prospect of doing so is poor, for two reasons. First, quality assurance of teaching has over time largely been standardised as a matter of scrutinising processes rather than outcomes. Research rankings, of course, focus on outcomes, not process. Second, and more fundamentally, just as there are many different ways of ranking research, there are many different definitions in the quality assurance world of what is meant by quality. Inevitably, then, different quality assurance agencies in different countries adopt different definitions, so they are not quite talking about the same thing.

None the less, we may investigate the conceptual question: What do we mean by quality? Do academics (and UUK) have some common conception of 'the best universities in the world'? Is there some consensus on quality in academia? And if so, what does it look like? If we want to substantiate any claims about some universities being 'amongst the best in the world', then presumably a common conception of quality would have to be a little stronger than 'I know it when I see it'. To this question, academics have come up with many answers, including the answer that no answer is possible.[9] That seems a little pessimistic. Even if no single comprehensive answer is commonly accepted, we can at least do some disambiguation, and survey some partial answers.

Let us focus on the excellence aspect of *arête*, and ask an apparently innocuous question. In principle, could every university be excellent?

We may treat the question as a thought experiment. If every university had academic freedom, and enough resources, and excellent staff, and good leadership, and all the rest – is it possible that they could all be excellent? The question is not limited to universities. In a class of students, or a team of athletes, or a shop floor of different makes of washing machines – could they all be excellent? If we say yes, then we have accepted one interpretation of quality; if we say no, another.

If we accept that, in principle, every university could be excellent, then we are buying into the idea that quality is a matter of exceeding a certain bar, or standard, or threshold. If the bar is high, then we say the performance is excellent. Excellence, on this line of thinking, is a substantive concept. Any university which gets over the bar may then be thought of as a good university. Every athlete who makes the Olympic team is an excellent athlete. If you make up a class of gifted students they will all be excellent. If you put on the shop floor only washing machines recommended by *Which?* magazine they would all be excellent.

If, however, we believe that excellence, in principle, cannot be attained by all, then we are adopting the view that to be excellent is to be better than the others. It is to excel. Excellence, on this view, is a comparative judgement, not a substantive one. Even among Olympic athletes, not everyone will win a medal, and only a few will win gold. Even among gifted students some will be better than others. And, having surveyed a shop floor full of excellent washing machines, you will only buy one of them.

With this distinction in mind, let us take quality to be, not a question, but the answer to a question. Let us say that quality – by which for the moment we mean quality of teaching and learning – is what you have when you can answer yes to the question 'Is it good?' There are then some plausible partial versions of the question 'Is this a good university?' Here are some of them.

- Does it have high standards?
- Is it better than the others?
- Does it have a good reputation?
- Is it good at what it does?
- Is it good for society?
- Does it deliver a good return on investment?
- Is it accredited by professional bodies?
- Is it efficient?
- Is it effective?

Each of these questions has been extensively analysed, debated and critiqued by quality assurance professionals, and various combinations of them have been formally adopted by state bodies responsible for higher education. I will discuss them one by one.

Does it have high standards?

When Jane and Joe Public are looking for a good university for their children, this is often the first question they ask. In doing so, they have reduced the question of quality to a question of excellence, and adopted a substantive interpretation of what excellence is. Quality assurance professionals, however, make a careful distinction between quality and standards. If quality is the answer to the question 'Is it good?', then standards give the answer to the question 'Is it good enough?' A standard is a threshold of some kind, in higher education as in other domains. For example, every Olympic athlete needs to qualify for the games by exceeding a certain minimum standard of performance, and we accept that these are all excellent athletes because the standard is so high.

For Jane and Joe Public a whole discussion could ensue about the further question 'standards of what?' It might be entry standards, or exit standards, or standards of teaching and learning, or any one of range of other things, or combinations of them, or all of them.

Even without burrowing further down that particular rabbit hole things quickly become confusing. One reason is a consensus which developed in the field that quality assurance is not really about answering the question 'Is it good?' in the sense of checking outcomes. Rather, quality assurance came to mean checking process – specifically, checking the effectiveness of the educational process. Taking the UUK *Guide to How the System Works* as an exemplar, we find the notion of quality defined as follows:

> Academic 'quality' describes the effectiveness of the learning experience provided by universities to their students, i.e. the appropriateness and effectiveness of learning, teaching, assessment and support opportunities provided to assist students achieve their learning objectives.

This UUK *Guide* definition of academic quality, although focused on process rather than outcomes, can still be made to fit with the idea of quality as high standards if we are prepared to stretch the point. If academic quality describes the effectiveness of the learning experience, then, given that effectiveness refers to outcomes, one may reasonably conclude that the outcome being sought is high standards. If so, then quality is about process, and standards are about outcomes, and the job of quality assurance would be to check that the educational process will ensure high standards, and thus excellence.

Unfortunately, this line of reasoning was torpedoed when quality assurance agencies – at least for a while – declined to comment on standards at all. In 2008, for example, the chief executive of the Quality Assurance Agency (QAA) in the UK went on record as follows:

> Clearly, standards are central to our mission and we are responsible for facilitating the way in which institutions describe them. We also need to be sure we have the means of monitoring and judging how they are being stewarded. But it is not our task to judge the standards themselves, second-guessing autonomous institutions' individual responsibilities in this area.[10]

This would lead us straight into a dead end, which is that standards are set by the universities themselves, and quality assurance is an external check on each university's internal processes for delivering on standards – but without the QAA actually making a judgement on those standards. So you could have very low standards, but as long as your processes for delivering to those low standards were effective you would get a tick from the QAA.

That would be a rather measly answer to the question 'Is it good?' No wonder Jane and Joe Public turn to rankings and league tables. These, of course, deliver an answer to a different question: not 'Is it good?', but 'Is it better than the others?' And the J. Publics are quite right to explore this option, because it fits the alternative answer, the 'no' answer, to the question whether every university can be excellent.

Is it better than the others?

The comparative approach says that the meaning of 'excellence' comes from the verb 'to excel', which means to distinguish yourself above everybody else. No matter at what level the bar is set, the question is who can jump higher than whom. Therefore, the accolade of excellence should be reserved for those who can jump the highest, no matter how high (or perhaps even how low) everybody else can jump. Very definitely, then, on this approach, not everybody can be excellent.

Rankings and league tables are founded on the idea of excellence as a comparative judgement. Excellence, on this way of thinking, is based on output measures. It means jumping higher, running faster, accumulating more points, winning the competition, coming first in the race. It is appealing in its simplicity. If you want to be excellent you don't just have to jump over some bar, you have to beat the other participants, who are your competitors. With that, we are back to all the issues around ranking discussed in Chapter Two. What is conceptually a comparative approach is in practice a competitive approach. Being seen as a good university is the prize you win for beating other universities. The game in which you choose to play has a set of rules, and you will make up strategy and tactics as much as necessary for doing well in the game, and gaining the rewards for doing well.

Does it have a good reputation?

Here is a different approach altogether. It not only ducks the question whether a university really is good, it also ducks the question whether it really is better than the others. It does not ask about reality, but about the perception of reality. (Recall from above, for example, UUK's opening sentence in its *Quality and Standards* pamphlet: 'UK Universities are widely regarded as being amongst the best in the world.') The question 'Is it good?' is replaced by the question 'Do people think it is good?'.

Perceptions matter, because perception will influence reality, perhaps just as much as reality influences perception. It is when perception fully replaces reality that we speak of a 'post-truth' society: there is no longer any question of truth, only a question of what people believe, and can be led to believe. So, the ramifications of the quality-as-reputation approach are not difficult to see. First, perceptions are easier to manipulate than reality, and doing so is the daily bread of professionals in marketing, communications and public relations. This does not fit well with the supposed academic mission of the search for truth. Second, using reputation as a proxy for excellence gives an immediate advantage to the old, the rich and the beautiful. Third, chasing reputation as an end in itself is usually based on envy and practised through imitation. There is an easy test for envy and imitation: just look out for those universities which characterise themselves by comparison, for example as the Oxbridge of Africa, or the Princeton of Europe, or the Harvard of the East, or some such.

Those who construct the opinion polls which form part of the rankings which create a reality may well make the point that they are simply trying to consult academics about academic work, in the spirit of peer review. And this point bears examination. Papers get published, or not published, on the basis of referee reports. Grants are awarded, or not awarded, on the basis of peer evaluation. Even the various national research assessment exercises would have a substantial component of peer review. So why not universities? But the comparison does not stand up to scrutiny, because the rankers ask a different question. Peer review of a paper, or a grant application, asks for a judgement on the substance of that particular piece of work. By contrast, a reputation survey, such as that carried out by Thomson Reuters for the *Times Higher Education*, asks for a comparative judgement. It is, again, the difference between asking 'Is it good?' and 'Is it better than the others?'

Is it good at what it does?

Of our several variations of the question 'Is it good?', this is the first one that begins to acknowledge that universities may differ. It really asks two questions of a university: 'What does it do?' and 'Is it good at it?'

Like all manifestations of a Platonic idea, universities differ. They teach different subjects and work in different areas of research. A university may have a Medical School but not an Engineering School, or vice versa, or both, or neither. It may or may not have an Agriculture School, or a Business School, or a Law School. One university may specialise in cancer research, another in social science. Some universities strive for an international footprint, others build a campus culture at home. Universities also differ in how they view their role in society. A university may, for example, aim to play a strong role in the social, cultural and economic development of its own city or region, or it may deliberately choose to project an image of being place-neutral.

Typically, a university would set out its stall through its vision statement, mission statement and strategic objectives. A vision statement says where you want to get to, in other words what kind of university you want to be, while a mission statement says what you are going to do to get there. Mostly, therefore, a university can give a reasonable articulation of what kind of an institution it wants to be, and a realistic report of what it is actually doing to realise that aim. The approach to quality that emanates from the question 'Is it good at what it does?' is premised on the idea that a university should have a clear sense of its purpose as an institution, and that a judgement of quality should involve an evaluation of the extent to which it succeeds in carrying out that purpose.

Quality assurance professionals refer to this approach to quality as 'fitness for purpose'. It allows for diversity among universities and relates quality to purpose. If this approach were to be universally adopted it would undercut the relentless linearity of rankings, by evaluating universities according to the extent to which they realise their institutional goals.

Is it good for society?

One drawback of the 'fitness for purpose' approach, however, is that it makes no judgement of the actual purpose itself. A university could, for example, set itself the purpose of delivering as many graduates as possible without worrying too much about exit standards – and might be very successful at delivering on this purpose (at least for a while). Would that make it a good university? Probably not, for most people. 'Fitness for purpose', therefore, needs a counterbalance, and quality assurance professionals found it in the concept of 'fitness *of* purpose'. Which is, essentially, a value judgement of the university's stated purpose.

This approach to quality is one that asks about the societal role of the university. On the standard model it is assumed that all universities, through their research and education, do in the fullness of time deliver societal value, through the hidden workings of the invisible hand. The 'fitness of purpose' approach to quality asks for something more than that. It asks for a formulation, not only of what all universities are assumed to deliver – by default, as it were – but more specifically what role this particular university sees itself as playing in society. Beyond that it is not meant to be prescriptive. 'Society' could, but need not be, the city or region within which the university is located. It could, but need not be, a particular community or group or section of society – for example a faith group, or a language group, or a cultural group. It could, but need not, refer to one or more of the global societal challenges. A university may, for example, devote itself to combating climate change, or tropical disease, or inner-city decline. Or it may take up a positive cause, promoting the open society, multilingualism or healthy ageing.

The world of rankings and league tables, and the idea of quality-as-excellence, and the idea of fitness for purpose, requires a university to say what it is good *at*. By contrast, the 'fitness *of* purpose' approach to quality raises the different question of what the university is good *for*. It is essentially a requirement on the university not only to formulate its purpose, but to put that purpose up for public scrutiny.[11] I will return to the good-at/good-for distinction in Chapter Eight.

Like all the others, the 'fitness of purpose' approach has a downside. Who evaluates the fitness of a university's purpose? And against what norms? The risk here is of creating a vacuum into which journalists, politicians and ministers of state would be keen to enter. Already it is the case that, in many countries, the government would decree some priority areas for research and development – usually based on an evaluation of what is required for economic development, or social change. And usually such policy priorities are backed up by levers of funding, through carrots and sticks. The danger is that this kind of government-led formulation of purpose may infringe on the universities' institutional autonomy, and that articulating the university's sense of purpose may become a matter of compliance rather than conviction.

It needs a mature relationship between government and higher education for 'fitness of purpose' to remain a check on societal value, and not to degenerate into sailing with the political wind. Infamously, the philosopher Martin Heidegger, who became Rector of Freiburg University shortly after Hitler became Chancellor of Germany, endorsed the *Führerprinzip*, and told his students:

> Let not propositions and 'ideas' be the rules of your being (*Sein*). The Führer alone *is* the present and future German reality and its law. Learn to know ever more deeply: that from now on every single thing demands decision, and every action responsibility. Heil Hitler![12]

Even when the sense of purpose emanates from the university itself, the question of purpose needs to pass the test of whether it benefits society as a whole, or is only narrowly focused on a particular section of society, perhaps to the detriment of others. In South Africa, Stellenbosch University had for most of the 20th century a very clear sense of purpose, which was the cause of Afrikaner nationalism. It pursued that purpose through the medium of apartheid, which has had a big impact on society – but not a beneficial one. I will return to this topic in Chapter Four.

Does it deliver a good return on investment?

This is a different approach altogether, focusing on the student as an investor in education, or even the purchaser of a degree. The question put into the mouth of the prospective student, Jenny or Jimmy Public, is this: 'If I come to study at this university, what will be the return on my investment of time and money in terms of career benefits?' This approach to quality is well suited to the school of thought which regards a university as a business, and students as its customers.

There are league tables for return on educational investment. A common one is about employability – the track record of how many graduates actually get a job within a certain time after graduating, and what kind of jobs they get.[13] On a bigger scale, various data sets are available about the 'graduate premium' – the extent to which career earnings of graduates are better than those of non-graduates. These can be specialised to differentiate between groups of universities, or even universities themselves. Prospective students, like any other prospective investor, can then weigh up what they can afford to invest against the likely returns over a suitable period of time, and this evaluation would constitute their judgement of quality.

'Return on investment' is not only about financial return. More generally, it is about the value of your degree in terms of social status and lifetime networks. It is more of a career advantage to be able say 'I have a degree from Cambridge' than just to say 'I have a degree', because Cambridge has worldwide brand value. It provides a label which people are keen to wear. With that, the idea of quality-as-value begins to fade back into the idea of quality-as-reputation, and the value of a degree becomes a matter of brand value at least as much a matter of what the student has learned.

Of course, the assumption would be that brand value is premised, among other things, on good-quality graduates. And that is perhaps the best that can be said for this approach: that brand value (or reputation) should be no more than a proxy for quality. Otherwise it would all be marvellously circular: a good brand is part of good quality, which is part of good value, which is part of a good brand.

Another way of thinking about the idea of quality-as-value (less often invoked) is to focus not so much on the value of the product as on the amount of value *added* to the product. To say that a good-quality university is one that produces good graduates is to neglect to ask how far those graduates have travelled intellectually since being freshmen. It is no great feat to take straight-A school leavers and turn them into straight-A graduates. It is therefore by no means clear that a university with an excellent intake should get credit for delivering an excellent output.

Yet this is exactly what is rewarded by many league tables. 'Quality of intake' is one of the parameters often used in the rankings game. This parameter suddenly came to the fore in 2012, when the UK government deregulated the recruitment of students at the top end of achievement (AAB or better), and it was suddenly a very pertinent matter what percentage of a university's intake were above the AAB threshold. When this is matched with another common rankings parameter, namely 'number of firsts and upper-seconds' (that is, top-end graduating scores), it is not surprising that there is a strong correlation. The surprise is rather the extent to which the fairly unremarkable process of turning high-achieving entrants into high-achieving graduates is esteemed and rewarded above the demanding task of raising performance from low to high.

Many universities, through conviction or circumstance, accept students with less than brilliant results, and many prospective students have less than brilliant results through no lack of ability or application, but through circumstances beyond their control. There is a difference between attainment and potential. Many who have a record of high attainment have had the benefit of every advantage in reaching that level. Many who don't have a high level of attainment have none the less accomplished what they did against every disadvantage, and may well have the potential to accomplish more under more favourable circumstances. The difficulty is that while attainment is easy to measure, being based on past performance, potential is impossible to measure, being based on future performance. And so we tend to go with what we can measure, because we see it as objective, rather than trust our judgement, because we fear subjectivity.

But let us return to the idea of quality, not just as good value, but as the ability to add value. As discussed earlier, standards are often used as a proxy for quality, and in particular entry standards have become one of the accepted measures of university league tables. These have rather overshadowed the question of exit standards, even though the latter can be measured at least as well as the former. Together, however, they have totally overshadowed the idea of added value. But if education is not about adding value, then what is it about?

On either approach – quality as good value, or quality as added value – we also have to ask: value for whom? There are two classic responses to this question: value to the individual, and value to society. If we focus on adding value to the individual, then we are talking about higher education essentially as a private benefit. With that, the value proposition is phrased in terms of a market economy, and the discourse is about customers and providers, competition and market forces, return on investment and lifetime premium. Many of these concepts are nicely measurable, and therefore easy to concentrate on.

If, on the other hand, we wish to talk about adding value to society, then we are talking about education as a public good. In this domain of discourse there are fewer measurables. It is not an evidence-free zone, and it is possible even here to invoke the idea of quality as value for money – correlations can be made, for example, between the general level of educational attainment and economic growth – but by and large the idea of education as a public good rests more on an intangible sense of the wellbeing of civil society. A well-educated citizenry, one would hope, can and should add value to the health, wealth and wellbeing of society – if we put our mind to making sure that it does.

I will return to these matters in Chapter Five. For the moment it will suffice to note that the question is one of private benefit vis-à-vis public good. This is not an abstract matter: it is directly related to the question of how universities are funded. In a system where the greater part of higher education is paid for by the taxpayer through some kind of state-funded subsidy to universities, society is fully entitled to demand a return on its investment in terms of the public good. In a different system based on a user-pays principle, the individual who bears the greater part of the expense of their own education may well want to maximise personal benefit, and be less inclined to see their education as a debt to society. When quality is seen as value, it is highly relevant to ask who the beneficiary of that value would be.

Is it accredited by professional bodies?

Many universities have a substantial offering of professional degrees. These are degrees leading to employment which require the imprimatur of some external professional body. Medical doctors in the UK, for example, need accreditation with the General Medical Council in order to practise. Similarly, accountants, architects, engineers, lawyers, psychologists, speech therapists and many others need the accreditation of their own professional organisation.

The professional bodies do not just put a stamp of approval on graduates. Usually, they accredit teaching programmes at particular universities. For this purpose they are often closely involved in the design and specification of curricula, and would carry out their own version of quality assurance through periodic visits, very much with the standards of the profession in mind. A university with a reasonable spread of professional degrees easily may have to satisfy the requirements of a few dozen of these professional bodies.

A minimal check on quality, then, at least in these professional subjects, is to make sure that they are suitably accredited. Beyond that, there are also networks of academic bodies which do some accreditation. Business schools, for example, have no less than three accreditations to chase: AMBA is the Association of MBAs, EQUIS is the European Quality Improvement System, run by the European Foundation for Management Development, and AACSB is the Association to Advance Collegiate Schools of Business. Each of these runs an extensive accreditation system, and triple accreditation is a sought-after and prestigious accolade.

Is it efficient and is it effective?

Any discussion of quality, in any domain of discourse, will of necessity involve the notions of efficiency and effectiveness. These are fundamental because they embody the distinction between process and product. Efficiency involves a judgement of how well a process works in delivering a product; effectiveness involves a judgement on whether satisfactory products have been delivered. In so far as education may be regarded as a process, low dropout rates and timely completion would be measures of efficiency, while a high proportion of first-class degrees and a good record of graduate employment would be measures of effectiveness.

As every academic knows, universities are often regarded as inefficient, particularly by business people and new government ministers. A university would typically only teach for about half the weeks in the year, a student may only receive 10–15 hours of formal instruction per week, and many universities may not even take the first year's work into account for computing the graduation result. Fairly regularly, then, some familiar ideas are recycled aimed at addressing these perceived inefficiencies: a third semester per year, guaranteed minimum lecture hours, modular courses and cumulative credits, two-year degrees and so on. None of these is without merit, and in some cases and places some of them have been made to work. It is fair to say, however, that in the regular campus-based university, where the bulk of the intake consists of school leavers, the perceived inefficiencies have been proved to be quite durable, despite accusations of complacency and recurrent warnings that new technologies will soon make old paradigms obsolete.

From the early days of the standard model era, almost every technological innovation in education has been greeted with confident announcements of the imminent demise of current teaching practice, and indeed the working of the university itself. Following the first mainframe computers in the late 1960s and early 1970s, conventional wisdom was that in future every educated person would have be able to program a computer. Children would therefore all have to learn Fortran or Algol. In fact, the opposite happened. People did not adapt to computers, computers adapted to people. And so now we all use very clever computing devices every day, without actually programming them, while leaving enough scope for those who like to do so. Similar evolutionary development took place with the arrival of electronic calculators, personal computers, the internet, the worldwide web, e-learning, mobile phones, apps, social media and MOOCs (massive open online courses). But somehow the end of teaching has never quite happened.

Experience shows that there is something quite durable about the way the university operates, which has allowed it to absorb and adapt to technological change without burying its head either in the sand or in the clouds. Rather the contrary: institutions which fundamentally changed their operational model to accommodate new technology have not always fared well, nor did new institutions which were created to serve it. UK academics may well remember, for example, the e-University which never actually happened.

Perhaps there is another way of looking at the matter. Perhaps the durability of the perceived inefficiencies and apparent slow pace of change at the university has something to do with educational effectiveness.

The fact is that more efficiency may mean less effectiveness, and vice versa. Thus, for example, teaching students in large lecture groups tightly timetabled is quite efficient in terms of resources, but from the perspective of individual learning not very effective. Small-group project work is an effective learning technique, but has inherent process inefficiencies, since the delivery of the project depends on the contribution of the slowest member of the group. From the point of view of pedagogical effectiveness it may seem an advantage to keep staff–student ratios low, but from the point of view of teaching efficiency the opposite argument may be made. It may be inefficient to teach only half the year, but it does effectively provide students with time to learn, and academics with time to do research.

Quality should be related to both efficiency and effectiveness, because neither guarantees the other. Education seems to be a case where you could not only be efficient without being effective, you can also be effective without being terribly efficient.

Education is not only a matter of process, it is also a matter of outcome. But the desired outcome is best seen not as a finished product – the graduate – but as having elicited a certain kind of autonomous behaviour. Teaching is not an end in itself, but a means to an end, which is learning. Or rather, the love of learning, which guarantees that learning will carry on beyond teaching. And the love of learning is the same driving force which we called curiosity when talking about research.

Learning is not something a teacher can give to a student, it is something students have to do for themselves. Perhaps this is the point which the UUK *Guide to How the System Works* is trying to get to when it says that quality is regarded as 'the effectiveness of the learning experience'. Teaching is effective in so far as it results in learning. And learning is effective if it results in a certain knowledge base, a certain set of intellectual skills, an ongoing desire to maintain and improve knowledge and skills, and an aptitude for using knowledge and skills both for private benefit and for the public good. These are outcomes, and so we have something against which we can consider effectiveness – as long as we accept that these outcomes are largely intangible.

More like a shape than a number

> It follows that we cannot in demonstrating pass from one genus to another. We cannot, for instance, prove geometrical truths by arithmetic.
> *Aristotle, Posterior Analytics, 75a38*

Rankers reduce quality to a number. This forces one-dimensionality upon diversity, and conformity to a standard model of what universities are supposed to be like. It thus creates a reality more than it reflects a reality.

Perhaps quality is more like a shape than a number. A shape gives a different kind of representation of reality from that of a number. Shapes are not, by their nature, linearly ordered. They *can* be ordered, and in various ways, if we really want to, but the exercise would always seem a bit forced.

So what would quality look like if we thought of it as a shape? We have already seen some examples. The idea of a 'quality profile' is not a new or radical invention. The RAE was always intended to deliver a research quality profile for each university, and that is still true of its later incarnation, the REF. To recall, there is a qualitative classification of research, as follows:

- Four star = Quality that is world-leading in terms of originality, significance and rigour.
- Three star = Quality that is internationally excellent in terms of originality, significance and rigour but which falls short of the highest standards of excellence.
- Two star = Quality that is recognised internationally in terms of originality, significance and rigour.
- One star = Quality that is recognised nationally in terms of originality, significance and rigour.
- Unclassified (zero stars) = Quality that falls below the standard of nationally recognised work. Or work which does not meet the published definition of research for the purposes of this assessment.[14]

An REF quality profile, then, is a histogram that shows what proportion of a university's research (perhaps in some specified area) is classified as four star, or three star and so on. Here is an example adapted from Chapter Two. Imagine that the REF profiles for the universities of Someburgh, Otherville, Thistown and Elseport are as shown in Figure 3.1.

Each profile gives a representation of the quality of research at that particular university, not as a single number, but as a distribution of numbers represented as a shape. Because these are shapes, we can differentiate between them and compare them to each other. In fact, we can draw conclusions – for example that Thistown has a lot of really good and also a lot of really poor research, with very little in the middle, which is the opposite of the situation at Someburgh. Because we can draw reasonable conclusions there is no incentive, other than vanity, to rank these profiles as the best, second best and so on. As the thought experiment of Chapter Two demonstrated, if you do wish to order such shapes you can pretty much achieve any result you want, but none of them would have any greater legitimacy than any of the others. There is no such thing as a 'correct' ordering of these four research profiles.

Figure 3.1: Imagined REF quality profiles for the Universities of Someburgh, Otherville, Thistown and Elseport

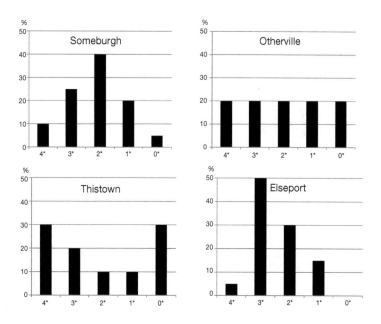

Another common representation of quality as a shape is so-called spider diagrams. Suppose, for example, you are interested in the publication record of universities. Specifically, because you know that mathematicians publish less than physicists, who publish less than biologists, who publish less than clinicians, and other such differentiations, you are interested in the average number of published papers per academic, per subject, per university. To structure this information, you define (say) six subject groups: Arts and Humanities, Social Sciences, Physical Sciences, Life Sciences, Engineering and Technology, and Clinical and Health Sciences. The typical ranking methodology would then give you six lists – the university rankings for each subject group. If you try to make a comparison between universities across all subject groups, the ranking methodology would just find some arithmetical formula for compounding the six lists into one – for example by computing the average publication output per university.

Instead, spider diagrams give a visual representation of what each university's output looks like across all six subject groups. For example, Figure 3.2 shows four universities from the data set used by Thomson Reuters for the 2013 *Times Higher* world ranking of universities.[15]

Figure 3.2: Examples of spider diagram representations of universities' research publication outputs

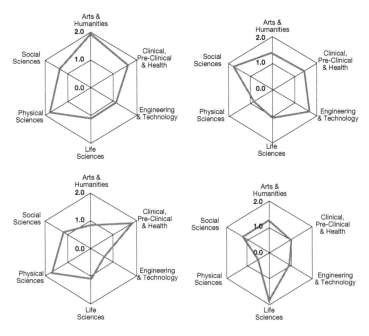

Such pictures give you a much better comparison between universities than six lists of numbers. You can immediately see how each university is positioned in terms of its subject concentration, and how these concentrations compare with each other. More importantly, the pictures also show that any ranking of the four universities in terms of average overall number of publications loses you a lot of information, and is therefore seriously misleading – just like any other attempt to rank shapes.

A real-life serious attempt at presenting quality as a shape rather than a number is the European Union-backed project U-Multirank,[16] already mentioned in Chapter Two. This is a large-scale exercise in visual representation of both the nature and the quality of a university. There are five categories of activity: research, teaching, knowledge transfer, international orientation and regional engagement. For each of these categories there are a number of parameters of measurement. Thus, for example, research is broken down into nine parameters,[17] such as research income, number of PhD graduates, number of research publications per academic FTE, and so on. Typically, the parameters of measurement are based on hard data, and so each single parameter generates a legitimate ranking.

The main differentiator between U-Multirank and standard rankings produced by the *Times Higher* or QS or Shanghai Jiao Tong, however, is that U-Multirank makes no attempt to aggregate its different single-parameter rankings into a single multiple-parameter ranking. On the contrary, the great virtue claimed for U-Multirank is exactly that it allows comparison without falling into the trap of aggregation.

> One principle of U-Multirank is the comparability of institutions. In rankings, institutions and programmes should only be compared when their purposes and activity profiles are sufficiently similar. Comparing institutions and programmes that have very different purposes is worthless. It makes no sense to compare the research performance of a major metropolitan research university with that of a remotely located University of Applied Science, or the internationalisation achievements of a national humanities college whose

major purpose is to develop and preserve its unique national language with an internationally orientated European university with branch campuses in Asia. This principle also derives from the need to make the diversity of higher education institutions' 'performance profiles' transparent. In our view the principle implies a two-step process: first, institutions with similar profiles have to be identified by 'mapping' their activities; a ranking of 'like with like' can only be applied afterwards.[18]

The notion of a 'performance profile' is congruent with what we have here called a quality profile. So what would a performance profile look like? U-Multirank uses a visual representation called a 'sunburst chart', an example of which is shown in Figure 3.3.

Each of the five categories of activity is codified by a shade of grey (see key). In the e-versions of this book, the coding is in colour, but the printed version has no colour, hence the adaptation. If you know the colour coding you immediately know what category of activity you are looking at. Within each category, each ray represents a single parameter, and the length of the ray represents the university's performance ranking on that single parameter. Across the five categories there are 44 parameters in all, which,

Figure 3.3: Example of a university performance profile as a 'sunburst chart'

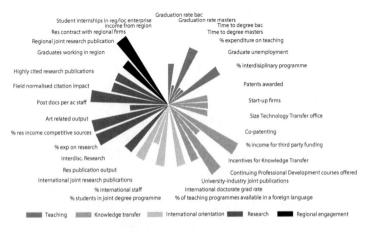

for any university to which all parameters apply, would make for a comprehensive picture, although quite a busy one.

The development of U-Multirank is an interesting illustration of the perils of trying to do something a little more subtle than reduce quality to a number. Its reception by the academic community is a sad but instructive story.

U-Multirank arose from an academic research project, commissioned by the Directorate General for Education and Culture of the European Commission. The project, including a three-year feasibility study with a sample of 150 institutions, was developed by researchers at the Centre for Higher Education Policy Studies (CHEPS)[19] at Twente University in the Netherlands and at the Centre for Higher Education (CHE)[20] in Germany. The final report[21] was published in June 2011 and led to a formal launch[22] of the U-Multirank implementation project at the end of January 2013.

Given its provenance as a legitimate piece of social science research you might think that U-Multirank would easily have gained respectability, or at least legitimacy, in the higher education sector. In fact, the opposite happened. U-Multirank was widely and variously condemned as (a) a waste of money, or (b) a conspiracy, or (c) the thin end of an undesirable wedge, or (d) unreliable.

I have already mentioned (early in Chapter Two) what happened after the publication of the final report. The *Times Higher Education* ran an article titled 'U-Multirank may be a waste of taxpayers' money',[23] authored by the person in charge of the *Times Higher* rankings. That article in turn reported the then-minister for universities and science as saying that U-Multirank could be viewed as 'an attempt by the EU Commission to fix a set of rankings in which [European universities] do better than they appear to do in the conventional rankings'.

Subsequently, at about the time of the launch of the U-Multirank implementation, the League of European Research Universities (LERU)[24] announced its decision to boycott U-Multirank, on the grounds that it was 'at best an unjustifiable use of taxpayers' money and at worst a serious threat to a healthy higher education system' – or at least so LERU's secretary general was quoted in the *Times Higher Education* as saying.[25] LERU consists of 21 research-intensive universities, including 5 Russell Group heavyweights. At that time,

17 members of LERU were in the *Times Higher* top 200 ranking, and all 5 UK members in the top 40.

Shortly afterwards, in May 2013, the UK International Unit,[26] one of the bodies funded by UUK and the HEFCE, issued a policy note titled 'Update on U-Multirank'. Under a heading 'What is the UK's position?', it mentions the following concerns:

- Public funding lends legitimacy to U-Multirank and performance as judged by the tool could become the basis for future funding decisions
- The league table market place is already crowded, with each ranking deploying its own methodologies
- The tool partially relies on self-reported data which lacks verifiability
- The tool risks being incapable of responding to rapidly changing circumstances in institutional profiles
- The multi-dimensional aspect of the tool means that incommensurate variables will be combined to create a league table, undermining efforts to go beyond rankings
- U-Multirank risks becoming a blunt instrument that would not allow different strengths across an institution to be recognised
- EU funds could be better spent on other EU priorities[27]

On the basis of these concerns, the UK International Unit concludes that 'U-Multirank may harm rather than benefit the sector'.

This is ironic in a number of ways. First, no other ranking had been deemed worthy of a policy note from the UK International Unit. So, the only serious academic attempt to develop a counterweight to 'conventional' rankings finds itself on the receiving end of academic censure, while those same 'conventional' rankings, including the ones concocted by newspapers and marketeers, pass without comment. Second, U-Multirank is attacked for combining incommensurate variables when that is a defining feature of virtually all 'conventional' rankings. Third, U-Multirank is suspected of being the thin end of a wedge, namely of rankings being used for funding purposes, when (a) both the REF and the Teaching Excellence Framework (TEF) are designed for that very purpose, and (b) many government agencies already use the *Times Higher* rankings to decide on funding allocations (such as student scholarships).

Fourth, U-Multirank is accused of partially relying on self-reported data which 'lack verifiability', while 50% of the QS ranking and 33% of the *Times Higher* ranking depend on unverifiable opinion polls. It is, above all, deeply ironic that a new and well-researched methodology was dismissed because 'the league table market place is already crowded', when the products in that market place are so poor. As noted before, a better response might be the exact opposite: to encourage a proliferation of league tables and rankings, precisely because they will all contradict each other.

There are various ways of interpreting the antipathy to U-Multirank. One such interpretation comes from a member of the International Expert Panel associated with the CHEPS/CHE final report, who wrote on their blog:

> U-Multirank is a creation of the European Union. Stung by the THE [*Times Higher Education*] and Shanghai rankings, which showed continental European (especially French) universities lagging badly, France took advantage of their EU Presidency in 2009 to announce that the EU would create a new rankings system, which, in the words of the French Minister of Higher Education, would create a new and fairer global ranking, one that would prove that French universities were the best. (Yes, seriously.)
>
> The people to whom this project was entrusted are among the smartest people in all of higher education: namely, the folks at the Centre for Higher Education (CHE) in Germany, and the Center for Higher Education Policy Studies (CHEPS) in the Netherlands. The system they have created is how rankings would look if universities had created rankings themselves, rather than left it to newspapers and magazines. It includes indicators on teaching and learning, research, knowledge transfer, international orientation, and regional engagement, and it portrays the data on each of these separately – no summing across indicators to come up with a single league table with a single 'winner'. ...
>
> It turns out, though, that not everyone likes the idea of rankings without winners. In one of the most cynical

pieces of university politics I've ever seen, the group known as the 'Leading European Research Universities' (LERU) announced[28] a couple of months ago that it would not participate – ostensibly this is because the rankings system is, 'ill-conceived and badly designed', but really it's because they don't like rankings in which they don't come out on top.

As you can tell, I'm a fan of the U-Multirank concept; but I'm cautious about its overall prospects for success. I think its ability to add non-European institutions will be limited because many of its indicators are euro-centric and will require non-european institutions to incur some cost in data collection. And I have my doubts about demand: after many years in this business, I'm increasingly convinced that, given the choice, consumers prefer the simplicity of league tables to the more accurate – but conceptually taxing – multi-dimensional rankings.[29]

So, universities prefer to squabble among themselves and jostle for position on a ranking rather than celebrate the diversity of the sector. It seems that, collectively, we prefer an illusion of certainty to the complexities of truth.

Reality check

> The Teaching Excellence Framework (TEF) is a new scheme for recognising excellent teaching, in addition to existing national quality requirements for universities, colleges and other higher education providers.
> *HEFCE, August 2017*[30]

If the idea of quality seems to be impossibly broad, should we try to narrow it down? For example, instead of looking at educational quality, why not just look at teaching? The Conservative Party in the UK, in its election manifesto of 2015, did exactly that, pledging to 'introduce a framework to recognize universities offering the highest teaching quality'.[31] After they unexpectedly won a majority, the promise became law in the Higher Education and Research Act of 2017.

The TEF started with four goals:

a. Better informing students' choices about what and where to study
b. Raising esteem for teaching
c. Recognising and rewarding excellent teaching
d. Better meeting the needs of employers, business, industry and the professions[32]

How does it work? There are six core metrics, all relying on available public data. The first three are about what students think of their teaching in terms of quality, assessment and feedback, and academic support, with data coming from the annual NSS. The fourth metric is about the proportion of dropouts, the data for which comes from the HESA. The last two metrics are about students' destination in terms of employment or further study, or *highly skilled* employment or further study (a distinction is made), with data coming from another survey, called the Destination of Leavers of Higher Education. The idea is that the first two of the six metrics report on teaching quality, the middle two on learning environment, and the last two on learning gain.

The TEF assessment structure is not under-engineered. The Powerpoint briefing given to universities and other 'HE [higher education] providers' by the TEF implementation team in 2016 consisted of 77 slides crammed with detail.[33] These briefing slides were prefaced with the comment that they do not provide definitive guidance, for which the 'provider' should turn to an Additional Guidance document (67 pages, annexes excluded).[34] The Additional Guidance in turn supplements an earlier Specification document (79 pages).[35] All of which was only about Year Two of the implementation process, 2016–17, which was the first full run of the TEF. More followed later, such as supplementary metrics, developing the TEF at subject level, and renaming it the Teaching Excellence and Student Outcomes Framework.

The metrics are the core of the assessment process, but they are considered in the light of contextual data (which, according to the briefing, 'will help the assessors understand the size, nature and context of the provider; but do not directly inform the ratings'.) The metrics for each 'provider' are then benchmarked, 'to allow fair comparison between providers by taking account of factors which may affect the metrics that are outside of providers' control'. Assessment is focused on whether the performance of a 'provider' is above or below benchmark for each metric. If it is *significantly* above or below benchmark (z-scores again) that metric gets flagged. All of which, with many other dotted i's and crossed t's, plus checks and balances, eventually, at the discretion of an overarching TEF panel, leads to a rating: gold, silver or bronze. For example, if your university gets a sufficient number of positive flags and no negative ones then you may provisionally put the champagne in the fridge in expectation of a gold award.

As with the REF, the outcome of the TEF is not supposed to be a ranking, but of course it can immediately be transmuted into one. Every 'provider' with a gold award clearly outranks everyone with a silver award, and likewise silver outranks bronze. Within each category, next, there is more than enough data available to perform some arithmetical magic and spells. Thus, for example, the *Times Higher Education* ranked the May 2017 outcome of the TEF as follows.

> *Times Higher Education* [*THE*] has run the numbers on these metrics and below is a (sortable) table of institutions ranked first by final TEF award but then by performance in the metrics.... *THE* counted the number of times an institution achieved a flag in each category (six being the maximum) and then sorted the final table according to TEF award, then flag performance and finally by average Z-score across the six metrics.[36]

The first ratings/rankings produced the usual PR flurry, with those who did well shouting about it and those who did poorly pointing out the limitations of the exercise. Thus, for example, the vice-chancellor of the University of Southampton (a Russell Group member which received a bronze rating) pointed out (accurately) that your rating does not just depend on how you performed in the metrics, but on your benchmarking. If your university had high benchmarks to begin with it would be almost impossible to outperform those benchmarks to the extent of accumulating sufficiently many positive flags for a gold rating.[37]

It would be hard to argue with the stated intentions of the TEF. Any effort towards parity of esteem between research and teaching, for example, should be welcomed. If we really wish our university to combine von Humboldt and Newman, then, whatever else we do (and I will argue that there is still another dimension to consider), we should begin by paying as much attention to the scholarship of teaching as we do to the scholarship of discovery. Recognising and rewarding excellent teaching is surely a good idea, and a necessary part of raising esteem. Also, 'more information' always plays well, and, while true, it seems a little defensive to say 'provided it adds value'.

There is no doubt that introducing the TEF was a brilliantly successful piece of politics. Partly this must be due to the vanilla flavour of the stated goals, partly because it is wonderful newspaper fodder, and partly because it fits so well into the increasing value-for-money ethos that followed in the wake of the post-2010 governments' push towards marketisation of higher education.

And yet, if you drill through the surface layer of the well-engineered technicalities there are some serious questions.

First, the TEF might not be the best way of achieving its stated aims. Take the matter of parity of esteem between research and teaching. You will not achieve parity of esteem in the public mind unless you first achieve it within the university. And you will not achieve it within the university unless and until academics can be promoted to full professor on the grounds of the scholarship of their teaching, just as they are commonly promoted on the grounds of research. So, instead of the intricacies of a TEF, it may be simpler and more productive to spend time on formulating and implementing fair and rigorous appointment and promotions criteria to reward scholarly teachers. And if you do want to use metrics, just count the number of such appointments and promotions per annum at each university. Most academic staff do both research and teaching, which is a good thing. But it remains common wisdom among academics (a consequence of the standard model university) that promotion comes primarily via research. Parity of esteem will require this particular piece of common wisdom to be refuted, and a TEF is unlikely to make much of a contribution towards doing so.

Second, it's a TEF, not a LEF. With the TEF we are talking about the teaching provided to students, not about any growth in their learning. The TEF is not a Learning Excellence Framework. The problem with this is that teaching is not an end in itself. Teaching is but a means towards an end, which is learning. So, with a TEF, we are evaluating the means, not the end. And terminology won't fix the problem. To say that the last two TEF metrics, regarding student destinations in the job market, represent 'learning gain' is over-complimentary, at best making sense if you believe that how much students learned is measured by what kind of job they do.

In fact, the TEF works with proxies: teaching as proxy for learning, student satisfaction as proxy for quality of education, employment destination as proxy for learning gain. In doing so, we are like the man who lost his car keys on a dark road, and goes looking for them under a streetlamp because that is where the light is. Can we do better? It is a fair question whether we can actually measure the effects of learning, rather than the input of teaching, but it is a credible position that doing so is possible, and worthwhile. For example, the director of education at the OECD, in the 2015 Annual Lecture of the Higher Education Policy Institute, makes a case for measuring student learning outcomes, both in a disciplinary and a transversal context, and warns:

> Without data on learning outcomes, judgements about the quality of teaching and learning at higher education institutions will continue to be made on the basis of flawed rankings, derived not from outcomes, nor even outputs – but from idiosyncratic inputs and reputation surveys....
>
> Let me conclude by stating that student learning outcomes should be in the critical path of assessing the outcomes of higher education. I really do not believe that we can find any shortcut to measuring the quality of higher education that bypasses students and student learning outcomes. We can find proxies and variables that correlate, but at the end of the day it is for learning gains that we go to university. Let me also affirm that

we can measure a sufficient range of learning outcomes in appropriate, valid and reliable ways to make such efforts worthwhile.[38]

Third, the TEF adds, but does not subtract. For example, in making the case for 'more information' for students and employers, the government of 2016 seems to have forgotten that, as lead partner in the government of 2010, it brought in an elaborate mandatory structure called the Key Information Set (KIS), to do exactly that. And the KIS was still there when the TEF came in. More broadly, the TEF comes 'in addition to existing national quality requirements'. So how do the two systems relate to each other? How, if at all, does 'teaching excellence' fit with the definition of quality we encountered earlier in the UUK *Guide to How the System Works*, as 'the effectiveness of the learning experience'? The HEFCE, under whose jurisdiction both these exercises fall, put a brave face on it:

> Quality assessment and the TEF form a coherent system but play distinctive roles. Quality assessment provides a foundation that ensures providers offer a high-quality student academic experience, deliver good student outcomes, and protect the interests of their students. It also delivers assurances about the integrity of degree standards to ensure that the value and reputation of UK degrees is safeguarded.
>
> The TEF will incentivise excellent teaching and provide better information for students to support them in making informed choices. Quality assessment and the TEF will therefore work together to promote, support and reward continuous improvement and better student outcomes.[39]

Universities, and other 'HE providers' subject to the quality assurance regime, may well beg to differ about the 'coherent system' claim. However, even if you accept the argument of complementarity, the fact remains that the assessment of educational quality now consists of two separate exercises. In bolting TEF and quality assurance together the whole seems less than the sum of the parts.

Finally, we cannot leave the TEF without taking account of the fact that, from the outset, it was linked to the contentious issue of student fees. The idea was that a university which does well enough in its TEF rating would thereby earn the right to raise their student fees.

That opens up a Pandora's box of debatable presuppositions. The argument for linking student fees to teaching excellence is premised on the idea of the student as a consumer of educational provision (which is why universities came to be called 'HE providers'). This premise is based on the presupposition that higher education is, or should be treated as, a market economy, which in turn is based on the conception that a university education is essentially a private benefit. The student will benefit, so the student should bear the cost, but should also have consumer rights, such as relating price to quality.

Such has been the post-financial-crash government view. It is almost exactly opposite to the view that prevailed for most of the standard model era, which was that students pay practically nothing. Instead, the government – that is, the taxpayer – will foot the bill. Such a policy is based on an entirely different conception, namely that higher education is essentially a public good. Everybody should help to pay for the university system because ultimately everybody will benefit from it, just as every taxpayer should contribute to, say, the roads network, even though perhaps they do not drive.

So which is it? Should we see higher education as a private benefit, or a public good? Many of us find it hard to see why this should be an either-or question. Surely the answer can be both. Which, in terms of funding, should mean that both the student and the taxpayer should pay for higher education. And fifty-fifty would seem like a reasonable starting point.

But that is not how things turned out. Instead, the pendulum swung from one extreme to the other. First students paid practically nothing, now they pay a lot. Why is that? One reason might be that, during the standard model period, the public lost faith in the public-good argument. Universities seemed disengaged from societal challenges, mere issuing offices for a passport to affluence. There was no noticeable educational trickle-down benefit. The gap between the haves and the have-nots was widening, and the haves all seemed to have degrees which they got with taxpayers' money.

Such disenchantment opened the door to the opposite view, and the global financial crash of 2007–8 provided a useful crisis under cover of which it could be implemented. But these are shifting sands. Following the 2017 election there were soon signs that the debate on student fees is by no means over. The question of higher education as a private benefit and/or a public good might well get a thorough airing, which would be welcome. With that, many of the presuppositions underpinning the TEF should come under scrutiny. And the same, more generally, for some of the inherent contradictions in what government policy says is a market economy but government practice treats as a public service. For example, it is a funny kind of market in which the price of every product is the same.[40] The undergraduate fee is fixed no matter what subject you study at which university. Yet the real cost of a course in sociology is a fraction of the real cost of a course in medicine, and in a free market the fee-charging ability of universities would vary greatly. Students therefore end their studies with much the same level of debt, but with quite different levels of value for money.

The overall point to note is that issues of quality in higher education are related to our conception of the role of higher education in society, which cannot be disengaged from issues of equality, fairness and social justice. I will follow up on this point from the next chapter onward.

A TEF of some kind is likely to become a permanent feature of the higher education landscape, even if for no better reason than being good politics on both sides of the political spectrum. If it leads towards increased multidimensionality in rankings, on top of adding a competing ranking, it might even have a beneficial side-effect. What it will not do, however, is reduce or streamline the regulatory environment for universities. It will be another good intention which has morphed into a compliance requirement.

The burden of good intentions

The road to hell is paved with good intentions.
English proverb

Good governance, accountability and transparency – these are good intentions, of which there are many in higher education. Too many, perhaps.

The pursuit of good intentions often seems to lead to a regime of regulation, monitoring and compliance. In principle that need not be a problem. In practice, universities find that their regulatory superstructure expands both in breadth and in depth, but not in a coordinated or coherent manner. Nothing gets subtracted, and little gets connected.

Here are some examples of regulation and compliance in higher education (limited to ten, so as not to stretch the reader's patience too far, but the list can easily be extended).

Example 1. Accepting the necessity – indeed, the value – of a regulatory regime, it would seem like a good idea if there were one central coordinating body for whatever regulations arise from whatever good intentions. In principle, this role has been played since 1992 by the HEFCE. (Similar bodies exist in Scotland, Wales and Northern Ireland.) As the name implies, the basic function of the HEFCE has been to disburse funding, and hence to demand accountability for funding. The core relationship between the HEFCE and universities, therefore, has long been through a detailed document called the Financial Memorandum.[41] Once a year each vice-chancellor, in their legal capacity as Accountable Officer, has to sign and take personal responsibility for an affidavit saying that the university has complied with all aspects of the Financial Memorandum. Since the entire operation of the university is summarised by that single signature, a lot of work goes into substantiating it. It would be worth the effort, if that were all. But there are two problems.

First, signing off for the HEFCE isn't quite the end of the story. The HEFCE has only been the 'lead regulator' – ominously but accurately pointing towards other regulators as well. Second, as already noted, with the advent of the user-pays principle of student fees and the idea of higher education as a market, the rug was pulled out from under the HEFCE as a funding body. It is due to be replaced in 2018 by a new body called the Office for Students (which will also take over responsibility for the TEF). It remains to be seen how that will turn out in terms of regulation and compliance, but the first signs are not encouraging. By the end of 2017 the documentation emanating from the Department for Education on the proposed regulatory framework for higher education ran to 544 pages across nine documents and five consultations. All of which only explains what the OfS (the inevitable acronym) intends to do, rather than how they will do it. Try this, for example:

> The OfS will be self-aware and, drawing from behavioural science, protect itself against the risk of internal biases and the resulting provider capture that can ensue.[42]

Example 2. With the marketisation of higher education, universities are to be regarded as 'HE providers' and students as customers. That brings into play another regulator, the Competition and Markets Authority (CMA). Just like any other business, universities are subject to the requirements of competition law, including the Competition Act 1998 and the Enterprise Act 2002, meaning that they must not engage in any conduct which has the object, or is likely to have the effect, of preventing, distorting or restricting competition. The CMA also take it as part of their remit to protect the consumer rights of students, and they are not shy about showing some muscle. In March 2015, for example, the CMA published 'guidance' for universities on their obligations under consumer protection law. In October 2015 it followed up with a review to assess compliance with the law and the effectiveness of their guidance. On 22 July 2016 the 'Senior Director, Consumer' of the CMA wrote to all vice-chancellors as follows:

> You may recall that in March 2015 the Competition and Markets Authority (CMA) wrote to Higher Education (HE) providers to highlight the publication of the CMA's advice to the HE undergraduate sector on consumer protection law. We asked HE providers

to read the advice and review, and, *where necessary, amend their practices to ensure they comply* with consumer protection law. We also made clear that we would follow up our advice with a compliance review, beginning in October 2015. More detail can be found on the case page. I am writing to draw your attention to the report that the CMA published today, summarising the review and *what we now expect of providers in light of it.* (My italics – CB)

Example 3. There are more than a quarter of a million international students in the UK, 'international' meaning from outside the UK and the EU. The Home Office has for some time been rather sensitive about immigration, but succeeded in scoring a massive own goal by counting international students within the official immigration figures. (This might well have had an influence on the Brexit vote.) Because of the political sensitivities there is a Home Office regulatory regime, enforced by a body called UK Visas and Immigration (UKVI), requiring any university to be able to prove, not only that each of its international students has the right academic credentials and can speak English, but that, at any snapshot moment when UKVI inspectors may choose to pay a campus visit, all these students are actively engaged in their studies. Should the university fail to have ready the required evidence to deliver on this burden of proof, it may lose its licence to recruit international students.

Example 4. Imagine a law which stipulates that a whim of mine may impose a burden on you, at no expense to myself. Such a law exists for universities in the shape of the Freedom of Information Act of 2000. It compels a university to comply with any request, from anybody, to supply any information about its affairs, in any stipulated format, at no expense to the asker, irrespective of the fact that compiling such a response takes somebody's time and therefore incurs a cost. Every university needs to employ some people whose job consists of responding to freedom of information requests.

There would seem to be an obvious solution, which is for the university proactively to make available all commonly sought-after information. Most do, but that does not actually solve the problem, because many people do not bother to look, finding it easier just to ask. Also, journalists like to present a story as the outcome of a freedom of information request rather than the prosaic result of looking something up on a website. In 2015, for example, the *Daily Mail* newspaper ran its annual exposé of vice-chancellors' salaries, 'based on thousands of freedom of information requests'.[43] That exact same information had been freely available in the universities' public accounts (and had at any rate already been reported in the *Times Higher Education* six months earlier).[44] If one freedom of information request takes, say, an hour's work to respond to, then the *Daily Mail's* 'thousands of freedom of information requests' will have generated thousands of hours of useless work – which did not cost the *Daily Mail* one penny.

Example 5. The Office of Fair Access (OFFA) is the independent regulator of fair access to higher education in England, acting on the principle that 'everyone with the potential and ambition to succeed in higher education should have equal opportunity to do so, whatever their income or background'. This laudable principle (on which more in later chapters) results in an obligation on universities to submit an annual document called an Access Agreement, accompanied by a Resource Plan, which sets out how they plan to improve/sustain access, success and progression for people from under-represented and disadvantaged groups.[45] (By law, the university must spend a certain proportion of student fee income on widening participation and fair access.) OFFA has the power to turn down a plan as insufficient, or to require amendments, and has the prerogative to force a university to lower its fees.[46]

Example 6. There is a person called the Independent Adjudicator, and a national body called the Office of the Independent Adjudicator, which provides a free external appeals service to students. On its website, it says: 'we are not a regulator'. None the less, no university can deny their request for full information on any student case, their findings are binding, and they can set levels of compensation.

Example 7. Every employer is subject to the Health and Safety at Work Act of 1974, overseen by a national body called the Health and Safety Executive. A medium-sized university may employ (say) 5,000 people, not all of whom sit at a desk all day, and some of whom may work in hazardous environments, like chemical engineering or anatomy. Somebody must therefore be responsible for health and safety at the institutional level, and likewise at faculty level and at departmental level. The university is likely to have a health and safety unit of some kind to coordinate all of this, to gather the obligatory statistics, work up an institutional health and safety policy, and provide an annual report. Health and safety will appear as a standing item on the agenda of every executive committee. Topics that fall under the health and safety regime include anything from slips, trips and falls to dealing with radioactive substances or human tissue (which has its own regulatory body, called the Human Tissue Authority).

Examples 8, 9 and 10. There are some regulatory bodies which have long worked through HEFCE, but none the less retain their own requirements.

- We have already encountered the QAA earlier in this chapter, and the fact that its periodic scrutiny of each university is a 'must not fail' exercise. Quality assurance compliance usually requires a permanently staffed organisational unit of quality assurance professionals, and a QAA audit would typically require 12 to 18 months of institutional preparation. The actual submission would be fronted by a comprehensive self-assessment document, backed up by around a thousand or so substantiating documents.
- Many universities in England are legally constituted as a charity. That requires compliance with the national regulatory framework of charities, which is overseen by the Charity Commission. As with the HEFCE's Financial Memorandum, once a year the vice-chancellor has to sign and take responsibility for having met all the obligations and exceeded none of the boundaries of charity law.
- In these days of radical fundamentalism national security is a big concern. The government has been worried that some young fundamentalists may have been radicalised while at university. It has therefore, in the Counter Terrorism and Security Act (2015) imposed an obligation on universities to 'have due regard to the need to prevent people from being drawn into terrorism'. This is enforced through something called the Prevent Duty, the Statutory Guidance Note for which[47] spells out what practical steps the duty entails: risk assessment, an action plan, staff training, relevant IT policies and so on. Understandably, there is a particular focus on visiting speakers, who may propound

fundamentalist ideas. At the same time, however, universities are equally obliged not to lose sight of their obligations on protecting free speech. According to Section 43(1) of the Education (No. 2) Act of 1986, universities must 'take such steps as are reasonably practicable to ensure that freedom of speech within the law is secured for members, students and employees of the establishment and for visiting speakers'.[48]

The first burden of good intentions, then, is their piecemeal accumulation. The examples above are all external, but we also inflict the same kind of burden upon ourselves internally. Within the university, and the academic community, the overriding good intention is collegiality, the value of which is beyond dispute. Collegiality easily transmutes, however, into the notion that anybody's business is everybody's business – or, more particularly, that my decision needs your permission. This can lead to complicated academic committee structures. Besides the university senate, which is the overall academic governance body, there will be a similar body within each faculty and likewise within each department. In addition, you need cross-departmental and cross-faculty structures for the core functions of research and teaching, and more besides to respond to external compliance requirements. On top of these, we invent various cross-disciplinary and interdisciplinary structures and activities, both for research and teaching. All to the good, but it means we inflict the same kind of cumulative burden on ourselves as is inflicted upon us from outside.

There is also another aspect to consider. If we're not careful, our good intentions on collegial academic governance can spiral into a situation where we all go and sit on committees for no better reason than to keep a watchful eye on our colleagues. In which case the first problem leads to the second, which is the erosion of trust.

Nowhere is the erosion of trust within the university more clear than in an apparent conflict between collegiality and what is easily condemned as 'managerialism'. There are many laments about this. Consider, for example, a book titled *For the University: Democracy and the Future of the Institution*,[49] by Thomas Docherty, Professor of English and Comparative Literature at Warwick University. It starts with the gloomy assertion that the university today finds itself increasingly 'besieged and beleaguered', with threats both internal and external.[50] Internally, the threat lies with the replacement of legitimate academic authority by bureaucratic authoritarianism.

> At the more local level of the University, we begin to see the hubris of individuals who start to style themselves not as vice-chancellors, but rather as chief executive officers. These individuals believed, possibly honestly, that they were running a business; and the logic then is that they establish a fundamental principle, for internal governance as for external self-preservation, of competition, aggression, ruthlessness and the bottom financial line.[51]

Externally, 'the culture of mistrust that dogs and threatens the sustained viability of the university is something that is at least tacitly endorsed, if not actually inaugurated, by political discourse'.

> And now, everyone mistrusts everyone. Teachers mistrust the Quality Assurance Agency; students question teachers; government questions everybody else; funding mechanisms have to be rendered 'transparent' because no one trusts the judgements made by funding bodies; examinations have to be mechanized into exercises governed by transparent criteria rather than judgement; and so on. Within the institution itself, likewise, everyone is now expected not only to do their work but also to justify their existence as workers, through endless monitoring processes and procedures. This is all well known.[52]

The culture of mistrust – or perhaps more accurately the culture of suspicion – is endemic. And we are part of it.

On the general topic there is an excellent little book by the philosopher Onora O'Neill, titled *A Question of Trust*,[53] which consists of the BBC Reith Lectures she delivered in 2002.

> We may not have evidence for a crisis of trust; but we have massive evidence of a culture of suspicion. Let me briefly join that culture of suspicion, and finish

by voicing some suspicions of my own that I shall trace in the next four chapters.... My suspicions fall secondly on our new conceptions of accountability, which superimpose managerial targets on bureaucratic process, burdening and even paralysing those who have to comply. My suspicions fall thirdly on the new ideal of the information age: transparency, which has marginalised the more basic obligation not to deceive.[54]

On these two topics, accountability and transparency, and her other two suspicions (about human rights and press freedom), Professor O'Neill goes on to show, with elegant simplicity, the burden that arises from such good intentions. On accountability, in particular, she is worth quoting at some length:

The diagnosis of a crisis of trust may be obscure: we are not sure whether there is a crisis of trust. But we are all agreed about the remedy. It lies in prevention and sanctions. Government, institutions and professionals should be made more accountable. And in the last two decades, the quest for greater accountability has penetrated all our lives, like great draughts of Heineken, reaching parts that supposedly less developed forms of accountability did not reach....

The new accountability has quite sharp teeth. Performance is monitored and subjected to quality control and quality assurance. The idea of *audit* has been exported from its original financial context to cover ever more detailed scrutiny of non-financial processes and systems. Performance indicators are used to measure adequate and inadequate performance with supposed precision....

In theory the new culture of accountability and audit makes professionals and institutions more accountable *to the public*. This is supposedly done by publishing targets and levels of attainment in league tables, and by establishing complaint procedures by which members of the public can seek redress for any professional or institutional failures. But underlying this ostensible aim of accountability *to the public* the real requirements are for accountability *to regulators, to departments of government, to funders, to legal standards....*

In theory again the new culture of accountability and audit makes professionals and institutions more accountable *for good performance.* This is manifest in the rhetoric of improvement and rising standards, of efficiency gains and best practice, of respect for patients and pupils and employees. But beneath this admirable rhetoric the real focus is on performance indicators chosen for ease of measurement and control rather than because they measure quality of performance accurately....

Perverse incentives are real incentives. I think we all know that from our daily lives. Much of the mistrust and criticism now directed at professionals and public institutions complains about their diligence in responding to incentives *to which they have been required to respond* rather than pursuing the intrinsic requirements for being good nurses and teachers, good doctors and police officers, good lecturers and social workers. But what else are they to do under present regimes of accountability?

In the end, the new culture of accountability provides incentives for arbitrary and unprofessional choices. Lecturers may publish prematurely because their department's research rating and its funding require it. Schools may promote certain subjects in which it is easier to get 'As' in public examinations. Hospital Trusts have to focus on waiting lists even where these are not the most significant measures of medical quality. To add to their grief, the Sisyphean task of pushing institutional performance up the league tables is made harder by constantly redefining and adding targets and introducing initiatives....

The pursuit of ever more perfect accountability provides citizens and consumers, patients and parents with more information, more comparisons, more complaint systems; but it also builds a culture of suspicion, low morale, and may ultimately lead to professional cynicism, and then we would have grounds for public mistrust.[55]

And that rather sums it up. Good governance, best practice, collegiality, transparency, accountability – these are all good intentions, but they all result in the accumulation of more work, which we experience as compliance obligations, bureaucracy and managerialism. If these good intentions were to add up to an overall good effect, then perhaps the extra admin would be a price worth paying. But they don't. Instead they add up to a bad effect, which is erosion of trust. So we lose twice. Our good intentions result in a burden of bureaucracy, and in addition bring a detriment rather than a benefit.

Professor O'Neill's reference to league tables is particularly telling. The quest for perfect accountability is pursued as an attempt to arithmetise the quality of what we do. Objectives, key performance indicators, benchmarks, targets, reports, audits – we are always counting our beans, and doing our sums. That, supposedly, yields objective evidence, which can be audited and presented for purposes of compliance or transparency. And that is how we meet the obligation of accountability. Rather than exercising our judgement, we are encouraged to exercise our calculators. It is an instance of defaulting into what, in Chapter Six, I will call linearism.

We should revisit our intentions, and think anew about the essence – the soul – of the university, and how to conceptualise it, rather than begin by asking how to measure it. I will return to this topic in the final chapter. But first I must redeem an earlier promise, and relate quality to equality and diversity.

4

Tales of Quality, Equality and Diversity

Cape Town

> In every man's writings, the character of the writer must lie recorded.
> *Thomas Carlyle*[1]

Any opinion on what constitutes the good is unlikely to be objective, and any attempt to make it so is likely to be boring. Plato reputedly once gave a public lecture titled 'On the Good', but since he delivered his discourse in mathematical terms most of the audience had left before he eventually reached the gnomic conclusion that 'the Good is One'.[2] An opinion on what makes a good university, particularly from a practising academic, is even less likely to be objective. At some point in a discourse on the good university, therefore, there should be a declaration of interest – some reference to the personal circumstances and social conditioning of the author which may impact on their judgement. For that reason, this chapter has a more personal slant, and relates some experiences of quality and equality. The first tale is about the University of Cape Town in the 1990s, and is set against the background of mathematics.[3]

To understand why mathematics is relevant to equality and diversity we have to go back to what happened in the South African Parliament in June 1954. This was when Dr Hendrik Verwoerd,

Minister of Native Affairs, introduced a piece of legislation called the Bantu Education Act. Dr Verwoerd addressed the Senate as follows:

> The school must equip the Bantu to meet the demands which the economic life of South Africa will impose on him... There is no place for him in the European Community above the level of certain forms of labour. Within his own community, however, all doors are open.... Until now he has been subject to a school system which drew him away from his own community and misled him by showing him the green pastures of European society in which he is not allowed to graze.... What is the use of teaching a Bantu child mathematics when it cannot use it in practice? ... That is absurd. Education is not, after all, something that hangs in the air. Education must train and teach people in accordance with their opportunities in life.... It is therefore necessary that native education should be controlled in such a way that it should be in accordance with the policies of the State.[4]

From Dr Verwoerd's point of view this probably looked very logical. Under apartheid, black people were never going to be allowed to do skilled jobs, or enter the 'green pastures of European society'. There was therefore no point in providing them with an education that would have made that possible.[5] But it is not Dr Verwoerd's reasoning for which this speech is known. What reverberated through South African history was 'Bantu education' – a swearword to black South Africans.

One particular phrase took on a life of its own. 'What is the use of teaching a Bantu child mathematics?', asked Dr Verwoerd. Mathematics, therefore, became a contentious subject, even a political one, with the teaching – or rather the non-teaching – of mathematics regarded as one of the tools of oppression deployed by the apartheid regime.

All of this was very relevant at universities in South Africa during the early 1990s, when it became clear that there would be a move towards a democratic dispensation. The university landscape was a fragmented one, as might be expected after decades of 'separate development'. But there were other factors too. For the best part of a century, South African universities had already been differentiated by language. The colonial-origin English-medium universities of Cape Town, Natal, Rhodes and Witwatersrand were, by evolution and by design, matched by Afrikaans-medium universities in Bloemfontein, Potchefstroom, Pretoria and Stellenbosch. To these the Nationalist government had in the 1960s added two more. The Randse Afrikaanse Universiteit[6] ('for Christian National Higher Education') in Johannesburg was intended to be a counterweight to the well-established University of the Witwatersrand, and the University of Port Elizabeth (with its fairly brief experiment in bilingualism) was likewise to be a counterweight to Rhodes University[7] in the Eastern Cape. In addition, however, the logic of apartheid dictated that there should also be universities for black people in the 'homelands', the places where they 'belonged' according to ethnic classifications. Thus, in apartheid-speak, there would be a University of Zululand for amaZulu, a University of the Transkei for amaXhosa, a University of Bophutatswana for Batswana, a University of Venda for VhaVenda, and so on. In addition, to be absolutely clear that everybody should be in their own box, the University of Durban-Westville was for Indian students, and the University of the Western Cape was for (so-called) coloured students.

It is necessary at this point to deal with a matter of record and terminology. In South Africa, not only under apartheid but to this day, 'coloured' is an official designation of ethnicity. The term 'coloured' does not, in South Africa, carry the connotations it would have in the UK or the USA. In particular, 'coloured' does not mean 'black'. It is still the case (for example in the 2011 census) that government statistics take into account four broad racial classifications: 'African Black', 'Coloured', 'Indian/Asian' and 'White'. In Afrikaans, coloured people are usually called 'brown people', rather than 'mixed-race', and this is a term that has been adopted by some coloured people. During apartheid most brown people were mother-tongue Afrikaans speakers, and the University of the Western Cape was originally established as an Afrikaans-medium university.

The fragmentation of higher education originated with another piece of apartheid legislation, called the Extension of University

Education Act of 1959. Like many other such acts, the intention was the opposite of what the title proclaimed. The intention – soon duly accomplished – was to get black students out of 'white' universities. The pretext was that black students, where in this case 'black' meant 'not white', would all have their own universities, neatly packaged into ethnic classifications. As the internal tensions and external pressures on apartheid mounted over time, the Nationalist government realised that it would be to their advantage if some homeland universities were seen to be doing well, but this never really materialised. The Verwoerdian reality was that the black universities, as long as they could only draw students coming out of Bantu education, were always going to be separate but never going to be equal.

There was persistent opposition from some universities:

> Once more the protests swelled. The University of the Witwatersrand pledged itself 'to uphold the principle that a university is a place where men and women, without regard to race and colour are welcome to join in the acquisition and advancement of knowledge.' In Cape Town three thousand demonstrated outside Parliament when the Bill came up, among them a recently retired Chief Justice of South Africa, the Chancellor of the University of Cape Town, his Principal, and vice-Principal, many of his teaching staff and most of the students. Inside, the Minister told members that 'the only possible inference is that this agitation is taking place under the influence of a leftist movement in our country.'[8]

Later, after the student uprising in Soweto in 1976, the University of the Western Cape started moving away from Afrikaans, and in the 1980s declared itself as the 'intellectual home of the left'. The apartheid government found resistance not only from the old English-medium universities, which they would have anticipated and discounted, but also from the very 'bush colleges' for which blacks were supposed to be grateful. None the less, by the 1980s higher education had successfully been segregated.

In this apartheid-induced maelstrom of higher education in the late 1980s and early 1990s, most academics were still trying to carry on as normal with the day job of research and teaching. But many were also beginning to think of a post-apartheid South Africa. And one thread of that thinking was about mathematics. It was clear that the country would, finally, not just need, but actually want, black scientists, engineers, accountants and other professionals of the kind Dr Verwoerd had tried to prevent. It was also clear that the generation of young blacks who had been deprived of mathematics at school were not interested in hearing that they were underqualified for entering the study of mathematics at university. The Freedom Charter had promised that the doors of learning would be open to all, that was their demand, and that demand would have to be met.

The University of Cape Town had been trying to prepare for this moment. The Academic Support Programme (ASP) was created specifically to cater for underprepared students entering disciplines like science, engineering and accountancy, and had already branched out into various innovative ventures. For example, the Alternative Admissions Research Project was designed specifically 'to provide a means of access for educationally disadvantaged students whose school results do not necessarily reveal their potential to succeed in higher education'.[9] The teaching of mathematics was central to much of the work of the ASP. Always the gatekeeper for science and engineering, mathematics could easily become an obstruction in what was already a bottleneck. But this was no moment to stand on the niceties of school-leaving results.

From 1991 onward, I was Head of the Department of Mathematics, which had the responsibility of teaching all mathematics courses in the university, including the 'service courses' which were a compulsory part of the curricula in science, engineering and commerce. If black students were to graduate in those disciplines they would first have to pass their maths modules. Conversely, if the Maths Department could not train up more black students to the requisite standard in mathematics, the university could not graduate them. This blunt reality taught me an important lesson about 'widening participation': what matters, in terms of both quantity and quality, is not entry, but exit. What matters is not so much the standard at which students enter your department, but, more importantly, the standard they have attained when they leave.

Of course there are caveats and uncertainties, and any university teacher in mathematics will be familiar with most of them. Taking on underprepared students is a lot of work. It is a risk, particularly to the student, because despite everybody's best efforts they might fail, which is demoralising and expensive. It is a challenge, because many of the standard teaching methods just do not work. It requires extra resources, because you will need to provide support both within and without the curriculum.

Against this were two factors. One was the inescapable fact that something had to be done, and it could not be done by anybody else. The other was a growing realisation that the joy and inspiration of teaching outstandingly gifted and well-prepared students (of which the university attracted plenty) had a counterpoint, which was the joy and satisfaction of opening doors to people who had the will to succeed but had not had the opportunity. The task of a mathematics department, and a university, is not only to take straight-A students and turn them into straight-A graduates. It is also to add value to those who most need it. There is professional pride in performing both these functions.

So, in the years around 1994, we invented, borrowed and experimented with every manner of teaching mathematics to underprepared students we could think of. The recruiters in the ASP scoured schools to find likely entrants to the university. We tried an extended degree programme, where the Bachelor's degree would be spread over four years instead of three, with less pressure and more support in the first two years. We experimented with teaching 'ASP students' in their own groups, which had the advantage of peer learning and the disadvantage of separation from the mainstream, as well as teaching them in a mix with everybody else, which had the advantage of diversity but piled yet more pressure on the lecturers. The ASP morphed into an Academic *Development* Programme (ADP), to make the point that we should move beyond remediation. We mounted more, and more intensive, tutorials. We appointed some teaching-only staff in a Maths Department which prided itself on research.[10] We made it clear that everybody was expected to pitch in, research or no research. We created a continuously staffed Maths Hot Seat, where any first-year student could wander in at any time and ask any question relating to their work. We set up a Quiet Room for studying, which had only one rule: absolute quiet. We invented computer-generated individual tutorial tests. We tried open-book exams, supplementary exams, extended exam times and fortnightly assessments. We realised that we had much in common with our sister Department of Applied Mathematics, and so did they, and so we voluntarily merged the two departments (an unheard-of choice at that time). The Science Faculty raised the profile of teaching through a Committee on Undergraduate Education in Science (CUES).[11] This made space for the Science ADP programme to operate as a central faculty initiative, rather than being seen as an adjunct activity. At university level we invented a new structure, called the Centre for Higher Education Development (CHED), which was a 'horizontal faculty', lying at the base of the six vertical pillars representing the subject-based faculties, bringing together a number of initiatives such as the ADP.[12]

Then we got a bit more radical. We realised that, while there was a problem with mathematics, there was a much wider problem with numeracy – or rather, innumeracy. Many students entering the university to study in the humanities or social sciences might, through the neglects of Bantu education, not have had any kind of exposure to anything mathematical for years. These students, hopefully, would not only graduate but would be leaders in the new South Africa. However, many of them were practically innumerate. So we set up a Numeracy Centre. The Numeracy Centre, for which we collaborated with the Statistics Department, offered a credit-bearing one-semester course in Effective Numeracy to students in the Faculties of Humanities and Social Sciences. Designing and teaching this course was a very satisfying thing to do, not least because it slaughtered so many holy cows.[13] The entry criterion was the inverse of the usual: you had to show that you did *not* have school-leaving mathematics qualifications (to avoid anybody taking the course as a soft option). There were no lectures, no handbooks, and in a sense no syllabus. Teaching consisted entirely of problem-solving. Students would sit around a table in groups of four, we would hand out a problem sheet, and they would try to figure out some answers, by whatever means came to hand. Tutors would move between the tables to give help and suggestions as needed, but no more than was needed. Problems would typically come from a newspaper, or advertising, or some facet of daily life. For example, most newspapers would carry a table of currency conversion every day. So a typical problem would be: 'As you can see, one US Dollar is worth R5.67 today. What is one Rand worth in Dollars?' Of course the students could not do it, which is why they were at the Numeracy Centre, so we had to learn to deconstruct a problem down to the very basics. 'Suppose a Dollar would buy you *two* Rand. Then what would one Rand be worth in Dollars? And how did you get to that answer?'

We always encouraged students to use calculators, and they liked to do so, but they did not always know what the calculator was doing. To understand why the button labelled x^{-1} was the right one to use to calculate what R5.67 is worth in dollars was a revelation. Once some confidence had been gained we moved on to teaching numeracy via spreadsheets. This gave the students some understanding of data, graphs and charts, and some computer proficiency, which they liked. At the same time, it gave us a platform to inculcate some understanding of the arithmetic behind spreadsheet manipulation.

The one piece of orthodoxy that we stuck to was that at the end of the semester students had to take an exam, and they had to do the exam individually. However, the exam had no time limit. Students would come in at 9 o'clock, get their exam problem sheet, sit down at a computer, and work away as long as they wanted – some brought their lunch. It was also open-book. They could bring any books, notes, other material, calculator or laptop they wanted. They could talk, but not confer. In the end, the exam was marked and graded just like any other, and the student would get a credit for the Effective Numeracy module just like any other.

In all of these activities of 'widening participation' and academic support we were trying, consciously or unconsciously, to match up quality with equality. We learnt that there was no silver-bullet solution, and no quick fix. We tried everything we could think of, and some things worked for some students and other things worked for other students, and sometimes nothing seemed to work. But on the whole, and over time, we made a contribution, and it was a worthwhile and satisfying thing to do.

Stellenbosch

The maternity ward of apartheid.
Rev. Simon Adams, Stellenbosch[14]

The Dutch Governor Simon van der Stel, venturing into the interior from the fort in Cape Town in 1679, was so enchanted with a pleasant wooded area on the banks of the *Eersterivier* (the 'first river') that he founded a settlement there, named after himself. The town of Stellenbosch is in a beautiful scenic setting, and is a popular tourist destination, being also at the centre of the Western Cape Wine Route. It is well known among rugby fans as the base of a renowned club which has produced many Springboks for the national rugby team.

Less well known is a fact which is also less pleasant. Stellenbosch was the birthplace and intellectual home of apartheid. Stellenbosch University was created by the Afrikaners, for the Afrikaners. It was their beacon of hope during the slow but grimly determined climb back into power after the defeat of the Boer war (which in my youth was still spoken of by my grandmother as 'the English war'). This drive for dominance took from 1901, when the two Boer republics accepted defeat, through 1910, when the Union of South Africa was founded, two world wars, the great depression and the 'poor white' problem of the 1930s, until 1948. That was when the National Party of D.F. Malan, a former *dominee* of the Dutch Reformed Church, defeated the United Party of Jan Smuts in a general election.

In the rise of Afrikanerdom to political power, Stellenbosch, and Stellenbosch University, played a considerable part. It was at Stellenbosch that the National Party was founded (in 1914, two years after the founding of its nemesis, the African National Congress). It was at Stellenbosch that some of the great Afrikaner businesses were founded, such as the insurance giant SANLAM (Suid-Afrikaanse Nasionale Lewens-Assuransie Maatskappy) and the Afrikaans newspaper company Nasionale Pers (now a global communications company renamed Naspers). It was here, also, that the institution that had previously existed as Victoria College became, in 1918, the University of Stellenbosch, dedicated to Afrikaans and Afrikanerdom. Deep within the psyche of

Stellenbosch is the story of how the university's founding was made possible by the bequest of £100,000 in the will of *Oom Jannie* J.H. Hofmeyr, stipulating that the bequest was to enable Afrikaans to have *geen mindere plaatz* – no lesser place – at the university than English. That is why, at the centre of Stellenbosch University campus, you will find the statue of J.H. Hofmeyr, with the simple inscription *Ons Weldoener* – Our Benefactor.

Surely it is one of the tragedies of the 20th century that the Afrikaners, who had the sympathy of the world after the Boer war, a strong case for self-determination, and the fortitude to overcome any adversity, went on to turn goodwill into global animosity because they could not see any route to survival other than through power and domination. And surely, within that narrative, we should take account of how and why a university became the standard-bearer for a narrow ethnic nationalism, proclaiming itself as the 'white Athens of the South'.

For most of the 20th century, the power brokers of apartheid were Stellenbosch men. D.F. Malan was a Stellenbosch resident. Hendrik Verwoerd, before he went into politics, was a professor of sociology at Stellenbosch University. When Verwoerd was assassinated in 1966, the National Party appointed as his successor John Vorster, Minister of Police, who had in his youth been president of the Students' Representative Council, and eventually became chancellor of Stellenbosch University. Vorster's brother Koot was the moderator of the Dutch Reformed Church, sometimes referred to as 'the National Party at prayer'. Koot Vorster's colleague *dominee* Kosie Gericke served as chair of the Council and vice-chancellor of Stellenbosch University (this position then being distinct from the position of rector). Vorster's successor as prime minister, the formidable P.W. Botha, also became chancellor of Stellenbosch University. Most of the rectors of Stellenbosch University were leading figures in the Broederbond, the secret organisation behind the National Party. H.B. Thom, rector during the 1960s and one-time leader of the Broederbond, declared Stellenbosch to be the *Volksuniversiteit* of the Afrikaners.

In a generous mood, one might say that during apartheid the Afrikaners wanted to give to black people exactly what they had so intensely desired for themselves – an ethnic university. Each perceived ethnic group would have its own. But the idea went wrong because the gift was not wanted. The liberal tradition, which most Afrikaners of the 20th century did not agree with, nor cared to explore, articulated 'the principle that a university is a place where men and women, without regard to race and colour [or indeed other markers of group identity] are welcome to join in the acquisition and advancement of knowledge'.[15] Instead, mainstream Afrikaner thinking considered a university as a manifestation of group identity. Therein lay the basis of Stellenbosch University's leading role in apartheid.

I took up office as rector and vice-chancellor of Stellenbosch University on 1 January 2002.[16] How, I wondered, does a university which had been in the forefront of apartheid become an integral part of the new multiracial South Africa? Many Afrikaners of the 20th century grew up in an apparently well-ordered world, in which God had authority over man, men had authority over women, older people had authority over younger people, and whites had authority over blacks. With a few notable and heroic exceptions, this world view was unchallenged from within, especially if you grew up on the *platteland*. You listened to SABC radio, read *Die Burger* daily, and went to church twice a week. These were the voices that informed your understanding of the world. I was conscious that many of the staff and most of the alumni of Stellenbosch University were, like me, apartheid's children. All the more reason, I felt, to engage with the new South Africa.[17]

The first lever of change was to get academic buy-in for a different approach. This took shape in a statement called Vision 2012, in which the university committed itself to an outward-oriented role in South Africa, Africa, and globally.

Stellenbosch University:

- Is an academic institution of excellence and a respected knowledge partner
- Contributes towards building the scientific, technological and intellectual capacity of Africa
- Is an active role-player in the development of the South African society
- Has a campus culture that welcomes a diversity of people and ideas

- Promotes Afrikaans as a language of teaching and science in a multilingual context

This five-point statement pointed the academic compass towards quality, but stood Verwoerdian ideology on its head by positioning diversity as an opportunity for increasing quality rather than a risk of losing it. It challenged the university to engage with the new South Africa. It recognised and celebrated Afrikaans-ness, but in the context of a society which now had 11 official languages.

Actions, however, would speak louder than words. And so, in December 2002, Stellenbosch University became the venue for the quadrennial conference of the African National Congress. This week-long event is attended by thousands of delegates, with white faces the exception. To organise a conference on this scale you need facilities: transport, accommodation, catering, at least one very large auditorium, plenty of seminar rooms and breakout spaces. Stellenbosch University campus could provide all of these. Here was an event which could be seen as closing a circle of history: the new black rulers of South Africa would have their plenary session in the D.F. Malan Hall at Stellenbosch University. The conference was diversity made manifest, up close and personal. Rarely, if ever, had Stellenbosch seen black people (as in 'African Black') other than cleaners or builders setting foot in the student halls of residence, let alone sleeping in the beds, or – in another reversal of an apartheid obsession – using the toilets.

Diversity needed to be followed by quality, and so we spent a lot of time and effort on raising academic performance. This was another one of the many ironies of that time and that place. To many Afrikaners, especially among the older alumni, Stellenbosch was literally peerless, because it was so much more than just a university. This led, over time, to a self-perception of excellence which was, unfortunately, more a reflection of the cultural insularity of the Afrikaner world than a realistic measure of the academic quality of the university. Moves towards increasing diversity therefore routinely invoked suspicion and distrust from the wider Afrikaner community, with many refrains of the 'standards will drop' variety.

Fortunately, most academics understood the matter rather better. The university started raising its academic game from around the mid-1980s, when national research metrics first appeared.

This was a process I was glad to inherit from my predecessors, and pleased to support, and it worked. By 2006 the deputy vice-chancellor for research could report that Stellenbosch produced more research publications and delivered more PhDs per academic than any other university in the country, was joint first with the University of Cape Town on papers in the *Science Citation Index*, first overall on weighted research outputs, and had bagged three of the first seven National Centres of Excellence and four of the first 15 National Research Chairs. The Business School had gained triple accreditation.[18] The new National Centre for Theoretical Physics was to be located at Stellenbosch. We had won an award as Technologically Most Innovative University in South Africa. Also, with a large grant from the Wallenberg Foundation in Sweden, we had established the Stellenbosch Institute for Advanced Study – the first such venture in Africa.[19]

All of these quality improvements took place in parallel with a concerted recruitment effort to raise the student diversity profile. Over a period of five years we raised the representation of coloured/black/Indian students at Stellenbosch University by 70% in terms of numbers, and from 19.7% of the total student population to 28.3%. Table 4.1 shows the growth curve.

In so far as comparisons can be drawn, these numbers would indicate a South African equivalent of what in the UK is called fair access – the idea that a good university should make a conscious effort to recruit, fund, educate and graduate a substantial number of students from disadvantaged backgrounds. The comparison should be treated with caution, because 'black or brown' does not necessarily equate to 'disadvantaged'. Indeed, it would be tragic if the new South Africa cannot over time invalidate such an equation. None the less, in the first decade of the 21st century the legacy issues of apartheid were still so prevalent that, by and large, black and brown students came from less affluent households than white students (and in some cases from poverty-stricken households, or from no households at all).

We therefore needed to reset the quality indicators for students. The standard indicators of 'what were your school-leaving grades?' or 'what school did you come from?' would clearly work against the disadvantaged. Exceptionalism would also not work. To treat disadvantaged students as an identifiable cohort to whom different standards and measures apply would be to stigmatise them as inferiors who need to be tolerated, rather than challengers who should be welcomed. While 'disadvantaged' was still visibly manifested by skin colour, such separation would confirm rather than overturn the prejudices of apartheid.

Table 4.1: Student diversity at Stellenbosch University 2001–2006

YEAR	2001	2002	2003	2004	2005	2006
Undergraduate Number	12,228	12,698	13,416	13,446	13,863	14,173
Race						
White	10,525	10,704	10,947	10,909	11,088	11,167
Coloured	1,346	1,518	1,776	1,890	2,036	2,195
Black	234	336	504	471	550	617
Indian	123	140	189	176	189	194
Percentage Coloured, Black and Indian	13.9%	15.7%	18.4%	18.9%	20.0%	21.2%
Postgraduate Number	6,031	6,160	6,341	6,857	7,244	7,420
Race						
White	4,132	4,091	4,124	4,172	4,213	4,315
Coloured	663	656	662	860	1,017	1,042
Black	1,050	1,160	1,289	1,586	1,782	1,838
Indian	186	253	266	239	232	225
Percentage Coloured, Black and Indian	31.5%	33.6%	35.0%	39.2%	41.8%	41.8%
All students Number	18,259	18,858	19,757	20,303	21,107	21,593
Race						
White	14,657	14,795	15,071	15,081	15,301	15,482
Coloured	2,009	2,174	2,438	2,750	3,053	3,237
Black	1,284	1,496	1,793	2,057	2,332	2,455
Indian	309	393	455	415	421	419
Percentage Coloured, Black & Indian	19.7%	21.5%	23.7%	25.7%	27.5%	28.3%

Note: a Special students excluded.

Source: Chris Brink, 'The State of the University', Chapter 1.3 in Amanda Botha (Ed.), Chris Brink, *Anatomy of a Transformer*, SUN Press, Stellenbosch, 2007.

The fact of the matter was that many of the black and brown students we admitted had faced hardships that students with the advantage of stable middle-class or affluent homes could not imagine, and might not have been able to overcome. Advantage creates opportunity, and can buy the preparation necessary to make the most of it. Conversely, disadvantage entails fewer opportunities and less ability to exploit them when they do arise. It is no use the doors of learning being open when those doors are at the top of a mountain you cannot climb.

We had to change the understanding of what quality means. This gave me the opportunity to do something I had long wanted to do. I initiated an award called the *Rektor se Uitstygtoekenning* – literally, the *Rector's Rise-Up Award*. This was a large cash award, double a normal full-cost bursary. The university already had the usual kinds of awards for attainment, including the very prestigious annual Chancellor's Medal for the graduate with the highest level of academic achievement. The Rise-Up Award was different. It gave recognition, not to a number, but to a story – a profile. The question was not what grades you had attained, either at school or at university. Your grades had to be good enough to get you into university, or to pass your exams, but this was not the determining factor. What qualified you for an award was the distance you had travelled, and the obstacles you had had to overcome, to reach your level of attainment. In short, the Rise-Up Award was based on a value-added understanding of quality: performance seen against context. When opportunity is not equally available to all, then merit cannot just be a number. The narrative, the profile, should also come into consideration.

Besides the money, and the conceptual clarity of the scheme, we also had to make sure that it enjoyed esteem. For that purpose we used the annual opening of the academic year, which at Stellenbosch is a formal event where the vice-chancellor delivers an address to the student community, including the entire intake of new students, in the company of senior academic staff. We endowed this event with the same kind of academic pomp and circumstance as would normally be used for a graduation ceremony, and we treated the Rise-Up awardees in the manner usually reserved for honorary graduates. The event started with an academic procession, in full academic dress, and was presided over by either the chancellor or the vice-chancellor. There would be words of welcome, in particular to the new students, followed by the vice-chancellor's address. The main moments of the ceremony, though, would be the presentation of the Rise-Up awards. Each awardee would be asked to step forward onto the podium, and the university orator would deliver an address essentially consisting of a short biography of their life and circumstances, and how, despite those circumstances, they had nevertheless managed to pursue successful academic studies.

It was never necessary to big it up. The stories were, without exception, absolutely compelling, and, to many in the audience an absolute revelation. At the first awards ceremony I put the matter thus:

> In line with our Vision Statement, Stellenbosch University strives to be an academic institution of excellence, with a national profile and an international reputation. Quality must be our benchmark. If so, we have to ask a simple but profound question: how do you judge quality relative to context? Some of us take for granted an environment which for others is only a dream. If so, is it not the case that our performance, no matter how well merited on the basis of our own efforts, also owes something to the environment within which we live and work?
>
> Consider two hypothetical cases. One is a student whose parents are well-educated professional people, reasonably affluent, and who comes to us from one of the so-called 'good schools', where she enjoyed every possible facility for sharpening the mind. The other is a student whose parents have had little formal education and who live in poverty, who comes to us from a historically disadvantaged school in a gang-infested area. If the former student comes to Stellenbosch with a school-leaving mark of 90%, and the latter comes with a school-leaving mark of 70%, is it possible for us to say that the former is a better student than the latter? And if we do, would that be right?[20]

Here is an example: the case of Ella Davids – not her real name, but a true story. She grew up in a deprived area of the *platteland*, where brown people are mostly agricultural labourers, went to a small rural school, under circumstances she described as 'frustrating', and matriculated with results which, on the numbers alone, would seem fairly mediocre. 'My childhood dreams and aspirations faded away', she said later, 'and I swore never again to read a book or learn something.' After leaving school she worked for a number of years as a fruit packer, in a grocery store, and as a nanny. Gradually, however, her dream of going to university was rekindled, in part through her involvement with a church group. Ten years after leaving school she plucked up the courage to go and see the local *dominee*. The *dominee* called a friend of his at Stellenbosch University, and a remarkable chain of events was set in motion.

Two weeks later Ella arrived in Stellenbosch, with R200 in her pocket 'and a word from the Lord'. She was 28 years old. She found accommodation in a back yard in Cloetesville, a 'coloured' neighbourhood of Stellenbosch, enrolled for a degree in theology, and walked to campus every day. By the end of that academic year she had completed 13 semester courses, 9 of them with distinction, including the obligatory Greek and Latin. In her second year her results were not quite as stellar, because she had had to take on a job to support herself, but she none the less again passed most of her subjects with distinction. The Rise-Up Award, which Ella won at the end of her second year, enabled her to realise her potential without the pressures of financial hardship. She later completed her Master's degree with distinction, and was working on her doctoral dissertation by the time I left Stellenbosch.

The Rise-Up Award brought to the fore many stories of succeeding against the odds. There was the black student who grew up in a corrugated iron shed in Khayelitsha in the troubled 1980s, wrote matric under the muzzles of police guns, stole train rides to get to the University of the Western Cape, and ended up with a PhD in physics from Stellenbosch University. There was the quadriplegic who went from Stellenbosch to Oxford. There was the young woman who lost her disabled father shortly after leaving school and found herself, at the age of 20, at the head of a household with a disabled mother and a disabled sister, both unemployed, and who none the less came to Stellenbosch and completed her degree with distinction.

Nobody can deny the merit of these students. But conventional means of admission and reward might not have picked them up, because when attainment is viewed without regard to context, others would at some crucial stage have outshone them, and without support the exigencies of their circumstances might have killed off any chance of success.

Two institutional change agents which I would never have anticipated were the Faculty of Theology and the Faculty of Military Sciences. By the time I arrived at Stellenbosch, the Faculty of Theology had undergone a complete mindset change from its days as the National Party at prayer. They had deeply engaged with their own past, had come to revere the anti-apartheid thought leaders their church had rejected in the apartheid days, and were a constant and steady example of neither complaining about the present nor fearing the future. They were by far the smallest faculty in the university, and on any organisational or financial analysis they really should not have existed as a separate faculty at all, but such was their symbolic value that I was more than pleased to give them every support.

The Faculty of Military Sciences, which was the academic face of the Military Academy of South Africa, had undergone an equally remarkable transformation from the days when it only educated young white men for the old apartheid Defence Force. After 1994, in an extraordinary fusion, that body was merged not only with the various liberation movements such as Umkhonto we Sizwe, but also the various homeland forces. At the time I arrived in Stellenbosch, the only substantial group of African black undergraduates at the university were in the Faculty of Military Sciences, and the only senior African black person associated with the university was the commandant of the Military Academy, a wise and wily man.[21] He understood what the new rector was trying to do, and he made an early symbolic gesture of support. For my first academic opening of the university, he brought the entire student body of the Military Academy in buses from the military base in Saldanha to the D.F. Malan Hall. I well remember getting goose pimples when that block of young men and women, black and brown and white and Indian, arose in full military uniform, in what was otherwise a sea of white faces, stood to attention, saluted, and sang in full voice all four verses of the national anthem.

Finally, although it does not fit the narrative of this book, for completeness I should mention the issue of Afrikaans at Stellenbosch. While many 'Coloured' people still spoke Afrikaans, very few 'African Black' people did, and they found a campus with an Afrikaans identity unconducive to study and culturally unwelcoming – particularly when those most vociferous in fighting for Afrikaans were Afrikaners. It was difficult, therefore, to disentangle the ideal of promoting Afrikaans as a language from the trappings of racial identity. The difficulty was compounded by the fact that for many Afrikaner alumni Stellenbosch was not only their university but the centre of their universe. Many of them perceived transformation as nothing but an attack on Afrikaans, and spineless political subservience on the part of the university management. There was therefore a lot of resistance to change among the Convocation (the body representing alumni), starting with the implementation of the new *taalbeleid* (language policy) of 2002. That resistance rumbled on for another decade or so after I had left in 2007, until eventually Convocation battled Council in court, and lost.

Transformation can be painful, particularly when it involves a mindset change about having to share something you regard as precious, and your own. And yet, by and large, the Stellenbosch academic community achieved it. This became clear to me when I read a statement from one of our students applying for a trip we organised annually to campuses in the US for upcoming student leaders.

> I am a black proud South African woman that prides herself in being an African, a South African, a Matie![22] ...
> I look forward to a time when my grandchildren will be Maties and I can say to them that I was one of the leaders of my time that pushed for diversity and multi-culturalism, cultural preservation and equality for all.[23]

England

> The English have a genius for turning diversity into hierarchy.
>
> *Professor Sir Howard Newby, former vice-chancellor of three English universities*

When my family and I moved to England I took only two books. One was the *Concise Oxford English Dictionary*. The other was by an anthropologist called Kate Fox, titled *Watching the English: The Hidden Rules of English Behaviour*.[24] That helped a lot, first in becoming aware of the English codes of behaviour, and then in trying to understand them.

Kate Fox helpfully summarises Englishness (see Figure 4.1). Social dis-ease, she says, is right at the centre of Englishness. As a consequence of social dis-ease, there are well-developed codes and protocols for social interaction. Politeness or, as (Kate Fox has it, 'courtesy') is an important component of these codes. I soon learnt that in England, if you are in a meeting and you wish to say something, you must always begin by fully agreeing with the previous speaker. Only after you have said 'I think Professor Took is quite right – that is a very valuable point' can you go on to say

Figure 4.1 Kate Fox's diagram of Englishness (from *Watching the English*, p 410)

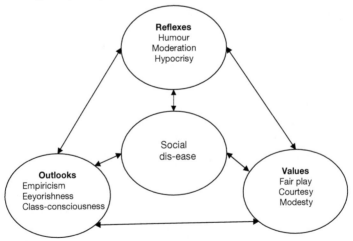

something like 'However, I just wonder whether, perhaps, we might also consider the possibility that, at some point ...' – after which you may then continue to say the exact opposite of what Professor Took had said.

One practical consequence of this politeness is that you have to learn to listen for the silences. Since outright contradiction is not part of the code, the strongest form of disapproval is total silence. English people draw their conclusions not only from what is said, but also from what is not said.

In that context, then, it is a bit worrying that while there are many voices arguing for greater equality, and expounding its merits, there is relative silence concerning the challenges and risks of actively pursuing an equality agenda. The case against an equality agenda is not articulated as often or as openly as the case in favour, but seems to manifest itself *sotto voce*, as lack of active support and perhaps some subversive activity. Such lop-sidedness in the debate does not do the equality agenda any favour. If there is anything wrong with or weak about the argument for equality it should be subject to challenge. Doing so is good Popperian methodology: you strengthen a theory by challenging it. It also helps in understanding whatever fears, doubts and anxieties there may be about the effects of an equality agenda.

It seems worthwhile, therefore, to summarise some of the common arguments *against* the equality agenda in higher education – those of the kind you could equally well have heard in South Africa in the 1990s or in England 20 years later.[25]

As a caveat, I should say that in many respects the South African experience is quite different from the UK. For example, in South Africa there is a national consensus about the need for rectifying the inequalities of the past, which is why the equality agenda is often referred to there as 'corrective action'. In the UK there does not seem to be such a national consensus. Also, the South African experience is one of race, while the English experience is anchored in a discourse of class. Class-consciousness, we may note, is one of the 'outlooks' in Kate Fox's Englishness diagram (Figure 4.1).

On the other hand, while we should allow for differences between the South African and UK manifestations of the fundamental issue, there is at least one aspect of the equality agenda which plays out similarly between countries and over time, namely the fears, doubts and anxieties of those who believe they stand to lose by it. This belief of impending loss is strongest among the semi-privileged. They are not weak enough to deserve a special dispensation, not strong enough to enforce one, and not rich enough to buy one. In England they would be called the middle class, possibly with finer distinctions such as upper middle, or middle middle, or lower middle class. Such gradings of hierarchy may inculcate a mindset of always striving upwards. It may also inculcate an aversion to anybody getting what is seen to be an unfair advantage in climbing up the ladder of success.

By way of preparation we should define some terms. In higher education in England, in terms of student participation, the equality agenda manifests itself through two key phrases: 'widening participation' and 'fair access'. These are different, and both differ from 'increasing participation'. The idea of increasing participation is about numbers. The question is how many people, or what percentage of the population, enter university, and if the number is considered to be too low then the agenda is that it should be increased. As noted in Chapter One, since the Robbins Report of 1963 participation in higher education increased from 5% to over 50% of young people. But these numbers do not say anything about where these extra students come from. Hence the idea of widening participation, which is about ratios. The question is whether entry into university from different social classes is in roughly the same ratio as those classes, and if it isn't then what, if anything, to do about it. But such ratios do not yet say which universities these students go. Hence the idea of fair access, which is about destination. The question here is whether sufficiently many, or a high enough ratio, of students from 'the lower socioeconomic classes' go to one of the 'good universities'.

To understand the debate, and more particularly the fears and anxieties underlying the debate, think of two hierarchies, one of social classes and another of universities. The question then becomes whether being in the lower echelons of the social hierarchy should be a consideration in gaining admission to a higher echelon university. If so, the fear of the semi-privileged is that those thus admitted will jump the queue ahead of those who have earned their place on graft and merit. And queue-jumping, in the code of Englishness, is not done. Here, then, are some of the common fears and anxieties about widening participation and fair access.

'Standards will drop'

This is the most stereotypical fear concerning widening participation. Its basis is the observation that the under-representation in higher education of some particular societal group correlates with the fact that people from that group do not meet university entry requirements to the same extent as the rest of the population. Consequently, admitting students from such groups into university – usually under some kind of special admission programme – has the effect that the average school-leaving results of the new cohort are lower than they would have been without such a programme. If 'standards will drop' means nothing more than that – that relaxing entry criteria result in the average entry qualification going down – then the point may be readily conceded. But the fear factor is more than that. 'Standards will drop' is usually code for a bigger claim, namely that the quality of education on offer will suffer as a consequence of widening participation.

We have already distinguished, in Chapter Three, between quality and standards, so we can respond to this fear in the language of standards rather than quality. And the way to do so is to distinguish entry standards from exit standards. It is when these two are conflated that the fear about dropping standards extrapolates from an observed change in entry standards to a postulated change in exit standards, and from there to a conclusion that the quality of education will decline. But that does not follow – at least not unless you believe that entry level predetermines exit level (in which case you would also have to wonder about the value of the educational experience).

Good value-adding measures can and should result in students with lesser entry standards attaining perfectly acceptable exit standards. My own experience at Cape Town and Stellenbosch was that value-adding measures can work even in very demanding environments, such as mathematics or medicine. In England, the first such effort I learnt about was an Extended Medical Degree Programme at King's College London.[26] Students coming from certain specified 'educationally deprived' boroughs in inner London were admitted with a school-leaving result of three C grades, rather than the usual two As and a B, and put through an extra year of study. Despite their lower entry grades, and slower start, in the later clinical years pass rates were comparable to those of conventional students.

'Our reputation will suffer'

This is a variation on the theme of 'standards will drop'. Essentially, it says: 'Other people will think our standards are dropping, so our reputation will suffer, which means we will not be able to attract the best students and staff, which means our standards will drop.' In an environment where reputation feeds into rankings, and the other way round, this argument cannot be lightly dismissed, circular as it is. *The Complete University Guide*, for example, uses entry scores as one of the parameters in calculating a ranking of UK universities.[27] In the 2015 *Guide*, which ranked Newcastle University as 20th overall and 9th for medicine, the entry tariff for medicine at Newcastle is quoted as 529 points, and their ranking on this particular parameter as joint 14th.[28] Without their cohort of 'widening participation' students, however, their entry score would have been 541 points, and their tariff ranking would have been 12th instead of 14th, thus improving also the ranking for medicine and thereby the overall university ranking. The widening participation programme, to which the university is firmly committed, therefore comes at a cost in terms of league table positions, and as such represents a reputational risk.

There is no easy answer. It depends on your values, and the value you attach to your values. It also depends on actively building and managing your reputation, internally and externally. Personal success stories, for example, go a long way. Cases such as that of Ella Davids, or other Rise-up Award winners at Stellenbosch, are so compelling that they can, if judiciously deployed, become reputation-enhancers. Successful alumni who came from a disadvantaged background often have a desire to give something back – not only money, but also a willingness to speak out in favour of the agenda that gave them a chance.

'It's not our problem'

This is the fear that universities may get sucked into a societal problem that is not of their making and to which they cannot provide a solution. The argument is that widening participation and fair access should be addressed by raising the exit standards of secondary schools, not lowering the entry standards of universities. In other words, the problem lies with the schools, and should be addressed in the schools.

In the UK the preferred route towards the so-called 'top universities' is still via school-leaving qualifications called 'A levels', typically earned around age 18. And the most common route towards A levels is via a qualification called the General Certificate of Secondary Education (GCSE), typically around age 16. The first question then is what percentage of GCSE students would obtain results suitable for leading on to A level study – usually thought to be five or more GCSEs at grade C or better, including maths and English. And the second question would be about the breakdown of those students.

The issue is not new. For example, here is a comment from a member of the Government's National Council for Educational Excellence (NCEE) in 2008:

> The class differences are stark. In the last year (2003) for which full details are available by socio-economic class, 42% of 16 year olds obtained 5 GCSEs A*–C including Maths and English. Yet for children from the higher socio- economic groups that figure was 57%, for lower groups it was 31%, and for those eligible for free school meals the figure falls to 16%. We know that once a student qualifies with A levels, eligibility for free school meals makes no difference to their going to university. Therefore, the critically important determinant is that they do not progress in education after 16, mainly because their GCSE grades are not good enough to get onto the right courses. If we want to widen participation the task is to increase the percentage of those from the lowest four socio-economic groups

going on to university and that requires raising their pass rate for five GCSEs, including Maths and English.[29]

Nor does the issue seem to go away. In 2014, during one of the periodic bursts of public attention to secondary education, *The Times* commented as follows:

> In the recent Pisa survey into education systems around the world, Britain had the best schools in the world. For the richest few percent of pupils. The country's overall performance is dragged down by poor provision for those at the bottom end. This is the problem to which Sir Michael Wilshaw, the chief inspector of schools in England, is referring when he says the biggest problem lies with the white working class.
>
> Sir Michael makes the point that parents of white working-class children do not create the conditions at home in which learning is prized. As people who have themselves had a poor experience of school, they are passing on a legacy of hostility to education that is damaging. This will not be true of all families but Sir Michael is only reflecting something that many teachers have experienced. It is also unfortunately true that the belief that working-class children are not likely to succeed has been confirmed in the low expectations that too many teachers have had of them.[30]

Two points are worth making. The first is that as long as everybody passes the buck we are not going to solve the problem. If the universities say the problem lies in the schools, and the schools say the problem lies at home, parents will probably say the problem lies with 'the system'. And they would probably be right, in the sense that unless we all take some responsibility, and do what we can, we are unlikely to make much progress. It is a systemic issue.

The second point is how easily the debate defaults into class terminology – and, more precisely, into an assumption of a hierarchy of classes. 'The class differences are stark', says the NCEE Report – and so they will be, while the reference point is 'the lowest four socio-economic groups'. Likewise, *The Times* has no compunction about speaking of 'those at the bottom end', clarifying that to be 'the white working class'.

'It's social engineering'

'Social engineering' is a term which expresses a value judgement. Typically, it is deployed as an accusation against government when behaviour-changing initiatives are considered to be harmful and/or coercive. There are, however, many such initiatives, and not all of them are tagged as social engineering. A ban on smoking in pubs, for example, could be called social engineering, but usually isn't, because most people agree with it. Likewise for inviting all males over the age of 65 to turn up for free prostate screening, or setting a national curriculum for children under 5 with 69 specified 'learning outcomes'. Under the premiership of David Cameron there was a government entity known as the Nudge Unit,[31] aimed at gently persuading people to make better choices. 'Social engineering', therefore, is used as a pejorative not so much in terms of the action as the intention. The term is deployed as an indication of disagreement.

For universities, the fear is that social engineering is a way of pressurising them into doing something they do not wish to do, or at least do not wish to do in the manner or to the extent that the state desires. Social engineering in that sense would be an infringement of academic freedom and institutional autonomy.

Apartheid was social engineering on a grand scale, including prescriptions and proscriptions on higher education. At the University of Cape Town such policies were opposed from the outset. The University of Cape Town vice-chancellor at the time, T.B. Davie, encapsulated the resistance of liberal universities against apartheid interference by his definition of academic freedom. Academic freedom, he said, is 'the right of each university to decide for itself who shall teach, who shall be taught, what shall be taught, and how it shall be taught'. On all these counts, the apartheid government was intent on interfering.

After 1994 the argument shifted in South Africa. There was broad national consensus that the legacy issues of apartheid had to be addressed. One manifestation of the government's intention of doing so was the national 'mergers and amalgamations' initiative of

2002–3, which consolidated the patchwork of 36 pre-1994 higher education institutions into 22 universities, often bringing formerly 'black' and formerly 'white' institutions together. Stellenbosch University was virtually untouched by this exercise, which, given its history, was generous of the post-1994 government. An intriguing paradox then confronted me. As much as I had supported the T.B. Davie definition of academic freedom while at the University of Cape Town, I was conscious of the fact that a strict adherence to that same definition at Stellenbosch, 20 years later, could be used to slow down or negate the corrective action required by the national consensus. Stellenbosch had no lack of good applicants for most of its degree programmes. Most of them, however, were young white Afrikaners from 'good schools'. If the university were to decide, after due academic consideration, that it was happy with this situation, made no effort to recruit outside of that cohort, justified its recruitment policy as being 'on merit' and only taught in Afrikaans, it would have been well within the T.B. Davie definition of academic freedom.

My view was that Stellenbosch *needed* more diversity, and so recruiting more black students and staff made good academic sense. I therefore did not face the risk of being told by the government to do something which I did not want to do. Rather, I faced the risk of government ordering me to do something which I *did* want to do. If that were to happen, which by and large it fortunately did not, it would have put me in an awkward position. The conservative Afrikaner view was that government was issuing orders to the university to implement positive discrimination, and that the spineless university leadership was meekly obeying such orders. I received many letters and emails and read many newspaper articles saying that we were selling out on academic freedom, playing politics with the university, or puppets of our political masters. (Most of these missives seemed to be from rather new converts to academic freedom and institutional autonomy, who had forgotten how willingly Stellenbosch had grasped the heavy hand of apartheid.) It was hard enough, therefore, to convince sceptical Afrikaners that the university was mounting equality initiatives of its own accord, for good academic reasons, with the full backing of its Senate, and was not being forced into social engineering initiatives by government orders. It would have been virtually impossible to make the same argument if government had indeed issued such orders.

'It's unfair'

Fairness is an integral part of Englishness. You would imagine, then, that a programme of 'fair access' will meet with general approval. But it doesn't, because many people – the threatened semi-privileged in particular – see it as *unfair* access.

Imagine a scenario where Jane and Joe Public lavish two decades of care, attention and money on the education of their children, Jimmy and Jenny. They plan it all very carefully, and meticulously execute their plan. They build their respective careers before starting a family. They take out the largest possible mortgage to buy a house in the vicinity of a good school – one which is selective and oversubscribed. From toddler stage onward, the children go to a nursery favoured by parents of children at their target school. They join a church group to build up a track record of community engagement. At home, they read to and play educational games with their children every day. Once each child has been selected by their preferred school, they studiously attend PTA meetings and participate in school activities. They encourage their child's participation in sport, music, cultural activities and volunteering, and they pay for participation and coaching in any possible extra-curricular or sporting activity the child might be good at. They go on outings and overseas trips to broaden the mind. At the crucial stages of GCSE and A level, they engage private tutors to help prepare for examinations. Through their social networks they are able to arrange work experience or internships for their children in high-status professional firms. These may be unpaid, but that is not a big concern, because Jane and Joe can afford to pay for the travel and maintenance costs of the children.

Fortunately, Jimmy and Jenny Public turn out to be a credit to their parents – well rounded, well networked, confident and accomplished. To nobody's surprise they achieve very good A level results at their good school. They therefore apply to a good university to study medicine – only to be knocked out by applicants of lesser attainment on the grounds of an equality agenda. Is that fair?

'Fair access', to remind ourselves, is the idea that prospective students should be judged not just in terms of the arithmetical fact of their school-leaving results, but in terms of the context within which those results were obtained. This is a line of thought I propounded myself when at Stellenbosch. The medical school provides a good case study. During my term of office, we crossed an important threshold when more than 50% of the intake for the medical degree came from previously disadvantaged groups – essentially black, 'coloured' and Indian students. Crossing that threshold could not have been accomplished by a simple algorithm of judging entry in terms of school-leaving results. It was necessary to design admissions criteria that looked at a variety of contextual data, such as school background, leadership qualities, and community work, and to supplement such data as far as possible with personal interviews.

Yet our success in 'fair access' brought to light quite vividly the other side of the coin, which is the argument that this kind of contextual judgement gives rise to *unfair* access. If you ignore context, it is easy to argue that school grades objectively reflect merit, and that admitting students with lower grades above students with higher grades – which is what special admissions programmes do – is a measure of discrimination. Every year, the dean of medicine and I had to deal with some irate parents who resented the fact that their child, who as they saw it had on the basis of their own hard work and perseverance achieved excellent school-leaving results, was not selected for medical studies, while others with lesser grades were. These discussions could become quite intense, and sometimes took surprising turns. One affluent parent offered the Faculty of Medicine a donation of R1 million should his child be admitted. There was no problem with the school-leaving results of the child, and R1 million, in South Africa, at that time, was a great deal of money. We knew we could do a lot of good with such a donation, even after covering the full cost of an extra student. None the less we turned it down. Was that wise? I still wonder, sometimes.

We were sometimes threatened with litigation, based on the accusation of unfair discrimination. Our response to this threat was twofold. First, we had a clear policy approved by Senate and Council, and we took great care to ensure that there were no procedural lapses in applying this policy. Second, however, we could rely on the fact that the Bill of Rights enshrined in the South African constitution allows the concept of *fair* discrimination.

Our efforts were also aided by the fact that we were operating in a context of increasing participation. The rate of participation of students from disadvantaged backgrounds increased rapidly – but the rate of participation of white students did not decline. Between 2001 and 2006 the total number of students at Stellenbosch grew 3% per year on average. During that time, the rate of growth for black/coloured/Indian students was 11.6% per year on average, while that of white students was about 1% per year on average. However, an increase of 1% p.a. roughly matches the growth rate of the white population over the same period. Thus, in crude terms, widening participation did not come at a cost to the previously advantaged.

Conceptually, there are two issues at play in this debate: fairness and merit.

Kate Fox lists 'fair play' as one of the values of Englishness, but, arguably, that is only one of the dimensions of fairness. A fuller breakdown might look like this:[32]

- fair share
- fair play
- fair go
- fair say

Fair share is about resources and resource allocation. It is founded on the belief that those who need more should get more. The intention is that those who are most disadvantaged should receive greater benefit, and more effort should go towards creating opportunities for them. Subscribing to this intention means accepting the principle that a fair distribution of resources may be an unequal one, because you would want proportionately more resources to flow to where the need is greater.

Fair play is about process, and the notion of even-handedness, but it is really a sporting metaphor. It is about playing the game, and about a level playing field. To say 'It's just not cricket' is to express a nuanced distaste for something that may be within the rules but is none the less unsportsmanlike to the extent of being unfair. Conversely, 'play the game' means transcending the narrowness of rules to strive for fairness even when the rules do not capture it.

Fair go is about equal opportunity. It is the idea that ability should be able to access opportunity regardless of circumstance. The principle of 'fair go' is the driving force behind widening participation and fair access. If some are expected to run the race while carrying a weight of disadvantage then they are not being given a fair go. Perhaps golf is the game that captures this best, where a 'handicap' is actually a means of fair discrimination: it allows players of unequal accomplishment to play against each other on something like equal terms.

Fair say is about being heard. In principle, it should be about people talking to each other, and hearing each other, as part of decision making. In practice, it is a difficult one for English people, because in order to be heard to you have to say something, which is then subject to the rules of politeness. None the less, they have found a way, which is the relentlessly critical scrutiny of their own institutions. In pursuit of fairness, the English are tireless in checking up on authority, through regulators, audits and reviews, thus strengthening the web of bureaucracy they complain of. But we have already covered this point at the end of Chapter Three.

A fair access agenda, properly motivated and implemented, stands up well on each of the dimensions of fairness. And that is perhaps the best response to the J. Publics. More work on articulating the case, more work towards a national consensus, more diversity of opportunity, should allow the J. Publics to do more contingency planning. That still leaves the issue of merit, to which I will return.

'It's a waste of time'

This fear has two flavours, mild and strong. The mild variation says that widening participation is a waste of time in the sense that the time and effort and money spent on it do not justify the returns. For example, when the Extended Medical Degree Programme at King's College London (mentioned above, under 'Standards will drop') was reported on in the *British Medical Journal,* an editorial in the same edition pointed out that the scheme cost £190,000 to run, and concluded by asking the question 'Is it worth our while to widen participation, particularly if this risks reducing standards?

Political ideology says yes, but the evidence is pending and costs are rising fast.'[33] Note the language: widening participation is driven by 'political ideology', but questioning the King's College programme is a cost–benefit analysis. None the less, the cost–benefit question cannot be shrugged off. Widening participation coupled with extra support does cost money, and – motives apart – it is legitimate to ask 'how much does it cost?' and 'who will pay?' Government has the mandate and the legitimacy to answer these questions – and a higher education sector which maintains its institutional autonomy has the right, collectively and individually, to decide whether or not to follow government policy.

There is also a stronger version of the fear that widening participation is a waste of time, which is the concern that it may be impossible. This is the view that widening participation and maintaining standards are inherently contradictory concepts – in short, that excellence and equality are mutually exclusive. We might call this the *strong* waste-of-time argument, to distinguish it from the mild version which only says that the costs outweigh the benefits. Implicitly or explicitly, the strong waste-of-time view is grounded in the idea that those societal groups for whom widening participation efforts are mounted are less capable intellectually, and hence less able to perform well at university, than those currently making up the norm. A short version of such an argument can be seen in the *British Medical Journal* editorial mentioned above, the opening sentence of which reads: 'UK medical students tend to come from higher socioeconomic classes, perhaps not surprisingly, as social class correlates with intellectual ability.'

At somewhat greater length, the strong waste-of-time argument can be unpacked into three parts. The first part claims to be an empirical observation, namely that standard IQ tests would show a correlation between test outcomes and social class: people from higher socioeconomic groups would have higher IQ scores, and conversely for lower socioeconomic groups. The second part of the argument consists of equating a quantitative measure, namely IQ scores, with a qualitative judgement regarding intellectual ability. The third part of the argument extrapolates from the qualitative judgement to a value judgement, namely that higher intellectual ability makes an individual more meritorious than lower intellectual ability.

I do not propose to discuss here the first part of the argument, that purports to correlate IQ with social class. I simply put it up as an observation that has been made,[34] and as an integral part of the strong waste-of-time argument.

About the second part of the argument, I would reiterate from Chapter Two the point that any translation between quantitative data and qualitative judgements involves imprecision. Quantifying qualitative information is a process of linearisation, which of necessity involves loss of information. In the other direction, when you give a qualitative interpretation to data you create meaning from numbers. Different outcomes are possible when you put words to numbers, meanings to words, and social categories to meanings.

To illustrate the point, consider the academic career of Nelson Mandela. In his autobiography, *Long Walk to Freedom*, Mandela recounts how he started his legal studies at the University of the Witwatersrand in 1943.

> The English-speaking universities of South Africa were great incubators of liberal values. It was a tribute to those institutions that they allowed black students. For the Afrikaans universities, such a thing was unthinkable.
>
> Despite the university's liberal values, I never felt entirely comfortable there. Always to be the only African, except for menial workers, to be regarded at best as a curiosity and at worst as an interloper, is not a congenial experience....
>
> Our law professor ... held a curious view of the law when it came to women and Africans: neither group, he said, was meant to be lawyers. His view was that law was a social science and that women and Africans were not disciplined enough to master its intricacies.... Although I disagreed with his views, I did little to disprove them. My performance as a law student was dismal.[35]

There can be little doubt about the intellectual ability of Nelson Mandela, and even less doubt about his merit. However, there can also be little doubt that if IQ tests had been carried out on African youths in the early 1930s in the Transkei, where Mandela came from, they would have scored no better than children from 'lower socioeconomic classes' score today. And, as Mandela attests, if admitted to university they might well struggle in an uncongenial environment. The question is to what extent we should equate Mandela's dismal performance as a law student with lack of intellectual ability, and then with lack of merit.

It is the third part of the strong waste-of-time argument, namely the identification of a qualitative judgement about ability with a value judgement concerning merit, which really deserves more scrutiny. The Nobel Prize-winning scientist James Watson, for example, once told the *Sunday Times* that he was 'inherently gloomy about the prospect of Africa', because 'all our social policies are based on the fact that their intelligence is the same as ours whereas all the testing says not really'.[36] These comments drew widespread condemnation. Yet it seems that exactly the same kind of comment can be made with impunity about 'lower socioeconomic classes'. While the discourse of racism has become unacceptable, the discourse of classism has not. It is not uncommon to encounter a line of argument that says admitting students to university solely on the grounds of school-leaving results is nothing more than the implementation of a meritocracy, with the corollary that if the 'lower social classes' are proportionately less successful, the only proper conclusion to draw is that they are less meritorious.

Consider again the pronouncement in the *British Medical Journal* editorial intimating that there is nothing surprising in the fact that UK medical students tend to come from higher socioeconomic groups, 'as social class correlates with intellectual ability'. It is uncontroversial to say that in an admissions system relying mostly or entirely on school-leaving results, children from socially disadvantaged backgrounds will not be successful to the same extent as children from a socially advantaged background. The difficulty arises when such a context-free numbers-based admissions system is called a 'merit-based' selection, and the successful and unsuccessful candidates, respectively, thereby included in or excluded from a presumed meritocracy. That could only be true if the playing field was level – which, by the very concept of 'lower socio- economic classes', it is not. To say that school-leavers whose parents could elbow their way into 'good schools' are of higher merit than school-leavers who struggled in adverse circumstances, on the sole evidence of their respective school-leaving results, seems a peculiarly narrow definition of the word 'merit'. So we need to talk about merit and I will do so in Chapter Five.

Quality needs diversity

> Socially diverse groups are more innovative than homogeneous groups.
>
> *Professor Katherine W. Phillips, Columbia Business School*[37]

Few would deny that a good higher education sector needs a diversity of universities, and all of us would like quality throughout that diversity. So there must be universities that are good, but different, and hence good in different ways. Each can and should strive to be good in its own way, while still sharing a common set of academic values. Mostly, however, our discussion of diversity in higher education is about diversity *within* a university – a diversity of people, very likely, but more importantly a diversity of ideas and talents.

I hold the view that diversity has an inherent educational value. For this view I would offer two reasons. First: a university is an institute of learning, and learning requires us to engage with the unknown. We will learn more from those people, those ideas, those phenomena and those circumstances that we do *not* know, than from those we know only too well. To enhance learning, we should encourage diversity, because it brings more unknowns. Socio-diversity is valuable to the intellectual environment of a university in somewhat the same way as biodiversity is valuable to the natural environment. Second, ability can arise anywhere. You could find a mathematical genius in a small town in India, a music legend from working-class Liverpool, a college dropout who becomes a global technology guru, or a world statesman among the amaXhosa.[38] Therefore, we should cast our net wide, and encourage the rise of ability without preconceived ideas as to where it may be found.

I would summarise the view that diversity has an inherent educational value in the phrase *quality needs diversity*.[39] Diversity is not a sufficient condition for quality, but it is necessary, in the sense that without allowing diversity into our frame of reference we will not attain true quality.

'Quality' should be distinguished from 'excellence'. Excellence is something like the performance of the Olympic sprinter, who runs down one lane and clocks up a measurable time against competitors of exactly the same kind. Quality, in the sense used here, is something like quality of life. It is *arête* – living up to your full potential. If excellence is like the Olympics, then quality is more like the Paralympics. Quality has many dimensions, which should be valued rather than measured, and these must hang together harmoniously and reinforce each other for us to experience quality. Excellence lends itself to ranking, because it is one-dimensional, but quality does not, because it is multidimensional. If you and I both feel that we have a good quality of life we would both be happy, and it would not normally occur to us that my quality of life must be better than yours, or vice versa. Excellence is about a relationship – typically a competitive relationship – with others. Quality is about our relationship with ourselves. We cannot all have excellence, but in principle we can all have quality.

However, when you have a diversity of people you also raise a risk, which is the risk of inequality. The risk is illustrated by the propensity to turn diversity into hierarchy.[40] Diversity turns into hierarchy when we force multidimensionality into one-dimensionality. Typically, this means that we turn from an obvious truth about difference of categories to a much less obvious supposition that those categories are not equal. In other words, we turn from an observation of fact to a value judgement. 'Different' is neutral, but 'unequal' is not. The risk, then, is that we will negate the very effects we seek, because the inequality inherent in a presumed hierarchical ordering is prejudicial both against learning from others and against leaving space for the unexpected. Hierarchy makes a mockery of diversity and is inimical to the pursuit of quality.

Inequality is a risk on moral grounds, on social grounds and on utilitarian grounds. It is a risk on moral grounds because it may signal a denial of natural rights or social justice. It is a risk on social grounds because unequal societies demonstrably have a higher incidence of social problems. And it is a risk on utilitarian grounds because it may signal a failure to turn diversity to advantage as a driver of learning and a source of innovation.

To mitigate the risk of inequality we may institute a countervailing force, which is an equality agenda. Equality is one of the axioms of a liberal democracy, as in the preamble of the American Declaration of Independence: all men are created equal. Fundamentally, as human beings, leaving aside all contingent circumstances, each of us is worth as much as any one of us. We are equally endowed with human dignity, we are equal before the law, as citizens we have equal rights and responsibilities, and we all have an equal vote in determining who should exercise governance over those rights and responsibilities.

Arguably, if there were no diversity there would be no need for an equality agenda. But there is, and so there is. The equality agenda has to do with making sure that the axiom of equality is not contravened. Like all axioms, the value of equality is a basic assumption rather than a self-evident truth. None the less, it is an assumption strongly and commonly held, because it guarantees natural rights and social justice. Not contravening the axiom of equality means that no individual should be either advantaged or disadvantaged simply by virtue of belonging to any particular group, or displaying any particular group characteristic. In the educational sphere, the equality agenda accepts that not all individuals have equal intellectual ability, just as we do not all have equal physical or artistic or musical ability. We know that we are different as people, yet we strongly believe that we are equal as humans. Therefore we have, over time and with some difficulty, decided to institute measures to ensure that the strong will not exploit the weak, or the many the few, or the able the unable. The equality agenda starts from the premise that natural ability is an individual trait, and that no conclusion regarding the ability of an individual should be drawn only on the basis of their belonging to or identifying with a particular group.[41]

Essentially, therefore, the aim of the equality agenda is to decouple circumstance from destiny. Where you were born, what culture or religion you belong to, how old you are, how rich or poor you or your parents are, what your sexual orientation is, whether or not you have any disability – no such manifestation of diversity should deny you any educational opportunity, nor impede your levels of attainment.

In short: ability should be able to access opportunity regardless of circumstance. This is true now, as it was in 1963 when Lord Robbins said that university places 'should be available to all who are qualified by ability and attainment to pursue them, and who wish to do so'.

5

Rank Order of Worth

On merit

> By merit raised
> To that bad eminence.
> *Milton, Paradise Lost*[1]

On 18 December 2012, as part of the year-long celebration of her Diamond Jubilee, the Queen attended a meeting of Prime Minister David Cameron's Cabinet – the first time a reigning monarch had done so since 1781. The next day, the *Daily Telegraph* published a rather cheeky front-page picture of the Queen and her Cabinet, not in formal pose, but getting ready for their formal pose. The Queen, in the middle of the front row, is quiet and composed. Everybody else is in high spirits, laughing, jostling and acting up a bit, in a schoolboy-ish kind of way.

It is a picture of a ruling elite at ease with itself. Besides the Queen, there are 32 people in the photograph. Thirty-one of them are white. Twenty-seven are men. All 32 have a higher education qualification. Twenty-seven went to a Russell Group university. Twenty-one went to Oxford or Cambridge. Twenty-three went to a selective school. Fifteen went to a 'public' (that is, private) school. Only six went to a comprehensive (that is, state) school. By way of comparison: out of the entire UK population only 7% of children go to public schools, and less than 1% of students go to Oxbridge.[2]

The press office of No. 10 Downing Street at the time had a standard response to questions about this membership profile of Cabinet: the prime minister selects his Cabinet and senior officers entirely on the basis of merit.

Mr Cameron was not the first prime minister to place a high premium on merit. His predecessor's predecessor, Tony Blair, on becoming prime minster, declared that New Labour would reconstruct Britain as a meritocracy. 'The Britain of the elite is over', he declared. 'The new Britain is a meritocracy.'[3]

In saying so, Mr Blair clearly thought that (a) everybody knows what a meritocracy is, and (b) a meritocracy is self-evidently a good thing. In at least the first respect he was mistaken. The word 'meritocracy' is not of long standing, and has changed meaning since it was first coined. It was made up in 1958 by a social activist called Michael Young, in a book titled *The Rise of the Meritocracy*,[4] and it was intended more as a pejorative than a compliment. In a new introduction to a reprint of 1994, Michael Young reflected on the provenance of the word:

> I had doubts about the key word which I made up. A friend, a classical scholar, said I would be breaking the rules of good usage to invent a new word out of one Latin and one Greek word. I would, she said, be laughed to scorn if I did. In the event the book has been subjected to much criticism but not on grounds of bad taste about the title – rather the opposite, I would say. The twentieth century had room for the word.

The book, or perhaps rather just the word 'meritocracy', had, to Michael Young's disappointment, almost exactly the opposite effect to what he had had in mind. 'I wanted to show how overweening a meritocracy could be', he lamented in his 1994 Introduction, 'how sad, and fragile'.

> If the rich and powerful were encouraged by the general culture to believe that they fully deserved all they had, how arrogant they could become, and if they were convinced it was all for the common good, how ruthless in pursuing their own advantage.... [A] meritocracy

could only exist in its full form if there were such a narrowing down of values that people could be put into rank order of worth.

The warning about a 'rank order of worth' was prescient, foreshadowing the now prevalent predilection for quality expressed as a position on some ranking. In this process, as Young had also pointed out, education played a central role.

> In all industrial societies the growth of massive educational systems has been one of the most significant phenomena of the [20th] century. A basic education has been regarded as a universal right. But after the basic education what? If there has to be selection at some rung on the educational ladder (as there always has to be), selection should surely not be on the basis of the parents' position or wealth but according to the merit of the child or youth. This is what educators like to think they are doing, and are often actually doing, with the aid of more or less elaborate systems of testing and examination.... Practically and ethically, a meritocratic education underpins a meritocratic society.

And so, one might ask, what is wrong with that? Here is Michael Young yet again, this time in 2001, writing in the heyday of the Blair years.[5]

> I have been sadly disappointed by my 1958 book, *The Rise of the Meritocracy*. I coined a word which has gone into general circulation, especially in the United States, and most recently found a prominent place in the speeches of Mr Blair. The book was a satire meant to be a warning (which needless to say has not been heeded).... It is highly unlikely the prime minister has read the book, but he has caught on to the word without realising the dangers of what he is advocating....
>
> It is good sense to appoint individual people to jobs on their merit. It is the opposite when those who are judged to have merit of a particular kind harden into a

new social class without room in it for others. Ability
of a conventional kind, which used to be distributed
between the classes more or less at random, has become
much more highly concentrated by the engine of
education. A social revolution has been accomplished by
harnessing schools and universities to the task of sieving
people according to education's narrow band of values.
With an amazing battery of certificates and degrees at
its disposal, education has put its seal of approval on a
minority, and its seal of disapproval on the many who
fail to shine from the time they are relegated to the
bottom streams at the age of seven or before. The new
class has the means at hand, and largely under its control,
by which it reproduces itself.

It is not an easy point to make, and in hindsight it is perhaps no
wonder that the word 'meritocracy' came to mean the opposite of
what its creator intended. How could anybody be against selection
on merit? If half the members of Cabinet went to a public school,
and two thirds graduated from Oxbridge, is that not simply an
indication of their merit? Is it not evident that the cream will rise
to the top?

Let us accept that merit does not – or at least should not – come
without effort. Indeed, Michael Young worked with the equation
that Merit = IQ + Effort. To avoid a detour on the notion of
intelligence quotient, we may take Young's intention to be that the
merit of an individual is a combination of their innate ability plus
the amount of hard work they put in to make that ability productive.
That sounds like quite a reasonable proposition. It tells us that there
ought to be some extent to which the meritorious deserve the
rewards they get. But then what do we have to say about the rest?
Where, in the meritocracy, do those feature who did not make the
cut? What about the non-meritorious?

Here is a more fundamental question: in principle, could
anybody have merit? This is essentially the same question we
posed about excellence in Chapter Three. As before, the question
is not whether everybody actually *does* have merit. The question
is whether, in principle, everybody *could* have merit. As before, we
may trace the consequences of saying yes or no.

If we say no, not everybody could have merit, then we are saying that for some people, no matter how hard they may try, merit is unattainable. This is certainly consistent with Young's equation. If merit equals ability plus effort, then those of no particular ability (or, as Young would have had it, a below-average IQ) are non-starters. This observation quickly gets us to the point Michael Young was trying to make: if not everybody can have merit then the meritocracy would be just a new kind of aristocracy, because it excludes some people through no fault of their own. It also shows up Mr Blair's definition of the new Britain as a meritocracy as rather harsh – especially coming from a politician – because being meritorious would then require being above average ability, thus excluding about half the population.

If, on the other hand, we say that yes, in principle anybody could have merit, then that raises a further question. Do we all already have it, in whatever small measure, or are we able to acquire it if we don't? Michael Young's equation says that those with merit have been born with ability, but they still needed to put in the effort to develop it. But now we find ourselves impaled on the horns of a dilemma. In so far as merit is innate, you cannot take credit for it, because you are just lucky with your genes. For the genetic part of merit your place in the meritocracy has no better justification than that of a hereditary lord in an aristocracy. On the other hand, in so far as merit is something you acquire, you can be helped to acquire it, in which case the extent of your merit depends on how much help you have had. Either way, if we could all have merit it is not clear how much credit any one of us can claim for it. And if that is the case, then it is also not clear how much reward should accrue to those with merit – which rather pulls the rug of fairness from under the show cabinet of meritocracy.

There is a good case for saying that in many cases those we consider to have merit have been lucky. Over and above whatever effort they themselves may have put in, they are either lucky in the gifts nature endowed them with, or they are lucky in the help they have had, or both. This point about luck and meritocracy has been made by Ben Bernanke, former Chair of the United States Federal Reserve. In a Commencement Address at Princeton on 3 June 2013, Bernanke said:

The concept of success leads me to consider so-called meritocracies and their implications. We have been taught that meritocratic institutions and societies are fair. Putting aside the reality that no system, including our own, is really entirely meritocratic, meritocracies may be fairer and more efficient than some alternatives. But fair in an absolute sense? Think about it. A meritocracy is a system in which the people who are the luckiest in their health and genetic endowment; luckiest in terms of family support, encouragement, and, probably, income; luckiest in their educational and career opportunities; and luckiest in so many other ways difficult to enumerate – these are the folks who reap the largest rewards.[6]

The point may be amplified at individual level. Undoubtedly most highly successful individuals have ability and also put in the effort. But there is a case to be made, on probabilistic terms if nothing else, that among the highly successful there must be a higher than usual proportion of individuals who have benefited from the pure blind luck of some chance events. The case is elaborated in a book titled *Success and Luck: Good Fortune and the Myth of the Meritocracy*, by Robert H. Frank, professor of economics at Cornell University.

How important is luck? Few questions more reliably divide conservatives from liberals. As conservatives correctly observe, people who amass great fortunes are almost always extremely talented and hardworking. But as liberals also rightly note, countless others have those same qualities yet never earn much.[7]

So, in England, who are these lucky folks? A 2014 report by the Social Mobility and Child Poverty Commission, titled *Elitist Britain*,[8] gives a detailed analysis of the educational background of 4,000 business, political, media and public sector leaders. It gives a very clear picture of the workings of what Michael Young called the engine of education.

71 per cent of senior judges, 62 per cent of senior armed forces officers, 55 per cent of Permanent Secretaries, 53 per cent of senior diplomats, 50 per cent of members of the House of Lords, 45 per cent of public body chairs, 44 per cent of the Sunday Times Rich List, 43 per cent of newspaper columnists, 36 per cent of the Cabinet, 35 per cent of the national rugby team, 33 per cent of MPs, 33 per cent of the England cricket team, 26 per cent of BBC executives and 22 per cent of the Shadow Cabinet attended independent schools – compared to 7 per cent of the public as a whole.

75 per cent of senior judges, 59 per cent of the Cabinet, 57 per cent of Permanent Secretaries, 50 per cent of diplomats, 47 per cent of newspaper columnists, 44 per cent of public body chairs, 38 per cent of members of the House of Lords, 33 per cent of BBC executives, 33 per cent of the Shadow Cabinet, 24 per cent of MPs and 12 per cent of the Sunday Times Rich List attended Oxbridge – compared to less than 1 per cent of the public as a whole.

No wonder that the Cabinet of David Cameron (ex-Eton and Oxford) looks the way it does. The political leadership is not out of line with the other leadership cadres in the top echelon of society – it is quite representative. Vernon Bogdanor, former Professor of Government at Oxford, and tutor of David Cameron, in reviewing a book on the radical right in Britain, writes:

> David Cameron is often mistakenly seen as a child of privilege. He is in fact, like Miliband and Clegg, a child of meritocracy, a product of academic success. All three party leaders belong to the exam-passing classes. This makes them ill-equipped to understand those who have not passed exams. The left behind have therefore become politically, as well as socially and economically, marginalised.[9]

The point about the educational system being a funnel towards privilege is becoming generally recognised. Here is another Oxford professor, Danny Dorling, author of a book titled *Inequality and the 1%*:

> In many ways, the pyramid of our examinations and qualifications system is coming to better and better resemble the ever-steepening pyramid of our wealth distribution.
>
> The problems of educational inequality continue after higher education. In the UK, elite employers use university name as the key selection criterion, above any more sensible measure of capacity to learn, enjoy and be good at a job. An ever more unequal society requires more and more mechanisms to divide our children and young people, to segregate the many and elevate the few. Yet the more exam-obsessed we become, the less qualifications show about what a person is truly able to do: they show only that, at a particular point in the past, they were found to have been successfully taught to do well at a particular test awarded by a particular institution.[10]

Does it matter? In the Foreword to *Elitist Britain*, the Chair of the Child Poverty and Social Mobility Commission draws an obvious conclusion.

> This research highlights a dramatic over-representation of those educated at independent schools and Oxbridge across the institutions that have such a profound influence on what happens in our country. It suggests that Britain is deeply elitist.
>
> That matters for a number of reasons. In a democratic society, institutions – from the law to the media – derive their authority in part from how inclusive and grounded they are. Locking out a diversity of talents and experiences makes Britain's leading institutions less informed, less representative and, ultimately, less credible than they should be. Where institutions rely on too narrow a range of people from too narrow a range of backgrounds with too narrow a range of experiences

they risk behaving in ways and focussing on issues that are of salience only to a minority but not the majority in society. Our research shows it is entirely possible for politicians to rely on advisors to advise, civil servants to devise policy solutions and journalists to report on their actions having all studied the same courses at the same universities, having read the same books, heard the same lectures and even being taught by the same tutors.

This is a powerful argument against the hegemony of the educational elite. And that hegemony is eerily familiar. We would do well to remember that Plato had pretty much the same idea in *The Republic*. A strenuous educational programme would be coupled with a careful breeding programme to secure a stratified society where those deemed to have intellectual merit would be securely positioned as a ruling elite at the top of society. To cover this up, the people would be sold a 'noble lie': the myth of the metals.

> Citizens, we shall say to them in our tale, you are brothers, yet God has framed you differently. Some of you have the power of command, and in the composition of these he has mingled gold, wherefore also they have the greatest honour; others he has made of silver, to be auxiliaries; others again who are to be husbandmen and craftsmen he has composed of brass and iron; and the species will generally be preserved in the children.[11]

As Professor Dorling points out,[12] it is no wonder that the noble lie has resonated down the centuries.

> The old myth about the ability and variability of potential in children is a comforting myth for those who are uneasy with the degree of inequality they see and would rather seek to justify it than confront it. The myth of inherent potential helps some explain to themselves why they are privileged.

Your professor of classical Greek will tell you that *arête* has the same etymological root as *aristos*. *The Republic* is about those with *arête* forming a ruling aristocracy. The worry is that in real life the causality also flows in the other direction. It is not only the case that those with merit form an aristocracy, but also, and perhaps increasingly, that those who have ascended into the new aristocracy, believing it all due to their own effort, claim the mantle of merit. *Arête* becomes identified with *aristos* – the meritocracy becomes the aristocracy.

Comparing the present-day educational elite to a *Republic*-style breeding programme is not divorced from reality. 'It's over, Cinders', reads a headline in the *Sunday Times* of 16 February 2014 – 'No prince is coming'.[13] The article is about a study of US census data for the National Bureau of Economic Research in the US, which found a rise in 'positive assortative mating'. In other words, high fliers increasingly tend to marry high fliers. This is the phenomenon of the power couple. Think of Amal and George, Bill and Hillary, Cherie and Tony, David and Victoria. No longer does the boss marry the secretary, or the doctor the nurse. In 2005, 48% of married men with university degrees had wed female graduates, up from 25% in 1960. The increase is also true for women: 44% of married female graduates were married to male graduates, up from 33% in 1960. By pairing off in this way, power couple graduates further increase the advantage they already had as individuals over non-graduates.

> A couple who both studied to postgraduate level in 1960 could earn 76% above the average income, but by 2005 they earned 119% more. By contrast, a household with a postgraduate wife and a high-school dropout husband had an income of 40% above the average in 1960, but 8% less than the average by 2005.[14]

Graduates graduate from a university, and unlike the 1960s more women than men now enter the university. There are therefore more opportunities than there used to be for 'positive assortative mating' of educational high fliers. And so, according to John Goldthorpe, an emeritus fellow of Nuffield College, Oxford:

> Education is functioning as a segregating force. It's
> healthy provided you are getting a greater equality of
> educational opportunity according to people's social
> class background. But we know that's not happening,
> which is the worrying thing.[15]

'The Britain of the elite is over', Mr Blair had said. 'The new Britain is a meritocracy.' But what if the meritocracy itself becomes an elite? Perhaps even a hereditary one? This is the problem that Michael Young had foreseen. When the meritocracy becomes self-reproducing it displays a disturbing number of characteristics of the aristocracy. Plus, as Michael Young had already pointed out in 1958, in a meritocracy those at the top of the pyramid have higher self-esteem, since they confidently believe they did it all on their own.

We should not think that England has become elitist *as opposed to* meritocratic. On the contrary, as Vernon Bogdanor says, it has become elitist *because* it has tried to be meritocratic. The concern of Michael Young has materialised. The engine of education has produced a social class to populate the top echelons of society, that class has become self-reproducing, but has convinced itself that membership is on merit, and that this is for the common good.

Schools

> Take the school system in England as an example: to an
> outsider, it often looks like a mile wide but an inch deep.
> *Andreas Schleicher, OECD Director of Education*[16]

To understand how education functions as the engine of meritocracy you need some understanding of the school system. And the first thing to note is that the word 'system' is an overstatement.

England is not a country where you should look for a rational design, or a consistent implementation, of some long-term national policy on primary and secondary education. English people like to let their decisions take shape gradually, on a case by case basis. (Kate Fox, in her diagram of Englishness, classifies this outlook as empiricism.) Their education system, therefore, like their legal system, is essentially an accrual of case histories. To outsiders and incomers, the intricacies and coded subtleties of its terminology are quite bewildering. To understand the concern about a dramatic over-representation among the elite of those coming out of 'independent' schools, and a corresponding under-representation of those coming out of 'comprehensive' schools, it helps to know what those terms mean, and what connotations they have.

Many parents, like the J. Publics, spend a lot of time thinking about schools for their children, starting even before the children are born. Here are some of the terms in the schooling lexicon which they need to be familiar with:

> Academies, city technology colleges, comprehensive schools, direct grant schools, faith schools, free schools, grammar schools, independent schools, maintained schools, public schools, secondary modern schools, selective schools, special schools, specialist schools, state schools, studio schools, university technical colleges, voluntary aided schools, voluntary controlled schools.

These terms can overlap, and may be ambiguous. All public schools are independent schools, but not all independent schools are public schools. A grammar school may be a public school, or it may be a state school. A free school is a kind of an academy, of which there are two different kinds. And so on. Also, there is a lot of historical background, as well as more recent social and political developments, to be aware of. To the mystification of foreigners, for example, 'public schools' are in fact highly elite private schools.

As you learn the language of English education you become aware of the extent to which the prestige of public schools overshadows the rest of the education system. The original public schools are the secondary school equivalents of Oxbridge, which draws a disproportionate part of its intake from them. The Public Schools Act of 1868 gave these schools independence from the Crown, the established (that is, Anglican) Church, and the government. The term 'public' was used to indicate that access was not restricted on the basis of religion, occupation, or home location. The schools mentioned were Charterhouse, Eton, Harrow, Rugby, Shrewsbury, Westminster and Winchester. All of these schools had been around for a long time before 1868. Westminster School was founded in 1179, Winchester in 1382, Eton in 1440, and similarly for the others, so they all had well-established reputations and a hereditary clientele. The following year, the Headmasters' Conference was established, which is today the Headmasters' and Headmistresses' Conference (HMC)[17] for head teachers of elite independent schools. Being one of the 289 members of the HMC is often considered to be what defines a school as a 'public' school, and therefore one of the elite, just as being a member of the Russell Group identifies you as an elite university.

As for grammar schools: a long time ago, the church – which was then the Catholic Church – established a few schools alongside cathedrals and monasteries to teach Latin to future priests and monks. The King's School at Canterbury, for example, was founded in 597, and the King's School at Rochester in 604. By medieval times many such schools had expanded into teaching the *trivium*, which (you may remember from Chapter One) was the lower part of the liberal arts education, consisting of grammar, logic and rhetoric, and this is where the term *scholae grammaticales* comes from.

The Conservative government of Winston Churchill, while still fighting the Second World War, introduced the so-called tripartite system in the Education Act of 1944, whereby schools were divided into three types: grammar schools, secondary technical schools, and secondary modern schools. This was a tiered system, where children were placed in rank order of worth. The children considered to be most intellectually able went to grammar schools, which focused on academic subjects like classics, literature and abstract mathematics, in Newmanesque style. Grammar schools thus became a sort of state-funded middle-class counterpart to public schools. Children deemed to be adept at scientific and mechanical matters went to secondary technical schools, which focused on subjects like physics, chemistry and more technical mathematics, to become engineers or technicians. And the rest went to a secondary modern school, to focus on practical skills. The allocation of children to one of these schools took place on the basis of an examination at the end of primary school, at age 11, universally known as the 'eleven plus'. This is very much like the gold/silver/brass classification in Plato's myth of the metals.

By the late 1960s and early 1970s the social and political winds were blowing from a different direction, and grammar schools went out of favour. The Labour government of Harold Wilson introduced the comprehensive system, where schools did not have an entry test but took all comers from its own locality. In 1975, the Direct Grant Grammar Schools (Cessation of Grant) Regulations sought to require all direct grant schools to decide whether to become comprehensive schools (and then be funded by the local government), or independent schools funded by whatever fees they could raise. One way or another, however, some schools retained the ability to select their pupils on some criteria for determining merit, while also being state-funded. Today, there are 164 secondary schools in England which could be called 'grammar schools' in that sense: merit-selective, but state-funded. They are highly sought after by parents, but their existence remains politically contentious, and so for some time there was a kind of truce between the main political parties, saying that no new grammar schools will be built.

In 2015 this truce was broken, as *The Times* announced on its front page: 'First new grammar in 50 years approved'.[18] Technically, it turned out, this was an extension of an existing grammar school, rather than a totally new one, but the pretext was fairly transparent. In its leader article on the same day, *The Times* expressed the view that this was a 'highly political decision' which could divide communities, and advised the prime minister to resist pressure from his backbenchers for a nationwide return to grammar schools. In 2016, with a different but still Conservative prime minister in office, a government initiative was launched to clear the way for more new grammar schools. That initiative was however scuppered by the Conservatives losing their majority in the election of 2017.

Once you have decoded the terminology of different kinds of schools in England, it becomes clear that there are four main distinguishing features. These are:

- Selection: whether or not the school can decide for itself who to admit, or must take all comers from its catchment area. If the former, the decision is typically taken 'on merit', but also sometimes on other criteria, such as faith.
- Governance: whether or not the school is state-controlled – typically via the 'local authority', which is the city or regional government – or has an independent board of governors or trustees.

- Finance: whether the school is mainly dependent on government funding, or mainly raises its own finances.
- Curriculum: whether or not the school can set its own curriculum, or must follow the national curriculum. (In parallel, there is also the question whether or not the school can appoint teachers of their choice, who may or may not have a national teaching qualification.)

One manifestation of navigating between these various questions are the schools called 'academies', which were first introduced by the Labour governments of Tony Blair and Gordon Brown. These are non-selective and state-funded, but free of local authority control. They do not need to follow the national curriculum but must meet the same core subject requirements in maths, science and English. The same idea was followed by the succeeding Coalition government of Conservatives and Liberal Democrats, led by Messrs Cameron and Clegg, who also started a variation called 'free schools', these being academies by law but in addition could appoint teachers who are not required to have qualified teacher status.

Such, then, is a rough outline of the categories into which the 3,268 secondary schools in England are divided.[19] As regards quality, the (national) Department of Education makes available data for all schools,[20] in the following categories:

- Attainment, with 56 measures for 'key stage 5', which is the age group 16–18
- Pupil absence rates
- Expenditure per pupil (in various classes of expenditure)
- School workforce (numbers of teachers, plus staff–student ratios and average salary)
- Census (the demographic distribution of the student population, including % with English not as first language)
- Education Destination measure (that is, which educational establishments pupils go to from secondary school)

In addition, there is an inspectorate of schools, called the Office for Standards in Education, Children's Services and Skills (Ofsted), which is responsible for inspecting and evaluating schools. Ofsted inspectors will visit a school to carry out an inspection, and produce a report which must, inter alia, cover the achievement of pupils at the school, the quality of teaching in the school, the behaviour and safety of the pupils, and the quality of leadership and management at the school. Inspectors must also consider 'the spiritual, moral, social and cultural development' of pupils at the school, and the extent to which the school caters for disabled pupils and those with special educational needs.[21] The report is summarised by a ranking on a four-point scale: 'outstanding', 'good', 'requires improvement' (formerly 'satisfactory') or 'inadequate'. The entire report, with the concluding judgement, of every school in the country is available on the Ofsted website, and usually the school website as well.

The fact that England has a wide variety of secondary schools has not served as any deterrent to ranking them. On the contrary, the rich data set from the Department of Education, plus the comprehensive Ofsted reports, have created a ranker's paradise. Most national newspapers publish an annual schools ranking, usually in terms of school-leaving results. Actually there are different school-leaving qualifications, ranging from A levels to more recent variations such as the International Baccalaureate, the BTEC national diploma (neither of which, despite the names, are bachelor's degrees) and the Cambridge Pre-U, not to mention the Scottish Highers. There are also different examining bodies. But no matter. Rankings just ignore all of that. *The Guardian*, for example, ranks over 4,000 schools in one list. The *Financial Times* only ranks about 2,000 schools. *The Independent* provides separate lists of their top 100 comprehensive schools, top 100 independent schools, and top 100 selective schools. To help your child get into a good secondary school, the *Sunday Times* will helpfully publish a ranking of their top 200 primary schools.[22] Naturally the newspaper rankings all use different methods, and so usually arrive at different results. Most rankings are available on the web, and most allow filtering by locality, so that parents, or even prospective parents, can check out schools in their vicinity online.

Equal opportunity?

> Ability is of little account without opportunity.
> *Napoleon Bonaparte*

It is easy to believe, as Mr Blair did, that a meritocracy must be a good thing. We assume that a meritocracy would be fair, and we assume that it would be for the common good. These assumptions suit our social conscience so well that they are usually left unexamined. If pressed, however, we would probably say that a meritocracy is fair in the sense of creating equal opportunity for everybody to have a go at getting to the top, and that it serves the common good by increasing social mobility.

A meritocracy would be virtuous, therefore, in so far as it is based on equal opportunity and delivers social mobility. To what extent is this the case in England? More particularly, in so far as the meritocracy is constructed by the engine of education, to what extent do we have equality of education and social mobility generated by education? When we look at the evidence, you have to wonder.

Let us rejoin Jane and Joe Public, and their children Jimmy and Jenny, whom we met in Chapter Three. In December 2013 the Sutton Trust, whose motto is 'Improving social mobility through education', published a study titled *Parent Power? Using Money and Information to Boost Children's Chances of Educational Success.* Based on a YouGov survey, the report shows that when it comes to securing a good education for their children, middle-class parents like the J. Publics have sharp elbows.

More than two thirds of professionals would pay for weekly music, drama or sporting lessons for their children (compared to 47% of working-class parents and 31% of the lowest-income parents). About one in three of professional parents have moved house to an area they consider to have good schools; 18% had moved to live in the catchment area of a specific school; 3% admitted to using a relative's address to get their children into a particular school; and 2% had bought a second home for the same purpose. Six per cent of parents admitted to attending church services when they did not previously do so, in order to get their child into a church school. The Chairman of the Sutton Trust commented:

This research suggests that those with money actively choose to live near good schools, employ tutors and ensure their children have extra lessons and enrichment activities that are often too expensive for other families to afford. This provides a significant advantage in school choice and in developing the cultural capital that is so important to social mobility and later success.[23]

One of the authors of the report, Prof Becky Francis, spoke in the same vein:

Our research shows just how far equality of opportunity is being undermined by the greater purchasing power of some parents. The ability for some parents but not others to use financial resources to secure their children's achievement poses real impediments for social mobility, which need to be recognised and addressed as detrimental to society.[24]

As an example of the advantage of greater purchasing power, the Social Mobility and Child Poverty Commission points out that unpaid internships give an advantage to those who can afford to work for free, and wants to ban them (against the wish of professional firms).[25]

Professor Dorling, in *Inequality and the 1%*, takes it further: 'although they will hope to keep it quiet, those at the top will use all the skills and advantages they have, honest and dishonest, to remain there'. But all parents, top or bottom, can be tigers. In what seems to be one of the first prosecutions of its kind, in September 2014 a mother was fined £500 and sentenced to 100 hours of community service after forging a tenancy agreement to secure a place at a successful school for her 11-year-old daughter. 'Mums just want the best for their children', the woman told a reporter afterwards – 'they want the best education for them possible. I am still shaken by this experience.'[26]

Dishonesty can come by degrees. Another couple lived about 5 miles away from the primary school they wanted their 4-year-old daughter to go to, but the husband's mother happened to live on the same street as the school. So the husband changed his address, registering himself on all official records as living with his mother. And it was his address that featured on the child's school application. After the application had been successful, he promptly changed his address back to the original – having continued to live in his own property throughout.[27]

All sorts of innovative ways can be found of gaming whatever system there is. Many schools, for example, give priority to admitting siblings of current pupils. The trick, therefore, is to get your first child into your school of choice, perhaps by renting a property in the catchment area for a sufficient period. After that the sibling clause comes into play, leaving the family free to move away – if, indeed, they had ever moved in. And it can get more sophisticated. Free schools, for example, must take all comers from their catchment area – but that just means catchment areas will shrink for successful schools, as parents compete to get closer to it. In January 2016 *The Times* reported[28] that 90 primary schools offered no places for children living further than 300 metres away, with the smallest catchment area a mere 92 metres from the school. Property prices around that school are correspondingly high, both for renting and for buying.

Schools, too, can quickly spot an opportunity. After the introduction of academies, a number of fee-paying private schools voluntarily converted to this mode. The school wins, because they now get government funding rather than having to rely on fee income alone. The parents win because they gain the established brand name of the school for their children without paying large fees. And the Russell Group wins because they can recruit more children from that school now that it no longer counts as a private school. Queen Elizabeth's Grammar School in Blackburn, for example, founded in 1509, had been a fee-paying school charging £10,000 a year. However, its numbers had been falling, from 1,200 in 1997 to 478 in 2012. At that time the headmaster was quoted as saying that it was becoming increasingly difficult even for high-earning parents to afford fees. The school opted to become a free school, which happened in September 2014. By January 2016, not only were student numbers up to more than 1,000, but Queen Elizabeth's Grammar had rocketed to the position of most oversubscribed primary school in the country.[29]

It is no surprise that mums – and dads – want the best for their children, and will do what they can to help them. In an article titled 'Milky Way kid sees his name written in the stars', *The Times* of 7 January 2013 reports on a 15-year-old boy who had just become co-author of a paper in *Nature*, having written a computer program to visualise the position and rotation speed of satellite galaxies.[30] He did that while on work experience at Strasbourg Observatory. The young man was modest about his achievement. 'It was my father's team', he said, 'who explained the implications.' His father is a researcher at the Observatory, and it was the father who set his son the assignment.

Another *Times* article[31] reports how a 19-year-old intern at an investment bank in London, through his own investment company, made a $46m deal to develop an oil field in Siberia. This precocious young man had already, three years earlier, been linked with a takeover bid for the Danish football champions FC Copenhagen. 'Like father, like son', is the comment from *The Times*. The young man is called Arkadiy Abramovich, and his father is the Russian oligarch Roman Abramovich, owner of Chelsea football club.

Our interpretation of merit can be quite flexible when family connections matter. What would we say, for example, about the election in 2009 of a young man of 27 as a Fellow of the Royal Society 'for services to science'? Becoming an FRS is very prestigious, and highly meritorious. There are 80 Nobel Laureates among the Fellows of the Royal Society.[32] So the young man elected as FRS must be truly exceptional. And so he is. His name is William, Duke of Cambridge, and he is second in line to the throne of the United Kingdom.

Now contrast these stories with the discovery of a phenomenon called the Mpemba effect. More than 50 years ago, a schoolboy called Erasto Mpemba, in what was then called Tanganyika, noticed something curious in his cookery class. When he put a hot ice cream mix in the freezer it froze faster than a mix put in at room temperature. He asked his physics teacher why this would be the case. The teacher said that he must be mistaken. So he tried it again and the hot liquid still froze faster. Later he moved to another school, and asked his new teacher the same question, but got pretty much the same answer. Then, however, he heard of a physics professor from Dar Es Salaam visiting his school. So, apparently to the embarrassment of his classmates, he asked the same question again. The professor, called Denis Osborne, had never heard of such a thing, but he told his laboratory technician to try it out with hot water. To everybody's astonishment, the hot water froze faster than water at room temperature. In 1969, Mr Mpemba and Professor Osborne published a joint paper on the phenomenon in *Physics Education*.[33] In 2012 the Royal Society of Chemistry held a competition to find the best explanation of the Mpemba effect. It elicited 22,000 entries, and Mr Mpemba himself went from Tanzania to award the prize.

Whether through the Sutton Trust report, or anecdotes such as those above, we know that parent power matters. More generally, influence matters. Somerset Maugham, in one of his short stories, casually observes 'It is one of the advantages of democratic government that, *if you have sufficient influence,* merit, which otherwise might pass unnoticed, generally receives its due reward'[34] (my italics – CB). Merit by itself may not suffice for success, but influence plus merit would practically guarantee it. The J. Publics know this. They also know that education and influence mutually reinforce each other. That is why they will use all the means at their disposal to get their child into a good school, and a good university. And so we have a new equation: Success = Merit + Influence. Which, expanding 'merit' in the Michael Young way, becomes: Success = Ability + Effort + Influence. There is probably still room for luck, in the sense of being in the right place at the right time with the right ideas or skills, but by and large these three components together would generally generate the 'due reward' which the meritocracy so easily lay claim to.

In addition, there is a long-term effect. Education is a mechanism whereby influence and connections are transmitted to the next generation. When the high fliers intermarry, not only is the sum of their advantages greater than the parts, they are also able to transmit their bundle of advantages to their children. That is how the meritocracy becomes hereditary. Again, the J. Publics know this. Procuring the best possible brand names on the pathway of a 'good education' yields an evolutionary advantage.

All of this leads us rather far away from equality of opportunity. The aim of the equality agenda, I said in Chapter Four, is to decouple circumstance from destiny. Parent power undermines that aim.

The idea of a meritocracy harbours an inherent contradiction. It claims the mantle of fairness, yet also undermines the equality of opportunity on which the fairness claim is based. And it does so on the basis of a putative virtue: mums and dads only want the best for their children. It is socially acceptable – even considered admirable – for parents to deploy their financial and social capital towards procuring a 'good education' for their children. We do not think of this practice as nepotism. But is that not somewhat curious? Nepotism, according to the eighth edition of the *Concise Oxford Dictionary*, is 'favouritism shown to relatives in conferring offices or privileges' – in other words, giving them jobs. Parent power does not consist of giving jobs to your children (or at least not mainly), but it does consist of giving them the advantages that will secure them a job when the time comes. Parent power secures the future employment of your children just as effectively as nepotism would secure their current employment. It thus renders nepotism unnecessary, and allows your children to claim the virtue of having succeeded on merit.

What must have seemed like a good idea at the time of Mr Blair has now been inverted. Instead of acquiring a good education on the basis of merit, you are now considered to acquire merit through a good education. That becomes a problem when the good education is not equally available to all.

> In the UK, good results can be bought through private education or by buying housing near to 'good' schools – so the cycle of rising domination by the richest continues, generation on generation. In no other OECD country, apart from Chile, is a higher proportion of national income spent on private education by so few – for so few. Half of all A and A* grades at A level in the UK are secured by the 7 percent of students who are privately educated, and 4.5 times as much is spent on teaching them as on the average state-educated student. The number of youngsters from the poorest backgrounds found in the most elite universities in both the US and the UK is similar to the number of people

who win large sums of money on national lotteries
– extremely low. Students from the most advantaged
areas are nearly 10 times more likely to take a place at a
'top' university than those from the most disadvantaged
neighbourhoods (and the gap grows even wider when
smaller areas of the country are compared). Four private
schools and one highly selective state sixth-form college
send more children to Oxbridge than do 2,000 other
secondary schools, while the average private school
fee is now £14,000 a year. But the richest 1 per cent
have access to so much spare wealth that, for many of
them, paying school and university fees up front is a
minor expense.[35]

The point is that a good education can be bought, and there are
many keen buyers who see it as the first step on a ladder of success.
As an added benefit, the purchase of a good education brings with it
social advantage, such as personal confidence and valuable networks.
Would David Cameron, with no long track record of political or
other achievement, have become leader of the opposition and then
prime minister without his easy breezy Eton confidence?

Influence will help merit to receive its due reward. When that
becomes an accepted fact, then the engine of education may, as
Michael Young feared, be doing exactly the opposite of what it was
supposed to do. It was supposed to create equality of opportunity
and a more egalitarian society. Instead, it is consolidating privilege.
Meritocracy, then, is not self-evidently a good thing.

Mind the gap

> In a grossly unequal society, the privileges of the
> parents unfailingly become the privileges of the
> children.
> *James Bloodworth, The Myth of the Meritocracy*[36]

To repeat: we assume that a meritocracy would be fair, in the
sense of creating equal opportunity, and that it would be for the
common good, in the sense of promoting social mobility. We have

questioned the presumption of equal opportunity. Now what about social mobility?

A meritocratic society, said Michael Young, is underpinned by a meritocratic education. So what is the role of higher education in social mobility?

Higher education, we may like to think, is both a private benefit and a public good, but we tend to pay more attention to the former than the latter. The reason why parents are so anxious for the children to go to a 'good school' and then on to a 'good university' are essentially utilitarian: it will serve them well in having a 'good career', which is a euphemism for earning more money. There does not seem to be much left of the Newmanesque idea of studying a subject for its own sake – let alone subjects of the kind Newman had in mind. Increasingly, it seems, we see education not so much as an end in itself, which is to expand your mind, but as a means to an end, which is to improve your prospects.

So clearly has the case been made for higher education as a private benefit, that this benefit has a name, and can be quantified. It is called the 'graduate premium' (briefly alluded to in Chapter Three), and defined as the average amount by which the lifetime earnings of graduates exceed the lifetime earnings of non-graduates. The idea has been around for some time. A 2004 report from the Higher Education Careers Services Unit,[37] for example, says: 'All the evidence suggests that employers continue to pay a premium to degree holders', and speaks of 'the graduate earnings premium – the additional earnings paid by employers to those who have a degree'. There is such strong evidence that this is the case that the discussion is more about the quantum of the graduate premium than about its existence. A recent OECD report says that 'Across OECD countries, 25-64 year-old adults with a tertiary degree earn on average 56% more than those with only upper secondary education'.[38] With that kind of information available – in many cases by subject – prospective students can do a calculation regarding return on investment: the cost of going to university against the quantum of the graduate premium.

Very well. But is there something similar on the public-good side? Is there something we could call a 'public-good premium', which would show the value of higher education not just to the individual, but to society? And if so, what is it? Again, utilitarian arguments can be made: an educated workforce is good for the economy; a strong base in research and development is an investment for innovation and so on. But the *moral* claim of the meritocracy, explicit or implicit, is that an important aspect – perhaps the most important aspect – of the public-good premium of higher education is that it will improve social mobility. More specifically, the assumption is that higher education contributes to social mobility in the sense of decreasing the gap between the advantaged and the disadvantaged – it helps to make society more egalitarian.

This interpretation of a public-good premium of higher education, however, is by no means as well supported by evidence as the graduate premium for the individual. We still need to ask the existential question: is there such a public-good premium at all? Does higher education really diminish the gap between the advantaged and the disadvantaged? Does it really contribute, not just towards a more prosperous, but also towards a more just society?

The question is broad and imprecise, but it can be made more specific. For example, we could narrow down the idea of 'the disadvantaged' to a specific cohort of students, namely those recruited into university under widening participation initiatives. What happens to them when they graduate? Are they then fully on a par, in terms of their career and life course, with those James and Jennifer Publics who entered with every advantage that parent power could procure? Or does the advantage gap persist despite having gone to the same university, and getting the same degree?

There is a growing literature on graduate outcomes and graduate employability, and some attention to the first destinations of graduates from under-represented groups, but a paucity of research on what happens to widening participation students in the long run after graduation.[39] Such research as is available, however, raises serious questions about whether higher education does indeed help to narrow the gap between the advantaged and the disadvantaged. Some of the evidence rather seem to point the other way.

In a research report titled *Mapping the Occupational Destinations of New Graduates*[40] the Centre for Analysis of Youth Transitions explored whether the chances of a graduate securing a 'high-status' job six months and then three years after graduation differ according to socioeconomic background. It found that access to higher status professions is unequal: graduates originally from disadvantaged backgrounds are less likely to secure such roles. Interestingly, the difference was not found after six months, but kicked in after three years – and particularly so for males.

A similar report, this time from the Institute of Education in London, titled *Who Gets the Top Jobs? The Role of Family Background and Networks in Recent Graduates' Access to High Status Professions*[41] concludes that privately educated graduates are a third more likely to enter into high-status occupations than state-educated graduates from similarly affluent families and neighbourhoods. They also found that the use of networks provides an additional advantage over and above background.

Lower down the hierarchy of social class, a PhD study at Cardiff University[42] explored the differences in employability between middle-class and working-class students. The project found that middle-class graduates were generally more successful in the graduate labour market than their working-class peers, even with similar credentials and from the same university. Academic barriers to the labour market affected all graduates equally, but middle-class graduates augmented their employability by drawing on economic, social and cultural capital to help get a job. Working-class graduates have less access to these forms of capital, which results in different outcomes in the labour market. The author concludes that:

> The widening participation agenda is premised upon a belief that higher education can be a force for social mobility but because social mobility is socially and culturally contingent, HE [higher education] can only be a force for social mobility if it provides the institutional conditions necessary to acquire social networks and dispositions upon which employability is based.

The researchers of *Who Gets the Top Jobs?* summarise the overall issue as follows:

> The UK government has stated that its aim is to create a society in which each individual, regardless of background, has an equal chance of realising their

potential (Cabinet Office, *Opening Doors Breaking Barriers: A Strategy for Social Mobility*). However, the UK labour market displays relatively low intergenerational income mobility, high income inequality and educational attainment varies significantly by socioeconomic background. Whilst the UK is not alone in facing these problems, they are arguably more acute in the UK than in many other European countries.[43]

One report after another of the Social Mobility and Child Poverty Commission makes the same point. Commenting on the 2014 report *Elitist Britain* (from which I quoted some stark numbers earlier in this chapter), its chair wrote on the centre page of *The Times*:[44]

> Young people are on the wrong side of the divide that is opening up in society.… The risk is real that this generation – from low-income families especially – will simply not have the same opportunities to progress as their parents' generation.
>
> I hope today's report makes uncomfortable reading for all political parties. Each of them has made too little effort to reconcile the social ends they say they want with the policy means to which they are committed.

A later report of June 2015, titled *Non-educational barriers to the elite profession evaluations*,[45] shows that working-class applicants struggle to get access to top jobs in the UK.

> The research is the product of extensive interviews with staff from 13 elite law, accountancy and financial services firms, who together are responsible for 45,000 of the best jobs in the country.
>
> It finds that elite firms are systematically excluding bright working-class applicants from their workforce. Data collected for the project showed that as much as 70% of job offers in 2014 were to graduates who had been educated at a selective state or fee-paying school, compared to 4% and 7% of the population as a whole.

> Rt Hon. Alan Milburn, the Chair of the Commission, said: "This research shows that young people with working-class backgrounds are being systematically locked out of top jobs. Elite firms seem to require applicants to pass a 'poshness test' to gain entry. Inevitably that ends up excluding youngsters who have the right sort of grades and abilities but whose parents do not have the right sort of bank balances."

We have already seen the effect of parent power getting the 'right' kids into the 'right' schools. The background of a good school then goes a long way towards helping with the poshness test. Here is the *Times* journalist Sathnam Sanghera – who grew up as 'the boy with the topknot' in a Punjabi Sikh community in Wolverhampton – commenting from personal experience:

> The only way to make it into established professions in the 21st century is either to be born in a particular class, or, as suggested by this week's report from the Social Mobility and Child Poverty Commission, to start mimicking the behaviour of the privileged few. The real value of my education, first as a boy on a fully assisted place at an independent grammar school, and then at Cambridge University, was not academic, but social.[46]

In view of all this, the easy assumption of the meritocracy that higher education increases social mobility begins to look rather thin. Origin and circumstance continue to play a large part in determining destiny.

Academics distinguish between 'intra-generational' social mobility, which is what happens when some children get to be better off in later life than those who were their peers when young, and 'inter-generational' social mobility, which is what happens when children are generally better off than their parents. Neither seems to be working. While origin and circumstance continue to determine the destiny of most children, intra-generational social mobility will not happen. As for inter-generational social mobility, the current cohort of young people may be the first generation in a long time who will not be better off than their parents.

The stalling of inter-generational social mobility is not confined to the UK. Having already quoted Chair of the US Federal Reserve Ben Bernanke on the meritocracy, here is his successor Janet L. Yellen on inequality:

> The extent of and continuing increase in inequality in the United States greatly concern me. The past several decades have seen the most sustained rise in inequality since the 19th century after more than 40 years of narrowing inequality following the Great Depression. By some estimates, income and wealth inequality are near their highest levels in the past hundred years, much higher than the average during that time span and probably higher than for much of American history before then. It is no secret that the past few decades of widening inequality can be summed up as significant income and wealth gains for those at the very top and stagnant living standards for the majority. I think it is appropriate to ask whether this trend is compatible with values rooted in our nation's history, among them the high value Americans have traditionally placed on equality of opportunity.[47]

To understand the failure of social mobility we should look not just at the numbers, but at the conceptual framework. We can do so by asking a question we have asked twice before: in principle, could everybody be socially mobile?

As before, the question is a thought experiment, not an empirical matter. Suppose we managed to wipe influence out of the success equation, to the point where we had really attained true equality of opportunity. Suppose further that we had an educational system where all schools were of equal standard, and treated everybody exactly the same. Under these ideal conditions, could everybody be upwardly socially mobile? If we say yes, then we have accepted one interpretation of social mobility; if we say no, another.

As was the case with the concept of excellence, the distinction we are led to is between a substantive (or absolute) and a comparative (that is, relative) interpretation of social mobility. It is similar to the distinction between excellence as high standards, and excellence as outperforming others. The substantive interpretation is what we have in mind when we say social mobility is about raising the standard of living for everyone. Doing so is perfectly possible, and indeed has been the normal expectation for a few generations. So, in that sense, everybody can indeed be socially mobile. However, this substantive interpretation of social mobility is not the common one of the J. Publics. The more common interpretation is the comparative version, where social mobility means doing better than others. These 'others' may be your childhood peers, or your parents, but in either case social mobility means climbing higher up the ladder than them. On this interpretation, it is clearly impossible for everyone to enjoy social mobility. To say that everybody can climb higher up the ladder than others would be like saying that every child can be above average.

Comparative social mobility may worsen even when substantive social mobility improves. It is quite possible that the gap between the top and the bottom may lengthen even while the average standard of living may be rising. And that is exactly what has been happening over the past few decades. Everybody is getting better off in absolute terms, but in relative terms some are getting *more* more better off, and more quickly. The rich are getting richer far more quickly than the poor are getting less poor.

The charity Oxfam uses a telling illustration of this phenomenon in its annual reports. The 2016 report points out that if you take the 62 richest people in the world and put them in a bus, then the net worth of the people in that bus would equal the combined wealth of all of the bottom half of the world population. The 2015 report required a bigger bus, taking 80 people. In 2010 you would have needed a few buses, or a Boeing, to take 388 people.[48]

So, in our stratified society, the gap is widening between the top and the bottom. In that sense, inequality is increasing. And there is a strong argument that this is a very bad thing indeed, for all concerned.

The key work in this regard is a book titled *The Spirit Level: Why Equality is Better for Everyone*, by Richard Wilkinson and Kate Pickett.[49] As health economists of considerable experience, Wilkinson and Pickett knew that health inequality follows social stratification: the poor are less healthy than the middle class, who are less healthy than the elite. Inequality, they point out, is known to be associated with lower life expectancy, higher rates of infant mortality, shorter stature, poor self-reported health, low birthweight, AIDS and depression.[50] They also knew that health inequality is worse in countries where social inequality is high. What they demonstrate, with a wealth of evidence, in *The Spirit Level* is that the same strong correlation exists between inequality and other social problems.

> It has been known for some years that poor health and violence are more common in more unequal societies. However, in the course of our research we became aware that almost all problems which are more common at the bottom of the social ladder are more common in more unequal societies. It is not just ill health and violence, but also, as we will show in later chapters, a host of other social problems. Almost all of them contribute to the widespread concern that modern societies are, despite their affluence, social failures.[51]

Wilkinson and Pickett use income inequality as a simple but powerful initial proxy for the broad concept of inequality. Specifically, they use the ratio between the income of the richest 20% of the population and the poorest 20% of the population, for which United Nations data is available. They are equally precise about social problems, sticking to those for which they could find reliable and internationally comparable data sets. These are: level of trust, mental illness (including drug and alcohol addiction), life expectancy and infant mortality, obesity, children's educational performance, teenage births, homicides, imprisonment rates and social mobility.

In each case, the graphs look the same: social desirables, such as trust, decrease as inequality increases, and social undesirables, such as imprisonment, increase as inequality increases.

> One of the points which emerge from Chapters 4–12 is a tendency for some countries to do well on just about everything and others to do badly. You can predict a country's performance on one outcome from a knowledge of others. If – for instance – a country

does badly on health, you can predict with some
confidence that it will also imprison a larger proportion
of its population, have more teenage pregnancies, lower
literacy scores, more obesity, worse mental health, and
so on. Inequality seems to make countries socially
dysfunctional across a wide range of outcomes.[52]

The point that hits home is that social ills are not a function of
poverty, but of inequality. What matters for the wellbeing of society
is not how rich or poor the country is. What matters is the distance
between the richest and the poorest. As wealth disparity grows, the
physical, mental and social health of society declines. Conversely,
the more equally wealth is distributed the better for the wellbeing
of society.

So which countries do well, and which do badly?

Internationally, at the healthy end of the distribution
we always seem to find the Scandinavian countries and
Japan. At the opposite end, suffering high rates of most
of the health and social problems, are usually the USA,
Portugal and the UK.[53]

One of the exemplars of social problems used by Wilkinson and
Pickett is children's educational performance. For comparison
between countries they use something called PISA scores. PISA is
the Programme for International Student Assessment, started by
the OECD in 2000, which does a three-yearly assessment of the
performance of 15-year-olds in reading, mathematics and science.
Inevitably, this leads to international PISA score league tables. Every
time PISA results come out there is consternation and lament in the
UK about its lowly ranking. In the 2012 PISA results, for example,
the UK was ranked 26th (out of 65 countries) for mathematics,
20th for science and 23rd for reading. The USA fared even worse,
coming 36th for mathematics, 28th for science and 24th for reading.
And it is not getting any better: in the 2009 results the UK came
28th, 16th and 25th, respectively, and in 2006 it was 24th, 14th
and 17th. Likewise for the USA.[54]

This raises an interesting point. The USA and the UK are, as
their politicians are fond of pointing out, way ahead of the pack

when it comes to university league tables. So what is going on? How can the same countries which perform outstandingly well on university rankings do so poorly on the performance of 15-year-olds? It is difficult to avoid the conclusion that there is a strong indication here of educational inequality. In the same way as income inequality is defined as the distance between the rich and the poor, we may define educational inequality as the distance between the low-performing masses at school level, and the top-performing elite at research level. In both cases, then, the UK and the USA stand out as affluent societies with high educational inequality. So the disparity between high performance in university league tables and low performance on PISA scores is not a paradox at all, but fits the overall pattern pointed out by Wilkinson and Pickett: another inequality indicator of affluent societies manifesting social dysfunction.

I distinguished earlier between the graduate premium and the public-good premium, the former being the extent to which universities bring benefit to the individual and the latter the extent to which they contribute to a more egalitarian society. It seems, now, that we have an inverse relationship: the higher the graduate premium, the lower the public-good premium. The better off graduates become, relative to their childhood peers or to their parents, the worse off society becomes in terms of the gap between the top and the bottom echelons of society. And the bigger the gap between the top and the bottom, the more symptoms there are of social dysfunction. Higher education thus becomes complicit in social inequality. And so the assumption that the meritocracy serves the common good does not stand up to scrutiny.

In summary: meritocracy is not working, and perhaps it cannot work at all.

> A vague commitment from our politicians to build a 'meritocracy' is not enough. Nor is it desirable: a perfectly stratified meritocracy, in which everyone knew their station based on 'merit', would be a deeply unpleasant place to live. Any genuine attempt to improve social mobility must start by reducing the gap between rich and poor.[55]

This quote (from James Bloodworth's *The Myth of the Meritocracy*) illustrates the chicken-and-egg nature of the two main policy arguments regarding merit and equality. Those who extol the virtues of the meritocracy say that a focus on merit will speed up social mobility and hence enhance equality. Opponents argue the reverse: a focus on reducing inequality will speed up social mobility and allow merit to flourish.

My view is that neither of these will work unless we understand and address a fundamental conceptual problem with 'social mobility', which is that we uncritically think of it as one-dimensional movement. Social mobility is seen as nothing but moving up (or down) a linear scale – like climbing up or down a ladder. Why is that? And is it right?

6

Linear Thinking

The idea of the ladder

We are for the ladder. Let all try their best to climb.
Winston Churchill[1]

Rankings and league tables, quality as a positional good, meritocracy as rank order of worth, society stratified into classes, hierarchy instead of diversity – what do these phenomena have in common? They are all linear representations. They compress reality into a ranked list, in which higher up means better and lower down means worse. They encourage us to fall into line. When we do, we acknowledge that the ranking, the list, the line-up, is an order of esteem. It is also called the ladder of success.

The idea of the ladder is strong, and promoted in many ways, particularly by those positioned on the highest rungs. Consider, for example, the case of Winston Churchill. Without detracting from our admiration for the great man, we may note that his career rather neatly illustrates Somerset Maugham's maxim that the ladder of success is more easily climbed when merit has the helping hand of influence.

The young Winston had illustrious family connections. His father was Lord Randolph Churchill, a younger son of the 7th Duke of Marlborough. The 1st Duke of Marlborough started life as just plain John Churchill, son of a minor squire called Sir Winston Churchill. This John Churchill played a key part in the

Glorious Revolution of 1688, and turned out to be a soldier of genius. He repeatedly defeated the allied forces of the Sun King Louis XIV, most famously at the Battle of Blenheim in 1704. In grateful appreciation, Queen Anne and Parliament awarded him a dukedom, a perpetual pension of £5,000, and a vast stately home called Blenheim Palace, which you can still visit at Woodstock in Oxfordshire. This is where the later Winston Churchill was born, in 1874. The 8th Duke, Lord Randolph's elder brother, died young, and was succeeded as the 9th Duke by his son, Winston's cousin and contemporary, called 'Sunny' after his courtesy birth title of the Earl of Sunderland.

> Winston Churchill did have family advantages, of course, and was determined to capitalise upon them. His parents' connections gave him immediate access to everyone who counted in the hierarchical society of the day. He had become a second lieutenant in the 4th Hussars in February 1895. But even in this lowly rank, he associated with the Prince of Wales, the Aylesbury scandal now forgotten. Winston also knew the prime minister – this was now Lord Roseberry, who would later invite the young politician to stay at one or other of his country houses. And Winston's mother, the vivacious Lady Randolph, seemed to know everyone. The young man only had to ask and the introductions were forthcoming. He instantly moved into the top social circles at a time when high society and high politics were still coterminous. 'Introduction – connections – powerful friends – a name – good advice well followed – all these things count', he acknowledged to his mother, ' – but they only lead to a certain point.'[2]

Churchill was no doubt correct in saying that influence can only get you so far, and you need merit to go all the way. The counterpoint, however, which he might well have acknowledged, is Maugham's observation that without influence merit might not get the opportunity to shine. Churchill himself actively and simultaneously leveraged ability, effort and connections. He found that he had a talent for writing, matching his inclination for self-promotion. So he started writing about his experiences in military campaigns, then became a war correspondent. These writings turned into successful books, and the consequent brand-name recognition was a contributory factor in a political career.

Connections helped with his literary career as well. His mother effectively became his agent. While still posted in India in early 1897, the young Winston became aware that Turkey had just declared war on Greece. He wanted to go there, not as a soldier but as a special correspondent. 'Of course nearly every paper has one there already', he wrote to his mother, 'but I have no doubt that you will find one to avail themselves of my services.' 'Lord Rothschild would be the person to arrange this for me as he knows everyone.' That particular effort did not work out, because the war was called off, but shortly afterwards Lady Churchill secured terms with the *Daily Telegraph* for her son to accompany the Malakand campaign, on the border of what is now Pakistan and Afghanistan. Winston's dispatches became his first book, *The Story of the Malakand Field Force*, on which a reviewer pleasingly connected the dots between family and personal merit: 'Lieut Winston Spencer Churchill, named if we mistake not, after the father of the first Duke of Marlborough, omits, indeed, the family hyphen from his name, but has evidently much of the genius of his uncle, of his father, and of their best-known progenitor.'

The matter of the missing hyphen is worth a small interlude. There was no 2nd Duke of Marlborough, because the 1st Duke had no surviving son, and the title passed through a daughter who had married a Spencer, Earl of Sunderland (the same Spencer family into which Princess Diana was later born). For almost a century, then, the family name of the Dukes of Marlborough was not Churchill, but Spencer. In 1817, however, the Churchill connection was reinvented by changing the family name to Spencer-Churchill, which is the name under which Winston was born. By dropping the hyphen Spencer came to be seen as merely a second Christian name, and thus the glory of the original name was restored. Clearly, every little bit helps.

'Let all try their best to climb', Churchill said – but in honesty he could have added 'with the aid of their family and friends.'

If, therefore, we are to conceptualise life as a perpetual effort to climb a ladder of success, we should acknowledge as part of that conceptualisation that some will have more help than others in getting on the ladder, or moving up from one rung to another. This is exactly the nature and function of parent power, exemplified by Winston Churchill's mother.

The idea of the ladder is a representation, a summary and a metaphor of the comparative (that is, relative) side of the various issues we have been discussing: quality, merit and social mobility. As regards quality, the idea of the ladder reflects and reinforces its interpretation as excellence: being better than the others. As discussed in Chapter Three, this means that not everybody can have quality, because not everybody could have climbed higher up the ladder of success than the others. Similarly, the idea of the ladder reflects and reinforces the conception of merit as nothing but a rank order of worth, as discussed in Chapter Five, which means that not everybody can have merit. And likewise, the ladder reflects and reinforces the idea of social mobility as relative rather than substantive – which, as we also saw in Chapter Five, forces us to conclude that not everybody could be socially mobile, not even in principle.

The ladder is not the only metaphor for the fundamental idea of worth as a linear order. We say that the cream will rise to the top. We talk about climbing up the greasy pole. We easily think of life as a race – a sprint towards success, in which the competitors separate into winners, also-rans, stragglers and losers. The *Times Higher Education*, in promoting yet another one of its many symposia on rankings, refers to 'The global higher education race' – with the subtitle 'Staying ahead of the chasing pack'.[3] The value judgement is much the same as with the ladder: winning is better than losing, and the top rung is a better place to be than the bottom ones. Or, conversely, winners deserve to be at the top. Even President Obama's $4.35 billion educational investment initiative of 2009 was called 'The Race to the Top'.

Whatever the metaphor of linearity, ladder, list, line, race or greasy pole, the fundamental characteristic of this way of thinking is that it is one-dimensional. It has no breadth. It does not allow any lateral movement. Somehow, we have allowed a lazy assumption to embed itself into our thinking about quality, merit and social mobility, namely that it is natural and inevitable for these concepts to be represented as a linear order. This lazy assumption, which I will call *linearism*, puts us at risk, because it rules out, even in principle, the possibility that quality, merit or social mobility can be attained by anybody. It rules out the possibility of equality of opportunity. It discriminates against equality, and legitimises inequality. On the assumption that everything is linearly ordered, of any two things one must perforce be 'better' than the other.

Some, indeed, having noticed that not everybody can be positioned at the top of the ladder, have then reached the rather depressing conclusion that in order for some to climb up others must slide down. *The Times*, for example, in an editorial commenting on the Social Mobility and Child Poverty Commission report of October 2014 (which I referenced in Chapter Six) draws exactly this conclusion: 'To encourage greater social mobility, it requires people to slide down the social ladder as well as climb it.'[4] The Social Mobility Commission Chair Alan Milburn deploys similar logic, expanding the metaphor of the glass ceiling preventing social mobility for some. There is a difficulty, he points out, in that while some are prevented from climbing the ladder of success by a glass ceiling, others – the advantaged – are saved by a glass floor from descending the ladder.[5] Therefore, he reckons, in order for social mobility to improve, not only the glass ceiling but also the glass floor needs to be shattered.

But this still leaves everybody stuck on that one-dimensional ladder, only being able to move up or down. Which raises a question: should we not consider the possibility of *lateral* social mobility? Similarly: should we not allow multiple dimensions of quality, or merit? Perhaps our problem lies not so much the conclusions we draw from the metaphor of the ladder, but the metaphor itself. Why should we confine ourselves to one-dimensionality?

The peril of arithmetic

> A good decision is based on knowledge and not on numbers.
>
> *Socrates to Melesias, in Plato's Laches*

It is a curious thing about mathematics that many people like to volunteer the information that they have never been any good at it.

By comparison, few people would, on meeting a novelist, begin the conversation by saying that they have always been rubbish at writing.

Along with their own presumed incompetence, most people are quite ready to believe that those who are mathematically competent must be right, and that formulas and calculation will always yield true results. In this belief they embrace the wrong half of an ambiguity. Performing a calculation is usually true in the sense of being correct; it is not necessarily true, however, in the sense of yielding a meaningful result. The distinction is important because the mere fact that you have correctly performed a calculation does not guarantee that the result means something. That is the peril of arithmetic: all too easily we confuse accuracy of calculation with validity of conclusion.

Rankings and league tables are usually correctly calculated, but they rely on many arbitrary choices, as outlined in Chapter Two. Therefore, the conclusions drawn from any ranking are only valid in so far as you believe that the choices made in constructing that ranking are somehow the right ones, or at least better than other choices. And the only test you have of your choices being the 'right' ones is if your calculation gives you the 'right' answer, which is the answer that you believed in at the outset anyway.

At the beginning of Chapter Two I quoted John Kay, first Director of the Said Business School at Oxford (earlier also Director of the Institute for Fiscal Studies, and a regular columnist for the *Financial Times*), on 'the modern curse of bogus quantification'. In his book *Obliquity* he goes on to give an example:

> The United Nations produces an index of human development ... under which countries are ranked from Iceland (at the top) to Sierra Leone (at the bottom). The high-level objective of human development is translated into three goals or states: longevity, educational standards and gross domestic product (GDP). The longevity measure, for example, takes life expectancy at birth (L) and then calculates $(L-25)/60$, so that if life expectancy is 82 years the score is 0.95. The educational score is the average of the literacy rate (with a weight of two-thirds) and the educational enrolment rate (with a

weight of one-third). The overall score is calculated by averaging the scores on the three intermediate states.

The intentions are admirable. But why should we measure human development in this particular way? Some people might suggest that a measure of human development should include personal freedom, or the strength of religious belief (or its absence), or environmental awareness. Why? Or why not? Even if we agree that health, education and income are the relevant criteria, then should we measure them in this way, and weight them in this way? Why? Or why not? The problem is not just that these are questions on which people might disagree. The problem is that it is difficult to see any criteria by which their disagreements might be resolved. The supposed objectivity of the measurement of human development – which is calculated to three places of decimals – is spurious.[6]

Numbers, and arithmetic, and mathematics generally, are great tools for helping us make decisions. But arithmetic cannot do your thinking for you. In using numbers and calculation to reach a decision, we should not fool ourselves into believing that the outcome of the calculation determines our choice. On the contrary, it is our choice of calculation that determines the outcome. Which numbers to use, by which algorithm to combine them, and how to interpret the result, these are all choices we make ourselves. To think, then, that the numerical outcome has some kind of objective reality over and above what we ourselves have built into it is a fallacy. It confuses accuracy of calculation with validity of conclusion.

By way of example, consider the idea of risk management and, more specifically, a document called a risk register (of which any university or large organisation would have several, corresponding to its various initiatives). The aim of such a register is to plan ahead, by identifying and keeping track of the envisaged risks to your enterprise and taking steps to mitigate these risks. Because it is important, we try to do it rigorously. Commonly, each risk would be evaluated by giving it a rating in two categories, namely *impact* (how bad would it be if it happens?) and *likelihood* (what are the chances of it happening?). For example, if you are out walking, the risk of being hit by lightning is of low likelihood but high impact, and you would mitigate it by not seeking shelter under a tree in a thunderstorm. On the other hand, the risk of getting wet in the rain is of high likelihood but low impact, and you would mitigate it by wearing a raincoat and taking your umbrella.

Risk ratings are usually quantified on a scale of 1 to 5. This is useful for shorthand, but not essential to the purpose of the exercise. In rating, say, impact, on a numerical scale of 1 to 5, we are not doing anything more clever or profound than using a qualitative scale starting with 'very low', then going on to 'fairly low', 'medium', 'fairly high' and 'very high'. Likewise for likelihood.

But the numbers game is seductive. Once we have given each risk two numbers, one for impact and one for likelihood, there is the temptation to combine those two numbers into one number, which would be our overall numerical evaluation of that risk. When this is done, and each risk on our very diverse risk register has just one number, then we automatically have a ranking of our risks. And so, miraculously but apparently scientifically, arithmetic has informed us which risks are more important.

Suppose, for example, our risk register has one item on the risk of flooding, and (somewhere else on the list) another item on the risk of our annual surplus coming in below budget. Suppose, further, that we rate the risk of flooding as 4 for impact (quite high, meaning flooding would severely affect our business) and 2 for likelihood (quite low, meaning that our location makes flooding fairly unlikely). And we rate the risk of reduced surplus as 3 for impact (because we think the loss will be noticeable but not critical) and 3 for likelihood (because we think it is a little more likely than an even chance).

Not yet content, we now want the items on our risk register to be ordered in a single list, from top (most risky) to bottom (least risky). Which means that, among others, we need a numerical comparison of the risks of flooding and the risk of reduced surplus. Which, in turn, means that the rating of each risk should be reduced from two numbers to one number. Which means, finally, that we have decide by which calculation we will combine those two numbers into one number.

I have never yet seen the question of which calculation to use surface at an audit committee meeting. Instead, I have many times seen it taken for granted that the way to combine the ratings for impact and likelihood is to multiply them. So, to continue the example above, the evaluation of the risk of flooding will be 4x2 = 8, and the evaluation of the risk of reduced surplus will be 3x3 = 9. And so, it seems, arithmetic has decided for us that a reduced surplus is a higher risk than flooding.

Arithmetic did no such thing. It was we who decided to *multiply* the ratings of impact and likelihood, and it was that choice of calculation that determined the two overall risk evaluations. But what is so special about multiplication? We might equally well have decided, say, to add up the two ratings. If we did so, the risk evaluation of flooding would be 4+2 = 6, and the risk evaluation of making a loss be 3+3 = 6, and so on this method the two risks are ranked exactly equal in importance.

But why restrict ourselves to multiplication or addition? There are infinitely many calculations by which you can combine two numbers into one number. We could easily amuse ourselves by making up some new calculation – particularly if it gives us the 'right' answer. Given two numbers I could for example decide to *pythagorise* them, which I would define as finding the square root of the sum of their squares. Performing this calculation for the same two risks, it turns out that flooding has a risk evaluation which is the square root of 20 and reduced surplus has a risk evaluation which is the square root of 18. So, on this calculation, which has just as much mathematical legitimacy as multiplication or addition, flooding comes out as a higher risk than reduced surplus.

Depending on your chosen calculation, therefore, for any two risks either one of them can be ranked above the other, or they could be equally ranked. Mathematically, there is no reason whatsoever why one calculation for combining two numbers into one number has any more meaning, or any less meaning, than any other such calculation. The arithmetical operation you choose to combine your two 'likelihood' and 'impact' numbers into a single risk evaluation number is entirely up to you. It is a matter of preference. And so your eventual risk evaluation is not a matter of substance but a matter of preference – it simply reflects the calculation you chose to use.

To labour the point a little: arithmetic will only deliver such outcomes as were built into a process by our own choice of which calculations to perform on which numbers. Arithmetic does not make your choices for you, it just delivers a numerical formulation of choices you have made yourself.

Recall that in Chapter Two we discussed exactly such a situation. Our experiment was to build a ranking of the Russell Group universities, and we noted that doing so involves various levels of choice. The fourth level of choice was to choose a calculation. Specifically: we evaluated each university in terms of seven categories, each of which was measurable, and hence represented by a number. The evaluation of each university therefore came out as a set of seven numbers. In order to rank the universities, then, we needed to choose a calculation which would combine seven numbers into one number.

All the comments above now apply. There are infinitely many choices of such a calculation. None of them have any greater validity than any other. They can produce wildly different results. If you know what result you want, it won't be too difficult to find a perfectly sensible-looking calculation that will give you exactly that result. And so, in the rankings game, your choice of calculation is just a proxy for your preference. Which, as we also saw in Chapter Two, is exactly what the rankers do. Under the heading of 'improved methodology', they simply tweak the various choices and parameters in order to get the outcome that seems right to them.

Whether for risks or for universities or anything else, given that there are so many different ways of arriving at a result, if you wish to argue that your ranking somehow represents reality you really need to argue that point at each level of choice. And so, specifically at the level of choice of calculation, you would really need to argue that some calculations are somehow more natural – more real, in a Platonic kind of way – than others, and hence to be preferred. In the case of our risk register, for example, you would have to make a case that multiplying the ratings for impact and likelihood is a more natural thing to do than, say, adding them.

But others may think differently. Here is an example where addition is preferred above multiplication. In 2015, the *Sportmail* section of the *Daily Mail* decided to seek the real answer to a burning question: which is the biggest football club in England?

So who, objectively, are the biggest clubs in England? That's the question *Sportsmail* answers today. We've used no opinion, just hard evidence to determine the answers.[7]

This objective investigation, under the subheading 'Sportsmail's forensic study finally settles football's great debate', proceeds as follows. First they choose a pool of candidates, which is done as follows: 'The starting point, to cast the net as widely as possible, is to narrow the field to "big" clubs who are currently among the 92 in the Premier League or Football League and who have played in England's top division for at least one season, ever.' This gives a pool of 59 clubs, and the *Mail* decides to rank the top 50 of these. Next, they choose some categories of evaluation.

> We ranked each of those 59 teams in six categories to assess how 'big' they are in each of them. We've considered trophies, all-time league performance by average finish since 1888–9, crowds (for this season and historically), calibre of players over time (counting England internationals, and World Cup stars), modern global popularity (using social media followings) and money, measuring income.

So far, then, the *Daily Mail* methodology displays all the characteristics of ad hoc choice already noted: they could have used ten categories instead of six, it could have been six different categories, each of the categories could have been measured in a different way, they could have used medians instead of averages, and so on. Next, they have to choose how to combine the six numbers yielded by their six categories into one number. And they decide to add them up.

> *Sportsmail's* exclusive table ranks the top 50 teams from the 59 who have played in the top flight for six categories: crowds, global fanbase, trophies, league finish, player quality and income. Their ranks are then added up for a final score – the lower the score, the better the club.

It turns out, then, that Manchester United is the biggest club, with Arsenal second, followed by Liverpool, then Chelsea and then Manchester City. On which the *Mail* comments:

> Manchester United come out top by some distance....
> It is who comes second that might cause most debate.
> Despite their incredible trophy record, Liverpool are
> pipped to second place by Arsenal.

What *Sportsmail* does not notice, however, is that Arsenal's second place is entirely due to their decision to use addition as a way of combining their six ratings into one. If they had used multiplication instead, Liverpool would have been second and Arsenal third. And if they thought multiplication is too artificial a way of combining six rankings into one, they could have taken the median of those six rankings, in which case again Liverpool would have been second and Arsenal third.

So then, the 'great debate' really should have been about the relative merits of using addition or multiplication to combine six numbers into one. Instead, there is a rather earnest discussion of the question 'How do Arsenal beat Liverpool?' And the answer is that 'Arsenal have consistently punched above Liverpool for most of the Premier League era, when the league has been a global commodity.' This is post hoc rationalisation. It is also a demonstration of the unthinking assumption that whatever result any calculation delivers, it must mean something. When *Sportsmail* boasts that 'we have used no opinion, just hard evidence' they are wrong. They did use an opinion, namely the opinion that there is a right way to combine six rankings into one, which is to add them up.

Sportsmail clearly believes that they have discovered a piece of reality. They have not. They have constructed some calculations which yield an outcome which they then believe to be reality, on the basis that it was delivered by numbers and arithmetic.

And that, to repeat, is the peril of arithmetic: we are tempted to endow its results with unwarranted meaning. The calculations we do are usually not wrong. What is wrong is when we so easily assume that calculations will relieve us from the burden of applying our minds. Too easily, mathematics – and even just plain arithmetic – has acquired such a mystique that it seen as some kind of magic.

It has become the sorcery of our time, conjuring up any conclusion you may desire through mathemagic. 'There is a formula for it' gives us reassurance, in somewhat the same way as 'there is a spell for it' must have given reassurance to our ancestors.

An even more scientific-sounding version of 'there is a formula for it' is 'there is an algorithm for it'. In early May 2016, for example, there was some controversy about how the social media platform Facebook determines which topics are or should be trending. When an expert was interviewed on the *Today* programme on BBC 4, the veteran commentator John Humphrys confessed himself puzzled. "One would assume", he said, "that there is just some kind of algorithm that decides, with no human intervention." As the expert then pointed out, an algorithm just calculates. But somebody wrote that algorithm, and the assumptions of that person are built into the algorithm.

As a final example, here is a real-life version of my thought experiment on culinary league tables in Chapter Two. Launched in 2015, and sanctioned by the French Foreign Ministry, *La Liste* provides us with a ranking of what they consider to be the 1,000 best restaurants in the world. And they do so, they proudly report, on the basis of an *algorithm*.

> At the heart of our rankings is an algorithm that quantifies the weighted average of reviews from critics, publications and diners like you. We believe that numbers speak for themselves, and we are here to translate them into a language for gourmands everywhere.[8]

Numbers do speak for themselves. But not in words. It is exactly in the 'translation' where choice and preference creep in.

Invented, not discovered

> The mathematician is an inventor, not a discoverer.
> *Ludwig Wittgenstein*[9]

In Chapter One I asked whether mathematical results are invented or discovered. When Euler first wrote down his famous equation, did he bring it into existence, or had it existed before as an undiscovered fact? When we say that $1+2 = 3$, is that just a convenient shorthand for expressing multiple observations, or does it express a truth about certain abstract objects called numbers? An orchard with 11 rows of 17 equally spaced trees is also an orchard with 17 rows of 11 equally spaced trees: is that an observation which adds evidence to our generalisation that $11x17 = 17x11$, or did we not even need to look at the trees to deduce that it must be so because of a fact about numbers?

Our later discussions about quality and merit have uncovered a similar question: to what extent is that which we call quality substantive, and to what extent is it normative? Do we discover quality, or do we define it?

We can ask the same question about each of the many rankings and linear orderings we are presented with every day: is this ranking substantive, or normative? Was it discovered, or invented?

John Kay (to continue the quote from the previous section) is clear in his opinion. Referring to the United Nations index of human development, he says:

> There is today a substantial industry preparing similar arbitrary indices. The annual rankings of national competitiveness published by the World Economic Forum and the business school IMD, receive a lot of attention, as do various rankings of the status of international universities. You can find the happy planet index or assessments of human freedom. These tables tell us something. Most people would agree that Iceland scores higher for human development than Sierra Leone. But if the index didn't give us that ranking, we would change the index, not our view of Iceland or Sierra Leone. Our judgements of what is a great poem or what is meant by human development determine the measures and the weights, rather than the weights and measures determining our assessment of the greatness of the poem or the meaning of human development.[10]

Some rankings are clearly substantive. When you rank Russell Group universities by, say, the size of their budget, you have done nothing more than obtain the numbers already published in various annual reports, and the numbers arrange themselves into an ordering, as numbers do. This is an example of a *single-parameter* ranking, where we only measure one particular aspect of a set of entities. When the aspect we measure is actually measurable, which is to say by nature expressible as a number, then we get a substantive ranking.

Provided we are careful enough in how we formulate what is being measured, even an opinion poll can yield a substantive ranking. The NSS, for example, gives an objective count of *the opinions expressed* by students. Likewise, as any academic who has had to face teaching evaluation by their students will know, the returns should be treated as an expression of students' *perceptions*.

The situation is different with multiple-parameter rankings. A multiple-parameter ranking is what you get when you compress a number of single-parameter rankings into one single ranking. And here is the important thing: even when those different single-parameter rankings are all substantive rankings, the combination of all of them into one multiple-parameter ranking will not be a substantive ranking. It will be a normative ranking – a ranking by preference. I have already pointed out the reason a number of times. To combine a number of different rankings of (say) universities into a single ranking you need to make a choice of calculation, and that choice is an expression of preference. The choice of calculation, in the hands of a skilled arithmetician, can pretty much get you to any preferred ranking you envisaged at the outset.

Each of the seven single-parameter rankings of Russell Group universities we saw in Chapter Two tells us something substantive about those universities. But they tell us different things. These different things cannot be combined into a single ranking *in any substantive manner*. They can indeed be combined, and in many different ways. But any such combination of those seven rankings into a single ranking will be normative, not substantive. Any such single ranking by different criteria will be invented, not discovered.

The same is true, by extension, for all the known multiple-criteria university rankings and league tables. They all involve many layers of choice, not least choice of calculation. They are therefore all normative, not substantive. They are invented, not discovered. Rankings create a reality, more than they represent a reality.

Even an opinion poll, we said above, can give a substantive ranking, provided we are very clear about saying that the outcome is a ranking of opinions. It is different for voting. Voting is an expression of choice, with the outcome of someone or some choice being selected, and as such is by definition normative.

In a democracy we do it all the time. I would rank all the candidates of all the political parties in my own order of preference, and so would you, and so would everybody else – and then we go out and vote. Some voters may think that they have made the 'right' choice, in the sense of having divined some deep-seated truth, but most of us understand exercising a choice as something different from making a discovery. Once voting is over, we then implement some system of aggregating the votes to construct a collective choice out of all these individual ones. There are many ways of doing so, and in fact the theory of voting systems is quite a complicated business, but the point here is just that the collective choice is a matter of preference in the same sense as the individual choices are. That is the essence of democracy: expressing the preference of the majority.

The same point applies whenever we vote on anything else. It could be a beauty parade, or a popularity poll, or a 'reputation survey'.

Consider for example the annual accolade called the BBC Sports Personality of the Year, awarded to the sportsperson 'whose actions have most captured the public's imagination'. The nominees can come from any sport. In 2012 the winner was Bradley Wiggins, the cyclist, who had then just won the Tour de France. He beat, among others, Jessica Ennis the heptathlete, Andy Murray the tennis player, Mo Farah the long-distance runner, David Weir the wheelchair athlete and Ellie Simmonds the paralympic swimmer – all of them, like Wiggins, gold medallists at the 2012 Olympics or Paralympics. The outcome was decided by 1,626,718 phone votes, of which Wiggins won 492,064 (30.25%). This is all very straightforward, and everybody takes it in good spirit for what it is: a popularity contest. What it does is to construct a linear ordering of the nominees through ranking voters' preferences. And the process has an outcome, which is that the first person in that ordering receives an award. What it does not do is to reveal an inherent ordering of quality. Few people would think that the vote proves that Bradley Wiggins is a better cyclist than Jessica Ennis is a heptathlete, or Andy Murray is a tennis player, for the same reason that few people would think that an apple really is a better fruit than an orange, or a rose intrinsically more beautiful than a carnation.

When we order things by preference, we impose rather than discover an ordering. It is as in a game: we make the rules, and the outcome of a match is determined not only by the skill of the players but also by the application of the rules. Take, for example, the women's heptathlon, won by Jessica Ennis at the London 2012 Olympics. This event (which is entirely different from the men's heptathlon) was created in the early 1980s, and is in fact not an event at all, but the calculation of a single outcome following seven different standard athletic events. The formula for that calculation is not trivial. The seven events are divided into three groups: running (100m hurdles, 200m and 800m), jumping (high and long) and throwing (javelin and shot put). For each event, and in each group, there is a weighting factor, specified to four decimal points, making 21 weightings in all. These are then combined with the times and distances achieved in the various events through three separate mathematical formulae to convert the athletes' performances into points scored out of a maximum of 1,000 for each event. The points are then totalled to give a ranking, whereby the winners are determined.

In each of the seven events of the heptathlon there is a clear winner, and a clear ranking of the contestants, because each separate event is a measurement of time or distance, and thus a number. The heptathlon is therefore similar to the seven different rankings we did of the Russell Group universities – each, separately, is a substantive single-parameter ranking. Also, while Jessica Ennis won on points, she did not win every one of the seven events, just as, among the Russell Group universities, no single one is first on all seven rankings. In both examples, therefore, the heptathlon and the Russell Group, we have seven respectable single-parameter rankings, and in both cases the question then arises of how these are combined into a single ranking. However, in the case of the heptathlon everybody accepts Jessica Ennis as the winner. Why, then, have I been arguing so strenuously against the legitimacy of linearising the seven Russell Group rankings into a single ranking? What is the difference?

The difference is that in the heptathlon the rules define the game. What we call the heptathlon is the outcome of a considered decision by a single governing body, the International Association of Athletics Federations (IAAF), on what method will be adopted to compound seven linear rankings into one. When the IAAF decided the rules, and made their various choices of events, parameters, weights and calculations, they were in effect exercising a number of preferences. The outcome of any heptathlon competition is therefore, through the application of those rules, a reflection of those preferences.

What makes this different from ranking universities is that the athletes, in participating, agree to submit to the authority of the IAAF, abide by the rules, and accept the outcome. The rules could have been different, and if they were the outcome might have been different. (We have seen earlier how easily small tweaks in weightings and calculations can give you almost any ranking you want.)

In the heptathlon the rules are accepted because the legitimacy of the IAAF is accepted, and therefore we all accept the outcome. Universities, however, have never accepted that they are bound by some overall governing body which sets universal rules of performance. Nor should they. For universities, it should never be the case that the rules define the entity. It should always be the case that the entity defines the rules. The strength of universities lies in institutional autonomy and academic freedom. The moment universities start playing the rankings game they tacitly accept the authority of the rankers to define the game. That is a dangerous thing to do.

Comparison ≠ ranking

> The admission of partial orderings vastly expands the applicability of social choice theory.
> *Amartya Sen*

Ranking is a form of comparison, but comparison is not restricted to ranking. We often confuse the two concepts. It is common wisdom, for example, that we should not compare apples with oranges. Actually, we can and we do compare them, in various ways: by taste, or by texture, or by colour. We just do not bother to rank them.

That is not to say that it cannot be done. If you really want to, you can linearly order all the fruit in a bowl by weighing or measuring them. Or you can preferentially order them in any way you like. However, if I happen to prefer apples to oranges, and oranges to pears, and pears to plums, and therefore consume the bowl in a certain order, this is not of any particular interest to you, and certainly does not constrain whatever different preference ranking you may wish to deploy for your own purposes. There is no *intrinsic* ranking of apples and oranges.

Many other things are like that – they are recognisably similar, and allow comparison, but they do not naturally present themselves in a ranked list. Shapes, for example. The whole point about making a toddler play with plastic cut-out shapes of a square, a triangle, a diamond, a rectangle and a circle is to compare the different shapes and learn about their geometric properties. Nobody would think that the child should be ranking those shapes as the best, second best, and so on. As with apples and oranges, if you really want to rank shapes you could easily do so, by counting the number of corners, or measuring the area, or calculating the ratio of circumference to area. But doing so won't tell you much about shape.

In Chapter Three I posited that quality may be better represented by a shape than by a number. Not perfectly, but better, because a shape gives more information than a number. And I gave some examples: quality profiles, spider diagrams and the 'sunburst chart' of U-Multirank (see Figures 3.1, 3.2, 3.3). Such representations are useful for purposes of comparison without any pretence to being linearly ordered.

Another example of how comparison is broader than ranking comes from our recent consideration of risk. If you know, for each of the items on your risk register, both the impact rating and the likelihood rating, then you can sensibly represent each risk as being located somewhere on a two-dimensional diagram as in Figure 6.1. (It does not matter which axis points which way, as long as you stick to the same arrangement for all risks.) So if the risk of flooding has likelihood 2 and impact 4, then it is represented as falling in the block second from the left and fourth from below. And if the risk of financial loss has likelihood 3 and impact 3 it is represented as falling in the middle block of the figure. Such a representation allows

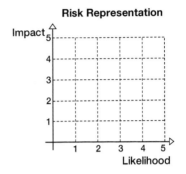

Figure 6.1: Two-dimensional diagram of risk representation

you to see at a glance how the two risks compare, so that you can make your own decisions about how you wish to treat them. It does not give you any false sense of security that one of them is a bigger risk overall than the other. (And you can make the diagram more sophisticated if you wish: allowing fractions of numbers for example, or colour-shading the diagram from green in the bottom left corner, through amber-green and then amber, to red in the top-most right corner.)

Comparison, then, does not need to invoke a ranking, and is often better done without it. One such way is to relax the key feature of rankings, which is that they are linear orderings. 'Linear' means 'as if on a line', which means a one-dimensional progression. However, as any mathematician can tell you, you can have an ordering without it being linear.

The defining feature of a linear ordering is this: if you pick any two things in that ordering, then one of them is bigger than the other. That is because of the one-dimensionality: of the two things, one must lie below (or to the left of) the other. There are, however, perfectly sensible orderings which do not have this property. One such is called a *partial* ordering. In a partial ordering, it is perfectly possible for two things to be different without either of them being bigger than the other. Which means that in a partial order you can compare things without ranking them.

This is true even for numbers. To illustrate, take for example the usual natural numbers up to 10. Conventionally, they are linearly ordered like this:

$$1 \rightarrow 2 \rightarrow 3 \rightarrow 4 \rightarrow 5 \rightarrow 6 \rightarrow 7 \rightarrow 8 \rightarrow 9 \rightarrow 10$$

The arrow is just a pictorial representation of the usual 'less than' ordering, which we denote in print by the symbol '<'. Now take the same set of numbers, 1 to 10, but with a different ordering. This time let 'A < B' mean that 'A is a divisor of B', or, equivalently, 'B is a multiple of A'. (There is no sleight of hand involved in giving a different meaning to a symbol like '<'. Mathematicians do it all the time. A symbol is just a symbol; it carries whatever meaning we ascribe to it, for whatever time we wish to do so.) Now, to draw a picture, we again represent 'A < B' by drawing an arrow from A to B, this time with the new meaning of '<'. The ordering then looks very different (Figure 6.2).

Figure 6.2: The numbers 1–10 partially ordered

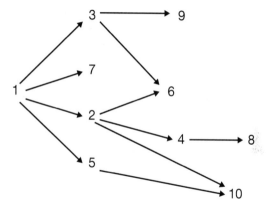

The spatial representation of the numbers is immaterial. You can position them on the page any way you like, as long as an arrow-path goes from one number to another if, and only if, the first is a divisor of the second. The ordering is represented by how the arrows go, not by where the numbers are positioned. Also, we adopt a minimalist approach: there is an arrow from 2 to 4 to indicate that 2 divides into 4, and likewise there is an arrow from 4 to 8, but we accept that this means also that 2 divides into 8, so we don't bother to draw another arrow from 2 to 8 because there is already an arrow-path from 2 to 8. Third, the fact that we have arrows going from left to right is just another convention: you could picture the same ordering with the arrows going top to bottom, or right to left, or any way you like, as long as the relationship of divisibility is faithfully portrayed.

The point of Figure 6.2 is just to exhibit an example of a perfectly sensible ordering which is not linear. That is, given any two things, it is not necessarily the case that one is 'less than' than the other (in this particular ordering).

Such partial orderings are more common than you might think. Your family tree, for example, is a partial order: if 'A < B' means that A is an ancestor of B (or, equivalently, B is a descendant of A) then while you are the ancestor of your children and grandchildren, and the descendant of your parents and grandparents, you are neither the ancestor nor the descendant of your siblings. Inside your university, the subcommittees of your Senate are partially ordered, because of any two subcommittees neither need be a subcommittee of the other. More generally, and more mathematically, the subsets of any set are partially ordered. You can have subsets of subsets, and subsets of subsets of subsets, and so on, but you can also have subsets neither of which includes the other. Kids learn this sort of thing in their set theory lessons at school.

At the other end of the scale, the use of partial orderings in a subject called social choice theory was a key factor in Amartya Sen winning the Nobel Prize for economics in 1998. (In the previous section I mentioned that the theory of voting systems is quite a complicated business – that is one aspect of social choice theory.) In the New Preface to the 2017 expanded edition of his seminal 1970 book *Collective Choice and Social Welfare*, Sen writes:

> One of the more important departures in this book (both in the original 1970 edition and in this expanded edition) is the use of *partial ordering* as the basic relation of social ranking (when such a ranking makes sense), rather than demanding, as the Arrovian framework does, the *completeness* of admissible social rankings. A complete ranking demands that every pair of alternatives can be ranked firmly against each other – either *x* is better than *y*, or worse than *y*, or exactly as good. A partial ranking, indeed even a partial ordering (satisfying the demands of transitivity), can leave some pairs unranked....
>
> The departure has big implications....
>
> The admission of partial orderings vastly expands the applicability of social choice theory. This makes

it possible, for example, to arrive at practical solutions despite some remaining disagreement, since the partial ranking of agreement may allow us to do many useful things. There may well be little hope of complete agreement, for example, on what to do in taking care of the global environment (or, more particularly, in trying to prevent global warming), or on what must be done urgently to try to curb global pandemics, or remove medical neglect across the world. And yet we can, with adequate public discussion and active advocacy, hope to get agreement on partial remedies that need not await the complete resolution of all our differences.[11]

To relate all of this talk of partial orderings to our earlier discussion, look again at the single-parameter rankings we compiled for the Russell Group universities in Chapter Two. To simplify the example, let us restrict ourselves to, say, the first 10 universities on the alphabet (Birmingham to King's), and restrict our attention to research. That leaves us with six single-parameter research-related rankings, as in Table 6.1.

Table 6.1: Research performance of ten universities

University	A: Research Income	B: Research Inc/FTE	C: Research citations	D: Citations /FTE	E: PhDs given	F: PhDs/FTE
Birmingham	101,540	80	9,348	7.35	555	0.44
Bristol	110,120	114	11,462	11.82	445	0.46
Cambridge	283,718	188	32,563	21.61	1095	0.73
Cardiff	84,633	64	9,222	7.02	380	0.29
Durham	48,740	66	7,060	9.61	310	0.42
Edinburgh	180,990	128	17,638	12.43	640	0.45
Exeter	46,327	71	5,700	8.69	265	0.40
Glasgow	128,047	117	10,983	10.04	350	0.32
Imperial	299,238	245	27,808	22.79	760	0.62
King's	147,099	94	14,988	9.53	520	0.33

Now order these 10 universities as follows: A < B if, and only if, A is ranked lower than B on *every one* of the six single-parameter research rankings. This seems quite a reasonable way of saying that, on the available data. B is definitely doing better than A in research. You then get a partial order as shown in Figure 6.3.

Figure 6.3: Ten universities partially ordered by research performance

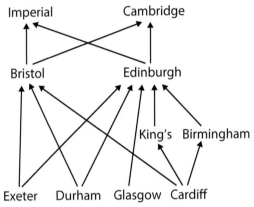

Figure 6.3 is a much more accurate representation of the facts (given the choice of parameters) than any linear ordering. That is because it did not lose information in the way a ranking does. It is a comparison of these 10 universities, and it is even an ordered comparison, but it is not a ranking. It is not as tidy as a ranking precisely because it is a better representation of the facts.

There are two further points worth making. First: in a linear ordering it is the case that if nothing is bigger than A, then A is bigger than everything else. In a partial ordering this need not be the case. For an example, look again at the 10 universities partially ordered above: nothing is bigger than Imperial, and also nothing is bigger than Cambridge, but neither of them is bigger than the other. Mathematicians would say that these two are *maximal* points in the partial ordering, precisely to make the point that neither of them is a *maximum* point. (A point is maximal if nothing is bigger than it; a point is a maximum if it is bigger than all the others.)[12]

Rankings insist on having a maximum point: the number one. They would be more credible if they used maximal points instead.

The second point worth noting is a variation on a theme I have mentioned before. It is always possible to compress a partial ordering into a linear ordering, and this can be done in various different ways, typically yielding various different outcomes, none of which has any better claim to being 'the right way' than any of the others. You always lose information by such a compression. It is as if you were to take the two-dimensional picture of a partial ordering and squash it flat, in which case any point may by happenstance slide in behind or in front of any other point.

The poverty of linearism

> A line is a breadthless length.
> *Euclid*

Whether for universities, or schools, or football clubs, or social classes, the habit of ranking in terms of presumed quality or merit is seductive in a number of ways. It is easy to do, it enjoys the precedent of some natural linear orderings, it can be given a veneer of mathematical respectability, and it allows an infinite variety of outcomes, thus enabling a covert exercise of our preferences. Overall, it just seems to make life easier.

It is also, however, an intellectually lazy habit, which commits a category error by reducing qualities to quantities. It is dishonest because it hides preference under the cloak of arithmetic. It is irresponsible because it fools us into believing that the normative is substantive. It is technically weak because it chooses, of all possible methods of comparison, one that loses the most information and conveys the least.

Yet the predilection for ranking is so widespread, and so deeply entrenched in our thinking, that it is more like a belief system than a habit. We now routinely treat quality, merit and social mobility as nothing but a matter of better or worse, higher up or lower down a ladder, or hierarchy, or stratification, of status and esteem.

This habit, this belief system, this predilection for listing things in presumed rank order of worth, we may refer to as *linearism,* because of its insistence that the world is or should be linearly ordered. If the concept needs a definition, I would offer the following: linearism is the lazy assumption that, given any two things, one of them must be inherently better, more meritorious or of higher worth than the other. It is the wilful adherence to a fallacy, namely that the most meaningful method of comparison is ranking. The key word here is 'inherently', used as an antonym for 'preferentially'. Linearism does not just say that we can linearly order the world according to our preference. At worst, it says that the world is structured by linear orderings. It insists, moreover, on finding a maximum element in any ordering, ignoring the possibility of different maximal elements.

Linearism impoverishes us in a number of ways:

- It deprives us of the possibility of laterality. By definition, a line is one-dimensional. It has no breadth. Linear thinking, therefore, is only ever in one dimension. It is like recognising north and south, but ignoring east and west. If you list world cities in terms of latitude only, it would be perfectly true to say that Paris is north of New York and south of London.[13] True, but misleading, because the geographical locations of these three cities are better compared on an east–west axis, and even better on both axes at once.
- In so far as it can see difference, linearism regards difference as a matter of degree, rather than allowing for difference in kind. Whether as cause or effect. or just as correlation, difference only in degree facilitates ranking. Difference in kind, on the other hand, goes with diversity and against uniformity.
- Quality needs diversity, I concluded in Chapter Four. That does not work when diversity is reduced to the one-dimensional concept of hierarchy. Hierarchy is a dangerous conception of diversity because the higher-ups will always consider the lower-downs to be inferior. For that reason, they will dismiss the possibility of learning from them, nor will they be interested in looking there for ability.
- Linearism turns the ideal of social mobility into an unsolvable problem. We went over this in Chapter Five. The question was whether, in principle, everybody could be socially mobile. The linearist conception of social mobility is the comparative one,

which says that social mobility means doing better than others – clambering higher up on the ladder. Since not everybody can be higher than everybody else, it follows that not everybody can achieve social mobility, not even in principle. This interpretation of social mobility does not recognise or give credence to any lateral movement. You can move up, or down, but there is no conception of moving sideways.

- Alan Ryan, Emeritus Professor of Political Theory at Oxford, has commented in the *Times Higher Education* that 'the knack of combining differentiation of function with equality of status continues to elude us'.[14] And no wonder, while we stick to a paradigm where differentiation can mean nothing other than ranking, which will always have the connotation of status. If equality of status only ever means being on the same rung of a social ladder, and differentiation means being on different rungs, the two concepts cannot go together.

- Linearism is reductivist. When we compress many modalities into one single list, we lose information. Typically, the process is irreversible. As noted before, you can compress a number of numbers into a single number in many different ways, but if you are only given the resulting number there is usually no sensible decoding whereby you can unpack it again into the different numbers it stemmed from.

- Linearism tempts us into believing that it is OK to abdicate our decision-making responsibilities. If the options from which you need to choose come to you in a ranked list, which you are led to believe is substantive, then there is nothing to decide. You will automatically go for the top of the list, or at least the highest item you can attain or afford. Doing so means ignoring the different dimensions of the decision-making process, some of which you might have weighted differently, for your own reasons, from whoever did the ranking.

If linearism were only to say that you can always rank things by exercising choice it would be a truism. Where linearism becomes a problem is when the predilection to rank things becomes a belief that all things are ranked, as if in some kind of Platonic universe. In particular, the fact that quantities come in ranked order does not mean that qualities do the same. The distinction is important, because exercising our judgement is more often a matter of dealing with qualities than quantities.

As regards universities, linearism manifests itself as the belief that quality can be presented as a linear ordering. In doing so, however, university rankings are invented, not discovered. In effect, a league table of universities is really a prescription on what a university should be like, legitimised halfway by some arithmetic and halfway by a popularity poll. It is not a reflection of reality as much as it is a decision on how to condense and frame and present reality. And that decision looks very much like the standard model university discussed in Chapter One.

Rankings work well for people who prefer certainty to truth. They should not work well for academics. To repeat: rankings create a reality more than they reflect a reality. When acceptance of the value and validity of rankings becomes so pervasive that it starts to dictate university strategy and national policy, then the normative has become the substantive. Policy enacted in the belief that 'the best universities' come in ranked order is likely to become a self-fulfilling prophecy.

So how do we escape the beguiling temptation of linearism? By realising that there are more dimensions than one, and that a multidimensional world allows for a sense of purpose other than just climbing up a ladder.

7

Another Dimension

A mathematician's contribution

> Some years ago I was researching on what might now
> be described as an investigation of the theoretical
> possibilities and limitations of digital computing
> machines.
>
> *Alan Turing, 1947*[1]

Perhaps you had not heard of G.H. Hardy before you read Chapter
One of this book. Very likely, however, you will have heard of
Alan Turing. One likely reason for knowing about Turing is that
he worked at Bletchley Park during the Second World War as
one of the code breakers in that secret establishment. The story
of how the Nazi war communication code was cracked, of the
Enigma machine, and Turing's part in it, has been told a number
of times,[2] not least in a movie starring Benedict Cumberbatch.[3]
But Turing was much more than a successful cryptanalyst. He was
a mathematician every bit as capable as G.H. Hardy of deep and
beautiful mathematics. The difference was that Hardy worked in a
field that has been studied at least since Pythagoras, whereas Turing
founded an entirely new discipline which we now call computing
science.

Turing enrolled as an undergraduate in King's College
Cambridge in 1931, the same year that Hardy returned from
Oxford to take up the Sadleirian Chair of Pure Mathematics. Upon

graduating he was immediately, at the age of 22, elected as a Fellow of King's, on the basis of his final-year dissertation. In 1936 he read a paper to the London Mathematical Society (published in its *Proceedings* the next year) with the title 'On computable numbers, with an application to the *Entscheidungsproblem*'. This is the seminal paper of computing science. It is also deeply rooted in mathematics.

To understand what computable numbers are, and what the *Entscheidungsproblem* is, requires a bit of explanation. For this purpose, it is best to go back to a speech made by another mathematician, David Hilbert, at the beginning of the 20th century. Hilbert was the most eminent mathematician of his time, and therefore a natural choice to give a keynote address at the Second International Congress of Mathematicians, in Paris in 1900. In his speech he outlined 23 mathematical problems which were unsolved at that time, and which he hoped would be solved during the coming century. These became known as Hilbert's problems, usually referred to by number. Thus, for example, Hilbert's eighth problem, which is known as the Riemann hypothesis, remains famous among mathematicians and is still unsolved today. Hilbert himself declared that: 'If I were to awaken after having slept for a thousand years, my first question would be: has the Riemann hypothesis been proven?'

Looking back, however, perhaps the most striking thing about Hilbert's speech is not the formulation of his 23 problems, but the conviction that any mathematical problem must be solvable. Hilbert believed that if you properly formulate any mathematical assertion, then, given enough inspiration and perspiration, that assertion can either be proved to be true or refuted as false. He spoke about:

> the conviction (which every mathematician shares, but which no one has as yet supported by a proof) that every definite mathematical problem must necessarily be susceptible of an exact settlement, either in the form of an actual answer to the question asked, or by the proof of the impossibility of its solution and therewith the necessary failure of all attempts.

If you take any definite unsolved problem, said Hilbert, then, no matter how difficult the problem may seem to us, 'we have, nevertheless, the firm conviction that their solution must follow by a finite number of purely logical processes'. From this follows the clarion call known to most mathematicians:

> This conviction of the solvability of every mathematical problem is a powerful incentive to the worker. We hear within us the perpetual call: There is the problem. Seek its solution. You can find it by pure reason, for in mathematics there is no *ignorabimus*.[4]

Twenty-eight years later Hilbert added another three problems to his original list. The third of these became known as the *Entscheidungsproblem*, which is German for 'decision problem'.

The *Entscheidungsproblem* was formulated in the context of what is known as 'Hilbert's programme', which was based on a view of mathematics called Formalism. G.H. Hardy, as we have seen, saw mathematics as a variation of Platonism, while Bertrand Russell saw mathematics as derivative from logic (a view called Logicism). Hilbert, however, believed that mathematics is essentially a kind of syntax, consisting of the manipulation of formal symbols. So, to illustrate, in Hardy's view the number 5 is an independently existing Platonic universal, and in Russell's view 5 is a logical construct, but for Hilbert 5 is just marks on paper, like this: | | | | |. Mathematics, Hilbert reputedly said, is like a game played according to certain simple rules with meaningless symbols. Moreover, Hilbert posited, mathematical results can in principle be derived mechanistically from a small set of axioms which could be proved to be consistent. And so Hilbert's programme was to try and build up all of mathematics from the simplest possible system, such as elementary arithmetic, and to prove arithmetic consistent.

The concern about consistency had arisen in the late 19th century, when paradoxes were found in the foundational discipline of set theory. A mathematical system is consistent if it is free from contradictions – that is, there is no proposition P such that both P and its negation not-P can be proved within the system. Conjoined with the question of consistency were two other questions, completeness and decidability.[5] A mathematical system is complete when it can be proved that, for every proposition P within the system, either P or not-P is provable. And a system is decidable if, as Hilbert thought, there is a mechanistic procedure – what we would now call an algorithm – which, given any statement within the system, will establish whether or not that statement follows from the axioms. The *Entscheidungsproblem*, then, was the question whether a mathematical system such as elementary arithmetic could be proved to be decidable.

As it turned out, the basic premise of Hilbert's programme was wrong. Not every mathematical problem is solvable. In 1931, a 25-year-old Austrian mathematician called Kurt Gödel published a paper titled 'On formally undecidable propositions of *Principia Mathematica* and related systems'. In it, he produced one of the deepest results, and one of the most imaginative proofs, of 20th-century mathematics. Gödel proved, namely, that elementary arithmetic, if it is consistent, must be incomplete. That is, there must be statements P within any consistent formal system of arithmetic for which neither P nor its negation not-P could be proved. Since one of P or not-P must be true, however, this showed that there are statements which are true but not provable.

The existence of 'formally undecidable' statements completely refuted Hilbert's 'conviction of the solvability of every mathematical problem'. If you had formulated such a statement as a hypothesis, it can neither be proved nor refuted.

So, what Gödel had shown is that any consistent system of arithmetic, and therefore of mathematics, must leave some truths unprovable. His result had thus settled the question of completeness, but not yet the question of mechanistic decidability.[6] That fell to Alan Turing.

What Turing did was to find a way of making quite precise the notion of 'mechanical procedure', or computability. He invented what has since become known to every undergraduate student of computer science as a Turing machine. This is very simple conceptualised computer – a paper computer. Moreover, he immediately generalised this to the notion of a 'universal' Turing machine, which could exactly represent and mimic the behaviour of any other Turing machine, and thus was provably capable of computing anything that is computable. He then went on to show that not even a universal Turing machine could compute the answer to a specific problem called the Halting Problem. As the name implies, the Halting Problem is the problem of determining, given an arbitrary computer program and an input, whether the program would ever stop, or would continue to run forever. The Halting Problem, therefore, was not computable.

So, arithmetic, and therefore mathematics, was neither complete nor decidable. And, from another result by Gödel, consistency is not straightforward either. The consistency of arithmetic cannot be proved by arithmetical means, but only within more complicated systems, the consistency of which was therefore less certain than that of arithmetic itself. With that, Hilbert's programme was ruined.

Even at that time, and certainly now with the benefit of hindsight, Turing's mathematical achievement was every bit as deep and profound as anything that G.H. Hardy, 'the fifth best mathematician in the world', had ever done. Any mathematician who solved any one of Hilbert's problems would be assured of lasting fame. Turing had done that. (Hardy, incidentally, had not, although he had worked, on and off, on the Riemann hypothesis for years.) Moreover, Turing had in fact solved the *Entscheidungsproblem* not by a direct attack, but as a by-product of something even more significant. He had explicated, with total rigour, a new concept, namely computability, which would form one of the most important bases of a new discipline, computing science. This new discipline would govern the computer revolution and change life for most people on the planet. Hardy thought of his mathematical results as discoveries. Turing, however, had clearly invented something.

Anybody could rest on their laurels after such an achievement. Or they could lament, as Hardy did, that after extreme mathematical creativity life becomes empty. That was not the case with Alan Turing.

From Cambridge Turing went to Princeton, where, in one of those coincidences that occur with such frequency in mathematics, an established mathematician called Alonzo Church had independently introduced a different but equivalent notion of computability. At Princeton, Turing could have furthered his career to the extent of becoming a regular research mathematician. He did do a PhD,[7] which was then still a fairly new-fangled idea (Hardy, for example, did not have a PhD), and he was offered a faculty position. However, his interests remained eclectic. He was interested, for example, in cryptography. He also, entirely unusually for a 'pure' mathematician, became interested in physical devices for computation.

> It was probably in the fall of 1937 that Turing first became alarmed about a possible war with Germany. He was at the time supposedly working hard on his famous thesis but nevertheless found time to take up the subject of cryptanalysis with characteristic vigour.... on this topic we had *many* discussions. He assumed that words would be replaced by numbers taken from an official code book and messages would be transmitted as numbers in the binary scale. But, to prevent the enemy from deciphering captured messages even if they had the code book, he would multiply the number corresponding to a specific message by a horrendously long but secret number and transmit the product. The length of the secret number was to be determined by the requirement that it should take 100 Germans working eight hours a day on desk calculators 100 years to discover the secret factor by routine search!
>
> Turing actually designed an electric multiplier and built the first three or four stages to see if it could be made to work. For the purpose he needed relay-operated switches which, not being commercially available at that time, he built himself. The Physics Department at Princeton had a small but well-equipped machine shop for its graduate students to use, and my small contribution to the project was to lend Turing my key to the shop, which was probably against all regulations, and show him how to use the lathe, drill, press etc. without chopping off his fingers. And so, he machined and wound the relays, and to our surprise and delight the calculator worked.[8]

Codes were indeed to be used during the war, and very heavily, by both sides, for transmitting military information and instructions. In the battle for the Atlantic, for example, the deadly game was between U-boats and Allied shipping. Here, and in the rest of the conduct of war, the German side used an encryption device called the Enigma machine. If the Allies could read the messages being transmitted and received by the German military command, they would know the movements of U-boats in the Atlantic, which would enable them to direct their warships towards the enemy and their supply ships away from them. If they could break the code of the Enigma machine they would be able to read the communications of their adversaries, which could (and did) help them to win the war.

There had been a British cryptography unit since the First World War, but, as with the rest of the country, it was unprepared for the new war. By 1939, however, those at the unit had realised that they needed some new recruits. Amazingly, they had no mathematicians working for them at that time. Alan Turing was the ideal recruit. On 4 September 1939, the day after Neville Chamberlain declared war on Germany, Turing reported for duty to the Government Code and Cypher School, recently evacuated from London to Bletchley Park. His biographer, Andrew Hodges, records that there were some complaints by local residents about the do-nothings at Bletchley Park, and that Turing's landlady was one of those who lamented that an able-bodied young man was not doing his bit.

Appearances to the contrary, however, Turing was doing much more than his bit. He became central to the code-breaking operation at Bletchley Park, which Churchill referred to as 'the geese who laid the golden eggs and never cackled'. The golden eggs were in the constant stream of information about the German conduct of war which, once they had cracked the Enigma code, and re-cracked it as it became more complicated, the Bletchley Park team was able to supply. In particular, as regards breaking the naval Enigma, Turing was the main intellectual force.

> The growing body of knowledge was rapidly put to use by the Admiralty. As June 1941 opened, and the naval traffic was read currently, it was able to make an almost clean sweep of the supply ships sent into the Atlantic in advance of the *Bismarck*, disposing of seven out of the eight.[9]

By December 1942 the code breakers had a clear idea of the location of all 84 U-boats operating in the North Atlantic. Decrypts were flooding in at the rate of 3,000 per day.[10] It is not too much to say that the battle for the Atlantic was won at Bletchley Park. Nor is it too much to say that a 'pure' mathematician was instrumental in achieving this victory. One wonders what G.H. Hardy would have made of that.

One side-effect of the war was an increased interest in 'computers', which hitherto had been a name for humans (usually women) performing calculations. For code breaking, for example, such as at Bletchley Park, these new devices were highly special-purpose, designed to do in reverse whatever encryption steps were taken by the other side. But if a *universal* machine could be built, then in principle any computation for any purpose could be done by the same machine. This was Turing's vision. As he wrote in 1945:

> There will positively be no internal arrangements to be made even if we wish suddenly to switch from calculating the energy levels of the neon atom to the enumeration of groups of order 720.

Or, as he put it in 1948:

> We do not need to have an infinity of different machines doing different jobs. A single one will suffice. The engineering problem of producing various machines for various jobs is replaced by the office work of 'programming' the universal machine to do these jobs.[11]

Implementation of these ideas rapidly started to take shape in a number of locations after the war. Turing took up a new position at the Victoria University of Manchester, where, on 21 June 1948, the world's first working program had run on an electronic stored-program computer.[12] Officially he held the position of reader[13] in mathematics and deputy director of the Royal Society Computing Laboratory. It was not a happy experience, because computer construction had taken on a momentum of its own and Turing was not really directing it. His creativity did not wane, however. He wrote the seminal paper[14] on what became known later as artificial intelligence, formulating what every computer science student now knows as the Turing Test for determining whether a machine exhibits intelligent behaviour.[15] He introduced the idea that a computer program can be proved to be correct,[16] 20 years ahead of anybody else thinking of something so bold. He branched out into biology, publishing a paper on morphogenetic theory. In 1951 he was elected a Fellow of the Royal Society.

In February 1952 Turing was prosecuted for homosexuality, which was then a criminal offence, and pleaded guilty to a charge of 'gross indecency'. He was placed on probation, on condition that he should submit to hormone treatment, which was effectively chemical castration. He died on 7 June 1954, two weeks before his 42nd birthday, from cyanide poisoning. The inquest determined that he had committed suicide. In 2013 Turing was given a posthumous royal pardon.[17]

Turing was different from Hardy in many respects, but perhaps most fundamentally in the sense that there was an additional dimension to his life and career: serving a societal purpose beyond the creation of new mathematics. In Turing's work at Bletchley Park, his mathematical skills and talents were brought to bear on a problem not defined by himself, but forced upon society by circumstances. The Enigma code had to be cracked, because the war effort demanded it. Lives depended on it. This was not a case of supplying new knowledge to the world irrespective of whether there was a need for it. This was a case of a very real and present need for knowledge to address a particular societal challenge. The creativity of the mathematician had to be utilised in a manner defined by the problem, and the problem did not come ready-packaged as a mathematical problem.

In addressing a societal challenge, Turing also integrated that experience into his own intellectual development. His creativity expanded as a result of meeting a need. The Enigma code, the devices required to make and break the code, the mathematics of cryptography, the development of electronics, the idea of computability – all these influences and no doubt many others flowed down feedback loops into his intellectual life. That connectedness with the world, and the willingness to learn from it, is what distinguishes Turing from Hardy. Turing could produce new mathematics at least as well as Hardy ever could, but in addition he was responsive to the world around him in a way that Hardy never was, and disdained to be.

Two Aristotelian precepts

> While we are men, we cannot help, to a great extent, being Aristotelians.
> *John Henry Newman*

The tale of two mathematicians, Hardy and Turing, illustrate the tension between the 'useless' and the 'useful', which is usually translated into academic language as the tension between pure and applied research. This is one of the 'binary oppositions' referred to by Professor Stefan Collini in his book *What Are Universities For?* It is worth re-quoting the relevant passage (from Chapter One):

> Anyone who attends to the history of debates about the values and purposes of universities needs to cultivate a high tolerance for repetition. The topic's capacity to generate eye-glazing truisms of various kinds seems matched by its tendency to recur to a small set of binary oppositions. In Britain, though also elsewhere, these debates fall into a particularly dispiriting pattern, which might be parodied as the conflict between the 'useful' and the 'useless'.

In one respect at least Professor Collini is understating the case: the perceived binary oppositions of higher education form a large set, not a small one. All too frequently debates in higher education come down to a presumed dichotomy. Here are some common examples:[18]

- Useless vs Useful
- Theoretical vs Practical
- Blue-sky vs Real-world
- Pure vs Applied
- Knowledge vs Action
- Understanding vs Decision
- Humanities vs Science
- Science vs Engineering
- Knowledge vs Skills
- Excellence vs Impact
- Analysis vs Synthesis

- Specialisation vs Generalisation
- Depth vs Breadth
- Disciplinary vs Cross-disciplinary
- Structure vs Function
- Qualitative vs Quantitative
- Research vs Teaching
- Education vs Training
- Managerial vs Collegial
- Private Benefit vs Public Good
- Platonic vs Aristotelian
- Gown vs Town

We do seem to have a habit of treating the juxtaposition of such apparent opposites as 'binary oppositions'. That immediately gets us into trouble. In the language of logic a binary opposition is called a dichotomy, which is what you have when two concepts are mutually exclusive and jointly exhaustive. This only really happens when they are contradictories – that is, one is the negation of the other. So, if we construe 'useless' as the negation of 'useful', in quite a strict way, so that everything that is not useful is useless, and vice versa, and everything is either useful or useless, then that would be a true dichotomy.

But the rest are not. Fundamentally, what is at play in presenting these paired concepts as 'binary oppositions' is the misapplication of one of Aristotle's laws of thought, which logicians call the law of excluded middle. It says that any proposition is either true or false, and none is both.[19] I have already quoted the relevant passage from the *Metaphysics* in Chapter Three as an example of Aristotle's prose; it now recurs as an example of his thinking: 'there cannot be an intermediate between contradictories, but of one subject we must either affirm or deny any one predicate'.[20] This may sound dry and abstract, but it is also fundamental. Relying on the law of excluded middle was the crucial logical underpinning of Gödel's theorem, for example.

The law of excluded middle, and other such laws of propositional logic, once fully understood, turned out to be a powerful modelling tool for computers. Indeed, as discussed in Chapter One, logic is one of the examples of apparently useless work that eventually, to our pleasant surprise, turns out to be really useful.

Aristotelian logic, phrased in terms of arguments called syllogisms, is only a limited and somewhat idiosyncratic part of what we now call logic, but it had a stranglehold on the formalisation of reasoning until Victorian times. That was when a self-taught mathematician called George Boole, Professor of Mathematics at Queen's College Cork, published a book titled *An Investigation of the Laws of Thought, on which are founded the Mathematical Theories of Logic and Probabilities*.[21] This changed the face of logic. Essentially, Boole conceived of logic as binary arithmetic – the arithmetic of a number system with base 2, rather than base 10. That was a stroke of genius, because the numbers 0 and 1 then serve as proxies for falsehood and truth, which are the 'truth values' we deal with in propositional logic, and arithmetical operations on 0 and 1 serve as proxies for logical connectives of propositions like 'and' and 'or'.

Later, in the early days of electronic engineering but before the arrival of computers, a 21-year-old Master's student at MIT called Claude Shannon made another connection. Shannon, in what has been called 'possibly the most important, and also the most famous, Master's thesis of the century',[22] pointed out that binary arithmetic, which came to be called Boolean algebra, or (equivalently) propositional logic, can also serve as a proxy for the workings of electronic switching circuits. When a switch is on we can give it the value 1, and when it is off we give it the value 0. Since a switch is either on or off, and never both, switches obey the law of excluded middle. More generally, the so-called 'logic gates' which make computers work mirror logical operations. An 'and-gate' will let current flow when two switches are both on (that is, they are in sequence), an 'or-gate' will let current flow when at least one of two switches is on (that is, they are in parallel) and so on.

It is all very beautiful and very precise, and it works a treat in a technological environment. Dichotomising, therefore, is a very useful tool. The fact that we can use this tool to build things like electronic circuits and computers, however, does not imply that all things in the world have been made by that tool, or conform to its dictates. The world tends to be more messy – 'stupidly constructed', said G.H. Hardy – and hardly ever neatly bivalent or even logical. And when we try to make it so, or behave as if it were so, problems often arise.

The either/or bivalent way of thinking can lead us down perilous paths. The 'binary opposition' of either/or easily morphs into positive-or-negative, left-or-right, right-or-wrong, black-or-white, us-or-them. Perhaps the ultimate socio-political experiment in bivalent thinking was apartheid, where the law of excluded middle was enacted in legislation, so that everybody who was not white must be black, and nobody was both. From that presumed dichotomy followed a number of consequences, in quite a logical fashion, as Dr Verwoerd would have thought. But the fact that it was logical did not mean that it was right.

The 'binary oppositions' so common in higher education, such as those in the list above, should therefore be treated for what they are: the juxtaposition of apparent opposites, with the emphasis on 'apparent'. Most of them are neither mutually exclusive nor jointly exhaustive, and so there are other and better ways of treating each than as a dichotomy. I will propose such a way in the next section.

The tendency to dichotomise is not our only bad habit in discussing the perceived oppositions of higher education. Those who have participated in enough of the many debates about such juxtapositions can discern another dispiriting pattern, namely that the debate usually ends in exhaustion dressed up as compromise. This ending typically manifests itself in the deployment of a metaphor such as 'striking a balance', or 'finding the middle ground', which has the saving grace of sounding rather virtuous. So, having started off as though there is no middle ground, we end up as if there is only middle ground. In management-speak: we have transitioned from an either/or approach to an and/and approach.

It is worth realising that with the second habit, just as much as the first, we are following an Aristotelian precept. Just as the first habit relates to an uncritical application of the law of excluded middle, the second relates to an uncritical application of the principle of the mean.

In the *Nicomachean Ethics,* Aristotle puts forward the idea of virtue, *arête,* as a mean between two extremes. Actually Aristotle thought of the two extremes in a particular way, as being extremes of excess and deficiency. Thus courage is the mean between recklessness and cowardice, truthfulness is the mean between boasting and understatement, modesty is the mean between shamelessness and shyness, and so on.

> In this way, then, every knowledgeable person avoids excess and deficiency, but looks for the mean and chooses it.... Virtue, then, is a mean condition.... It is

> a mean between two kinds of vice, one of excess and
> the other of deficiency ...[23]

But the idea of 'the golden mean' (as it is commonly known, though Aristotle did not use the term) is deeply entrenched in a wider sense, as the virtue of two protagonists meeting each other halfway. The principle of the mean is ingrained in our thinking at least as much as the law of excluded middle, in the shape of an assumption that finding a compromise is always a virtuous outcome. In this respect, the English are natural Aristotelians. Kate Fox, in *Watching the English* (see Chapter Four), speaks of moderation as an English reflex. That is just another version of the doctrine of the mean: virtue resides in the middle ground between too much and too little.

The assumption that virtue lies in the middle can only hold good, however, when the metaphor is applicable. Often it is not. So, when considering our 'binary oppositions', we should question the applicability of the principle of the mean for the same reason we question the applicability of the law of excluded middle.

Just as the law of excluded middle can lead us astray by dichotomising two juxtaposed apparent opposites, the principle of the mean can lead us into the temptation of *linearising* those two apparent opposites. 'Linearising' means placing on the same line, or the same axis, so that we have a mental picture of one concept to the left and the other to the right. And that is what we do when we talk about finding the balance, or the middle ground, or the mean, between two concepts: we line them up, in order to find the middle. In other words, we put them in opposing positions, in order to balance them. This is what happens when we default into the metaphor of striking a balance between pure and applied, or specialisation and generalisation, or humanities and science, or research and teaching, or any of the others. So, in the 'binary oppositions' of higher education, the 'binary' aspects relate to the uncritical application of the law of excluded middle, and the 'opposition' part relates to the uncritical application of the principle of the mean.

But instead of dichotomising and linearising, perhaps we can find another metaphor for dealing with the juxtaposition of apparent opposites, which may serve at least as well in most cases and sometimes better. Perhaps we can think of two apparent opposites to be, not on the same axis, but on *orthogonal* axes.

Orthogonality

orthogonal adj. of or involving right angles.
Concise Oxford Dictionary

In the Vatican Museum in Rome, in the Raphael rooms of the Apostolic Palace, there is a large fresco known as *The School of Athens*. It was painted by Raphael between 1509 and 1511, on a commission from Pope Julius II, who envisaged using the room as his private library. If you do not have the opportunity to go there yourself, you can easily see the painting on the internet. It is an allegory of the main ideas from classical philosophy, depicted by a number of well-known philosophers gathered in clusters of conversation inside a very imposing, very symmetric building. The fresco appears under the theme of Philosophy, to match three other large frescoes in the same room, representing other branches of knowledge: Poetry, Theology and Law. It displays the motto *causarum cognitio* – 'seeking knowledge of causes'.

It is reasonably clear who most of the represented philosophers are, and even which of Raphael's contemporaries were models for some of them. It is also clear that various 'binary oppositions' of philosophy are represented. There is Parmenides, who said that nothing ever moves, and Heraclitus, who said that everything is always in flux. As 'the weeping philosopher', Heraclitus is also in opposition to Democritus, 'the laughing philosopher'. There is Epicurus, who said that the good is pleasure, and Diogenes the cynic, who called himself 'the dog' and lived in a barrel. These are what we would now call philosophers, but there are also a number of what we would call scientists, like Euclid and Archimedes.

The painting is, among other things, a marvellously rigorous example of perspective. The tiled floor of the building within which the philosophers are gathered, its steps and walls and cornices, all lead the eye to a vanishing point in the centre. Exactly on either side of that vanishing point, side by side, framed by an archway, are the central figures of Plato and Aristotle. They are standing at the midpoint of the allegory about Western philosophy and science. It is possible to think of their philosophies as the fundamental 'binary opposition' of Western thinking: the esoteric theory of ideas versus the empiricist view of concrete particulars – philosophy versus science.

Their body language, however, tells a more subtle story than that of opposing forces. Plato has his right arm raised and is pointing with his finger at the heavens above, while Aristotle is gesturing with outstretched arm and flat palm at the world around him. The symbolism of 'blue skies' and 'real world' is too obvious to miss.

In fact, the symbolism is so obvious that it is often exaggerated to fit a stereotype. The philosopher Simon Blackburn, for example, writing about Plato's *Republic*, observes casually that 'in Raphael's painting *The School of Athens*, Plato and Aristotle together hold centre-stage, but while Aristotle points to the earth, Plato points upwards to the Heavens'.[24] But that is not quite right. Just have a look at the painting. Plato is indeed pointing up to the sky, but Aristotle is not pointing down to the ground. He is pointing to the world around him. The two gestures are not in opposite directions. They are at right angles to each other.

Through the body language of Plato and Aristotle Raphael clearly represents Platonic idealism and Aristotelian empiricism as being at right angles to each other. The two schools of thought are not painted as opposite directions in one dimension, but as the juxtaposition of different dimensions: vertical and horizontal. The blue sky above us is not opposite to the world around us; it is *orthogonal* to it.

Raphael must have had an instinct about this, that the two giants of philosophy and science should not be represented as opposites. Plato and Aristotle are each carrying a copy of one of their works, with the titles visibly displayed. If Raphael had wanted to make a clichéd point about 'binary opposites' of philosophy and science he could, for example, have depicted Plato with one of his more metaphysical dialogues, and Aristotle with his *Physics*. Instead, rather ostentatiously, Plato is carrying his most scientific work, the *Timaeus*, long considered a major work on cosmology, and Aristotle is carrying one of his most philosophical works, the *Nicomachean Ethics*.

The *School of Athens* resonates with the academic unconscious in somewhat the same way as Newman's *Idea of a University*, or G.H. Hardy's Oxbridge. It strikes a subliminal chord. It is often referenced, in print or visually. There are copies in many academic institutions: the University of Virginia, the University of North Carolina, Immanuel Kant's birthplace of Kaliningrad (formerly Königsberg) and the Bibliothèque Sainte-Geneviève in Paris.

Let us therefore explore the visual metaphor of Plato and Aristotle pointing in two orthogonal directions. 'Orthogonal' is just a mathematical term meaning 'at right angles to each other', which is how we visualise different dimensions. So, for example, east–west is orthogonal to north–south, left–right is orthogonal to up–down, the warp in any woven cloth is orthogonal to the weft, and on any graph the x-axis and the y-axis are orthogonal to each other.

Orthogonality is the key motif of *The School of Athens*. Not only do Plato and Aristotle gesture on the orthogonal axes of vertical and horizontal, but the symmetry of the architecture within which the philosophers find themselves is defined by orthogonal lines. In fact, the building in the painting is constructed as a Greek cross – orthogonal axes of the same length, like a plus sign. So, while the allegory about philosophy and science concerns different schools of thought, it is not about *opposing* schools of thought, but about *different dimensions* of thought.

The allegory of orthogonality fits quite nicely with a number of the 'binary oppositions' of higher education. 'Blue-sky vs Real-world' are on the orthogonal axes of vertical and horizontal. 'Depth vs Breadth' is clearly a case of orthogonality, and it makes essentially the same distinction as 'Specialisation vs Generalisation' or 'Analysis vs Synthesis'. In 'Disciplinary vs Cross-disciplinary' the common picture is one of vertical disciplinary silos, with horizontal cross-cutting activities. The same kind of picture is often used in organisational diagrams for 'Structure vs Function' – and for good measure we often speak of the 'matrix management' of such interactions (on which more in Chapter Eight).

The advantages of orthogonality become more apparent when we think dynamically rather than statically – that is, in terms of forces rather than numbers, or, in mathematical terms, vectors rather than scalars. 'Binary oppositions', such as those listed above, are often considered as opposing forces: 'A *versus* B'. Obviously, however, there is a self-defeating aspect to opposing forces, which is that they cancel each other out. Opposing forces either collide with each other head-on, stopping both movements, or pull away from each other, like a tug-of-war contest at the market fair. Two teams of burly men can do a lot of grunting and sweating pulling on a rope in opposite directions, while the midpoint of the rope barely moves. There is little effect from all that effort because the forces work on the same axis but in opposite directions. What this means is that 'finding a balance', is not a productive metaphor in the dynamic interpretation, because it means finding a *counter*-balance, which really just means striving for a stalemate.

Different forces can, however, become quite productive when they are positioned orthogonally, rather than in opposite directions. If the husband wants to push the easy chair against the north wall of the living room, and the wife wants to push it against the east wall, then they can both push at the same time, and between the two of them they will move that chair into the north-east corner, thus satisfying both their requirements. This additivity of effort would not happen if one was pushing north and the other pushing south. Likewise, if 'useless' research is propelling you upward, towards the blue sky, and 'useful' research takes you across the road, towards civil society, then the combination of these two forces will yield a resultant vector which moves you towards a position where theory has combined with practice. As discussed previously, this may happen in fits and starts, over time. It also happens non-deterministically and unpredictably, because you never quite know which advance in theory will respond to which of the needs and demands of society. But by and large, conceiving the force of theory to be orthogonal to the force of practice will get you into a better position than conceiving of them as being one versus the other.

The principle of the mean is an Aristotelian precept ingrained in our thinking, which it would not be if we did not find it useful. But it is not *always* useful, because it is essentially one-dimensional. Statically, it means finding a point somewhere around the middle[25] of two other points on a line. Dynamically, it means counterbalancing one force with an opposing force.

In many cases, and in particular as regards the 'binary oppositions' of higher education, it may be more productive to deploy the metaphor of the resultant vector. That becomes possible when we think two-dimensionally rather than linearly, and dynamically rather than statically. Two-dimensional thinking, in turn, requires orthogonal axes of thought. So orthogonality is the key idea.

And it will suffice. As any mathematician will tell you, once you know how to deploy orthogonality you can have as many dimensions as you want, should you need them. Mathematically, there is nothing strange in having any number of dimensions, each orthogonal to all the others. For reconfiguring any 'binary opposition', however, two dimensions will suffice.

Lateral research

> Rightness is what matters in vertical thinking. Richness
> is what matters in lateral thinking.
> *Edward de Bono*

I now want to use the ideas above to rethink the common binary oppositions of Useless vs Useful, Theoretical vs Practical, Blue-sky vs Real-world and so on, to arrive at a two-dimensional conceptual framework for research. Recall from Chapter One that the standard model of the university is based on a dominant paradigm of research. The dominant paradigm says that research is about the creation of knowledge within a framework of academic disciplines. G.H. Hardy is a good example. His entire life was about the creation of beautiful new mathematics, and when he was no longer creative his life was over. So dominant is this paradigm that it has established its own discourse, with its own standard vocabulary, and this language has become our default medium of communication when we talk about research. We speak with appreciation of knowledge creation in the disciplinary framework as 'pure', or 'basic', or 'fundamental', or 'curiosity-driven', or 'blue-sky'. We thereby afford such work the highest esteem, and the more so when it is happens in mathematics, which retains its reputation as the pinnacle of intellectual achievement.

Any attempt to consider another paradigm of research suffers from a significant initial disadvantage. For common understanding it can only be phrased in terms of – or at the very least by reference to – the language we all understand, which is the default language of the dominant paradigm. From the outset, therefore, a discussion that is meant to break new ground appears to be derivative. When we speak of 'cross-disciplinary' research, for example, we implicitly acknowledge the primacy of the disciplines that this kind of research is supposed to be crossing. When we speak of 'applied' research we implicitly accept that there has been some kind of prior creation of knowledge which we are now trying to make use of. And when we refer to disciplinary research as 'pure', we accept a connotation that any different kind of research must be tainted with impurity.

The second disadvantage in attempting a paradigm change is that we are easily trapped, not only by our language but by our thinking. I refer specifically to an over-reliance on the Aristotelian precepts of the excluded middle and the virtuous mean, even when these are not applicable. As seen above, the excluded middle leads us into the trap of viewing the juxtaposition of apparent opposites as binary oppositions, and the principle of the mean, through the metaphor of 'finding a balance', leads us into linear thinking. Our debates then soon fall into a dispiriting pattern of cliché and repetition.

To escape, we need to devise a language of discourse within which the disciplinary paradigm of the standard model can find a place, but will not be assured from the outset of a dominant place. I propose to think in different dimensions, and use the language of orthogonality. For simplicity, and for the advantage of neutral terminology, I will refer to 'vertical' and 'lateral' research.

We can easily think of 'blue-sky' research as having a vertical orientation. All the synonyms and connotations of 'blue-sky' research – 'pure', 'basic', 'theoretical', 'fundamental', 'disciplinary', 'curiosity-driven' and so on – are then likewise thought of as operating on a vertical axis. A common way of visualising this metaphor is to think of the disciplines as vertical silos within which the creative force of curiosity is either reaching upwards towards the rarefied atmosphere of the blue sky or digging downwards towards the foundations of the subject.

Hardy's work in number theory, then, is blue-sky oriented, and Gödel's theorem is foundational, but they are on the same vertical axis. Likewise, Hilbert's problems, the Riemann hypothesis, the *Entscheidungsproblem* and Turing machines are examples of vertical research. So is the original 'academic' work on graphene, and so is the work done at the Large Hadron Collider to prove the existence of the Higgs boson. This kind of work exemplifies our dominant paradigm of research.

To this standard model of vertical research we can now juxtapose the idea of research on a horizontal axis: lateral research. The challenge is to characterise it, and I will do so through a 'compare and contrast' approach.

- *Vertical research is focused on the supply of knowledge; lateral research is focused on the demand for knowledge.* Researchers on the supply side of the knowledge economy, such as G.H. Hardy, or Gödel, or the scientists at the Large Hadron Collider, see their job primarily as creating new knowledge and pushing it out into the world, without concerning themselves much with whether or not this will be picked up by anybody. In Chapter One we rehearsed the reasons why this is an entirely justifiable position; these essentially come down to a measure of faith in the workings of the invisible hand.

  Lateral research, in contrast, typically arises from the needs and demands of society. It operates on the demand side of the knowledge economy, aiming to generate knowledge suitable for addressing societal challenges. Such challenges can be local, but increasingly local difficulties are manifestations of global challenges.

  It is not difficult, though it can be depressing, to make a list of grand challenges facing global society. You could start with global warming, climate change and loss of biodiversity, then go on to challenges such as renewable energy, or anti-microbial resistance, or urbanisation, or overfishing. There are pandemics such as HIV/Aids, malaria and ebola, public health issues like smoking, obesity and drug addiction, and social issues like migration, refugees and human trafficking. Continuing this trajectory, you come to existential threats such as war, fundamentalism and terrorism.

  The social reformer Martin Luther King was an early identifier of global challenges, which formed the *leitmotiv* of his work.

There are three urgent and indeed great problems that
we face not only in the United States of America but
all over the world today. That is the problem of racism,
the problem of poverty and the problem of war. And
the things that I have been trying to do in our struggle
at home and in the struggle that is taking place all over
the world, has been to deal forthrightly and in depth
with these great and grave problems that pervade our
world.[26]

Since then there have been many cases of highlighting the 'great
and grave problems that pervade our world'. The United Nations
Millennium Development Goals, for example, formulated at the
Millennium Summit in 2000, committed all member states to
addressing eight global challenges by 2015: to eradicate extreme
poverty and hunger; to achieve universal primary education; to
promote gender equality; to reduce child mortality; to improve
maternal health; to combat HIV/AIDS, malaria, and other
diseases; to ensure environmental sustainability; and to develop
a global partnership for development.

These have since been superseded by 17 Sustainable
Development Goals, to be delivered by 2030. Research capacity,
knowledge creation, money and other resources are required
to address these societal challenges just as much as resources
are required for a Large Hadron Collider. But the conceptual
framework and the tools are different. I will return to the topic
of societal challenges in Chapter Eight.

- *Vertical research is in production mode; lateral research is in responsive
  mode.* This is really a restatement of the previous point. By
  'production mode' I mean that vertical research is focused on
  the creation of new knowledge without regard to the question
  whether or not there is any need for it. By 'responsive mode' I
  mean that lateral research typically arises from some societal issue
  we feel needs addressing, and to which the purposeful creation
  of new knowledge would make a contribution.

- *Vertical research is curiosity-driven; lateral research is challenge-led.*
  Vertical research arises from a push factor, which is curiosity –

typically the curiosity of the individual. Lateral research arises from a pull factor, which is the societal challenge to which we are responding. The old-fashioned description of lateral research would be that it is *teleological*, which means that it strives towards a *telos*, a final end or purpose. I will return to the topic of purpose in Chapter Eight.

- *Vertical research has a sense of purpose emanating from the individual; lateral research has a sense of purpose emanating from society.* In vertical research, the individual's sense of purpose may be about the creation of new knowledge within an academic discipline, or it may be about solving a problem within that discipline. The work is done, however, for personal gratification: the desire to know. In lateral research the need for knowledge, or the problem to be addressed, comes from outside the researcher, as a challenge facing society, and the response to that challenge is a matter of public good.

- *Vertical research has the creation of knowledge as an end in itself; lateral research has the creation of knowledge as a means to an end.* In vertical research, the act of creation needs no justification. With lateral research there is a reason why we are doing it, which is usually to try to make life better, or at least prevent it getting worse. In order to do so, new knowledge may need to be created, but the purpose of doing so is not the act of creation itself. Drug discovery, for example (if we leave aside any commercial motive), is not just about the joy of discovering new chemical compounds. It is about creating drugs that will prevent or ameliorate a particular disease and infirmity, and help to preserve and extend life.

- *Vertical research is about the true; lateral research is about the good.* There are many articulations of the idea that the search for truth and understanding elevates the mind. Here, for example, is a quote from the annual report of the US National Science Foundation of 1953:

> A worker in basic scientific research is motivated by a driving curiosity about the unknown. When his explorations yield new knowledge, he experiences

the satisfaction of those who first attain the summit of a mountain or the upper reaches of a river flowing through unmapped territory. Discovery of truth and understanding of nature are his objectives. His professional standing among his fellows depends upon the originality and soundness of his work. Creativeness in science is of a cloth with that of the poet or painter.[27]

This is very Hardyesque. By contrast, any articulation of lateral research may seem as prosaic as the writing of Aristotle when compared to that of Plato. Lateral research is, however, as necessary a counterpart to vertical research as Aristotle ever was to Plato. In so far as this kind of research is a *search*, the search would be for decision and action. To borrow from Marx, while the point of vertical research is to understand the world, the point of lateral research is to change it – hopefully for the better. If vertical research is about elevating the mind, then lateral research is about improving the conditions of life. What are we going to do about climate change? Can we find a drug to ameliorate HIV/AIDS, or a vaccine against ebola? How should we react to fundamentalism, terrorism and war? More to the point, what is our own contribution to any of the 'great and grave' problems that pervade the world?

- *Vertical research is strongly individualistic; lateral research is commonly collective.* The archetype of the lone scholar is firmly entrenched in academia, and the favourable image of the individual genius is a common one. There is a romantic side to the story of Newton inventing calculus while in retreat from the plague, or the young Einstein working away on three miracle papers while employed as a clerk in a Swiss patent office. Many academics prefer to work in that way: they want their own office, and to be able to close the door in order to concentrate.

  Lateral research, in contrast, is typically carried out by teams – sometimes large teams – with disparate efforts directed towards the same end. This can be seen in most universities now. It is common to set up an institute of some kind, with members bringing expertise from various different disciplines across the university, to work on (say) renewable energy, or climate change issues, or the digital economy. Such institutes are often not the usual line management structure, and may or may not have their own budget. For cohesion, such institutes rely instead on common purpose and mutual benefit.

- *Vertical research has little interaction with society; lateral research relies upon it.* The lone scholar operating on the supply side of the knowledge economy usually values isolation above interaction. Lateral research, on the other hand, which starts with a societal challenge, needs and values the input of society in addressing that challenge. Social scientists now commonly speak of the co-creation of knowledge arising from interaction with the third sector – charities, social enterprises, not-for-profit organisations, policy bodies and the like. Even the natural sciences are discovering the value of deploying 'citizen scientists' on investigating ecological issues, or the movement of stars, or the erosion of the coastline, or the migration of birds.

- *Vertical research emanates from disciplines; lateral research cuts across them.* None of the grand challenges of society come to us neatly packaged in a disciplinary wrapping. Consider, for example, the challenge of population ageing. Across the developed world, average life expectancy is rising by about five hours every day, which is a triumph of medical science and public health initiatives. But increased longevity is also a societal challenge. It is a challenge to make sure that the extra years are not years of decrepitude. It is a challenge to figure out the social, economic and political consequences of a changing age demography. It is a challenge when there are increasing numbers of old people and decreasing numbers of young people. And so, to address the challenge of ageing we need more than just the disciplines and ologies of science. We need the architects and the engineers to work on assisted living. We need the computer scientists to work with designers to produce smart gadgets that can be handled with clumsy fingers, poor eyesight and short memory. We need entrepreneurs who see the business opportunities in a cohort of elderly people who are demanding consumers, and by no means all poor. We need social care policies and structures that address loneliness. All of this demand a way of thinking that requires more than curiosity-driven, individualistic, vertical research. It needs some concerted purpose-driven, collective, lateral research.

Lateral research is not defined by disciplines, but draws upon them as needed. It can be 'cross-disciplinary', in the sense of cutting across the vertical silos of the disciplines, it can be 'interdisciplinary', in the sense of drawing upon them, and 'multidisciplinary', in the sense of using more than one. It may even be 'transdisciplinary', although we are still trying to figure out what this new term might mean. Vertical research, in contrast, can only really get at interdisciplinarity through the overlap between disciplines. To denote such overlap, we often use prefixes, as in biomathematics or geochemistry or hydrogeology, and may even concatenate them, as in psychoneuropharmacology or bioelectrochemical engineering.

- *Vertical research is objective; lateral research is participatory.* Vertical research, and indeed the standard model of the university, is strongly associated with the ideal of the academic or scientist as a dispassionate observer and objective thinker. 'Objectivity', indeed, is almost universally considered to be a virtue, and is then contrasted with 'subjectivity', which has the derogatory implication of allowing your own preferences to colour your scientific conclusions. That contrast, however, is in turn part of the linear dichotomising approach we are trying to expand into another dimension. When we adopt a two-dimensional approach, contrasting vertical research with lateral research, and the supply side of knowledge production with the demand side, a different juxtaposition emerges. With purpose-driven demand-side research we have to note at the outset that often we ourselves are participants in and agents of the very phenomena we are studying. Understanding climate change is different from understanding the laws of physics, because nothing we do will alter the laws of physics, but many things we do could change the climate.

The contrast with 'objective' then, if contrast is the right word, is not 'subjective' but 'participatory'. And the counterpart of the dispassionate observer is the committed contributor. Many of the grand challenges facing us arise, not from acts of God, but acts of humans. When we take it as our purpose to address such challenges, we are to some extent trying to undo side-effects or unintended consequences of what we have done before. In such a situation, to adopt the stance of the dispassionate observer is not to be scientific but to duck responsibility.

- *Vertical research has a sense of freedom; lateral research has a sense of responsibility.* Particularly in the social sciences and humanities, vertical research is sometimes coupled with academic freedom. Indeed, the idea of the individual academic being able to investigate any topic they wish and disseminate the results without fear or favour fits nicely with the idea of curiosity-driven research. As with the other contrasts, however, we need to be careful not to fall into the dichotomy trap. Lateral research is not about letting go of the idea of academic freedom. It is about juxtaposing to it the idea of academic responsibility.

  Academic freedom, as a concept, is well developed, well understood, frequently articulated and almost universally subscribed to. 'Academic freedom' as a piece of terminology is also, however, part of the discourse of the dominant paradigm. In consequence, its counterpart on the horizontal dimension, which is academic responsibility, is less developed, not often articulated, and might be contested. If you are G.H. Hardy you might well argue that academics have no responsibility other than creativity. But that is to refuse to leave the safe linearity of the vertical approach. If we do venture into a second dimension, of societal purpose, then the question of responsibility becomes inescapable.

In summary: starting from the visual metaphor of Plato pointing upwards and Aristotle gesturing sideways, I have tried to construct a vocabulary of lateral research as a counterpart to the dominant language of verticality. Vertical research is situated on the supply side of the knowledge economy. It is creative, curiosity-driven, disciplinary, individualistic and objective. Lateral research is situated on the demand side of the knowledge economy. It is responsive, purpose-driven, challenge-led, team-based and participatory. Where vertical research is about depth, lateral research is about breadth. Where vertical research aims for the blue skies, lateral research scans the horizon for societal needs and demands. If vertical research is considered to be an exercise in academic freedom, then lateral research is an exercise in academic responsibility. And finally, if vertical research is considered to be 'pure', then perhaps lateral research is best considered as 'complex'.

So much about what lateral research is. It will be helpful to consider also what it is not.

- *Lateral research is not 'applied research'.* It is certainly not 'applied' in the sense in which applied mathematics is another name for theoretical physics, or applied physics is engineering, or applied logic is theoretical computer science. Application, in this sense, as a linear gradation of 'theoretical', remains in the vertical dimension. Lateral research is also not 'applied' in the sense commonly understood and discussed in Chapter One, which is that we take knowledge produced on the supply-side vertical axis and then go out looking for where or how it may be useful. The gold rush for graphene is of this kind. So was the application of lasers – the original 'solution looking for a problem'. So is the idea of 'technology transfer' – that there is continuous process of transformation and refinement turning raw knowledge into sophisticated products or services. As we know, in many respects tech transfer works very well indeed. We just need to note in addition that the standard process of 'applying' research remains on the supply side of the knowledge economy. It still operates within a linear process of pushing out knowledge, but now with the added intention of pushing it far enough to make a connection – any connection – with the world around us. 'Applied' research, therefore, is still about push. Lateral research, on the other hand, is about pull.

- *Lateral research is not new.* Any doctor searching for a cure, any engineer looking for a solution, any economist proposing policy, is in some measure working on the demand side. The key idea of lateral research is that it starts with a challenge – not an intellectual one, like proving the Riemann hypothesis, but one involving society, such as a new pandemic, and then reasons backwards to figure out what is needed to address it. What is new about lateral research is not the practice of doing it. What is new is the conceptual framework of a second dimension rather than a binary opposition, and the terminology to express that conceptual framework without treating it as derivative from the standard model.

- *Lateral research is not in opposition to, or an intended replacement of, vertical research.* The demand side does not call into question the legitimacy or value of the supply side. It is not a call to decrease curiosity-driven research, or an attempt to diminish it. To work on the horizontal, demand-side axis is just to recognise that vertical, supply-side work by itself may not suffice to meet societal needs and demands – at least not in a timeframe within which solutions to the grand challenges must be sought. Turing's demand-side code-breaking work was not a denial of, nor in opposition to, his supply-side work on defining computability. Arguably, it was his ability to do both, and the way he could both move upward on the vertical axis and forward on the horizontal axis that resulted in him being regarded as the founder of a new branch of science.

- *'Demand side' does not mean 'market forces' – at least not if market forces are equated with the corporate sector, or the bottom line.* The demand side of the knowledge economy is not a matter of increasing the share price of multinational corporations, or meeting a consumer demand for more products or services, or marketising the university. It is matter of consciously steering and directing our academic work to respond to the needs and demands of civil society. Likewise, working on the demand side is not a matter of falling in line with governmental pressure, or participating in social engineering. It does not compromise academic freedom. It acknowledges, in a way that the supply side does not, that the university is an integral part of civil society, and on that basis calls for the university to exercise its freedom with a sense of civic responsibility. It is a reciprocal interaction with civil society, from which the university stands to gain as much as it gives.

It is worth noting, finally, that the distinction between supply and demand in the knowledge economy, and the attempt to contribute on both sides, is not an issue in our research portfolio only. It is relevant as much to the dissemination of knowledge as to its creation. In our portfolio of teaching and learning, we focus both on broadening the mind and on preparing for a career. When they graduate, we want our students to have enjoyed two benefits: the accumulation of knowledge for its own sake, and the skills and expertise attractive to employers. The former is a supply-side endeavour, the latter a demand-side one.

As for structures, by and large the supply-side discipline-based division of a university into faculties/schools/departments has served us well. The challenge is not to replace the supply-side structures, but to define and acknowledge an orthogonal demand-side taxonomy, which is functional rather than structural. 'Does your university have a physics department?' is a supply-side question about structures. 'Does your university deal with climate change?' is a demand-side question about functionality. In academia, these two questions, and what they represent, do not yet enjoy parity of esteem. In the next and final chapter I try to address this issue, and pull together the various threads spun in the preceding chapters.

8

Ideas of a Civic University

A sense of purpose

> Knowledge is the object of our enquiry, and men do
> not think they know a thing until they have grasped
> the 'why' of it.
>
> *Aristotle, Physics, Book II*

There are two key questions every university should ask itself about its academic work. The first is: What are we good *at*? And the second is: What are we good *for*?

The good-at question takes us back to the standard model university and the closing discussion of Chapter One. With Wilhelm von Humboldt we believe that research is a core function of the university, and with John Henry Newman we believe that teaching is a core function of the university. Our response to the question 'What are we good at?' is therefore usually phrased in terms of these two core functions. More specifically, it is phrased in terms of our academic disciplines: what we teach, and which subjects we do research in.

So, in response to the question 'What is your university really good at?', the standard model academic will reply that it is really good at mathematics, or biology, or history, or medicine or engineering. The first subtext of that response is usually that the university is really good at research in these disciplines, an assertion which can then be substantiated by metrics of publications, citations, rankings and league tables. Alternatively, but not excluding the first answer, the second subtext is about the education offered within the disciplinary structures: the university has a really good law faculty, or business school, or philosophy department, or conservatory of music. Which again can be substantiated by metrics: perhaps a national student satisfaction survey, or teaching rankings, or employment statistics, or eminent alumni.

Now what about the good-for question? As discussed in Chapter One, there are many standard model academics who believe that a strong response to the good-at question will suffice, by itself, as a response to the good-for question as well. This is the argument about knowledge for its own sake, so eloquently articulated by Newman, and supplemented by the evidence of the invisible hand at work in the long-term usefulness of curiosity-driven research.

There are also, however, many voices that argue that although the good-at response is true, it is not the whole truth. These voices argue that the good-for question should also, and perhaps primarily, be answered in terms of a more direct response to the needs and demands of civil society. We heard some of these voices at the end of Chapter One. After a long detour it is time now to return to them.

Gibbons et al introduced the mode1/mode 2 distinction in 1994 to argue that the standard mode 1 practice (in what I have called the standard model) of curiosity-driven disciplinary research does not suffice to articulate fully what academics do, or should be doing. We should also consider, they argued, mode 2 knowledge, which 'is created in a broader, transdisciplinary social and economic context'. However, the Gibbons et al model is still mostly situated on the supply side, in production mode, focused on 'application'. In Chapter Seven I have made the case for focusing more on knowledge arising from the demand side, in what I called lateral research.

A key characteristic of lateral, or challenge-led, research, I have argued, is that it is responsive. Specifically, it is responsive to the challenges faced by civil society, globally, nationally or regionally. In order for us to be responsive in this way, as academics we need to *engage* with civil society. Our response to the 'good-for' question is, I would argue, best articulated in terms of civic engagement as another core function of the university.

Immediately there is then a terminological problem – one we need to address before moving on. Engagement is a core function in the same sense as research and teaching are core functions, but it is not a 'third strand' – a terminology which has often been used, but overall not to good effect. That is, engagement with civil society is not a separate activity from research and teaching. Nor would it suffice to say that it 'overlaps' with research and teaching. Engagement is better characterised as *orthogonal* to research and teaching. It is the deployment of our research and teaching, for the purpose of (a) responding to societal challenges, and (b) learning from them. Research and teaching are vertical core functions, engagement is a horizontal core function, cutting across the other two. Thus, in accepting engagement with civil society as a third core function of the academy, we accept it as one that is in a feedback loop with the other two. Engagement has a sense of purpose: it does not just analyse a societal challenge, but hopes to help address them. We deploy our expertise, the subjects and disciplines that we are good at, in order to be able to give a reasonable response to the question of what we are good for.

Another voice to recall from Chapter One is that of Ernest L. Boyer, author of the 1990 Carnegie Report *Scholarship Reconsidered*. It is worth repeating a quote from Boyer:

> Beyond the campus, America's social and economic crises are growing – troubled schools, budget deficits, pollution, urban decay, and neglected children, to highlight problems that are most apparent. Other concerns such as acid rain, AIDS, dwindling energy supplies, and population shifts are truly global, transcending national boundaries. Given these realities, the conviction is growing that the vision of service that once so energized the nation's campuses must be given a new legitimacy. The challenge then is this: Can America's colleges and universities, with all the richness of their resources, be of greater service to the nation and the world? Can we define scholarship in ways that respond more adequately to the urgent new realities both within the academy and beyond?

The question remains pertinent – even more so than in 1990. The challenges are more pervasive and more global. At the same time, a rampant rankings culture is overtly and covertly coercing the academy back into concentrating on supply-side knowledge production. Can we define scholarship in such a way that it gives credence and legitimacy to responding to the question of what we are good for?

As we have seen, attempts have been made. Various responses are known, some with their own terminology: 'service', 'outreach', 'third strand', 'university social responsibility', 'the entrepreneurial university', the university as an 'anchor institution' in its city and region – and so on. Terminology is here following expectations, and the expectations of what universities could and should be doing in relation to society are ever-increasing. Universities should serve their communities. They should engage with secondary schools. They should widen participation and ensure fair access. They should work with their cities on local needs. They should engage more actively with business and industry. They should produce skills-ready graduates. They should support small and medium-sized enterprises. They should engage with the 'third sector'. They should play a role in economic development. They should be more entrepreneurial, particularly in terms of spin-out companies. They should recruit internationally, but not exacerbate perceived problems with immigration. They should operate in a market. They should collaborate, but not in such a manner that they fall foul of anti-competition law.

No university can do it all. So, as Boyer said, we need multiple models of success. But we also need a conceptual framework within which those multiple models of success may enjoy parity of esteem. The standard model won't do it. Rankings won't do it. We need an academic ecosystem. We need a landscape of purposes, not just a ladder of esteem.

After the success of his *Scholarship Reconsidered* book, Boyer's last publication (approved by him just before his death in December 1995, and sent off for publication posthumously by his staff) was a paper on 'The scholarship of engagement', in which he said:

> Still, our outstanding universities and colleges remain,
> in my opinion, one of the greatest hopes for intellectual

and civic progress in this country. I'm convinced that for this hope to be fulfilled, the academy must become a more vigorous partner in the search for answers to our most pressing social, civic, economic and moral problems, and must reaffirm its historic commitment to what I call the scholarship of engagement.[1]

It is not quite clear whether Boyer intended the scholarship of engagement to be added as a fifth variety to his other four, or whether he saw it as an amalgam of the others. But no matter: the key point is that engagement is about a sense of civic purpose: accepting the responsibility of being responsive to the challenges faced by civil society, and deploying our knowledge and expertise to that end.

Perhaps the most fundamental question in academia is: 'What are universities for?' I have proposed that we unpack this into two questions, 'What are we good at?' and 'What are we good for?' In doing so, we begin to work towards an answer that embraces both excellence and purpose. Remember we have said that anything, and anybody, can have *arête*, if you live up to your full potential, or truly fulfil your core purpose. It is the same for universities. So we need to unpack the idea of 'a sense of purpose' – what Aristotle called the 'why'. And this leads us straight to Aristotle's theory of causality, because he believes that we have knowledge of a thing only when we have grasped its causes.[2]

Aristotle starts from a premise called the principle of sufficient reason, which says that things don't just happen; they happen for a reason. For anything to move, something must *cause* that movement. A football must be kicked; a frisbee must be thrown; an aeroplane will fly because of the propulsion of its engines and the shape of the wings. More generally: any effect must have a cause. The relationship between cause and effect constitutes the theory of causality. Whenever we say 'be*cause*', we are invoking a notion of causality.

What Aristotle came up with (repeatedly: in the *Physics,* and the *Metaphysics,* and the *Posterior Analytics*)[3] is that there are four kinds of causes. These are called the *material* cause, the *formal* cause, the *efficient cause*, and the *final* cause.

The material cause is essentially the stuff out of which a thing is made.

> In one sense, then, (1) that out of which a thing comes to be and which persists, is called 'cause', e.g. the bronze of the statue, the silver of the bowl ...[4]

In other words, when you ask what caused a statue, for Aristotle one possible answer is 'the material out of which it was made'. A second kind of answer – and this would be the formal cause – refers to the *essence* of the object or phenomenon under discussion (as opposed to its *substance*). For a statue, this would be the form that it represents – the form of an athlete, or the form of a warrior, or the form of a lion.

> In another sense (2) the form or the archetype, i.e. the statement of the essence, and its genera, are called 'causes' (e.g. of the octave the relation of 2:1, and generally number).

An octave is a series of eight notes occupying the interval between two notes, one of which has twice the frequency of vibration of the other. According to Aristotle, the essence of an octave – its formal cause – is the numerical relationship of two to one. Next we come to the efficient cause; this, essentially, is what gives impetus to change.

> Again (3) the primary source of the change or coming to rest; e.g. the man who gave advice is a cause, the father is cause of the child, and generally what makes of what is made and what causes change of what is changed.

The efficient cause, thus, is something dynamic: it is the kick of the football, the throw of the frisbee, the thrust of the jet engine. It is what pushes change along. And its opposite, so to speak, is the reason for which things are done – this being the final cause.

> Again (4) in the sense of end or 'that for the sake of which' a thing is done, e.g. health is the cause of walking about. ('Why is he walking about?' we say. 'To

be healthy', and, having said that, we think we have assigned the cause.)

There is another Greek word to know about all this: *telos,* which means 'purpose' or 'end' or 'goal'. We give a *teleological* explanation of the production of a bronze statue when we phrase its cause in terms of the *telos,* or goal, of the process, for example to honour someone or to commemorate an event.

Nowadays Aristotle's four-way explanation of causality is not much used. For this we can blame Newton, whose notion of a universe subject only to mechanical laws has led us to think almost exclusively in terms of the efficient cause. The ball went into the net, we say, because Rooney kicked it. That is however just the efficient cause. We tend to forget about the formal cause (the rules of the game), the material cause (the pitch; the posts; the ball), and the final cause (winning the game; moving up in the Premier League).

Now what has all this got to do with universities? Quite a bit, if we match our terminology of strategic planning to it. Strategy starts with an institutional vision statement, which tells you what kind of place the university wants to be. Ideally, the vision statement is phrased in such a manner that people are inspired by it, they become enthusiastic, they buy in, they are pulled along by it. That is why many vision statements start with the words 'Our aim is to be ...' The whole idea is that for the people making up the organisation, the vision should become their aspiration, their goal, their passion, their dream, their sense of purpose. It becomes, in short, their final cause.

Recall, also, that we raised the good-at/good-for distinction in Chapter Three when trying to get to grips with the idea of quality. In the language of quality assurance (and hence in the context of teaching and learning), that distinction led to notions of quality called 'fitness for purpose' and 'fitness of purpose'. Both of these relate to qualitative questions about the vision, the sense of purpose, the *telos,* which the university has articulated for itself.

Defining and moving an organisation along towards a final cause is the primary test of leadership. When Aristotle's former pupil Alexander left Macedonia, his vision was to conquer Persia. That was compelling enough for 36,000 troops from the various Greek states to join him. And, in the event, they conquered far more.

A university's vision statement is usually followed by a mission statement: the former says where the university wants to be, the latter says what it is going to do to get there. The real meat, however, is in the institutional strategic plan, which maps out a campaign for implementing the mission and realising the vision. That plan matches the idea of an efficient cause: it is the propulsion of the vehicle, the Newtonian force that moves it along.

To complete the picture, we can easily think of the material cause of the university as its asset base: the buildings, the labs, the lecture halls, the campus. And finally, the formal cause consists of those 'duller routines of universities' so disdained by G.H. Hardy: the formalities of governance, management and admin.

Of course, all of this is just an amusing little thought experiment. For example, it says nothing about the centrality of the academics in whatever the vision and mission of plan of the university might be. It is standard HR-speak to say 'our staff is our biggest asset', but the staff will not be charmed to be thought of as a material cause.

None the less, it is instructive to think of a vision as a final cause, because it is an articulation of the university's sense of purpose. If our vision statement stipulates, as part of the purpose of the university, the aim of being responsive to the needs and demands of civil society, then we have an idea of a civic university.

Redbrick and the like

> He gets degrees in making jam, at Liverpool and Birmingham.
> *Comment at Oxford, 1914*[5]

During the 12th and early 13th centuries, England established two universities.[6] Exhausted by this spurt of innovation, it then founded no more for the next 600 years, only adding more colleges to the two existing ones.

So, by the early 19th century, England still only had Oxford and Cambridge. By that time Scotland had St Andrews (1413), Glasgow (1451), Aberdeen (1495) and Edinburgh (1582). Italy had Bologna (1088), Padua (1222), Naples (1224), Siena (1240), Sapienza (1303), Florence (1321), Pisa (1343) and more than half a dozen other smaller city universities and specialist institutions (such as the medical school at Salerno). Iberia had Salamanca (1134), Valladolid (1241), Coimbra (1290), Alcala de Henares (1393), Barcelona (1450), Santiago de Compostela (1495), Valencia (1499) and Seville (1505). Besides the towering presence of Paris (1200), France had, or had had in various manifestations, Toulouse (1229), Montpellier (1289), Orleans (1306), Cahors (1331), Grenoble (1339) and Angers (1356). German-speakers had Vienna (1365), Heidelberg (1368), Erfurt (1379), Leipzig (1409), Freiburg (1457), Munich (1472) and Tübingen (1477). Eastern Europe had Charles University in Prague (1347–8), Jagiellonian University in Kraków (1364), Pécs (1367) and what is now known as Eötvös Loránd University in Budapest (1635). The tiny Netherlands, England's onetime rival as a naval, imperial and commercial power, had Leiden (1575), Groningen (1614), Amsterdam (1632) and Utrecht (1636).[7] The ten oldest universities in America were all founded before the Declaration of Independence on 4 July 1776, including Harvard (1636), Yale (1701), Pennsylvania (1740), Delaware (1743), Princeton (1746), Columbia (1754) and Brown (1764).[8]

In Chapter One, I discussed the worldwide sudden expansion of the university sector in the 1960s and 1970s, and identified three causal factors – the cold war, computers and the welfare state. That was not the first time such a growth spurt had occurred. In the UK, the first such expansion, confused but significant, started a decade or so before the coronation of Queen Victoria and lasted until a decade or so after her death. Suddenly, from the 1820s onward, two universities were no longer enough, and a hundred years later each of the major English cities had a university. We can again identify three causal factors: the industrial revolution, the vote and greater religious freedom.

The industrial revolution gave rise to the new industrial cities, particularly in the north of England. Greater concentration of people allowed greater concentration of effort, not only in manufacturing but also in a practical, non-donnish kind of intellectualism. An early example was the Lunar Society of Birmingham, a dining club and informal learned society in the 'Midlands Enlightenment' (which met during the full moon, so that members could have more light when travelling home afterwards), boasting such prominent figures as Matthew Boulton, the commercial manufacturer of steam engines, Erasmus Darwin the physician, Joseph Priestley the chemist, James Watt the engineer and Josiah Wedgwood the potter. A 'Literary and Philosophical Society' of some kind could be found in many cities: Bath, Hull, Leicester, Leeds, Liverpool, Manchester, Newcastle, Sheffield, Whitby. Politically, the Great Reform Act of 1832 (passed under the aegis of a prime minister from Newcastle, whose statue still stands high on a gratefully-inscribed column in the centre of the city) started the process whereby the previously disenfranchised began to develop as a 'working class' in the industrial cities. 'Working Men's Clubs' developed as societies of self-help, education and recreation, providing an upward push towards institutions of higher education.

Also, the Church – now the Anglican Church – was beginning to lose its grip on the regimentation of thought. As regards higher education, that process is perhaps best illustrated by what happened in London, in the 1820s.

The title of 'first English university after Oxbridge' has various claimants, so it may be better to start the story at a later point in the chronology. Consider, therefore, the case of what is now the University of Sheffield. In 1902 a pamphlet was circulated in the factories of the 'steel city', soliciting a contribution of one penny from each worker towards establishing a university in the city. Headed 'A University for Sheffield', it said:

You should support the University because:

1. The UNIVERSITY will be for the people.
2. The UNIVERSITY will bring the highest education within the reach of the child of the working man.
3. The UNIVERSITY will help the local industries.
4. The UNIVERSITY will be the centre where the treatment of accidents and diseases will be studied.
5. SHEFFIELD is the only large City in England without a University. Sheffield cannot afford to remain in this position.
6. The UNIVERSITY will not only benefit this district, it will assist the nation in its trade competition with other nations.[9]

The pamphlet nicely summarises a number of earlier points about ideas of a civic university. It says that the university will be a civic institution. It talks about widening participation, interacting with industry, and addressing societal challenges. It speaks of the city, and of global impact. All in all, it says a lot about what the university will be *for*. And mainly, what it says is that the university will be *for the people*. That is why even the poorest factory worker may be asked for a penny towards its establishment. And evidently the workers responded: the *Sheffield Independent* felt that they made 'a very creditable display of the proper sense of citizenship'.[10]

By the time Sheffield got around to it, similar stories had already unfolded in other industrial cities, such as Manchester, Birmingham, Liverpool and Leeds. Further north, Newcastle, long known for coal and latterly for building ships and armaments, also had the advantage of its own Literary and Philosophical Society, established in 1793. Here, in April 1831, a local surgeon called Thomas Greenhow delivered a paper titled 'The expediency of establishing in Newcastle an academical institution of the nature of a college or university for the promotion of literature and science, more especially among the middle classes of the community'. In making this proposal, Greenhow was following a theme already raised in 1802 by one of the vice-presidents of the Lit and Phil (as it is known to this day), urging the establishment of educational institutions based on 'the application of scientific principles to the process of trade and manufacture', including 'the systematic training of the younger mining pupils'.[11]

Greenhow's paper is seen as the founding document of what became in effect a private medical school. It was joined in 1871 by a College of Physical Science, where the theoretical chairs of mathematics, physics and the like were balanced by chairs devoted to regional needs, such as mining, naval architecture, and agriculture.

> Unthinkable as it may have been to many members of England's oldest universities, Oxford and Cambridge, there was a new spirit of higher education developing in the large provincial cities in the last decades of the nineteenth century. New universities were in the making. Often called 'redbrick', their better name is 'civic' universities, since this exactly describes their

symbiotic relationship with the urban area which created them....

The earliest northern civic college of higher education was Owens College, Manchester, set up in 1851. Its founder aimed at a model derived from Oxford and Cambridge, with emphasis on the classics, but there was little demand among Mancunians. The college struggled until it changed its syllabus to more practical subjects and secured the backing of a wealthy local industrialist. Thereafter it went from strength to strength, establishing particular excellence in chemistry....

Sheffield, Leeds, Newcastle and Bristol formed higher education colleges in the 1870s; Birmingham, Liverpool and Nottingham followed soon afterwards. Mason Science College, Birmingham, opened in 1880 but quickly secured generous funding and was the first to gain an independent charter, as the University of Birmingham in 1900. Liverpool began life as University College in 1881 and also developed speedily, forming the federated Victoria University with Manchester and Leeds. These three became separate universities between the years 1902 and 1904. Sheffield followed in 1905.[12]

Developments in London actually preceded those in the provincial cities, but quickly became quite confused. Part of the confusion was about the role of the Church in higher education. In order to study at Oxbridge, you needed to 'conform' to the 39 Articles of the Church of England. 'Non-conformists' – Methodists, Congregationalists, Unitarians, Quakers and Presbyterians, let alone Catholics and non-Christians – naturally began to wonder where they should go. (John Henry Newman, we saw in Chapter One, went to Dublin.)

What is now University College London traces its founding back to 11 February 1826, under the name London University. Or at least that was the intention. Founded as a joint stock company, it was completely secular, and had a broad support base outside the Anglican Church, containing Jews, Roman Catholics, Baptists and Utilitarians. Its official motto translates from Latin as 'Let all come who by merit deserve the most reward'. Famously, the body of the utilitarian philosopher Jeremy Bentham, considered the spiritual father of UCL, remains to this day on public display in a glass case in the main building.

The establishment of such a company, soon referred to as 'that Godless institution in Gower Street', with a bold claim to being London's University, was bound to evoke both a religious and an intellectual counter-reaction. (Newman, in his second discourse, was scathing: 'It is the fashion just now, as you very well know, to erect so-called Universities, without making any provision in them at all for Theological Chairs.... Such a procedure ... seems to me an intellectual absurdity.')[13] So, when the council of the new institution sought a royal charter which would officially confer the title of 'university' and enable them to grant degrees, their application was successfully blocked by Oxford and Cambridge. They tried again in 1833, only to meet with an even broader front of opposition, Oxbridge now being joined by the Church and the medical profession. Concurrently, while the 'University of London' was trying to live up to its name, a more god-fearing Tory institution was founded in 1829, supported by the prime minister (the Duke of Wellington), and under the patronage of King George IV, who soon issued the necessary Royal Charter. King's College, as it was known then and now, made its point plain through its own motto: 'With holiness and wisdom', and through its opening ceremony being presided over by the Archbishop of Canterbury. Even at King's, however, non-Anglican students were admitted, though the staff had to be members of the Church.

The matter of degree-granting powers was resolved, after a fashion, in 1836, by the creation of a new body called the University of London, of which King's College and the now-renamed University College London became constituent colleges. That body eventually became the federal University of London, which still exists. (UCL and King's only gained their own degree-awarding powers in 2005 and 2006 respectively.)

Whether Anglican, non-conformist or secular, however, the London colleges, just like the redbrick universities, were clearly different from Oxbridge.

The strongest, single, intellectual influence was that of Edinburgh, and, from the example of the Scottish

Universities, London drew many of its most distinctive features. The extended range of the subjects of the university study, the lecture system, the non-residence of students, their admission to single courses, the absence of religious texts, the dependence of the professors upon fees and the democratic character of the institutions, were all deliberate imitations of Scottish practice.[14]

More generally, whether in London or in the industrial cities, but especially in the latter, the new universities differed from Oxbridge in having a sense of place, a sense of people, and a sense of purpose. They were not just *in* the city, but *of* the city. They knew they were catering to a different clientele from Oxbridge, and they knew pretty much what they were there for.[15]

It is worth remembering that Oxbridge played no part whatsoever in the industrial revolution, neither in contribution nor in response. By contrast, most of the new universities were part of the new industrial society, perhaps more as an outcome than as an influence, but connected to it in a way that Oxbridge was not. Most but not all, because the Oxbridge model, and the Church, and the 'collegiate system', still had their adherents. Durham, for example (another claimant to the title of being the third university in England) was founded in 1832 by the Anglican Church, very much in imitation of Oxbridge, and partly in reaction against what was happening in the neighbouring industrial city of Newcastle. In Dublin, John Henry Newman's intention was similar: cloning Oxbridge, but for the Catholic Church.

The 'new spirit of higher education' took shape in the context of serving the needs and demands of a broader society. It was a demand-led model, rather than a supply-driven model.

This kind of thinking did not happen only in England. A near parallel is the creation of the land-grant universities in the United States, from the time of the civil war onward. In 1862, President Abraham Lincoln signed into law what became known as the Land-grant Act, or the Morrill Act, titled 'An Act donating Public Lands to the several States and Territories which may provide Colleges for the Benefit of Agriculture and the Mechanic Arts'. One key asset of the federal government at that time was that it had made itself the owner of enormous tracts of land, and the Land-grant Act monetised that asset for the benefit of education. Each eligible state received 30,000 acres of land, to be sold or developed in order to fund the new institutions.

> *Provided*, That the moneys so invested or loaned shall constitute a perpetual fund ... to the endowment, support, and maintenance of at least one college where the leading object shall be, without excluding other scientific and classical studies and including military tactics, to teach such branches of learning as are related to agriculture and the mechanic arts, in such manner as the legislatures of the States may respectively prescribe, in order to promote the liberal and practical education of the industrial classes in the several pursuits and professions in life.[16]

So, just as industrial development provided the stimulus for civic universities in England, agriculture and the 'mechanic arts' provided the stimulus for similar institutions in the US. The Morrill Act of 1862 excluded what counted as the Confederate states at that time, but the model was re-invoked after the civil war with a second and similar Morrill Act in 1890. Many American universities, both public and private, still proudly fly the flag of a land-grant university. Cornell, for example, situates itself as 'New York State's Land Grant University', and states: 'Cornell was founded on the principle that our labs, classrooms and extension programs focus on societal challenges'.[17]

The civic universities of England established a new academic pathway: arising from and serving their cities, responsive to the new industrial era, and admitting students who lived at home rather than cloistered together in college. Durham and Dublin sought to imitate the Oxbridge aura, Manchester, Birmingham, Liverpool, Newcastle and Sheffield did not. The civic university model worked, for what it was intended to do.

But in England there is always a but. The big but for the civic universities was the matter of esteem. Was a university that was not Oxbridge really a university? Or just, as John Henry Newman sneered, a 'so-called university'? Were these new institutions not just about degrees in making jam? One can hear, even from this distance, the ghostly refrains of a 'standards are dropping' chorus.

That nagging doubt did not go away easily. It is expressed with great clarity in a book titled *Red Brick University*, first published in 1943, which was followed by a sequel, *Redbrick and these Vital Days*, in 1945, with the two volumes combined (and amended) under the original title in 1951.[18] The author was one 'Bruce Truscot', a deliberate pseudonym. The dust jacket of the 1951 edition takes some pride in the fact that 'the enigmatic personality of Bruce Truscot has excited much curiosity in University circles'. This claim is slightly curious, because the supposedly enigmatic author drops plenty of hints as to his identity: 'One who, besides having long experience at Oxbridge and Redbrick, has both studied and taught in foreign universities, served as a delegate to conferences held at universities in Europe, visited almost all the universities of one of the Dominions and made an intimate study of university life in the United States'.[19] Known or anonymous, however, Bruce Truscot clearly projected himself as a gentleman worth listening to.

Unfortunately, it is quite hard, at this distance, to distinguish in Bruce Truscot's writing satire from prejudice, or conviction from provocation. The thrust of the book can none the less be summarised as follows: there are at present (which is 1943) 12 universities in England: 2 of Oxbridge, the ancients, and 10 of redbrick, the moderns. (That immediately disregards what was then already well established as the University of London, with its constituent colleges, but let that pass.) The first chapter is titled 'The battle of the ancients and the moderns', and it soon becomes clear that this is a very unequal battle indeed.

> ... not one Etonian or Harrovian in a thousand would consider entering a shabby modern university, unlovely in appearance, unmellowed by tradition and attended by men who actually live with their families and probably have only the faintest idea of the respective significance of a dinner jacket and a white waistcoat.

Consider, for example, the life of poor Bill Jones at Redbrick University.

Poor Bill Jones! No Hall and Chapel and oak-sporting for him; no invitations to breakfast at the Master's Lodgings; no hilarious bump suppers or moonlight strolls in romantic quadrangles; no all-night sittings with a congenial group round his own – his very own – fireplace. No: Bill goes off five mornings a week to Redbrick University exactly as he went to Back Street Council School and Drabtown Municipal Secondary School for Boys – and he goes on his bicycle to save the twopenny tram-fare. Exactly as in those earlier institutions, he climbs the similar flights of dirty, sordid stairs (only there are more of them), sits in a rather larger classroom of the same type and with the same grimy outlook and answers to his name called from very much the same kind of register. His lunch consists, according to the state of his finances, of a shilling made-up meat dish, or of a roll and a cup of coffee, taken hurriedly at the University Union and followed by the meeting of some society sandwiched between lunch and afternoon lectures because no society that meets in the late afternoon can hope for more than the most diminutive attendance. Between four and five o'clock he goes home to the same sort of high tea as he has had all his life and then attempts to settle down to an evening's work, either alone in an unused sitting room, in his unheated bedroom or, more probably, in the living room, where Lizzie, at the same table, is wrestling with her algebra, Bertie is continually appealing to him for help with his French, and at all too frequent intervals the wireless is turned on for the entertainment or edification of the rest of the family.

All of this, however, is not Bill Jones' fault, nor is the fault of Redbrick University. And it needs to change.

So year after year, to an increasing extent, Redbrick has the chagrin of seeing all the best boys and girls from its schools making for Oxbridge and the dubious consolation of welcoming those who had tried to do the same, and, for lack of brain, or possibly of application or efficient teaching, had failed.

The same process goes on to this day, 'Oxbridge if I can and Redbrick if I can't'. Headmasters almost to a man, and headmistresses almost to a woman, encourage their pupils to think of the local university as second-best.... So Redbrick loses two groups of undergraduates, each superior to the group it gets, and with the help of which it could very soon challenge Oxbridge everywhere. The first group is of children who leave the district young, for expensive boarding schools elsewhere, and, having gone through them, would never dream of going on (or should one say 'back'?) to the local university; the second group is of boys and girls educated, usually at no cost to their parents, in local schools, who leave their native town just as they have the chance of repaying something of the debt they owe it.

That is the state of things which the new world must remedy.

'Oxbridge if I can and Redbrick if I can't' – you have to wonder what has changed over the past three-quarters of a century. Substitute 'Russell Group' for 'Redbrick', and Bruce Truscot's observation still rings true. Then observe that you could in like manner say 'Russell Group if I can and 1960s university if I can't', or '1960s university if I can and post-1992 university if I can't', and we may conclude that the main change since 1943 is that the ladder of esteem has become longer.

So, what to do? Bruce Truscot's prescription is that all should be level. 'What is the ideal', he asks, 'towards which we need to work?'

An England, surely, in which there are no longer two large residential universities for those who are either well-to-do or brilliant, and ten smaller universities, mainly non-residential, for those who are neither. Let there be twelve, of approximately equal size, all in the main residential, and each having certain Schools in which it excels the rest. Let the standard of admission at all universities, as well as the minimum standard for graduation, be raised, as nearly as is possible, to the same level.... Let every boy or girl entering a university go where his or her particular subject is best taught. And finally, let a levelling of standards pave the way for the interchange of pupils where this is in the interest of the pupils themselves.

In short, then, Bruce Truscot's proposed remedy for inequality is uniformity. Let all be the same.

In fact, the moderns started to imitate the ancients, not in terms of structure, but in striving for more academic esteem. And so, in the English way of turning diversity into hierarchy, they sought to climb the ladder rather than cement the new paradigm of a civic university. Chronologically, the esteem-chasing process accelerates at about the time when Sputnik was launched, which, as discussed in Chapter One, was the beginning of the era of the ologies and the rise of the standard model university. The redbrick universities increasingly focused on research, and particularly pure research. All else – teaching in particular – became secondary. Being secondary still left teaching better off than the original civic mission of the redbrick universities, which all but disappeared as they effectively turned their back on their cities.[20] Today, the original redbricks, together with Oxbridge and London, comprise the majority of the Russell Group.

To give credit to Bruce Truscot, neglect of civic engagement is not what he would have wanted. On the contrary, within the context of his various prejudices and preoccupations, Bruce was an advocate of the civic mission. In his levelling process, Oxbridge was supposed to learn more about the civic mission from Redbrick, just as Redbrick had to learn more about excellence from Oxbridge. That did not happen – or at least not in that phase. Instead, the redbricks were replaced as new entrants by the 'plateglass' universities of the 1960s and 1970s, which very soon started to play the imitation game, conforming to the standard model. And the same happened again after 1992, when the polytechnics became universities. There seems to be a kind of gravitational pull towards the standard model.

Finally, just when some cracks started appearing in the ivory tower, with Boyer's idea of the four scholarships, and Gibbons et al discoursing on mode 2 knowledge generation, and various voices calling for a return to the value of civic responsibility – at that moment rankings and league tables appeared on the scene, and seduced or coerced universities back to the standard model. And so England still has a hierarchical and stratified university sector, and everybody still tries to climb the ladder of esteem.

It is the one-dimensionality of the ladder that is the difficulty. Bruce Truscot's proposed solution of uniformity clearly did not work. Which is fine: we do want differentiation. So, somehow, we should try to construct a sector where differentiation of purpose does not entail stratification of esteem. To do so, we need to think in more than one dimension. We must allow for lateral developments.

To see how that can be done, it is worth going even further back into history, to the very early days of universities.

Paris, 1277

> From the twelfth century onwards Paris was the acknowledged intellectual capital of Europe; during the thirteenth and early fourteenth centuries it was the arena of combat for the ablest and most daring minds of the age.
>
> *Friedrich Heer, The Medieval World*

On 7 March 1277, in Paris, there was an attack on academic freedom. The Bishop of Paris, Stephen Tempier, issued a condemnation of 219 propositions associated with various aspects of Aristotelian teaching. Essentially, the condemnation sought to stop some of the masters of arts of the University of Paris from interpreting the works of Aristotle in ways that were not agreeable to the Church. Not explicitly named in the condemnation, but clearly a target, were two of these masters: Siger of Brabant and Boethius of Dacia.

We are a bit dismissive nowadays about medieval scholarship, and scholastic philosophers in particular. We easily invoke the stereotype of angels dancing on the head of a pin, or an alchemical search for the philosopher's stone, or a vague remembrance of arguments for the existence of God. And yet the medieval period, from the 12th century onwards, saw the first real awakening of European thought since the fall of Rome. This was a long time before what we call the Renaissance, and showed the first glimmerings of the scientific method.

In the early medieval period, those who tried to think for themselves, beyond Church doctrine, did not have much to work with. They knew no disciplines other than the liberal arts, or the 'practical arts' of medicine, architecture or law. They had no laboratories for conducting experiments, nor would they have had any clear idea of experimentation as different from magic and sorcery They had little grasp of empirical research or the analysis of data, and almost no quantitative methods. Intellectual endeavour took place within a theological frame of reference, in somewhat the same way as Greek intellectual endeavour one and a half millennia earlier took place within a philosophical framework. What they did have, though, was their faculty of reasoning. They learnt to doubt, to ask questions, to analyse, and to dispute. And so most of that first wave of independent thinkers, who fell upon the recently rediscovered works of Aristotle with a voracious intellectual appetite, were logicians of some sort.

For centuries, Aristotle had been largely unknown in Europe. Plato had had somewhat better fortune. Already in the 5th century AD, St Augustine of Hippo had done a good job of relating Platonic realism to Church doctrine. In chapter ten of Book 8 of his *City of God*, postponing his arguments with the Platonists, St Augustine makes it clear that he far prefers them to the other pagan philosophers. It is not difficult to see why. Plato's otherworldliness and insistence on a supra-world of universals, understood only by philosophers, away from the grubby everyday world around us, can be made to mesh rather nicely with the teachings of a Church which believed that the Kingdom of God could be entered only after leaving the sinful world into which we were born.

Aristotle, who was interested in physics at least as much as metaphysics, and in particulars at least as much as universals, had no similar champion at that time. And so he largely disappeared from view. Largely, but not entirely. His eventual reappearance came via a different trajectory. Intellectually, his work was preserved by the scholarship of Islam, through which his corpus was translated into Arabic. Chronologically and geographically, he followed in the wake of the Islamic conquest of North Africa, and then of a large part of Spain. Toledo, which was under Muslim rule from 712 to 1085, was a cosmopolitan city with a diverse population of Jews, Moors and Spaniards, both Muslim and Christian, and by the 12th century it had a renowned school of translators. The entire Aristotelian corpus was translated from Arabic into Latin, and thus became available to Christian scholars.

The bridging figure was a Muslim jurist, physician and scholar known as Averroes of Cordoba (1126–98), 'Averroes' being a latinised version of his Arabic name Abu al-Walid Muhammad ibn Ahmad ibn Rushd (usually shortened to Ibn Rushd). He is the only Islamic thinker to appear in Raphael's *School of Athens*, where, with a sublime disregard for chronology, he is peering over the shoulder of Pythagoras. Averroes produced extensive commentaries on the works of Aristotle, in some cases line by line. These were in addition to his own philosophical works, which were considered to be controversial within Islam for a reason we might still recognise: he gave more weight to reason than some of the faithful considered appropriate. (He was considered the main philosophical opponent of a previous scholar called Al-Ghazali, still famous for a tome titled *The Incoherence of the Philosophers* – to which Averroes produced a response titled *The Incoherence of Incoherence*.) Averroes argued, essentially, that it is wrong for religion to forbid the study of philosophy – a point of view relevant to all three the major religions of that time. In the end, he had a greater influence on emerging thought in Christian Europe than on later Islamic thought, precisely because of his stance on reason vis-à-vis faith. So great was his influence that the scholastics referred to Averroes as 'the Commentator'. Aristotle had by that time long been known simply as 'the Philosopher'.

So, when the Bishop of Paris issued his condemnation of 1277, it was a continuation, in a different faith, of the clash between religious and rational thought. It was in fact the bishop's second go at eradicating Aristotelianism, having already issued a first condemnation in 1270. But this time the bishop overreached himself: his scattergun condemnation of 219 propositions included some from a renowned scholar who was supposed to have been on the side of the Church. This man was a Dominican friar called Thomas Aquinas, later Saint Thomas, who had been engaged in a fierce intellectual contest with Siger of Brabant.

The battle between Siger and Aquinas was a Christian replay of the battle between Averroes and more orthodox Islamists. It was also an academic spat between the masters of arts and the doctors of theology at the University of Paris.

> By far the largest faculty in the university was that of the arts, the 'philosophical' faculty. The curriculum was based on the seven liberal arts, grammar, rhetoric and dialectics, which made up the trivium, and music, arithmetic, geometry and astronomy, which were the quadrivium.... Study in the faculty of arts was really intended as a prologue to the study of theology. The only 'full' professors at Paris were the doctors of theology, who had completed sixteen years of study, of which the years spent in the faculty of arts were only a necessary preliminary, to be looked back on with contempt in after years. Nevertheless, the theologians regarded the 'artists' with disquiet and displeasure, often not untinged with envy.... At Paris the masters of arts were the permanent element of intellectual unrest and the driving force of intellectual revolutions.[21]

If the masters of arts were the radicals, then the doctors of theology were the conservatives. Having made it to the top of the academic pyramid, the doctors were not keen on being overtaken in esteem by mere masters of arts. Chief among the artists was Siger (or Sigebert) of Brabant, the leading Averroist. He is quoted as saying: 'We are not discussing God's miracles; what we have to do is to discuss what is natural in a natural way.'

> Siger was at the heart of the intellectual storm raging in Paris during the second half of the thirteenth century. His party, the 'party of Siger', for some years refused to accept the result of the rectorial election of 1271. Siger fascinated students and scholars as the

unequivocal champion of the autonomy of reason, of 'pure' knowledge free of any intellectual limitation.[22]

So alarming had been the advance of the Averroist front that something had to be done. And so, back in 1269, the doctors of theology had brought back to Paris their most renowned scholar, the 'Sicilian ox', Thomas Aquinas, for a second spell of teaching. (The move was somewhat against their own statutes, it must be said, which allowed friar doctors only one such period.) This may have been a mistake on their part, because Aquinas had as much in common with Siger as he had in opposition to him. He did write a treatise *De unitate intellectus, contra Averroistas,* and he attacked Averroes as the 'the perverter of Aristotle', but that was because he himself was a true Aristotelian. Unlike St Augustine, and not quite in line with what the Bishop of Paris would have wanted, Aquinas taught the primacy of the intellect over the emotions. He regarded God as the 'most perfect of intellectual beings' – a kind of Supreme Professor of Logic.

The disagreement between Siger and Aquinas, therefore, was not a case of being pro- or contra-Aristotelian. They were both pro. Rather, the disagreement was the extent to which the world-based philosophy initiated by Aristotle could or should be brought into line with theological dogma. Aquinas wanted to do for Aristotle what St Augustine had done for Plato 800 years earlier: reconcile him with the Church. The outcome of this endeavour, a kind of Aristotelian counterpoint to Augustine's *City of God*, was his *Summa Theologica* (which among other things gives five proofs of the existence of God). Siger, on the other hand, could not be bothered much with the theological superstructure. He was for rational investigation on its own terms.

Somewhere within this intellectual firestorm was a quiet but important voice from someone we know tantalisingly little about: Boethius of Dacia.[23]

> While relatively little is known about the life and career of Boethius of Dacia, considerable progress has been made in recent decades with respect to his writings. As a consequence, more light has been cast on his important role within the Faculty of Arts at the University of

Paris in the early 1270s. He is emerging as a leading representative of the movement often referred to as Latin Averroism or as Radical Aristotlelianism which had developed there at about that time. It is now clear that a number of the propositions condemned in March 1277 by the Bishop of Paris, Stephen Tempier, were taken from his writings.[24]

Just to be clear: Boethius (or Boetius) of Dacia was not the Boethius you may have heard about, the one who wrote the *Consolation of Philosophy* in the early 6th century. The 13th-century Boethius was probably from Denmark or Sweden, because he is also referred to as *Danske Bo* – 'Bo the Dane'. (Confusingly, the Dominican province of the three Scandinavian kingdoms of Denmark, Norway and Sweden was called 'Dacia' rather than 'Dania'.)[25] At the University of Paris he was one of the scholars, like Siger, who chose not to progress his studies beyond Master of Arts by entering for a Doctorate in Theology. These 'artists' preferred the freedom of philosophical enquiry to the strictures of theological doctrine.

Someone who heard Boetius of Dacia lecture described him in his lecture-notes as *naturalis*; his interest was confined to 'things, their motion and matter'. Boetius was silenced by the condemnation of 1277; so little is known of him personally that it is not certain exactly where he came from or when he died. He was the author of one of the most interesting medieval treatises on grammatical theory (*De modis significandi*) and of a small work On the Sovereign Good (*De summo bono*), which Mandonnet has described as the 'purest, clearest and most resolute rationalism one could possibly find'.[26]

So what did he say? *De summo bono* (which was only rediscovered in 1924) is not a long treatise, and it is reprinted in its entirety as an Epilogue at the end of this book, so you can read it for yourself. In summary, however, what he says is that our most supreme human fulfilment is to be found in combining clear thought and virtuous action. His conclusion comes, as one would expect, as the outcome of a logical argument, which goes like this. The supreme good for man should be in terms of his highest power, which is his reason and intellect. One part of the intellect is speculative – what we might call theoretical, or 'pure' reasoning, through which we try to gain understanding. The other part of the intellect is practical, where, in any given circumstance, we try to decide what is the right thing to do. The highest good that can be attained in terms of the speculative intellect is knowledge of what is true.[27] The highest good that can be attained in terms of the practical intellect is the pursuit of virtue. It follows, then, that the supreme good consists in the cognition of the true and the practice of the good – 'and taking delight in both'.

Behind *De summo bono* we can distinguish the inspiration of that work which Aristotle, the Philosopher, carries in his hand in Raphael's *School of Athens*: the *Nicomachean Ethics*. In Book X Aristotle deals with human happiness, which is an end in itself, as 'the best, noblest and most pleasant thing in the world', and is identified with the good. Moreover, the pursuit of philosophy – that is, the exercise of reason – is the best way of achieving it. Agreeing with that sentiment, Boethius asserted that 'There is no more excellent kind of life than to give oneself to philosophy.' That must have riled the bishop no end – it is one of the propositions featuring in his condemnation of 1277.

Reasoning from the work of the Philosopher, Boethius concludes that human happiness – quality of life – consists in the enjoyment of two things: knowing the true and doing the good. We come back here to the ambiguity discussed at the beginning of Chapter Three. This is what I wrote there:

> When we talk about the good, therefore, and we take the concept back to Plato or Aristotle, we should know that in their language they were talking about *arête*. Our translation comes out either as excellence or as virtue, and we experience this as an ambiguity to be cleared up, but the original sense of *arête* would encompass both nuances, as separate dimensions rather than separate meanings.

I am going to take seriously the thought of excellence and virtue positioned in separate dimensions. Before proceeding, however, we need an interlude to talk about risk.

Reality check

> It's your fault, Eeyore. You've never been to see any of us. You just stay here in this one corner of the Forest waiting for the others to come to you. Why don't you go to them sometimes?
>
> *Rabbit talking to Eeyore, in The House at Pooh Corner*

Let us continue to expand the thought that the pursuit of virtue, for a university, involves engagement with society. Hard-headed realists and sober pragmatists will tell you that positioning civic engagement as a core function of your university involves certain risks. These are not inconsiderable.

As you would expect, there are books about civic engagement. Already in 1982 Derek Bok (25th President of Harvard University, 1971–91) published a book titled *Beyond the Ivory Tower: Social Responsibilities of the Modern University*,[28] described by the *Los Angeles Times Book Review* as 'the first serious attempt since Clark Kerr's 1963 *The Uses of the University* to analyze the role of the university in modern society'.[29] Incidentally, it was Clark Kerr (12th President of the University of California, 1958–1967) who, in coining the term 'multiversity', said that the university no longer has a soul.

> The university started as a single community – a community of masters and students. It may even be said to *have had a soul* in the sense of a central animating principle. Today, the large American university is, rather, a whole series of communities and activities held together by a common name, a common Governing Board, and related purposes.[30] (My italics – CB)

Later, in the millennium year 2000, the Association of Commonwealth Universities started a project to explore how universities engage with society. It resulted in a book titled *The Idea of Engagement*[31] with a wider aim: not just to learn what happens, but 'to lead, and contribute to, an international debate on why it is imperative for universities and institutions of higher learning to be actively involved in the society of which they are part'. The book is partitioned into various sections, the first of which is 'The Idea'. One of the contributors here is Michael Gibbons – that same Michael Gibbons of the mode1/mode2 distinction – writing about 'engagement as a core value in a mode 2 society'. Another contributor, David Watson, followed up with a book of his own, *Managing Civic and Community Engagement*.[32] David Watson is also one of the editors of a later book titled *The Engaged University: International Perspectives on Civic Engagement,*[33] which is really a book about an organisation called the Talloires Network.

Headquartered at Tufts University in Massachusetts, the Talloires Network grew out of a meeting organised by Tufts at its European Centre in the alpine village of Talloires, France, in September 2005. It was the first international gathering of the heads of universities devoted to strengthening the civic roles and social responsibilities of higher education.

> Although the conference participants represented starkly different contexts and types of universities, they found that they embraced very similar visions and strategic orientations. The conference produced the Talloires Declaration on the Civic Roles and Social Responsibilities of Higher Education.[34] All signatories of the Declaration have committed their institutions to educating for social responsibility and civic engagement, and to strengthening the application of university resources to the needs of local and global communities.[35]

Since then the Talloires Network has grown considerably, to over 360 member universities in 77 countries. It has a defined set of aims and activities,[36] and as a network it works very well.

Other collaborations along the same lines may be more focused. The (much smaller) University Social Responsibility Network,[37] for example, adapts the idea of corporate social responsibility. Like Talloires, it arose from a founding conference, organised by Hong

Kong Polytechnic University in 2014. Besides further meetings and collaborative arrangements it has also produced a book titled *University Social Responsibility and Quality of Life*,[38] the Preface of which neatly summarises the idea that universities should be responsive to global challenges.

> The contemporary world is facing many problems such as global warming, poverty, income disparities, refugees, aging populations, and new diseases. Obviously, how to solve these problems is a challenging task for leaders in the national, regional, and global contexts. As universities are commonly regarded as incubators for knowledge and solutions to promote quality of life, it is important to ask how universities can help to build a better world. In fact, it is the public expectation that universities should generate knowledge which can solve real-life problems which can eventually promote quality of life.

As another example, The Research University Civic Engagement Network (TRUCEN)[39] consists of around 40 universities in the US. The secretariat for TRUCEN is a much bigger body called Campus Compact, which is 'a national coalition of nearly 1,100 colleges and universities committed to the public purposes of higher education'.[40] An article titled 'The History of TRUCEN' lifts out the core issue quite clearly:

> By the early years of this new century it was evident that increasing numbers of colleges and universities had undertaken numerous innovative efforts to reinvigorate and prioritize students' civic and community engagement in their surrounding communities.... However, a number of individuals involved with these movements had noticed that much of the most ambitious and innovative work was taking place in teaching-focused community and liberal arts colleges and state universities. Research universities were relatively less involved, despite the significant efforts of many of their faculty and staff members

who had undertaken to promote and advance civic engagement in these institutions.[41]

So, 'recognising the need to encourage engaged scholarship at research universities and these institutions' potential to provide leadership in this arena', a meeting on this topic was organised in 2005 by Campus Contact and Tufts University, and TRUCEN grew out of that meeting. The interesting point here is the motivation of that first meeting: 'the opportunities and special challenges relating to civic engagement work at research-intensive universities'. Which leads us to the question of the challenges, and more specifically the risks, of civic engagement. Why are research universities 'relatively less involved' in civic engagement?

The fairly obvious answer to this question is that the risk of doing civic engagement is higher for research-intensive universities. History points out the most obvious risk of adopting civic engagement as a core function of your university: lack of esteem. The standard model school of thought, in both the Humboldtian and Newmanesque traditions, holds that accomplishment in pure research and subject-based teaching is of higher intellectual merit than engaging with the world around us, and therefore deserves higher esteem. It is a powerful Platonic belief that the discovery and dissemination of 'knowledge for its own sake' is more worthy, more exalted, more *pure*, than any deployment of knowledge in responsive mode. Remember, for example, G.H. Hardy's dismissive comment about the work of the applied mathematician as being 'in some ways a little pathetic'.

The story of the redbrick universities illustrates the point. Faced by an esteem deficit and sneering comments about degrees in making jam, they turned their face away from society in order to emulate Oxbridge. Today they are the backbone of the Russell Group. In that sense, the strategy worked for them. And history repeats itself, with later universities likewise trying to climb the greasy pole of rankings and league tables. On this one-dimensional strategy, the tag of 'civic university' is nothing but an unnecessary risk.

The second risk is a contemporary version of the first: positioning yourself as a civic university will bring you no benefit whatsoever in terms of rankings and league tables. Have a look again at Table 2.1 in Chapter Two setting out the measures of evaluation for some of the standard world rankings: there is virtually nothing in there that connects with the idea of responding to the needs and demands of civil society. The measurements are all on the supply side, and, as discussed before, mostly on output measures of research. The only attempt at giving some credence to measures of civic engagement was the U-Multirank scheme, discussed in Chapters Two and Three. Two of its five categories of evaluation can be thought of as being in responsive mode: knowledge transfer and regional engagement. (The other three are research and teaching, as expected, and internationalisation.) However, as we have seen, U-Multirank had difficulty getting off the ground, partly because politicians and the academic community did their best to clip its wings, and partly because participating in U-Multirank turned out to be a lot of work.

'A lot of work' is a third risk worth reckoning with. Civic engagement is a lot of work: it is diffuse, disorganised, even somewhat chaotic. When academics engage with other academics they know the rules of the game, so they can be fairly efficient about it. This is not the case when they engage with civil society, because civil society does not know what the academic rules are, nor does it much care. Business and industry have their own set of rules of engagement, so do charities, social enterprises, faith groups, community organisations and local government. 'Civil society' is not homogeneous, and the needs and demands of civil society do not come to us neatly packaged into academic disciplines. So there is a quite a lot of translation going on to match needs with expertise.

That brings up the fourth risk: any activity which requires a lot of work can easily become a displacement activity, offered in lieu of other work. When a university adopts civic engagement as a core academic function, there is the risk that some academics will step away from research and/or teaching on the grounds that they are busy with engagement. The risk is exacerbated when engagement is characterised as a 'third strand' activity. The view taken here is the opposite: engagement is premised on research and teaching, not distinct from them. A university should engage with societal challenges on the basis of its academic expertise. It should deploy what it is good at if it wishes to be able to say what, distinctively, it is good for. Any large organisation could set up a soup kitchen as an expression of corporate social responsibility. A university, to add academic value, should do so only if there is some connection between soup kitchens and its research or teaching.

Selectivity, I would argue, is a key factor in successful civic engagement. It helps to mitigate another risk, which is the risk of raised expectations. The number of societal issues that a university *could* engage with is potentially infinite. Besides the big global challenges, there is almost always a list of local challenges as well. It might be poverty or homelessness, industrial decline or urban decay, drug use or public health issues, poor schooling or lack of opportunity, the protection of a minority culture or the preservation of a small language. Whatever the issue, those who suffer from it might well feel that a university which has set out its stall for responding to societal challenges should feel itself under an obligation to take up their cause. The only way out of this conundrum is for the university, in making its commitment to address the good-for question, to be very clear that it cannot do everything, and that it will try to make its contribution to society through deploying what it is good at. The manner and extent of societal engagement must remain an academic choice, made on academic grounds, and the choice must be exercised by the university itself, not by any interest group on behalf of the university.

Overall, there is a risk of simplistic assumptions about the civic university 'serving its community'. 'Which community?' should be the first question, and 'to what purpose?' the second. Surely no university served its own community more assiduously than Stellenbosch served Afrikanerdom. But to what effect? In positioning itself as a *Volksuniversiteit*, Stellenbosch served as the maternity ward of apartheid and the intellectual muse of the Broederbond. As we saw in Chapter Three, something similar happened at Freiburg in the 1930s, when Heidegger, as rector, endorsed the *Führerprinzip*. And, lest the English feel a little smug in this respect, it is worth remembering how effectively and for how long Oxbridge has served its own community, the English upper class. Serving a community is not necessarily, in itself, an expression of the good. There needs to be a broader test of whether serving that community in the way it may wish to be served is also a service to society.

As we saw in our earlier discussion of risk management, the presence of risk need not deter us. Instead, we should be aware of risk, evaluate it, and take whatever steps we can to mitigate it. So, then, how do we mitigate the risks of civic engagement?

The first step is clarity of thought. We need a conceptual framework. For that, we may go back to the advice of Boethius of Dacia, that we should take delight in two things: to know the true and to do the good.

The good orthogonal to the true

Unum, verum, bonum. [One, true, good.]
The transcendental aspects of being, in medieval philosophy

The key idea of this section, and this book, is that we may think of the true and the good as orthogonal concepts. In such a conceptual framework, the true and the good define a two-dimensional landscape. Within this landscape each university may respond to the question of quality by determining its own coordinates.

More concretely, following on from the early part of this chapter, we may think of societal purpose as orthogonal to academic excellence. What we are good *for* is at right angles to what we are good *at*. The demand side of our knowledge business is orthogonal to the supply side. Which is just to say that the core function of civic engagement cuts across, draws upon, and feeds back into both the two classic vertical functions of research and teaching. Concretising this idea further in terms of research, and following on from the discussion in Chapter Seven, we conceptualise curiosity-driven blue-sky research as operating vertically and challenge-led responsive research as operating horizontally. Our disciplinary research is located within our subject-based pillars of wisdom, the departments, schools and faculties which make up the academic structures of the university, while our response to global or local challenges emanate from cross-faculty and cross-disciplinary groupings. Like Plato and Aristotle in the *School of Athens*, we point at the heavens above and also reach out to the world around us.

Positioning the true and the good on orthogonal axes gives us a conceptual framework within which to resolve some earlier conundrums. We struggled with the notion of quality in Chapter Three. What Boethius of Dacia tells us is that quality – our 'supreme good' as universities – can be conceived of as a combination of two things, excellence and virtue. That allows us to draw upon both, as in the original idea of *arête,* rather than dwelling on an apparent ambiguity between them. It also allows us to avoid the 'binary oppositions' of which Professor Collini speaks, by recognising that the apparent opposition is often better thought of as orthogonal juxtaposition. In addition, orthogonality gives us a way of taking simultaneous delight in the true and the good. It yields an alternative to 'finding a balance' as a way of resolving the tension between our 'binary oppositions'. It gives us a way, therefore, of handling the two Aristotelian precepts of Chapter Seven.

Imagine, now, that you actually need to run a university. How could these ideas be implemented? First, you should have clarity of purpose. What are you good at, or trying to be good at? And what would you hope to be good for? 'Good at' is a matter of verticality, of supply-side work in research and teaching, as per the standard model university. We are very much accustomed to responding to this question, boasting about our disciplinary strengths, and having metrics and data to back up our boasts. 'Good for' is a matter of laterality, of responsiveness and challenge-led demand-side work, as per the contrasts drawn in Chapter Seven. It is also, specifically, about your university's response to the needs and demands of society. We are less accustomed to responding to this question.

We should recognise, however, that the question of responsiveness is a recurring and important one. Of all the many grand challenges facing global society, to which ones will your university respond? To what extent, and in what manner, will you deploy your institutional good-at expertise to help provide solutions? Which of the grand challenges manifest themselves particularly in your own city or region or community? And what steps are you taking to build local partnerships and collaborations in order to play a role in addressing these?

Perhaps the answer is none, at both the global and the local level, which would be the case if you are satisfied that the standard model university will suffice for you. That is a legitimate choice, provided it is consciously made, but it is not the choice we are interested in here.

If you do wish to articulate a societal purpose, and be responsive to societal challenges, the next question is which ones to focus on. I have already argued that selectivity is a key risk-mitigation strategy, which means that you need to identify some thematic areas within which to concentrate your engagement activities. Let us call them *societal challenge themes* – a neutral enough term which you could make more precise, according to preference or circumstance, as 'grand challenges' or 'civic engagement topics' or 'societal focus areas'. It would be sensible to select these themes on the basis of available academic expertise, so that you can connect your response to the 'good-for' question to the evidence of what you are good at.

Your societal challenge themes could relate to either or both of your research and teaching portfolios. The key point is just that it should not be divorced from research or teaching – not a 'third strand' activity. Challenges like climate change or renewable energy or antimicrobial resistance are best addressed from a research base, but should not rule out an educational aspect. Widening participation, fair access and social mobility, on the other hand, are societal challenges better tackled from the base of teaching and learning – but without neglecting good research into the topic. Suppose for example that your university is situated in a city or region with low levels of entry into higher education. You may well decide, then, that widening participation is one of the societal challenges you choose to address. If so, you will, for example, need to deploy expertise in dealing with the issues outlined earlier on quality and standards – not only in the recruitment and admission of students with potential, but also in providing teaching and support to ensure parity of exit standards.

In any case, the point of departure is a deliberate institutional decision to focus on certain societal challenges, and an implementation process for doing so. Conventional wisdom will tell you that a university strategy on societal challenge themes is best implemented with as much of an overlap between a 'top-down' and a 'bottom-up' approach as you can achieve. This is good as far as the intention goes, but sub-optimal in terms of its one-dimensionality. 'Top-down' also translates into academic language as 'managerial', while 'bottom-up' translates into 'collegial'. When phrased in one-dimensional language you have the usual problem of binary opposition: forces going in opposite directions cancel each other out, rather than complementing each other. Better, then, to conceive of 'managerial' and 'collegial' as orthogonal forces, with the consequent resultant vector. For implementing societal challenge themes the managerial force works towards efficiency, deploying benchmarking, data analysis, financial considerations and hierarchical decision making. The collegial approach cuts across all of that, working towards effectiveness, generating a collective sense of purpose among the academic body for responding to this particular challenge in their own particular way.

You also need to decide at which geographic levels you wish to operate: city, region, national or global. Loss of biodiversity, for example, is a global challenge, which may or may not be a particularly strong issue in your own region. Or there may be a particularly pressing issue in your own city or region: economic issues like high unemployment, or public health issues like too much smoking and drinking, or infrastructural issues like risk of flooding. Of course, local and global issues usually overlap, hence the idea of a second filter: of all the global challenges you have the academic expertise to contribute to, which ones are particularly relevant in your own city or region?

Once your university has determined its societal challenge themes, you need to build an identity for each of them. At this point, the ideas on lateral research become relevant. Your societal challenge themes are purpose-driven, which means they each have certain objectives, which means your organisational approach to creating an identity is more functional than structural. You are building teams, consisting of individuals who are already situated within disciplinary structures, to work towards a common purpose, usually with some specific objectives aimed at addressing a particular challenge.

Suppose for example that you have decided on urban sustainability as one of your societal challenge themes. You would do so on the basis of having academic expertise in the kind of things that make a city work: energy, transport, water, waste, infrastructure and so on. You may also have picked this topic particularly in regard to your own city. For example, if you are in one of the cities where the redbrick universities grew up, you may ask: how do we re-engineer an old industrial city to become a sustainable city? And so you would wish to work with the city in deploying your expertise to make tangible changes, aimed at lower and more efficient energy consumption, smart transport systems, less waste going into landfill, better digital infrastructure and generally more sustainable living. You may even invent a name for this conglomeration of objectives and activities: urban science.

All of that takes organisation, and leadership, and a budget, and staffing, and branding. So let us suppose you set up an Institute for Urban Science, with the aim of re-engineering your city as a sustainable city for the future. What would this institute look like, and how would it operate?

The Institute for Urban Science would be what we might call a *soft institute,* which is a kind of virtual structure. That is to say, it will consist of a team, or possibly teams, of people who are already located in 'hard structures', which typically will be discipline-based departments or schools.

The 'hard structures' are the constituent parts of the organisational diagram of the university. In the standard model, a university is organised into faculties, and each faculty is organised into schools or departments. An organisational diagram shows how these all fit together, and who reports to whom, in a hierarchical manner. When an academic says 'I am a senior lecturer in mathematics' that usually means that there is a department or school of mathematics to which they 'belong', where they perform certain duties according to a departmental workload schedule, and with a head to whom they report. The head will typically have a budget and, besides exercising academic leadership, will also be responsible for those 'duller routines of universities' without which the university cannot function.

If we identify 'hard structures' (more or less) with 'disciplines', then 'soft structures' are best identified with 'societal challenges'. An Institute for Urban Science, for example, is focused on the challenge of making your city (and cities in general) more sustainable in terms of energy, transport, water, waste and so on. It is a 'soft structure' in the sense that its participants come from different disciplines and contribute different kinds of expertise towards a collective purpose of addressing a societal challenge.

Soft structures would seem to create a management conundrum. Imagine, for example, that Dr Proudfoot is a member of the Mathematics Department, and also a member of the Institute for Urban Science. Who then is Dr Proudfoot's line manager? Who funds her research? Who signs her leave form, agrees her workload plan, and carries out her annual performance and development review?

This is not an A-grade problem. Say, for example, that Dr Proudfoot is an expert on the mathematics of transportation networks. Academic papers in that subject, which would be valued by the head of the Department of Mathematics, can and will be advantaged by case studies on transport which Dr Proudfoot participated in as a member of the Institute for Urban Science.

There are various practical ways of making such an arrangement work. Conceptually, it is perhaps easiest to conceive of the Institute for Urban Science as a university-wide endeavour, pursuing a university-wide purpose. That means that participation should be sought not only from scientists and engineers but also from academics in the social sciences, humanities, medical sciences, the business school and so on. Usually, however, there is a preponderance of expertise on the topic in question in some particular part of the university. Say, for example, that in the case of the Institute for Urban Science most of the expertise lies in the Faculty of Engineering. It would then be feasible to task the Faculty of Engineering with leading, *on behalf of the whole university*, on the topic of addressing the challenge of urban sustainability. That means that the dean of the Faculty of Engineering will have both a vertical line-management 'excellence' responsibility and a horizontal responsive 'purpose' responsibility.

And so, in principle, does everybody else. In particular, other deans will have similar horizontal responsibilities for other societal challenge themes. Deans are usually budget-holders, and so each dean will devote part of their budget to the pursuit of horizontal aims – something for which they are held responsible and accountable by the university at large. Within each faculty, in the vertical line, each dean would pass on the same expectations, both vertical and horizontal, to which they themselves are subject, to the various heads of department who report to them. That creates a matrix of vertical lines of accountability and horizontal lines of responsibility.

Such a matrix of orthogonal lines of accountability and responsibility requires careful coordination, and this role falls quite naturally to the director of the 'soft' institute. This director works with heads of department across the university to help them exercise their horizontal responsibility for urban science. In terms of line management, the director of the Institute for Urban Science reports to the dean of the Faculty of Engineering, who holds the university-wide responsibility for this theme.

Such arrangements can work not only for research but also for teaching and learning. Laterality is beneficial educationally just as much as in knowledge production. 'Service learning', for example, is an experiential learning pedagogy that aims to integrate students' academic studies with a contribution to society.[42] The Institute for Urban Science would be a natural ally and champion of such endeavours, in parallel with arranging suitable industry-based internships and incorporating project-based modules into the engineering curriculum. It would do so on the pedagogically solid grounds of adding breadth to the standard model type discipline-based teaching. Beyond the curriculum, and beyond the institute, the university can encourage further civic interaction initiatives, such as student volunteering, social enterprise and international exchange programmes. Such initiatives fit well with the idea of responsiveness, particularly when coordinated with the chosen societal challenge themes.

Whether in research or in teaching and learning, the overall idea is that all academics, and academic managers in particular, have two orthogonal lines of responsibility: excellence and purpose. Some will focus more on one axis than the others, but the idea of orthogonality would be common cause. Running the university, then, is an exercise in matrix management.

The idea of matrix management entered business language in the late 1970s. For a while it was somewhat overhyped as a panacea for strategies that require multiple simultaneous management capabilities. To a mathematician, a matrix is just a rectangular arrangement of numbers into rows and columns. This tidy picture encouraged an approach to matrix management that was mainly structural, rather than cultural. In consequence, early implementations of matrix management were not encouraging. The remedy, certainly for universities, is to think of matrix management primarily as a way of permeating a lateral sense of purpose and responsiveness throughout the vertical discipline-based structures of the organisation.

A 1990 article in the *Harvard Business Review* summarised matrix management as 'not a structure, a frame of mind'.[43]

> As formal, hierarchical structure gives way to networks of personal relationships that work through informal, horizontal communication channels, the image of top management in an isolated corner office moving boxes and charts on an organization chart becomes increasingly anachronistic.

This passage is not far removed from, and easily translates into, the views expressed by Gibbons et al in distinguishing the vertical mode 1 discipline-based approach from the cross-disciplinary mode 2 approach of teams and networks. The *Harvard Business Review* authors go on to talk about inculcating a sense of purpose in the organisation:

> The surest way to break down such insularity is to develop and communicate a clear sense of corporate purpose that extends into every corner of the company and gives context and meaning to each manager's particular roles and responsibilities. We are not talking about a slogan, however catchy and pointed. We are talking about a company vision, which must be crafted and articulated with clarity, continuity, and consistency.

Again, while this was written in the context of multinational business, the spirit is in line with the argument about positioning societal purpose orthogonally to disciplinary excellence. The trick is to articulate the 'why' of what we are doing, and make it permeate the university.

There are some practical dos and don'ts to make matrix management manageable in a university.

- *Keep the matrix small*. With matrix management, the crucial actions happen at the nodes of intersection (where the rows and the columns cross). The more nodes of interaction you have, the more complicated it becomes to manage them all simultaneously. It is worth keeping in mind, therefore, that adding even just one more item on either the vertical or the horizontal axis generates many more nodes of interaction. In practice, for a university that wishes to pursue both excellence and purpose, it is usually better to have only a small number of faculties, and only a small number of societal challenge themes.

- *Make the money flow horizontally as well as vertically.* Standard practice dictates that money cascades down from the university budget to the faculty, from the faculty to the schools and departments, and from there to disciplinary subgroups and individuals. At each stage, however, part of the budget can be earmarked for horizontal activities. The dean of the Faculty of Engineering is responsible to the vice-chancellor for the university's response to the societal challenge of urban sustainability. Exercising that responsibility involves supporting the Institute for Urban Sustainability to engage in cross-faculty interactions, with a budget to back that up.

- *Evaluate in two dimensions.* We may legitimately have expectations of a collective which we cannot have of every individual. For example, it is generally accepted that some academics are better at teaching than research, and others the other way around. However, it is realistic to expect of a department or a school or a faculty that it should perform equally well at both teaching and research, because it should be of sufficient critical mass to balance out different contributions from its staff. Likewise with excellence and purpose. It is reasonable to expect the Faculty of Engineering, which is a large unit, to deliver results both on the excellence axis and on the purpose axis. The School of Mathematics may perhaps deliver more on the excellence axis, but cannot be devoid of contribution on the purpose axis, and with the Institute for Urban Sustainability the expectation would be the other way around.

- *Distribute support throughout the matrix.* Matrix management could easily generate a lot of admin, which could negatively influence the purpose-orientation of the university. To counteract such a tendency, put as much of your admin as close to the academics as is feasible. As a general rule, affection for administrators is inversely proportional to distance. Academics are more likely to see an administrator next door as a colleague and a welcome source of support, and less likely to have the same view of those in the central admin block. These localised administrators, too, can have orthogonal lines of responsibility: up towards the head of the school or faculty, and across towards their peers in central admin. The heads of admin in each faculty, for example, could be line-managed by the registrar, even though they are physically positioned next to the faculty deans.

The conceptual framework of orthogonality, the formulation of societal challenge themes running across disciplinary structures, and the implementation of some kind of matrix management give us a way of thinking in practical terms of the good as positioned orthogonally to the true. It is probably not the only way in which a university can try to give a coherent response to the question of societal purpose – the 'good-for' question. By whatever means, however, there is a name for the kind of university that sees responsiveness to the needs and demands of civil society as part of its institutional purpose, and adopts engagement with civil society as an academic core function. It is called a civic university.

Happily, 'civic' is ambiguous in a good way. In England, for many people, civic means city. Indeed, the building housing the city council is usually called the civic centre, or perhaps just the civic. So, 'by civic university' we may mean a university strongly related to the city – which is what the redbrick universities initially were. As quoted in Chapter Eight, 'their better name is "civic" universities, since this exactly describes their symbiotic relationship with the urban area which created them'.

But 'civic' also comes from *civitas*, which is the social body of the citizens comprising the state. In that sense 'civic' refers to what I have called civil society, which is not geographically specific. It is perfectly feasible to think of civil society in national or even global terms, and we commonly do so when we talk of the global challenges confronting civil society. And so the civic university is one that has special reference to civil society. It may or may not, in addition, have a special relationship with a city (if indeed it is located in a city), but clearly there is no conflict between the two concepts and they could happily coexist.

I have taken the defining feature of a civic university to be a sense of purpose in responding to the needs and demands of civil society. That is not meant to articulate in some Newmanesque sense 'the idea of a civic university'. Very likely there is a plurality of such ideas (which explains the heading of this chapter). Indeed, writing a book on civic universities would present the authors or editors with a methodological choice at the outset. One approach would be to do an empirical study of some likely candidate universities, such as those in the Talloires Network or the University Social Responsibility Network, and then try to extract some common themes. The book emanating from the University Social Responsibility Network, for example, is subtitled *A Global Survey of Concepts and Experiences*, and has a final chapter titled 'Global experience to date and future directions'.[44] Likewise, Burton Clark adopted a case study approach in his seminal book on the entrepreneurial university, and we saw in Chapter One the electrifying effect which that slim volume had on the sector.

Alternatively, and somewhat at the other end of the spectrum, a book about civic universities could adopt a normative approach, which is essentially to offer a definition and then challenge likely candidates to measure up to it. Such an approach can be found in *The Civic University: The Policy and Leadership Challenges*, edited and authored by John Goddard et al.[45] These editor-authors give a definition of the contemporary civic university in terms of seven dimensions, which are in their view best practice characteristics, and then look at the extent to which eight universities in four countries meet this characterisation. You will find in that volume various scholarly references to civic engagement, such as the idea of a 'quadruple helix' of interactions between universities, the government, business and industry, and civil society.

All too easily, however, the normative approach becomes an endeavour to capture some Platonic idea, and is therefore about the way the world ought to be more than the way the world is. The reader may well agree with the overall intention, and still be left wondering how to make it work, and how to deal with the risks, given all the other pressures on universities, particularly the relentless pressure of rankings and league tables.

That takes us back to the quality question. What makes a university a good university? Chapter Two explored the approach of rankings and league tables, and Chapter Three explored the approach of quality assurance, but neither seemed satisfactory. Ranking is a numbers game which illustrates the peril of arithmetic: it parades accuracy of calculation as legitimacy of conclusion. As demonstrated, ranking can pretty much give you any answer you want, and so it creates a reality more than it reflects a reality. Quality assurance, on the other hand, does not really *measure* anything, being more interested in process than in outcome. Our consideration of quality did, however, open up a different pathway, which has now culminated in distinguishing an excellence dimension (the good-at question) from a dimension of purpose (the good-for question). These two key questions, through various historical digressions, led in turn to the orthogonal juxtaposition of the true and the good.

All of which brings us to a fundamental conclusion: for a good university, responding to the question of societal purpose should be just as important as responding to the question of academic excellence. Society is entitled to expect, and therefore may demand, an answer to both the good-at and the good-for question from each university. Universities are not only about academic excellence. The workings of the invisible hand to deliver societal benefit from academic excellence cannot be denied, but it is too slow and too unpredictable to be the only causal factor we rely on. It is, by definition, without purpose – without *telos*.

In practical terms, then, for each university and for all universities, the question 'Which societal challenges do you respond to?' should be made as common, and as insistent, as the question 'Which disciplines do you excel at?'

This (horizontal) question about the extent to which your university responds to societal challenges is not as well developed as the (vertical) question of academic performance, but there is no strong reason why it couldn't be. And it is beginning to happen. Through various incentives, the idea of a challenge-led approach towards knowledge generation and dissemination is gaining traction. The Bill and Melinda Gates Foundation, for example, with tens of billions of dollars to spend, runs a Global Grand Challenges scheme. Interestingly, they credit the Hilbert problems of 1900 as their inspiration:

Grand Challenges is a family of initiatives fostering innovation to solve key global health and development problems.... These initiatives use challenges to focus attention and effort on specific problems, and they can be traced back to the mathematician David Hilbert, who over a century ago defined a set of unsolved problems to spark progress in the field of mathematics.... In 2003, the Bill & Melinda Gates Foundation launched Grand Challenges in Global Health, which came to include multiple funding partners. This initiative focused on 14 major scientific challenges that, if solved, could lead to key advances in preventing, treating, and curing diseases of the developing world.... Funding included an additional supporting project addressing ethical, social, and cultural issues across the initiative.[46]

Governments, too, are beginning to target research funding towards societal challenges. Societal challenges are central, for example, to the European Commission's Horizon 2020 research programme. In the UK, adding 'impact' as a parameter in the REF was a first move in this direction. It took a while for the penny to drop that 'societal impact' is what is meant, not 'impact on other academics', and also the impact statements were still boxed into disciplinary 'units of assessment' – but it is a start. In its 2015 Spending Review the UK government then went further, committing £1.5 billion over five years to a Global Challenges Research Fund, 'to ensure UK research takes a leading role in addressing the problems faced by developing countries', explicitly mentioning 'challenge-led research' and 'an agile response to emergencies'.[47] This move was reinforced in 2016 when Prime Minister Theresa May announced an Industrial Strategy Challenge Fund, to respond to core industrial challenges through research and innovation.[48]

And so, via the question of quality, back to rankings and league tables. In Chapter Two I said that at a tactical level we should encourage their proliferation, and at a strategic level we should try to understand the drivers behind the phenomenon in order to figure out how to respond to it. The analysis has now been completed: behind rankings we found an appetite for the oversimplifications of linearism: bogus quantification, rank order of worth, a ladder of esteem, hierarchy instead of diversity. And the response is becoming clear: to overcome one-dimensionality we need more dimensions. And different dimensions, as any mathematician will tell you, are orthogonal to each other, so we need the concept of orthogonality. There may be many dimensions to be explored, but for this book my argument has been based on two: excellence and purpose.

Rankings is an evaluation tool on the excellence axis. Crude, simplistic and wrong-headed as they are, they will not go away. As they are presented at the moment, rankings cannot really be 'improved', because that just means more fine-grained mechanisms for capturing the preferences of the rankers. But perhaps they can be complemented. Perhaps we can juxtapose lateral purpose-based evaluations to the current vertical excellence-based rankings. In particular, perhaps we can develop the quality question along the horizontal axis of societal purpose.

Imagine, therefore, that we can increase the expectation on universities to respond to the 'good-for' question. Imagine, further, that it becomes a common expectation on universities to report on the societal challenge themes they have adopted. It will not be long, then, before these effects begin to be compared. If there must be rankings, then perhaps we can engineer a situation where there will also be demand-side narratives, not only supply-side parameters. Recall that current rankings are all on the supply side: they have no criteria for evaluating responsiveness to societal issues. The first attempt to do so (U-Multirank) had a hostile reception, but it showed what is possible. As the expectation of responsiveness gathers momentum, through 'grand challenge' incentives or whatever other means, such attempts may well be revived. Rankers will begin paying attention to the demand side as soon as they get a whiff of their being a market for it.

Perhaps, for the demand side, we need not think only of ranking. Comparison is what we really want, and comparison is not the same as ranking. In the 2014 REF, for example, impact case studies were presented as narratives, not as metrics. The experiment showed that it is perfectly feasible for universities to report on the societal effect of their academic work, and it is perfectly feasible for such case studies to be evaluated. So perhaps we could, on the demand side, pay more attention to words as a means of comparison and less attention to numbers. Most universities, after REF 2014, would have turned their best REF impact case studies into some kind of marketing or public relations brochure. It is not a big step from there to a kind of who-does-what comparative overview of the impact of the sector, with examples – perhaps even measurements – of the extent of their impact on society.

To repeat: the question 'Which societal challenges do you respond to?' should be made as common, and as insistent, as the question 'Which disciplines do you excel at?' By giving the responsiveness question parity of esteem with the excellence question, we open it up to further analysis, so that the question of purpose becomes just as exhaustively scrutinised as the question of excellence. How do you respond to societal challenges? To what extent is responsiveness part of the institutional ethos? With whom do you collaborate? What resources do you deploy? What effects can you demonstrate?

With such an approach, the question of what makes a good university becomes more nuanced, more multidimensional, less of an exercise in linearism. We should expect a response in the sense of *arête*: being very good at what you are supposed to be, and doing well at what you are supposed to be doing. In other words, a good university will have both excellence and purpose. To paraphrase Boethius of Dacia: the supreme good for universities should be to pursue academic excellence, to serve a societal purpose, and to delight in both.

Not a ladder but a landscape

> Now I re-examine philosophies and religions,
>   They may prove well in lecture-rooms, yet not
>   prove at all under the spacious clouds and
>   along the landscape and flowing currents.
>   *Walt Whitman, Song of the Open Road.*

If we are not going to remain stuck in the one-dimensional metaphor of the ladder, we need some lateral movement. Hence the idea of a landscape.

Any university has an internal landscape. In fact, it has different landscapes, depending on your point of view. When we juxtapose challenge-led lateral research to curiosity-driven disciplinary research we conceptualise a research landscape, and we give practical effect to this research landscape by adopting societal challenge themes as horizontal complements to the vertical faculty structures. Instead of speaking of depth vs breadth of knowledge, either in teaching or in research, we can conceptualise a landscape by speaking of depth *and* breadth. Likewise for many of the other common binary oppositions of academia: disciplinary vs cross-disciplinary, specialisation vs generalisation, structure vs function, managerial vs collegial. The key move is to get away from the linear 'versus' juxtaposition into an orthogonal complementary juxtaposition.

Nationally, the higher education sector should be conceived of as a landscape – not just geographically, but conceptually. At the moment we all fall into line, and the line is a ranking, and the ranking is a ladder everybody desperately tries to climb. Could we try, instead, for each university to plot its own coordinates on an academic landscape defined by the axes of excellence and purpose? Could we each give a considered response to the two key questions of what we are good at and what we are good for?

We could encourage society to demand of us to be clear about which societal challenges we are addressing, and how we develop and deploy our academic excellence in order to do so. Since there is no lack of societal challenges, this will encourage differentiation. With different sets of expertise, different local conditions, different interests in global conditions, we could each occupy our own region of the higher education landscape, and be valued accordingly. The quality question – is this a good university? – should be about both excellence and purpose, and so become more differentiated, more multidimensional. Quality is not just about what you are good at, it is also about what you are good for. Quality needs diversity, and diversity manifests itself better in different dimensions.

Globally, universities form a landscape which transcends languages, cultures, religions and national boundaries. The idea of a *Volksuniversiteit* as the manifestation of some kind of national or cultural identity runs contrary to the soul of the university as well as the historical record. It does not fit the original idea of the *universitas magistrorum et scholarium*; it does not fit the 'republic of letters' in the age of enlightenment; it does not fit the Humboldtian idea of *Freiheit der Lehre und des Lernens*; and it does not fit the Newmanesque Platonic idea of a university. Ever since Bologna received from Pope Honorius III in 1220 the right to style itself 'the teacher of Europe' the university has been international; it still is today. From the earliest times universities attracted wandering scholars, intent only on finding the best place to learn; they still do so today. Universities have never found any contradiction between being place-based and being part of an international network.

Universities have proved to be one of the most durable and successful constructs of civil society. How many European entities today can trace their lineage back almost a thousand years? The Catholic Church, the crown of England, some of the institutions of democracy – it is not a long list. Many universities are older than the nation-states within which they now find themselves. Oxbridge and the four Scottish ancients predate the 1707 Act of Union which formed the United Kingdom. Italian universities arose in city states before there was an Italy, German universities before there was a Germany, American universities before the States declared themselves United. Most universities will outlast most governments.

Is there not more we can make of such a successful model? The landscape of universities spans the globe. The soul of a university remains universally recognisable. Any academic from any country can find some commonality in almost any other university anywhere. If we are to address the grand challenges facing global society we need to make best use of this worldwide network. We must invest both in excellence and in purpose. To do so we must facilitate what has always been the strength of universities: making welcome the wandering scholar, who adds to the diversity of ideas.

Imagine this: an international academic passport, to facilitate ease of movement between centres of learning in order to address societal challenges. Many academics already hold long-term visas, or more than one passport. They acquire this facility because they add value – they contribute to quality – regarding some issue common to different places in the world. It cannot be too hard to extrapolate from there. Create a Universitas passport, premised on two things: academic excellence, and a contribution to society. It will help those who strive to know the true and do the good to continue to take delight in both. In this increasingly fractured world, that might help to bind us all together in a stronger network of mutuality.

EPILOGUE

On the Supreme Good (De Summo Bono)

Boethius of Dacia, ca.1270s[1]

Since in every kind of being there is a supreme possible good, and since man too is a certain kind [*lit.* species] of being, there must be a supreme possible good for man. I do not speak of a good which is supreme in the absolute sense, but one that is supreme for man; for the goods which are accessible to man are limited and do not extend to infinity. By reason let us seek to determine what the supreme good is which is accessible to man.

The supreme good for man should be in terms of his highest power, and not according to the vegetative soul, which is [also] found in plants, nor according to the sensitive soul, which is [also] found in animals and from which their sensual pleasures arises. But man's highest power is his reason and intellect. For this is the supreme director of human life both in the order of speculation and in the order of action. Therefore, the supreme good attainable by man must be his by means of his intellect. Therefore, men who are so weighed down by sense pleasures that they lose intellectual goods should grieve. For they never attain their supreme good. They are so given to the senses that they do not seek that which is the good of the intellect itself. Against these the Philosopher protests,

335

saying: "Woe to you men who are numbered among beasts and who do not attend to that which is divine within you!" He calls the intellect that which is divine in man. For if there is anything divine in man, it is right for it to be the intellect. Just as that which is best among all beings is the divine, so also that which is best in man we call divine.

Moreover, one power of the human intellect is speculative and the other practical. This is clear from this fact, that man theorises about certain objects which he does not actively cause, for example, eternal things, and actively causes others under the intellect's direction whereby he realises a means which can be chosen in human acts. From this, then, we know in general that these two intellectual powers are present in man. But the supreme good accessible to man in terms of the speculative power of this intellect is knowledge of what is true and delight in the same. Knowledge of what is true gives delight. An intelligible object gives delight to the one who knows it. And the more wondrous and noble the intelligible object and the greater the power of the apprehending intellect to comprehend perfectly, the greater the intellectual delight. One who has tasted such delight spurns every lesser pleasure, such as that of sense. The latter is, in truth, less, and is more base. And the man who chooses such pleasure is, because of that pleasure, more base than one who chooses the former.

It is because of this, because the object known gives delight to the one who knows, that the Philosopher [Aristotle] in Book 12 of the *Metaphysics* maintains that the first intellect enjoys the most pleasurable life. For since the first intellect is the most powerful in understanding and the object which it knows is the noblest, its essence itself – for what nobler object can the divine intellect have than the divine essence? – therefore, it has the life of greatest delight. No greater good can befall man in terms of his speculative intellect than knowledge of the totality of beings which come from the first principle and, by means of this, knowledge of the first principle in so far as such is possible, and delight in it. Therefore, our conclusion above follows: that the supreme good available to man by means of his speculative intellect is knowledge of what is true in individual cases, and delight in the same.

Likewise, the supreme good available to man in terms of his practical intellect is the doing of good, and delight in the same.

For what greater good can befall man in terms of his practical intellect than to realise a fitting means in human action and to delight therein?

No man is just save him who takes delight in acts of justice. The same must be said of the acts of the other moral virtues. From what has been said one can evidently conclude that the supreme good open to man is to know the true, to do the good, and to delight in both.

And because the highest good possible for man is happiness, it follows that human happiness consists in knowing the true, doing the good, and taking delight in both. The military profession is prescribed in a state by the lawmaker for this reason, that when enemies have been expelled, citizens may devote themselves to intellectual virtues in contemplating the true, and to moral virtues in doing good, and thus live a happy life; for the happy life consists in these two. This then is a greater good, which man can receive from God and which God can give to man in this life. With reason does a man desire a long life who desires it for this, to become more perfect in this good. He who shares more perfectly in that happiness which reason tells us is possible for man in this life draws closer to that happiness which we expect in the life to come on the authority of faith.

And since so great a good is possible for man, as has been said, it is right for all human actions to be directed toward that good, so as to attain it. All actions regarding a certain law are right and proper when they tend toward the end of the law, and better the more closely they approach the end of the law. Actions which are opposed to the end of the law or which are weak (and not perfect according to the precepts of the law) or even indifferent (without either being opposed to the end of the law or in accord with its precepts), all such actions are sin against that law to a greater or lesser degree as is clear from what has been said. The same is true in man himself. All designs and deliberations, all actions and desires of man which tend to this supreme good which is available to man according to the above, these are right and proper. When man so acts, he acts in accord with nature. For he acts for the sake of the supreme good, to which he is ordered by nature. And when he so acts he is properly ordered, for then he is ordered to his best and his ultimate end. But all actions of man which are not ordered to this good, or which are not such as to render man stronger and better disposed for actions which are ordered to this good, all such actions in man are sin.

Wherefore the happy man never does anything except works of happiness, or works by means of which he becomes stronger and better fitted for works of happiness. Therefore, whether the happy man sleeps or is awake or is eating, he lives in happiness so long as he does those things in order to be rendered stronger for the works of happiness. Therefore, all acts of man which are not directed to this supreme good of man which has been described, whether they are opposed to it or whether they are indifferent, all such acts constitute sin in man to a greater or lesser degree, as is clear. The cause of all such acts is inordinate desire. It is also the cause of all moral evil. Moreover, inordinate desire in man is the cause which most greatly prevents him from attaining that which is desired naturally. For all men naturally desire to know. But only the smallest number of men, sad to say, devote themselves to the pursuit of wisdom. Inordinate desire bars the others from such a good. Thus we find certain men pursuing a life of laziness, others detestable sense pleasures, and others giving themselves to the desire for riches. So it is that all today are prevented by inordinate desire from attaining to their supreme good, with the exception of a very small number of men, men who should be honoured.

I say they are to be honoured because they despise sense desire and pursue the delight of reason and intellectual desire, labouring after knowledge of the truth of things. Again I say they are to be honoured because they live according to the natural order. All lower powers found in man naturally are for the sake of the highest power. Thus the nutritive power is there for the sake of the sensitive. For the sensitive power is a perfection of an animated body, and an animated body cannot live without food. But it is the nutritive power which changes and assimilates food. Therefore, it follows that the nutritive power exists in man for the sake of the sensitive. And the sensitive power is for the sake of the intellective since, in us, intelligibles are derived from things imagined. Wherefore, we understand with greater difficulty things which of themselves cannot be imagined by us. But imagination presupposes the senses. The proof of this is that one who imagines is also affected on the level of sense. Wherefore, according to the Philisopher [sic], imagination or *phantasia* is a movement arising from an actual exercise of sense. [Just as all lower powers in man are for the sake of the highest] [*sic*], so too the operations of all man's lower powers are for the sake of the operations of his highest power, the intellect. And if, among the operations of the intellective power, there is one which is best and most perfect, all others naturally exist for its sake. When a man performs such an operation, he enjoys the highest state possible for man.

Such men are the philosophers, who spend their lives in the pursuit of wisdom. Wherefore, all powers found in the philosopher operate according to the natural order, the prior for the sake of the posterior, the lower for the sake of the higher and more perfect. But all other men, who live according to lower powers and choose their operations and the pleasures found in such operations, are not ordered in accord with nature. They sin against the natural order. For man to turn away from the natural order is sin in man. Because the philosopher does not turn away from this order, for this reason he does not sin against the natural order.

Morally speaking, the philosopher is virtuous for three reasons. *First*, because he recognises the baseness of action in which vice consists and the nobility of action in which virtue consists. Therefore, he can more easily choose the one and avoid the other and always act according to right reason. He who so acts never sins. But such is not true of the ignorant man. It is difficult for him to act rightly. *Secondly*, because he who has tasted a greater delight despises every lesser delight. But the philosopher has tasted intellectual delight in theoretical consideration of the truths of beings. This delight is greater than that of sense. Therefore, he despises sense pleasures. But many sins and vices consist in excessive sense pleasure. *Thirdly*, because there is no sin in understanding and theorising. There is no possibility of excess and of sin in the order of absolute goods. But the action of the philosopher is such a contemplation of truth. Therefore, it is easier for the philosopher to be virtuous than for another.

So it is that the philosopher lives as man was born to live, and according to the natural order. Since in man all lower powers and their operations are for the sake of higher powers and their operations, and all taken together for the highest power and that highest action, which is contemplation of truth and delight in the same, above all, the first truth, the desire to know will never be satisfied until the uncreated being is known. As the Commentator says, all men naturally desire to know about the divine intellect.

Desire for any knowable object is a kind of desire for the first knowable object. This is the proof. The closer beings are to the first knowable being, the more we desire to know them and the more we delight in thinking of them. Therefore, by studying the caused beings which are in the world and their natures and relationships to one another, the philosopher is led to consider the highest causes of things. For a knowledge of effects leads to a knowledge of the cause. And in noting that higher causes and their natures are such that they must have another cause, he is led to a knowledge of the first cause. And because there is pleasure in speculative knowledge, and all the more so the nobler the objects known, the philosopher leads a life of very great pleasure.

The philosopher also knows and observes that it is necessary for this cause to be its own cause of being, that is to say, not to have another cause. If there were nothing in the universe which was not caused by another, then there would be nothing at all. He also notes that this cause must be eternal and unchangeable, always remaining the same. For if it were not eternal, then nothing whatsoever would be eternal. And again, since certain things in the world have begun to be, and since one being which begins to be cannot be a sufficient cause of another being which begins to be, as is evident, it clearly follows that all things in this world which begin to be must derive from an eternal cause. This cause is also unchangeable and always remains the same, for change is possible only in imperfect things. And if there is some most perfect being in the universe, it is right for this to be the first cause.

The philosopher also notes that the entire being of the universe, with the exception of this first cause itself, must come from it and thus, just as this first cause is the cause which produces beings, so it orders them to one another and maintains them in existence – certain ones in terms of their individual identity and without any kind of change (as the separated substances); certain ones according to their individual identity, but as subject to change (as the heavenly bodies); and certain ones in terms of their species alone (as those which are below the sphere of [the moon] such as the lowest levels of beings).

He also notes that just as all things derive from this first cause, so too, all things are ordered to it. For that being in which the principle from which all things [come] is joined to the end to which all things [return], that is the first being according to the philosophers and God the Blessed according to the holy men. Nevertheless, in this order there is great range. Those beings which are closest to the first principle are nobler and more perfect. Those things which are farther removed from the first principle are lower and less perfect.

This first principle is to this world as the father of a family is to his household, as a commander is to his army, and as the common good is to the state. Just as the army is one because of the unity of its commander, and just as the good of the army is in the commander essentially and in others according to their relationship to him, so too, from the unity of this first principle derives the unity of the world, and the good of this world is in this first principle essentially, and in other beings of this world in so far as they participate in the first principle and are ordered to it. So it is that there is no good in any being in this world which is not participated [sic] from the first principle.

Considering all these things, the philosopher is moved to wonder at this first principle and to love it. For we love that from which our goods derive, and we love that to the greatest degree from which our greatest goods derive.

Therefore, the philosopher, noting that all goods come to him from this first principle and are preserved for him in so far as they are preserved by this first principle, is moved to the greatest love for this first principle. This is in accord with the right order of nature and with right reason from the side of the intellect. And since everyone takes delight in that which he loves and maximum delight in that which he loves to the maximum degree, and since the philosopher has the greatest love for this first principle, as has been indicated, it follows that the philosopher takes maximum delight in this first principle and in contemplating its goodness, and that this alone is right pleasure. This is the life of the philosopher. Whoever does not lead such a life does not live rightly. However, I call "philosopher" any man who lives according to the right order of nature and who has acquired the best and ultimate end of human life. And the first principle of whom we have spoken is the glorious and most high God, who is blessed forever and ever. Amen.

Notes

Author's Note: There are many weblinks in the notes below. All of these were live and functioning at the time of writing, but the reader will be aware that weblinks are ephemeral. Institutions may change, rebrand or even disappear, and when that happens the web pages of the original organisation may no longer be accessible, or the weblinks may change. For example, the HEFCE, the Higher Education Funding Council for England, became a new organisation, the Office for Students, in 2018.

1 *The standard Model University*

[1] G.H. Hardy, *A Mathematician's Apology*, Cambridge University Press, Cambridge, first edition, 1940; reprinted with Foreword by C.P. Snow 1967; Cambridge University Press, Cambridge, available in the public domain from the University of Alberta at www.math.ualberta.ca/mss/misc/.

[2] For some background, there is a useful paper titled 'Three Sadleirian professors' by H.T.H. Piaggio, which appeared in *The Mathematical Gazette* 15(215) (1931): 461–5, and is available online at www-history.mcs.st-and.ac.uk/Extras/Sadleirian_Professors.html.

[3] Bertrand Russell, 'The study of mathematics', in his collection *Mysticism and Logic and Other Essays,* first published by George Allen and Unwin, London, 1917, and still easily available. See also https://en.wikisource.org/wiki/Mysticism_and_Logic_and_Other_Essays .

[4] Bertrand Russell, 'Recent work on the principles of mathematics', *International Monthly* 4 (1901), 83–101. Reprinted as 'Mathematics and the metaphysicians' in his book *Mysticism and Logic*, also Longmans Green, London, 1918, pp 74–96.

[5] E.C. Titchmarsh, 'Godfrey Harold Hardy', *Journal of the London Mathematical Society* 25 (1950): 81–138, available online at www.numbertheory.org/obituaries/LMS/hardy/page96.html.

[6] www.sciencemag.org/content/28/706/49.

[7] When I was a schoolboy my mathematics teacher taught us that the value of π is 22/7. This was wrong, both numerically and conceptually. If you enter 22/7 into your calculator you will see that the result differs from π already

in the third decimal. In retrospect, however, the really worrying thing was that my teacher did not know that π is irrational, and so presumably did not know about the existence of irrational numbers either. Later, when I started teaching mathematics in South Africa, I found that many students still believed that π equals 22/7.

8   G.H. Hardy, *Apology*, p 41.

9   Paul R. Halmos, 'Applied mathematics is bad mathematics'. In: *Mathematics Tomorrow*, Lynn Arthur Steen (ed.), Springer-Verlag, New York, 1981. See also www.jstor.org/stable/2320989 for a riposte by F.F. Bonsall.

10   'Mathematics as a creative art', lecture, Edinburgh, 1973. See www-history. mcs.st-and.ac.uk/Extras/Creative_art.html.

11   www.maa.org/news/100306halmos.html.

12   G.H. Hardy, *Apology*, p 35.

13   Teresa Iglesias (ed.) *The Idea of a University by John Henry Newman: The Integral Text Unabridged*, University College Dublin Centre for Newman Studies, Dublin, second edn, 2009. All subsequent quotes of Newman are from this source.

14   W. von Humboldt, 'Ueber die innere und aeussere Organisation der hoeheren wissenschaftlichen Anstalten in Berlin' (1810). In: *Wilhelm von Humboldts Gesammelte Schriften*, Leitzmann et al (eds), Band X, B. Behr, Berlin, 1903–35. See https://archive.org/details/gesammelteschri03berlgoog.

15   Geoffrey Boulton and Colin Lucas, 'What are universities for?', position paper for the League of European Research Universities, September 2008. See www.leru.org/files/general/%E2%80%A2What%20are%20universities%20for%20(September%202008).pdf .

16   In this respect, Martianus Capella had a predecessor, by a few hundred years, a prolific Roman scholar called Marcus Terentius Varro (116–27 BC), who defined nine basic disciplines in a book titled *De Novem Disciplines*. These were the seven topics later adopted by Capella, plus medicine and architecture. Capella thought that the last two were too practical for inclusion in his list – an early instance of the familiar divide between the theoretical and the practical. See Peter Watson, *Ideas: A History from Fire to Freud*, Phoenix, London, 2005, p 498.

17   Sister Miriam Joseph, CSC, PhD, *The Trivium: The Liberal Arts of Logic, Grammar and Rhetoric: Understanding the Nature and Function of Language*, first published 1937, edited by Margaret McGlinn and published by Paul Dry Books, Philadelphia, 2002.

18   J.H. Newman, *The Idea of a University*, Discourse V, pp 101–2.

19   Newman, *The Idea of a University*, p 153.

20   Newman, *The Idea of a University*, p 163–4.

21   Newman, *The Idea of a University*, p 165–6.

22   Stefan Collini, *What Are Universities For?*, Harmondsworth, Penguin, 2012.

23   Yet another and no less striking piece of repetition is for academics to pen an essay or a monograph on the question 'What are universities for?'. Professor Collini has done so. So have Boulton and Lucas, so have I, and so have many others. It is a question worth grappling with.

[24] Hilary Mantel, writing in the *Sunday Times News Review* of 25 January 2015, says: 'If you strip away hindsight, and try to imagine the Tudors living their lives as we live, without knowledge of how their stories will end, then in a heartbeat they leap out of the history books: you find them next to you, in the street' (p 2).

[25] Patricia J. Gumport, Maria Iannozzi, Susan Shaman and Robert Zemsky, *The United States Country Report: Trends in Higher Education from Massification to Post-massification*, National Centre for Postsecondary Improvement, School of Education, Stanford University, Stanford, CA, 1997. Available at http://web.stanford.edu/group/ncpi/documents/pdfs/1-04_massification.pdf.

[26] Published on 31 May 2012. For an electronic version of the entire supplement, see http://europe.nxtbook.com/nxteu/tsl/100under50/index.php#/8 . For the list with live web links see www.timeshighereducation.co.uk/world-university-rankings/2012/one-hundred-under-fifty .

[27] The full text of the Robbins Report is available at www.educationengland.org.uk/documents/robbins/robbins1963.html. The quoted Robbins Principle occurs in item 31 on page 8.

[28] Peter Drucker, *The Age of Discontinuity: Guidelines to Our Changing Society*, first published in 1969 by Harper and Row, London, 8th printing by Transaction Publishers, Piscataway, NJ, 2008.

[29] Originally published in 1776. The full title is *An Enquiry into the Nature and Causes of the Wealth of Nations*. It is widely available in book stores, and as a pdf file in Penn State University's Electronic Classics Series, www2.hn.psu.edu/faculty/jmanis/adamsmith.htm.

[30] Smith, *Wealth of Nations*, from Book 4, chapter two, 'Of restraints upon importation from foreign countries of such goods as can be produced at home', p 364 of the Electronic Classics Edition.

[31] See www.press.uchicago.edu/Misc/Chicago/284158_townes.html , where Charles H. Townes gives an overview of Theodore Maiman's 1960 paper in *Nature* announcing the construction of a laser device. Townes writes: 'When the first laser appeared, scientists and engineers were not really prepared for it. Many people said to me – partly as a joke but also as a challenge – that the laser was "a solution looking for a problem." But by bringing together optics and electronics, lasers opened up vast new fields of science and technology.' He adds: 'Maiman's paper is so short, and has so many powerful ramifications, that I believe it might be considered the most important per word of any of the wonderful papers in *Nature* over the past century.' Tantalisingly, he also asks: 'This raises the question: why weren't lasers invented long ago, perhaps by 1930 when all the necessary physics was already understood, at least by some people? What other important phenomena are we blindly missing today?'

[32] The quote is from a short summary of the WorldWideWeb project posted by Tim Berners-Lee, its creator, on an early internet forum. It is available at https://qz.com/750688/heres-the-message-announcing-the-world-wide-web-25-years-ago/.

33 Case study 32 in the Russell Group publication, *The Economic Impact of Research Conducted in Russell Group Universities,* Russell Group Papers 1, London, 2010, p 35. See http://russellgroup.ac.uk/policy/publications/the-economic-impact-of-research-conducted-in-russell-group-universities/ (but note that the 2010 report can no longer be downloaded, having been superseded by a report [available at the same web address] dated October 2017).

34 Home page at www.nature.com/nature/index.html.

35 Laura Garwin and Tim Lincoln (eds) *A Century of Nature: Twenty-one Discoveries that Changed Science and the World,* University of Chicago Press, Chicago, 2003. See also www.nature.com/nature/history/century.html.

36 This quote, and the next, are from the editors' Preface to *A Century of Nature,* pp xii–xiii.

37 A.K. Geim and K.S. Novoselov, 'The rise of graphene', *Nature Materials* 6(3) (2007): 183–91. See www.nature.com/nmat/journal/v6/n3/full/nmat1849.html.

38 www.nature.com/nphys/journal/v6/n11/full/nphys1836.html.

39 Michael Gibbons, Camille Limoges, Helga Nowotny, Simon Schwartzman, Peter Scott and Martin Trow, *The New Production of Knowledge: The Dynamics of Science and Research in Contemporary Societies,* Sage, London, 2012 (first published 1994).

40 This quote, and the two that follow, come from Gibbons et al, *The New Production of Knowledge,* pp 1–3.

41 Ernest L. Boyer, *Scholarship Reconsidered: Priorities of the Professoriate,* Carnegie Foundation for the Advancement of Teaching, 1990. See http://www.hadinur.com/paper/BoyerScholarshipReconsidered.pdf. Boyer was at that time president of the foundation.

42 Chapter one of Boyer, *Scholarship Reconsidered,* pp 1–3.

43 Chapter two of Boyer, *Scholarship Reconsidered,* pp 16–17.

44 Gibbons et al, *The New Production of Knowledge,* p 49.

45 The term was coined by Henry Chesbrough, in his book *Open Innovation: The New Imperative for Creating and Profiting from Technology,* Harvard Business School Publishing, Cambridge, MA, 2003.

46 Burton R. Clark, *Creating Entrepreneurial Universities: Organisational Pathways of Transformation,* Emerald Group Publishing, Bingley, 1998.

47 Clark, *Creating Entrepreneurial Universities,* pp 3–4.

48 The OECD, created in 1961, now has 35 countries as members. See www.oecd.org/.

49 Burton R. Clark, 'The entrepreneurial university: new foundations for collegiality, autonomy, and achievement', keynote address at the 2000 IMHE General Conference in Paris, published in *Higher Education Management* (the Journal of the Programme on Institutional Management in Higher Education) 13(2) (2001): 9–24. See www.oecd.org/edu/imhe/37446098.pdf.

[50] Holden Thorp and Buck Goldstein, *Engines of Innovation: The Entrepreneurial University in the Twenty-first Century*, University of North Carolina Press, Chapel Hill, NC, 2010.

[51] Clayton M. Christensen and Henry J. Eyring, *The Innovative University: Changing the DNA of the Higher Education from the Inside Out*, Jossey Bass, San Francisco, 2011.

[52] Ben Wildavsky, Andrew Kelly and Kavin Carey, *Reinventing Higher Education: The Promise of Innovation*, Harvard Educational Publishing Group, Cambridge, MA, 2011.

[53] Derek Bok, *Universities in the Marketplace: The Commercialization of Higher Education*, Princeton University Press, Princeton, NJ, 2003.

[54] Jennifer Washburn, *University Inc.: The Corporate Corruption of American Higher Education*, Basic Books, New York, 2005.

[55] Sheila Slaughter and Gary Rhoades, *Academic Capitalism and the New Economy: Markets, State and Higher Education*, Johns Hopkins University Press, Baltimore, MD, 2004.

[56] Benjamin Ginsberg, *The Fall of the Faculty: The Rise of the All-administrative University and Why It Matters*, Oxford University Press, Oxford, 2011.

2 Rankings and League Tables

[1] John Kay, *Obliquity: Why Our Goals Are Best Achieved Indirectly*, Profile Books, London , 2011. On p 71 Kay writes:'"When you cannot measure something", said Lord Kelvin, "your knowledge is of a meagre and unsatisfactory kind".... But Kelvin was wrong. What Solon and Aristotle knew about human flourishing, or Dame Helen Gardner knew about poetry, was not meagre or unsatisfactory.... Kelvin's approach leads directly to the modern curse of bogus quantification.'

[2] This phrase is from the page produced by Google for 'webometrics', not from the Webometrics website.

[3] www.i-graduate.org/services/international-student-barometer-and-student-barometer/ .

[4] www.u-multirank.eu/.

[5] *Times Higher Education*, 22 March 2012. See www.timeshighereducation.co.uk/story.asp?storycode=419431.

[6] See https://www.tesglobal.com/content/tes-global-welcomes-rt-hon-david-willetts-mp-chair-its-new-higher-education-advisory-board.

[7] We are on shifting sands here, because, as mentioned a few times, the various rankings agencies change their mind every so often. What follows was mostly written around 2012, and was correct at that time.

[8] Or Fields Medal winners. There is no Nobel Prize in Mathematics, but the Fields Medal is often regarded as the equivalent honour for mathematicians. Fields Medals are awarded once every four years at the Congress of the International Mathematical Union. They are only awarded to mathematicians younger than 40.

[9] This example dates from 2017, but it is not much different from what the same table looked like in 2012, a decade after rankings first appeared. Some

of the weightings change over time, but the kind of differences illustrated here remain. Note that the Leiden ranking does not come with simple weighting factors, like the other rankings. It actually represents five different rankings, each of which is based on different indicators. For an explanation, see www.leidenranking.com/.

[10] Quoted in *The Guardian*, 15 September 2015, www.theguardian.com/education/2015/sep/15/british-universities-slip-downing-global-rankings. See also the article in *The Times*, 15 September 2015, p 21.

[11] *Times Higher Education*, 15 October 2015, p 7.

[12] Based on a grade point average calculation. See *Times Higher Education*, 18 December 2008, pp 28–41.

[13] The Russell Group is an alliance of 24 universities in the UK, generally regarded as 'leading universities'. See www.russellgroup.ac.uk.

[14] The NSS is conducted by Ipsos Mori, polling final-year undergraduate students across the UK.

[15] Most of the data in the table come from the Higher Education Statistics Agency (HESA) returns for 2010/11, published in spring 2012. HESA data is published in the Higher Education Information Database for Institutions (HEIDI, https://heidi.hesa.ac.uk/), but they are not freely published. To get access, it is necessary to subscribe to HEIDI, paying an annual fee. Or one can purchase specific data sets as required, which is what the ranking compilers do. Criterion A gives total income from research grants and contracts for 2010/11, from the HESA Finance return. Criterion B gives 'A' divided by the FTE of academic staff with a 'teaching and research' contract of employment, 2010/11, from the published HESA Staff return. Criterion C gives the number of citations received between publication and December 2011, on papers published in 2010, from the Web of Science. Criterion D is 'C' divided by the FTE of academic staff with a 'teaching and research' contract of employment, 2010/11, from the published HESA Staff return. Criterion E gives doctorates awarded in 2010/11, from the published HESA Student return. Criterion F is 'E' divided by the FTE of academic staff with a 'teaching and research' contract of employment, 2010/11, from the published HESA Staff return. Finally, criterion G is the percentage of respondents who stated that they agreed with Question 22 of the NSS, conducted in January to March 2012, and published in September 2012. NSS data are freely available from the HEFCE, at www.hefce.ac.uk/lt/nss/results/2012/.

[16] Since there are infinitely many possible weightings, there are already infinitely many possible outcomes even just on this one particular method.

[17] See the HEFCE website at www.hefce.ac.uk/rsrch/funding/, under 'Principles of research funding'.

[18] www.rae.ac.uk/news/2008/results.asp.

[19] www.rae.ac.uk/aboutus/quality.asp.

[20] As in 2008, the top-ranked institution for 'quality' in the UK was again the Institute of Cancer Research, which submitted just over 100 researchers, compared to over 2,400 from Cambridge. (Actually, this statement needs

to be qualified. The Institute for Cancer Research was top of the list of institutions which submitted researchers *in more than one subject*. If you make a list including even single-subject institutions, then the top-ranked higher education institute for 'quality' in the entire UK in REF 2014 was the Courtauld Institute of Art, which submitted 32.5 researchers.)

21 *Times Higher Education*, 22 January 2015, p 58.

22 Peter W.A. West, 'A Faustian bargain? Institutional responses to national and international rankings', *Higher Education Management and Policy* 21(1) (2009): 11–18.

23 The last four examples come from: Ellen Hazelkorn, *Rankings and the Reshaping of Higher Education: The Battle for World-class Excellence,* Palgrave Macmillan, Basingstoke, 2011.

24 Ellen Hazelkorn, 'Rankings and the battle for world-class excellence: institutional strategies and policy choices', *Higher Education Management and Policy* 21(1) (2009): 55-76.

25 All the quotes in this paragraph are from Hazelkorn, *Rankings and the Reshaping of Higher Education.*

26 See, for example, 'Building Singapore's scientific excellence', *Straits Times*, 19 October 2016, on the occasion of the Nanyang Technological University President, Prof. Bertil Andersson, being awarded the Singapore President's Science and Technology Medal.

27 Quoted in Hazelkorn, *Rankings and the Reshaping of Higher Education.* Also referred to in Hazelkorn, 'Rankings and the battle for world-class excellence', p 155.

28 Quoted in West, 'A Faustian bargain?'

29 References given in Hazelkorn, *Rankings and the Reshaping of Higher Education.*

30 *Times Higher Education,* 22 January 2015.

31 All the examples (up to here) in this paragraph and the preceding one are from Hazelkorn, *Rankings and the Reshaping of Higher Education.*

32 www.kaust.edu.sa/about/kingsmessage.html .

33 Hazelkorn, *Rankings and the Reshaping of Higher Education*, p 75.

34 Hazelkorn, *Rankings and the Reshaping of Higher Education*, p 210.

35 See www.chatham.edu/about/.

36 See http://snu.edu/about .

37 *Times Higher Education*, 13 October 2016, p 32, reporting on the first *Wall Street Journal/Times Higher Education* College Rankings. The survey of 100,000 US students was carried out by *Times Higher Education*, which is based in London.

38 Andrejs Rauhvargers, *Global University Rankings and Their Impact*, European University Association, Brussels, 2011, http://www.eua.be/Libraries/publications-homepage-list/Global_University_Rankings_and_Their_Impact.pdf?sfvrsn=4this. See p 39.

39 Hazelkorn, *Rankings and the Reshaping of Higher Education*, p 106, p 62.

40 West, 'A Faustian bargain?', p 14.

41 Email from a representative of Thomson Reuters, 11 December 2012.

42 See www.hefce.ac.uk/pubs/year/2008/200814/. *Counting What Is Measured, or Measuring What Counts?*, Report to HEFCE by the Centre for Higher Education Research and Information (CHERI), Open University, and Hobson's Research, HEFCE Issues Paper 14, see http://webarchive. nationalarchives.gov.uk/20120716102534/https://www.hefce.ac.uk/ media/hefce1/pubs/hefce/2008/0814/08_14.pdf 2008.

43 Rauhvargers, *Global University Rankings*.

44 S. Marginson and M. van der Wende, 'To rank or to be ranked: the impact of global rankings in higher education', *Journal of Studies in International Education* 11(3/4) (2007): 306–29.

45 S. Marginson, 'Rankings, marketing mania or menace? The big picture', paper presented at the 16th Annual New Zealand International Education Conference, Christchurch, New Zealand, 8–10 August 2007, www.cshe. unimelb.edu.au/people/marginson.html#RecentPaperPres.

46 Andrejs Rauvhargers, *Global University Rankings and Their Impact: Report II*, European University Association, Brussels, 2013, http://www.eua.be/ Libraries/publications-homepage-list/EUA_Global_University_Rankings_ and_Their_Impact_-_Report_II .

47 Ellen Hazelkorn, *Rankings and the Reshaping of Higher Education: The Battle for World-class Excellence*, Palgrave MacMillan, Basingstoke, 2011.

48 Ellen Hazelkorn (ed.) *Global Rankings and the Geopolitics of Higher Education: Understanding the Influence and Impact of Rankings on Higher Education, Policy and Society,* International Studies in Higher Education, Routledge, Oxford, 2017.

49 Hazelkorn, *Rankings and the Reshaping of Higher Education*, pp 4–5.

50 Hazelkorn, *Rankings and the Reshaping of Higher Education*, pp 200–3.

51 For example, COREHEG, the Tertiary Education Community of Practice at the World Bank Group, organised a seminar in January 2015 on: 'The Obsession with Rankings in Tertiary Education: Implications for Public Policy'. The main speaker was Ellen Hazelkorn. (Email communication: Francisco Marmolejo, 23 January 2015.)

3 Quality in Higher Education

1 See the entry on Plato in the *Stanford Encyclopaedia of Philosophy*, more particularly the section on 'Plato's indirectness', https://plato.stanford.edu/ entries/plato/.

2 This quote is from the Harvard Classics Edition, in the translation by Benjamin Jowett, published by P.F. Collier & Son, New York, 62nd printing, 1969. See also http://classics.mit.edu/Plato/apology.html.

3 Karl Popper, *The Open Society and its Enemies*, first published by Routledge, London, 1945.

4 Aristotle, *Metaphysics*, Book IV, chapter seven. I quote from *The Basic Works of Aristotle*, edited by Richard McKeon, with an Introduction by C.D.C. Reeve, published in the Modern Library Paperback Edition, Random House, New York, 2001 (first published by Random House New York in 1941).

[5] Here and in the next two quotations I use the translation of W.D. Ross, from my trusty copy of *The Basic Works of Aristotle*, edited by Richard McKeon.

[6] Robert M. Pirsig, *Zen and the Art of Motorcycle Maintenance*, 40th Anniversary Edition, Vintage Books, London, 2004, p 362.

[7] http://dera.ioe.ac.uk/26289/1/QualityStandardsGuide.pdf.

[8] The International Network for Quality Assurance Agencies in Higher Education (INQAAHE), www.inqaahe.org/index.php.,

[9] On this matter I have found the following article very useful: Jethro Newton, 'What is quality?', in *Embedding Quality Culture in Higher Education, A Selection of Papers from the 1st European Forum for Quality Assurance*, 23–25 November 2006, hosted by the Technische Universität München, published by the European University Association, Brussels, 2007, pp 14–20.

[10] Peter Williams, 'Debating standards', *Higher Quality* 28 (November 2008).

[11] We need to watch our prepositions here. Fitness-*for*-purpose matches with the good-*at* question, while fitness-*of*-purpose matches with the good-*for* question.

[12] Martin Heidegger, 'German students', speech delivered on 3 November 1933 at Freiburg University. English translation in R. Wolin (ed.) *The Heidegger Controversy*, Cambridge, MA, MIT Press, 1993, chapter two.

[13] The UK variation is called Destinations of Leavers from Higher Education, which is compiled by the HESA, and essentially asks what proportion of graduates (who do not go on to further degrees) are in employment within six months of graduating. Of course, the results can then be turned into a league table.

[14] www.ref.ac.uk/panels/assessmentcriteriaandleveldefinitions/.

[15] The data (from the Thomson Reuters Incites database) was available by subscription at the time. However, in 2015 Thomson Reuters and the *Times Higher* dissolved their relationship, so while the Incites website is still active, at http://ipscience.thomsonreuters.com/product/incites/, the data is no longer accessible in this format.

[16] See the U-Multirank website at www.umultirank.org/, and the 'Key questions and answers' at www.u-multirank.eu/fileadmin/user_upload/documents/UMR_key_questions_and_answers.pdf. See also Frans A. van Vught and Frank Ziegele (eds) *Multidimensional Ranking: the Design and Development of U-Multirank*, Springer, Berlin, 2012, http://books.google.co.uk/books?id=CpsgEyO_kpUC&pg=PA173&lpg=PA173&dq=u-multirank+sunburst+charts&source=bl&ots=KIi_OSTP0Z&sig=0f3oczUNKontv6_Vm5n4waQ8Kag&hl=en&sa=X&ei=ncKNUr7qK4GVhQe2_ICgDg&ved=0CD4Q6AEwAg#v=onepage&q=u-multirank%20sunburst%20charts&f=false.

[17] www.umultirank.org/our-project/indicators/.

[18] www.umultirank.org/methodology/indicators/mapping-indicators/.

[19] www.utwente.nl/mb/cheps/.

[20] www.che.de/cms/?getObject=302&getLang=en.

[21] Frans van Vught and Frank Ziegele (eds) *Design and Testing the Feasibility of a Multidimensional Global University Ranking: Final Report*, Education and

Culture DG, 2011,https://www.eurashe.eu/library/u-multirank_design-and-testing-the-feasibility-of-a-multidimensional-global-university-ranking-pdf/ .

22 www.education.ie/en/Press-Events/Conferences/Ireland-s-Presidency-of-the-EU/Conference-30-31-Jan-2013/.The sample sunburst chart (Figure 3.3 in Chapter Three) is taken from this report.

23 www.timeshighereducation.co.uk/story.asp?storycode=419431.

24 www.leru.org/index.php/public/home/.

25 www.timeshighereducation.co.uk/news/leru-pulls-out-of-eus-u-multirank-scheme/2001361.article. I could not find a corresponding quote on the LERU website.

26 www.international.ac.uk/home.

27 Available at www.international.ac.uk/research-and-publications/research-and-publications.aspx (but only accessible by registered users of the UK International Unit website).The policy note was circulated by email from the UK International Unit director directly to all UK vice-chancellors on 15 May 2013.

28 https://www.timeshighereducation.com/news/leru-pulls-out-of-eus-u-multirankscheme/2001361.article .

29 Alex Usher, http://higheredstrategy.com/u-multirank/, posted on 23 April 2013.

30 www.hefce.ac.uk/lt/tef/whatistef/.

31 See the Conservative Party Manifesto for the 2015 general election, at www.conservatives.com/manifesto2015, p 35.

32 See the HEFCE document *Teaching Excellence Framework: Year Two Additional Guidance*, HEFCE, Bristol, 2016, www.hefce.ac.uk/pubs/year/2016/201632/.

33 The briefing slides can be downloaded from www.hefce.ac.uk/lt/tef/tefproviders/tef2/.

34 HEFCE, *Teaching Excellence Framework:Year Two*.

35 First published on 16 August 2016, then periodically updated.The version of 9 October 2017 can be found at www.gov.uk/government/uploads/system/uploads/attachment_data/file/651155/Teaching_Excellence_and_Student_Outcomes_Framework_Specification.pdf.

36 See www.timeshighereducation.com/news/tef-results-times-higher-education-metrics-ranking and www.timeshighereducation.com/sites/default/files/breaking_news_files/tef_results_-_institutions_ranked_on_metrics.pdf .

37 www.timeshighereducation.com/news/tef-meaningless-results-devoid-credibility-says-v-c.

38 Andreas Schleicher, OECD Director of Education, 'Value-added: how do you measure whether universities are delivering for their students?', Higher Education Policy Institute Annual Lecture 2015, www.hepi.ac.uk/wp-content/uploads/2016/01/Andreas-Schleicher-lecture.pdf.

[39] This quote too is from the HEFCE document *Teaching Excellence Framework: Year Two Additional Guidance*. I have omitted the explanatory diagram, but the determined reader will find it on the next page of the *Additional Guidance*.

[40] As far as I know this comment was first made by Professor Andy Hamilton, former Vice-chancellor of Oxford University.

[41] Officially, the *Memorandum of Assurance and Accountability between HEFCE and Institutions: Terms and Conditions for payment of HEFCE Grants to Higher Education Institutions*. See www.hefce.ac.uk/pubs/year/2014/201412/.

[42] From a 182-page document titled *Securing Student Success: Risk-based Regulation for Teaching Excellence, Social Mobility and Informed Choice in Higher Education*, a government consultation (by the Department for Education) on behalf of the Office for Students (OfS), launch date 19 October 2017, p 39, paragraph 40. See https://consult.education.gov.uk/higher-education/higher-education-regulatory-framework/supporting_documents/HE%20reg%20framework%20condoc%20FINAL%2018%20October%20FINAL%20FINAL.pdf.

[43] *Daily Mail*, 12 November 2015.

[44] As was pointed out in the *Times Higher Education*, 19 November 2015, p 4.

[45] www.offa.org.uk/about/.

[46] OFFA is due to be subsumed under the new OfS in 2018.

[47] www.gov.uk/government/uploads/system/uploads/attachment_data/file/445916/Prevent_Duty_Guidance_For_Higher_Education__England__Wales_.pdf.

[48] As explained by Oxford University, see www.admin.ox.ac.uk/councilsec/prevent/legal/.

[49] Thomas Docherty, *For the University: Democracy and the Future of the Institution*, Bloomsbury Academic, London, 2011.

[50] Docherty, *For the University*, p 1.

[51] Docherty, *For the University*, p 113–14.

[52] Docherty, *For the University*, p 3.

[53] Onora O'Neill, *A Question of Trust*, BBC Reith Lectures 2002, Cambridge University Press, Cambridge, 2002.

[54] O'Neill, *A Question of Trust*, p 18.

[55] O'Neill, *A Question of Trust*, extracts from pp 45–57.

4 *Tales of Quality, Equality and Diversity*

[1] Thomas Carlyle, 'Goethe [1828]', in *Essays on Goethe*, Cassell's National Library, Cassell and Company, London, Paris, New York and Melbourne, MCMV (1905), p 78. Available online at https://archive.org/details/essaysongoethe00carluoft .

[2] Apparently the story was first told by Aristotle. See Konrad Gaiser, 'Plato's enigmatic lecture "On the Good"', *Phronesis* 25(1) (1980): 5–37, www.jstor.org/stable/4182081?__redirected.

[3] The material about the Universities of Cape Town and Stellenbosch largely come from a chapter I wrote for a book produced by the Council for Higher Education of South Africa: *Reflections of South African University Leaders, 1981*

to 2014, published by African Minds, Cape Town, 2016 (chapter five, 'Two tales of quality and equality', pp 93–118).

4   Quoted from David Harrison, *The White Tribe of Africa: South Africa in Perspective*, Southern Book Publishers, Johannesburg, 1987, p 191. (This is a South African edition. The book was previously published by the BBC in London, and the first South African edition was published in 1981 by MacMillan South Africa.)

5   For a somewhat different interpretation by the Afrikaner historian Hermann Giliomee, see 'Education in SA: is Verwoerd to blame?', 3 September 2012, politicsweb, http://politicsweb.co.za/politicsweb/view/politicsweb/en/pa ge71619?oid=323686&sn=Detail&pid=71619 .

6   I am an alumnus of the Randse Afrikaanse Universiteit.

7   I am an alumnus of Rhodes University.

8   Harrison, *The White Tribe of Africa,* p 193.

9   This project is still (in 2016) functioning at the University of Cape Town. See www.ched.uct.ac.za/departments/adp/interfac_proj/aarp/ .

10 For the benefit of any readers not acquainted with the South African research system: the National Research Foundation at that time, and still today, rated individual academics according to their research performance. The top rating is an A, which means 'world-leading researcher'. In the 1990s there were fewer than 50 of these A-rated researchers in the entire country, across all scientific disciplines. Five of them were in the Mathematics Department at the University of Cape Town.

11 I was the first Chair of CUES.

12 If you visualise CHED as a set of steps at the base of six pillars, and you put a triangular apex on top of those pillars to represent admin/management, you get a picture that looks uncannily like the front of Jameson Hall, the great hall of the University of Cape Town at the centre of the campus (renamed Sarah Baartman Hall in 2017). Accordingly, the new model of six faculties plus CHED was known as the Jameson Hall model. (This greatly confused an international adviser on university restructuring, who went searching through the literature for two experts called Jameson and Hall.)

13 For a summary, see Chris Brink, 'Effective numeracy', *Transactions of the Royal Society of South Africa* 54(2) (1999): 247–56.

14 The Reverend Simon Adams is a social activist and the long-time pastor of a small church in Ida's Valley, one of the 'coloured' neighbourhoods of Stellenbosch.

15 David Harrison, *The White Tribe of Africa*, p 193.

16 I was only the seventh rector of Stellenbosch University since 1918, the first rector to be appointed from outside the university, the first who was not an alumnus, and the first who had never been a member of the Broederbond or any of the Afrikaner cultural organisations.

17 The story of how my time at Stellenbosch unfolded is told in a valedictory volume: Amanda Botha (ed.) *Chris Brink: Anatomy of a Transformer*, SUN Press, Stellenbosch, 2007.

18 'Triple accreditation' is a sought-after accolade among business schools. It means being accredited simultaneously and independently by EQUIS (the European Quality Improvement System), AMBA (the Association of MBAs), and AACSB (the Association to Advance Collegiate Schools of Business).

19 The results mentioned in this paragraph are quoted from my 2007 paper 'The state of the university' in Botha, *Anatomy of a Transformer*, pp 29–30. For the Stellenbosch Institute for Advanced Study, see www.stias.ac.za.

20 This quote, and the following example, from Botha, *Anatomy of a Transformer*, pp 5–6.

21 Brigadier General Lekoa Solly Mollo, later Major-General and South African High Commissioner in Uganda.

22 Students at Stellenbosch University are called Maties.

23 Quoted in my public Annual Report, 27 July 2005, 'On transformation and quality at Stellenbosch University' (see Botha, *Anatomy of a Transformer*, p 120).

24 Kate Fox, *Watching the English: The Hidden Rules of English Behaviour*, Hodder and Stoughton, London, 2004.

25 I formulated these thoughts in the year after my arrival in the UK, as a way of trying to understand my new environment. The argument was first presented as a keynote address at the September 2008 Conference of the Institutional Management in Higher Education (IMHE) programme of the OECD in Paris, under the title '"Standards will drop" – and other fears about the equality agenda'. A slightly revised version was presented at a plenary session of the UK Conference of the Equality Challenge Unit (ECU) in Manchester in November 2008. The paper was subsequently published in the journal *Higher Education Management and Policy* 21(1) (2009): 19–37.

26 Pamela B. Garlick and Gavin Brown, 'Widening participation in medicine', *British Medical Journal* 336(7653) (17 May 2008):1111–13. See www.bmj. com/cgi/content/extract/336/7653/1111.

27 www.thecompleteuniversityguide.co.uk/league-tables/key/.

28 www.thecompleteuniversityguide.co.uk/league-tables/ rankings?o=Entry&s=Medicine.

29 Professor Steve Smith, Vice-Chancellor of Exeter University, 'Focus on real access issues', Guest leader in *Times Higher Education*, 24 April 2008. This was written in the run-up to the NCEE presenting a set of recommendations to government, dated October 2008, in which Professor Smith authored the section on higher education engaging with schools and colleges. See www.dcsf.gov.uk/ncee/docs/7898-DCSF-NatCouncilEd.pdf.

30 *The Times*, leading article, 17 June 2014, p 26.

31 The Behavioural Insights Team, part of the Cabinet Office. See www.gov. uk/government/organisations/behavioural-insights-team.

32 I take this breakdown from the *Report of the Newcastle Fairness Commission*, July 2012. I chaired the commission, drafted the principles of fairness, and co-authored the report. See www.ncl.ac.uk/socialrenewal/engagement/ fairnesscommission/documents/.

33 Hugh Ip and I.C. McManus, 'Increasing diversity among clinicians', *British Medical Journal* 336(7653) (17 May 2008): 1082–3. See www.bmj.com/cgi/content/extract/336/7653/1082. In a short response, the authors of the original paper point out that the places reserved for widening participation are additional to the normal number of entrants to the medical school, and the extra cost was funded not by the university but by the HEFCE.

34 See for example Bruce G. Charlton, 'Social class differences in IQ: implications for the government's "fair access" political agenda', *Times Higher Education*, 22 May 2008: 'Yet in all this debate a simple and vital fact has been missed: higher social classes have a significantly higher average IQ than lower social classes.' See www.timeshighereducation.co.uk/Journals/THE/THE/22_May_2008/attachments/Times%20Higher%20IQ%20Social%20Class.doc.

35 Nelson Mandela, *Long Walk to Freedom*, Abacus, London 1994, pp 103–4. Mandela eventually dropped out of his LLB studies at Wits, after failing his exams several times, and took the (separate) qualification exam for an attorney in 1952 (*Long Walk to Freedom*, p 171).

36 www.timesonline.co.uk/tol/news/uk/article2677098.ece .

37 Katherine W. Phillips, 'How diversity makes us smarter', *Scientific American*, 1 October 2014. See www.scientificamerican.com/article/how-diversity-makes-us-smarter/. The article was originally published with the title 'How diversity works'. I shortened the quote a little; the full version reads: 'Decades of research by organizational scientists, psychologists, sociologists, economists and demographers show that socially diverse groups (that is, those with a diversity of race, ethnicity, gender and sexual orientation) are more innovative than homogeneous groups.'

38 Ramanujan, John Lennon, Steve Jobs and Nelson Mandela.

39 I coined this phrase in the title of a speech at the centenary celebrations of the Rhodes Trust at Stellenbosch University in 2003. The speech appears in full in Botha, *Anatomy of a Transformer*, pp 83–7. I also used 'Quality needs diversity' as the title of a keynote address at a meeting of Universities UK on 10 September 2014. See www.youtube.com/watch?v=fnAHdDbZtUo.

40 Comment made by Sir Howard Newby, former vice-chancellor of Liverpool University, the University of the West of England and Southampton University. Quoted as an epigraph to the section on England in this chapter.

41 I should emphasise that by 'group' I mean an identifiable social group, not just an artificially defined collection of people. Otherwise it would not be difficult to construct counterexamples.

5 Rank Order of Worth

1 John Milton, *Paradise Lost*, Book II, l.5.

2 These figures are from the report *Elitist Britain?*, published by the Social Mobility and Child Poverty Commission on 28 August 2014. See www.gov.uk/government/news/elitist-britain-report-published. Members of Parliament have a similar profile. Of the MPs returned after the May 2015 election, nine out of ten are university graduates, more than half studied

at a Russell Group university, just under a third had some kind of private schooling, and more than a quarter hold a degree from Oxbridge. (These figures are cited in the *Times Higher Education* of 14 May 2015, following a Sutton Trust report titled *Parliamentary Privilege: The MPs 2015*. The figure of just under a third of MPs having received some kind of private schooling comes from *The Week*, 16 May 2015, p 5.)

3   Quoted in www.flintoff.org/what-happened-to-meritocracy and in www. theguardian.com/theguardian/2001/feb/14/features11.g21.

4   Michael Young, *The Rise of the Meritocracy*, with a new introduction by the author, Transaction Publishers, New Brunswick, NJ, 1994, 11th printing 2008. Originally published in 1958 by Thames & Hudson. The next three quotes are from the Introduction.

5   Michael Young, 'Down with meritocracy', *The Guardian*, 29 June 2001, www.theguardian.com/politics/2001/jun/29/comment.

6   See www.usnews.com/opinion/blogs/noah-kristula-green/2013/06/04/ben-bernankes-discusses-meritocracy-at-the-elite-princeton-university.

7   Robert H. Frank, *Success and Luck: Good Fortune and the Myth of Meritocracy*, Princeton University Press, Princeton, NJ, 2016, p xi.

8   *Elitist Britain*, Report of the Social Mobility and Child Poverty Commission, 28 August 2014, www.gov.uk/government/uploads/system/uploads/attachment_data/file/347915/Elitist_Britain_-_Final.pdf.

9   Vernon Bogdanor, book review in *The Spectator*, 5 April 2014, p 44, of Robert Ford and Matthew Goodwin, *Revolt on the Right: Explaining Support for the Radical Right in Britain*.

10 Danny Dorling, Halford Mackinder Professor of Geography at Oxford, writing in *Times Higher Education*, 25 September 2014, pp 35–41.

11 Plato, *The Republic*, Book III, 415a. This is the translation of Benjamin Jowett.

12 In another paper, with Sally Tomlinson: 'The creation of inequality: myths of potential and ability'. See www.jceps.com/archives/3204. I am grateful to Professor Dorling for drawing my attention to the noble lie analogy.

13 *The Sunday Times*, 16 February 2014, p 9.

14 *The Sunday Times*, 16 February 2014, p 9.

15 *The Sunday Times*, 16 February 2014, p 9.

16 Andreas Schleicher, OECD Director of Education, 'Value-added: how do you measure whether universities are delivering for their students?', Higher Education Policy Institute Annual Lecture 2015, www.hepi.ac.uk/wp-content/uploads/2016/01/Andreas-Schleicher-lecture.pdf .

17 www.hmc.org.uk/.

18 *The Times*, 15 October 2015.

19 www.gov.uk/government/publications/number-of-secondary-schools-and-their-size-in-student-numbers.

20 www.education.gov.uk/schools/performance/download_data.html.

21 This is from an Ofsted document titled 'The Framework for School Inspection', available at www.ofsted.gov.uk/resources/framework-for-school-inspection.

22 *The Sunday Times*, 15 November 2015, 'Parent power'.

23 I quote from a BBC report at www.bbc.co.uk/news/education-25415231. (The original study is referenced elsewhere as: B. Francis and M. Hutchings, *Parent Power? Using Money and Information to Boost Children's Chances of Educational Success*, Sutton Trust, London, 2013, but it no longer appears at the web reference given: www.suttontrust.com/our-work/research/item/parent-power/.) Other media summaries of the study appeared in the *Daily Telegraph*, see www.telegraph.co.uk/education/educationnews/10523029/Middle-class-parents-cheating-to-secure-school-places.html , and *The Independent,* see www.independent.co.uk/news/education/education-news/well-off-parents-resorting-to-ethically-dubious-practices-to-get-their-children-into-good-school-9011520.html .

24 Quoted in both the *Daily Telegraph* and *The Independent*, as in the preceding note 23.

25 *The Independent*, 16 October 2014: '"Ban unpaid internships to end elitist closed shop", urges social mobility watchdog'.

26 Reported in *The Times*, 23 September 2014: Gabriella Swerling, 'Parent forged document to get place at chosen school'.

27 *Daily Mail*, 20 January 2016, pp 28–9.

28 *The Times*, 14 January 2016, front page.

29 *The Times*, 14 January 2016, p 4.

30 *The Times*, 7 January 2013, p 5.

31 *The Times*, 20 March 2013, p 35.

32 https://royalsociety.org/about-us/fellowship/ .

33 Erasto B. Mpemba and Denis G. Osborne, 'Cool?', *Physics Education* (Institute of Physics) 4 (1969): 172–5. Republished as E.B. Mpemba and D.G. Osborne, 'The Mpemba effect', *Physics Education* (Institute of Physics) 14 (1979): 410–12.

34 W. Somerset Maugham, 'A marriage of convenience', in *The Complete Short Stories of W. Somerset Maugham,* vol. III, William Heinemann, London, 1952.

35 Danny Dorling, Halford Mackinder Professor of Geography at Oxford University, writing in *The Times Higher Education*, 25 September 2014, p 38.

36 James Bloodworth, *The Myth of the Meritocracy*, Biteback Publishing, London, 2016, inside cover.

37 Higher Education Careers Service Unit, *Seven Years On: Graduate Careers in a Changing Labour Market*, 2004, http://ww2.prospects.ac.uk/downloads/csdesk/members/reports/seven_years_on.pdf.

38 See 'Education at a Glance 2017: OECD Indicators', http://www.oecd.org/edu/education-at-a-glance-19991487.htm, p.104.

39 Here and for the remainder of this topic I draw on an internal report produced for the Student Policy Network of Universities UK by Fiona Waye, titled 'Social mobility project: Does higher education really diminish the gap between the advantaged and the disadvantaged?', UUK paper number SPN-2014-19. As a declaration of interest, I should mention that I was at that time the Chair of the Student Policy Network.

40 Lindsey Macmillan and Anna Vignoles, *Mapping the Occupational Destinations of New Graduates*, research report produced by the Centre for Analysis of

Youth Transitions for the Social Mobility and Child Poverty Commission. Available at www.gov.uk/government/uploads/system/uploads/attachment_data/file/259380/Mapping_the_occupational_destinations_of_new_graduates_Final.pdf .

41 Lindsey Macmillan, Clare Tyler and Anna Vignoles, *Who Gets the Top Jobs? The Role of Family Background and Networks in Recent Graduates' Access to High Status Professions*, Working Paper 13-15, Department of Quantitative Social Science, Institute of Education, December 2013. Available at http://repec.ioe.ac.uk/REPEc/pdf/qsswp1315.pdf .

42 Daniel Andrew Gordon, *Employability and Social Class in the Graduate Labour Market*, PhD thesis, Cardiff University, 2013. See http://orca.cf.ac.uk/46473/.

43 Macmillan et al, *Who Gets the Top Jobs?*

44 Alan Milburn, 'No political party is facing up to worsening poverty', *The Times*, 20 October 2014, p 26, www.thetimes.co.uk/tto/opinion/thunderer/article4241362.ece.

45 *Non-educational Barriers to the Elite Professions Evaluation*, Social Mobility and Child Poverty Commission, 14 June 2015, www.gov.uk/government/news/study-into-non-educational-barriers-to-top-jobs-published.

46 Sathnam Sanghera, commenting in *The Times* of 16 June 2015 on the report of 14 June 2015 by the Child Poverty and Social Mobility Commission (see note 45). His autobiography is *The Boy with the Topknot: A Memoir of Love, Secrets and Lies in Wolverhampton*, Penguin Books, London, 2008.

47 Janet L. Yellen, Chair of the Board of Governors of the Federal Reserve, 'Perspectives on inequality and opportunity from the survey of consumer finances', speech at the Conference on Economic Opportunity and Inequality, Federal Reserve Bank of Boston, Boston, MA, 17 October 2014. See www.federalreserve.gov/newsevents/speech/yellen20141017a.htm.

48 www.oxfam.org.uk/media-centre/press-releases/2016/01/62-people-own-same-as-half-world-says-oxfam-inequality-report-davos-world-economic-forum. See also the report in *The Times*, 18 January 2016, p 21, and the article by the columnist Matthew Parris in *The Times*, 23 January, p 19.

49 Richard Wilkinson and Kate Pickett: *The Spirit Level: Why Equality Is Better for Everyone*, Penguin Books, London, 2009.

50 Wilkinson and Pickett, *Spirit Level*, p 81.

51 Wilkinson and Pickett, *Spirit Level*, p 18.

52 Wilkinson and Pickett, *Spirit Level*, pp 173–4.

53 Wilkinson and Pickett, *Spirit Level*, p 174.

54 See www.oecd.org/pisa/keyfindings/pisa-2012-results.htm and www.oecd.org/pisa/keyfindings/pisa2009keyfindings.htm.

55 James Bloodworth, *The Myth of the Meritocracy*.

6 Linear Thinking

1 Cited on the Conservative website www.conservativeforum.org/authquot.asp?ID=26 as former US Senator Jack Kemp quoting Churchill during

a speech to the International Churchill Society on 7 November 1993. Churchill was describing the difference between capitalists and socialists:'We are for the ladder. Let all try their best to climb.They are for the queue. Let each wait his place until his turn comes.' Both ladder and queue, I would note, are one-dimensional.

2   Quoted from Peter Clarke, *Mr Churchill's Profession: Statesman, Orator,Writer,* Bloomsbury, London, 2013.

3   *Times Higher Education,* 19 May 2016, p 54.

4   Editorial, *The Times,* 20 October 2014.

5   See www.gov.uk/government/news/new-research-exposes-the-glass-floor-in-british-society , 26 July 2015.

6   John Kay, *Obliquity:Why Our Goals Are Best Achieved Indirectly,* Profile Books, London, 2011, p 73.

7   'So how big is your club?', Special Report by Nick Harris, *Daily Mail,* 26 March 2015, pp 86–7.

8   *La Liste* website, www.laliste.com/.

9   Ludwig Wittgenstein, *Remarks on the Foundations of Mathematics,* edited by G.H. von Wright, R. Rhees and G.E.M. Anscombe, translated by G.E.M. Anscombe, Basil Blackwell, Oxford, 1956.

10   John Kay, *Obliquity,* p 73.

11   Amartya Sen, *Collective Choice and Social Welfare,* expanded edition, Penguin, London, 2017. First published by Holden Day 1970; revised edition published by North-Holland Publishing Company 1979.

12   For example, in Figure 6.3 showing the partial ordering of the numbers up to 10, you can see that the maximal points are 6, 8, 9 and 10, none of which is a maximum.

13   The geographical location of London is pinpointed as $51.5072°N$, $0.1275°W$; Paris at $48.8567°N$, $2.3508°E$, and New York at $40.7127°N$, $74.0059°W$.

14   *Times Higher Education,* 10 September 2015, p 28.

7 *Another Dimension*

1   Quoted in Andrew Hodges, *Alan Turing:The Enigma,* first published 1983; centenary edition by Vintage Books, London, 2012, p 318.

2   Hodges, *Alan Turing:The Enigma.*

3   *The Imitation Game,* loosely based on Hodges' biography, about Turing's Bletchley Park code-breaking exploits, with Benedict Cumberbatch playing Turing.The title of the movie comes fromTuring's paper in *Mind* 59(236) (1950), where he first put forward what came to be known as the Turing Test for artificial intelligence. Earlier, Turing had also been the hero of a 1986 play by Hugh Whitemore, *Breaking the Code,* which had a successful run both in the West End and on Broadway, and was subsequently made into a television film. In both the play and the TV production Turing was played by Derek Jacobi. In fairness, it should be mentioned that G.H. Hardy also features in a movie, *The Man Who Knew Infinity,* about Hardy's protégé the Indian genius Srinivasa Ramanujan. Hardy is played by Jeremy Irons.

[4] From Hilbert's address at the Second International Congress of Mathematicians in Paris, 1900, subsequently published as 'Mathematical problems', *Bulletin of the American Mathematical Society* 8 (1902): 437–79.

[5] There is a useful short overview at www.philocomp.net/home/hilbert.

[6] There is some risk of terminological confusion here. When Gödel wrote about 'formally undecidable' *propositions,* he meant propositions which can neither be proved nor refuted, never mind whether mechanistically or not. When we speak of the undecidability of arithmetic as a *system,* we refer to the question of whether there is a mechanistic procedure which will deliver proofs of all provable results (but not prove anything that should not be provable).

[7] Turing's PhD thesis of 1938, titled 'Systems of logic based on ordinals', envisions a logical system to formalise mathematical proofs so they can be checked mechanically. This was visionary: automated theorem-proving is now a reality. There is a book about Turing's PhD thesis: *Alan Turing's Systems of Logic: The Princeton Thesis,* edited and introduced by Andrew W. Appel. It is a beautiful little circle of history that Andrew Appel is the son of Kenneth Appel, who, in 1976, with Wolfgang Haken, proved perhaps the most famous unsolved mathematical problem at that time, the Four-Colour Theorem – using a computer.

[8] Hodges, *Alan Turing,* p 138 and note 22 of chapter three. The speaker here is a Dr Malcolm McPhail, a Canadian physicist who was at Princeton with Turing.

[9] Hodges, *Alan Turing,* p 201.

[10] Hodges, *Alan Turing,* p 244.

[11] These two quotes, and their concatenation, come directly from Hodges, *Alan Turing,* p 293. The original references are given there.

[12] Hodges, *Alan Turing,* p 392.

[13] 'Reader' is a very particular British academic title, with no real equivalent anywhere else. 'Associate professor' comes closest. Turing never held a professorship, although he was known to friends and co-workers as 'the Prof'.

[14] Alan Turing, 'Computing machinery and intelligence', *Mind* October (1950).

[15] The Turing Test is deceptively simple. It says that if you have an online conversation with an unidentified someone, and despite your best efforts you cannot tell whether that someone is a computer or a human being, and it turns out to be a computer, then that computer has exhibited artificial intelligence. Turing referred to 'the imitation game', which became the title of the movie about him.

[16] In a talk on 24 June 1949 titled 'Checking a large routine'. See Hodges, *Alan Turing,* p 407.

[17] The pardon was granted under the Royal Prerogative of Mercy after a request by Justice Minister Chris Grayling, following an online petition. The request was initially denied by the Justice Secretary, Lord McNally, who said Turing was 'properly convicted' for what was at the time a criminal offence. Earlier, in 2009, following another petition, Prime Minister Gordon

Brown had tendered an official apology, and said that the way Turing was persecuted over his homosexuality was 'appalling'.

18 Based on examples I gave in a public lecture at Newcastle University on 27 November 2007, titled 'What are universities for?' See www.ncl.ac.uk/executive/assets/documents/WhatareUniversitiesfor.pdf.

19 To be precise (and pedantic): the law of excluded middle says that one of a proposition and its negation must be true: either *P* or *not-P* must be the case. When we say that it is not the case that both a proposition and its negation can be true that is called the law of non-contradiction: *P* and *not-P* cannot both be the case. Aristotle distinguished between these two laws, and in fact thought of the law of non-contradiction as 'the most certain of all' (*Metaphysics*, Book IV, chapter three, para 15), but in standard logic they are logically equivalent. For more on Aristotle on non-contradiction, see http://plato.stanford.edu/entries/aristotle-noncontradiction/.

20 Aristotle, *Metaphysics*, Book IV, chapter seven.

21 George Boole, *An Investigation of the Laws of Thought on Which are Founded the Mathematical Theories of Logic and Probability*, first published in 1854. It is still freely available.

22 Claude Shannon, 'A symbolic analysis of relay and switching circuits', Master's thesis, MIT, 1937. The key idea was subsequently published in the 1938 issue of the *Transactions of the American Institute of Electrical Engineers*.

23 The quote is from Book II, chapter six of the *Nichomachean Ethics*. The exact formulation depends on which translation you use. This one comes from the 1976 Penguin Classics edition of the translation of J.A.K. Thomson, as revised by Hugh Tredennick. Richard McKeon's *The Basic Works of Aristotle* (first published by Random House in 1941, paperback 2001) uses the translation of W.D. Ross, where it comes out as 'Thus a master of any art avoids excess and defect, but seeks the intermediate and chooses this.'

24 Simon Blackburn, *Plato's Republic: A Biography*, Books that Changed the World, Grove Press, New York, 2006. See also Professor Blackburn's newspaper article about the book: www.theguardian.com/books/2006/aug/05/shopping.plato.

25 I say 'somewhere around the middle' because Aristotle is very explicit that finding the mean is not a matter of arithmetic. See for example http://plato.stanford.edu/entries/aristotle-ethics/ or http://ir.stthomas.edu/cgi/viewcontent.cgi?article=1000&context=cas_cojo_pub.

26 Martin Luther King, speech made at the University of Newcastle upon Tyne on 13 November 1967, on the occasion of accepting an Honorary Doctorate. (This was the only honorary degree conferred upon him by a British university during his lifetime.) See www.ncl.ac.uk/congregations/ceremonies/honorary/martinlutherking.php.

27 Third annual report of the National Science Foundation, 1953. See www.nsf.gov/pubs/1953/annualreports/ar_1953_sec6.pdf.

8 *Ideas of a Civic University*

1 Ernest L. Boyer, 'The scholarship of engagement', *Journal of Public Service and Outreach* 1(1) (1996): 11–20. Reprinted in the *Journal of Higher Education Outreach and Engagement* 20(1) (2016): 15–27.

2 *Posterior Analytics* 71 b 9–11, and 94 a 20. (I found this reference in the *Stanford Encyclopedia of Philosophy*, http://plato.stanford.edu/entries/aristotle-causality/).

3 *Physics*, Book II, chapter three; *Metaphysics*, Book V, chapter two; *Posterior Analytics*, Book II, chapter ten.

4 This quote, and the next three, are from *Physics*, Book II, chapter three, in Richard McKeon, *The Basic Works of Aristotle*, pp 240-241.

5 Quoted in Adam R. Nelson and Ian P. Wei (eds) *The Global University: Past, Present and Future Perspectives*, Palgrave Macmillan, Basingstoke, 2012, p 228.

6 The first recorded date of teaching at Oxford is 1096, but (according to L. W. B. Brockliss, *The University of Oxford: A History*, Oxford University Press, Oxford, 2016) the effective founding of the university was in 1214, when a Papal Bull gave legal status to the students, their tutors and chancellor. Cambridge University has adopted 1208 as its founding year.

7 Friedrich Heer, *The Medieval World: Europe 1100–1350*, translated from the German by Janet Sondheimer, Weidenfeld and Nicolson, London, 1963 (initially for sale only to members of the Readers Union in London). See chapter nine. There is also a useful Wikipedia article at https://en.wikipedia.org/wiki/List_of_oldest_universities_in_continuous_operation, listing the oldest universities in continuous operation established before 1500. The information given there can easily be cross-checked against the current websites of the universities in question.

8 www.topuniversities.com/blog/10-oldest-universities-us.

9 Helen Mathers, *Steel City Scholars: The Centenary History of the University of Sheffield*, James and James, London, 2005, p 47. See also www.sheffield.ac.uk/about/the-university-of-the-year/civic-university .

10 Mathers, *Steel City Scholars*, p 47.

11 The references to the 1831 and 1802 papers are from A. L. Short and T. W. J. Lennard, 'Thomas Michael Greenhow M.D., F.R.C.S., a man born out of time', *Durham University Journal* 87(2) (1995): 195–211.

12 Mathers, *Steel City Scholars*, p 2.

13 Iglesias (ed.), *The Idea of a University by John Henry Newman*, Discourse II, p 19.

14 H. Hale Bellot, *University College, London 1826–1926*, University of London Press, London, 1929.

15 See, for example, chapter five, 'The making of a modern university', in William Whyte, *Redbrick: A Social and Architectural History of Britain's Civic Universities*, Oxford University Press, Oxford, 2015.

16 See www.law.cornell.edu/uscode/text/7/304: 7 U.S. Code § 304 – Investment of proceeds of sale of land or scrip.

17 http://landgrant.cornell.edu/; https://www.johnson.cornell.edu/CornellEnterprise/Article/ArticleId/44524/Launched-and-ready .

18 'Bruce Truscot', *Red Brick University: A Critical Discussion of the Working of a Modern Civic University which Describes its History, Analyses its Achievements, and Outlines a Programme for its Future*, Pelican Books, London, 1951. My editor asked me to mention that 'Redbrick University' is a metaphor used synonymously with 'the redbrick universities'.

19 The identity of 'Bruce Truscott' was only revealed after his death in 1952. He was Edgar Allison Peers, Professor of Hispanic Studies at Liverpool University. He coined the term 'redbrick university', reputedly after the Victoria Building, completed in 1892, the first purpose-built building for what became the University of Liverpool.

20 This is true physically as well as metaphorically. In Newcastle, for example, the redbrick Armstrong Building which is the heart of the campus is only a few hundred metres away from the city's Civic Centre, but looks away from it.

21 Heer, *The Medieval World*, p 200.

22 Heer, *The Medieval World*, p 216.

23 For an encyclopaedia entry, see 'Boethius of Dacia' in *Mediaeval Science, Technology and Medicine: An Encyclopaedia*, edited by Thomas F. Glick, Stephen Livesey and Faith Wallis, Routledge, London, 2014, p 94.

24 J.F. Wippel (trans.), *Boethius of Dacia, On the Supreme Good, On the Eternity of the World, On Dreams*, Pontifical Institute of Mediaeval Studies, Toronto, 1987. The quote is from Wippel's Introduction.

25 www.jggj.dk/Dacia.htm.

26 Heer, *The Medieval World*, p 215.

27 The philosophically minded reader will see a connection here with the work of Immanuel Kant: *Critique of Pure Reason* and *Critique of Practical Reason*.

28 Derek Bok, *Beyond the Ivory Tower: Social Responsibilities of the Modern University*, Harvard University Press, Cambridge, MA, 1982.

29 See www.hup.harvard.edu/catalog.php?isbn=9780674068988&content=reviews for the quote. The reference is: Clark Kerr, *The Uses of the University*, 5th edn, Harvard University Press, Cambridge, MA, 2001. The book originated as the Godkin Lectures on the Essentials of Free Government and Duties of the Citizen, delivered by Kerr at Harvard University in 1963, and published in book form later that year.

30 For a pdf copy, see https://porter.ucsc.edu/pdfs/Kerr%20The%20Idea%20of%20the%20Multiversity%201963.pdf.

31 Svava Bjarnason and Patrick Coldstream (eds) *The Idea of Engagement: Universities in Society*, Policy Research Unit of the Association of Commonwealth Universities, London, 2003.

32 David Watson, *Managing Civic and Community Engagement*, Open University Press, Maidenhead, 2007.

33 David Watson, Robert M. Hollister, Susan E. Stroud and Elizabeth Babcock, *The Engaged University: International Perspectives on Civic Engagement*, International Studies in Higher Education, Routledge, Abingdon, 2011.

34 http://talloiresnetwork.tufts.edu/who-we-are/talloires-declaration/?c=7.

35 http://talloiresnetwork.tufts.edu/who-we-are/.

36 http://talloiresnetwork.tufts.edu/what-we-do/.

37 www.usrnetwork.org/.

38 Daniel T.L. Shek and Robert M. Hollister (eds) *University Social Responsibility and Quality of Life: A Global Survey of Concepts and Experiences*, Springer Nature, Singapore, 2017.

39 http://compact.org/initiatives/trucen/.

40 http://compact.org/who-we-are/ .

41 Maureen F. Curley and Timothy K. Stanton, 'The history of TRUCEN', *Journal of Higher Education Outreach and Engagement* 16(4) (2012): 3–9. The two quotes in the next paragraph are also from this article.

42 I adapt here the definition of service learning given in the Head's Message, Office of Service-Learning at the Hong Kong Polytechnic University. See https://www.polyu.edu.hk/osl/01b_introduction.html. Service learning courses have been credit-bearing and mandatory at Hong Kong Polytechnic University since 2012–13.

43 Christopher A. Bartlett and Sumantra Ghosal, 'Matrix management: not a structure, a frame of mind'. See https://hbr.org/1990/07/matrix-management-not-a-structure-a-frame-of-mind. This is a version of an article that appeared in the July–August 1990 issue of *Harvard Business Review*.

44 Shek and Hollister, *University Social Responsibility*.

45 John Goddard, Ellen Hazelkorn, Louise Kempton and Paul Vallance (eds) *The Civic University: The Policy and Leadership Challenges*, Edward Elgar, London, 2016. I should declare an interest: I am co-author of one of the chapters (on Newcastle University), and I wrote the Foreword.

46 http://gcgh.grandchallenges.org/about.

47 www.gov.uk/government/uploads/system/uploads/attachment_data/file/505308/bis-16-160-allocation-science-research-funding-2016-17-2019-20.pdf and www.rcuk.ac.uk/funding/gcrf/.

48 www.rcuk.ac.uk/funding/iscf/ and www.rcuk.ac.uk/media/news/170116/.

Epilogue *On the Supreme Good*

1 This reproduction of the text of *De Summo Bono* is by kind permission of the copyright holder, the Pontifical Institute of Mediaeval Studies at St Michael's College, University of Toronto, http://www.pims.ca. The text (without the translator's footnotes) comes from: Boethius of Dacia, *On the Supreme Good; On the Eternity of the World; On Dreams,* a translation of *De Summo Bono; De Aeternitate Mundi; De Somniis* by John F. Wippel, published by the Pontifical Institute of Mediaeval Studies, Toronto, 1987.

Index